The Emperor Hadrian: a picture of the Graeco-Roman world in his time. ... Translated by Mary E. Robinson. [With a bibliography.]

Ferdinand Gregorovius, Mary E. Robinson

The Emperor Hadrian: a picture of the Graeco-Roman world in his time. ... Translated by Mary E. Robinson. [With a bibliography.]

Gregorovius, Ferdinand
British Library, Historical Print Editions
British Library
Robinson, Mary E.
1898
xviii, 414 p. ; 8°.
9041.m.12.

The Emperor Hadrian

The
Emperor Hadrian

A Picture of the
Graeco-Roman World in his Time

By

Ferdinand Gregorovius

Translated by

Mary E. Robinson

London
Macmillan and Co., Limited
New York: The Macmillan Company
1898

GLASGOW : PRINTED AT THE UNIVERSITY PRESS BY
ROBERT MACLEHOSE AND CO.

TRANSLATOR'S PREFACE.

THIS translation of Gregorovius' *Life of Hadrian* has been written in the hope that it may prove useful to the students of this period of Roman history.

In publishing it I have to express my obligations to Professor Pelham for his valuable introduction; to Mr. Herbert Fisher, Fellow of New College, Oxford, who kindly looked through my manuscript, and to whose encouragement the work is due; and to Mr. Martin Trietschel, who has rendered me great assistance, especially with the notes and index.

MARY E. ROBINSON.

HOLMFIELD,
AIGBURTH, LIVERPOOL,
November, 1898.

AUTHOR'S PREFACE

MY first studies in the field of history were devoted to the age of the emperor Hadrian. Encouraged by the celebrated historian Drumann, I collected and published these studies in a book which appeared in Königsberg in the year 1851, under the rather ambitious title of *History of the Roman Emperor Hadrian and his Time.* This work soon became my guide to Rome, where I arrived in 1852. There, however, I was enthralled, not by the ancient, but by the mediaeval genius of the Eternal City, and I gave the best work and the best years of my life to the study of the history of Rome in the Middle Ages.

A generation has since then passed away—the most eventful period of our century—and I am not a little gratified to have found leisure to perform an act of piety toward the first-fruits of my youth by presenting my work in a new form.

This undertaking was, in the first instance, suggested by my travels in Greece and in the East, where I frequently followed the footsteps of the great world-traveller Hadrian. Another reason was, that since the appearance of my monograph, this remarkable ruler has not found another biographer either in Germany or abroad. But the ceaseless researches of science have produced new documentary evidence, and the fresh light thus thrown on this epoch of Roman history has tended to fill the gaps in the hitherto very fragmentary accounts of the life of Hadrian.

With the help of this evidence, especially of the inscriptions, I have rewritten my first work, so thoroughly indeed that little more than the plan has been preserved. I now call these studies *A Picture of the Graeco-Roman World in the Time of Hadrian*, although I am afraid that this title is still too ambitious. In view of the scanty notice which, generally speaking, the history of the emperors subsequent to the twelve Caesars still receives—and this is not surprising—I venture to think that every serious attempt at its elucidation will meet with the sympathy of all lovers of history.

THE AUTHOR.

MUNICH, November, 1883.

CONTENTS

FIRST BOOK—POLITICAL HISTORY

CHAPTER I

An Ancient Portrait of Hadrian. - - - - - -
PAGE
1

CHAPTER II

Circumstances in the Life of Hadrian until the Accession of Trajan. - - - - - - - - - - 6

CHAPTER III

Circumstances in the Life of Hadrian during the Reign of Trajan. 11

CHAPTER IV

Hadrian accompanies the Emperor in the Parthian War. Rising of the Jews. Lusius Quietus. Death of Trajan and Adoption of Hadrian. - - - - - - - - - - 16

CHAPTER V

Hadrian gives up the lately acquired Provinces of Trajan. The State of Judaea. Fall of Lusius Quietus. - - - - 23

CHAPTER VI

Return of Hadrian to Rome by way of Illyricum. War with the Roxolani. Arrangement of Affairs in Pannonia and Dacia. Conspiracy and Execution of the Four Consulars. Arrival of Hadrian in Rome in August 118 A.D. - - - - 30

CHAPTER VII

PAGE

Hadrian's First Acts in Rome. The Great Remission of Debt. The Third Consulate of the Emperor. Fall of Attianus. Marcius Turbo becomes Prefect. Death of Matidia Augusta. The Palilia of the year 121 A.D. - - - - - - 37

CHAPTER VIII

General Remarks on Hadrian's Journeys. Coins which commemorate them. - - - - - - - - 45

CHAPTER IX

Hadrian's Journeys into Gaul and Germany as far as the Danubian Provinces. The Condition of these Countries. - - - 53

CHAPTER X

Hadrian in Britain. He goes through Gaul to Spain and Mauretania. - - - - - - - - - - - 60

CHAPTER XI

Hadrian's First Journey to the East. The Countries on the Pontus. Ilium. Pergamum. Cyzicus. Rhodes. - - 67

CHAPTER XII

Hadrian's Residence in Athens and in other cities of Greece. Return of the Emperor to Rome by way of Sicily. - - 77

CHAPTER XIII

Hadrian in Rome. The Title *Pater Patriae*. The Emperor goes to Africa. Condition of this Province. Carthage. Lambaesis. 87

CHAPTER XIV

Second Journey to the East. Hadrian in Athens and Eleusis. Journey to Asia. Ephesus. Smyrna. Sardis. - - - 93

CHAPTER XV

Hadrian in Syria. Antioch. Phoenicia. Heliopolis. Damascus. Palmyra. - - - - - - - - - - 104

CHAPTER XVI

PAGE

Hadrian in Judaea. Condition of Jerusalem. Foundation of the Colony Aelia Capitolina. Hadrian in Arabia. Bostra. Petra. The Country of Peraea. Gaza. Pelusium. - - - - 111

CHAPTER XVII

Hadrian in Egypt. Condition of the Country. Alexandria. Letter of Hadrian to Servianus. Influence of Egypt and Alexandria on the West. - - - - - - - 120

CHAPTER XVIII

Hadrian's Journey on the Nile. Heliopolis. Death of Antinous. Thebes. The Colossus of Memnon. Coptus. Myus Hormus. Mons Claudianus. Return to Alexandria. - - - - 128

CHAPTER XIX

Hadrian returns from Egypt to Syria. He revisits Athens. Dedication of the Olympieum. Hadrian's divine Honours. - - 138

CHAPTER XX

The Rising of the Jews under Barcocheba. - - - - 143

CHAPTER XXI

The Jewish War. Julius Severus assumes the Command of the Roman Army. The Fall of Bether. The Destruction of Judaea. - - - - - - - - - - - 150

CHAPTER XXII

The Colony Aelia Capitolina. - - - - - - - 159

CHAPTER XXIII

The War with the Alani. Arrian's Periplus of the Black Sea. 165

CHAPTER XXIV

Hadrian's Last Years in Rome. Death of Sabina Augusta. Adoption and Death of Aelius Verus. - - - - - 173

CHAPTER XXV

Adoption of Antoninus. Death of the Emperor Hadrian. - - 181

Contents

SECOND BOOK

THE STATE AND GENERAL CULTURE

CHAPTER I

PAGE

The Roman Empire. - - - - - - - - - 191

CHAPTER II

The Provinces of the Empire, their Government and their Relation to the Central Power. The Peaceful Development of their Civilization. Slavery. - - - - - - - - 195

CHAPTER III

Cities. Municipia. Colonies. - - - - - - 206

CHAPTER IV

Italy and Rome. - - - - - - - - - 211

CHAPTER V

The Equestrian Order. The Senate and the Princeps. The Imperial Cabinet. - - - - - - - - 216

CHAPTER VI

Roman Law. The *Edictum Perpetuum*. The *Responsa*. Roman Jurists. The Resolutions of the Senate and the Imperial Constitutions. The Reforming Spirit of Hadrian's Legislation. - - - - - - - - - - - 226

CHAPTER VII

Science and the Learned Professions. Latin and Greek Literature. The Schools. Athens. Smyrna. Alexandria. Rome. 234

CHAPTER VIII

Plutarch. Arrian. The *Tactica*. Philo of Byblus. Appian. Phlegon. Hadrian's Memoirs. - - - - - - 243

CHAPTER IX

Florus. Suetonius. Geography. Philology. - - - - 250

CHAPTER X

PAGE

The Schools of Roman Oratory. Roman Orators. Cornelius
Fronto. - - - - - - - - - - - - 253

CHAPTER XI

Greek Sophistry. Favorinus. Dionysius of Miletus. Polemon.
Herodes Atticus and other Sophists. - - - - - 260

CHAPTER XII

Polite Literature. Hadrian as a Poet. Florus. Latin Poets.
Greek Poets. Pancrates. Mesomedes. The Musician
Dionysius of Halicarnassus. Greek Epigrams of Hadrian.
Phlegon. Artemidorus and His Dream Books. The
Romance of the Golden Ass. - - - - - - 273

CHAPTER XIII

Philosophy. The Stoa. Epictetus and the *Enchiridion.* Stoicism
and Cynicism. Demonax of Athens. - - - - - 282

CHAPTER XIV

Peregrinus Proteus. - - - - - - - - - 290

CHAPTER XV

Alexander of Abonotichus. - - - - - - - - 294

CHAPTER XVI

Oracles. Plutarch their Apologist. Hadrian's Mysticism. The
Deification of Antinous. - - - - - - - 301

CHAPTER XVII

Attempts to Restore Paganism. Plutarch and Lucian. - - 313

CHAPTER XVIII

The Spread of Christianity. The Christian Religion a *Religio
Illicita.* Hadrian's Toleration of the Christians. Rescript
of Hadrian to the Proconsul Fundanus. The Christian
Apologists. - - - - - - - - - - 322

Contents

CHAPTER XIX

PAGE

Art among the Romans. Hadrian's Relation to Art. Activity of Art in the Empire. Greek Artists in Rome. Character of the Art of Hadrian's Age. - - - - - - - 332

CHAPTER XX

The Progress and Production of Art. Furniture. Gems. Medals. Precious Stones. Paintings. Portraits in Marble. Historical Relievo. - - - - - - - - - - 339

CHAPTER XXI

Ideal Sculpture. Its Cosmopolitan Character. Imitation of Ancient Masterpieces. Review of the Works of Art found in Hadrian's Villa. The Statues of Antinous. - - - - 346

CHAPTER XXII

Architecture. Munificent Civic Spirit of the Cities. Hadrian's Love of Building. Antinoe. Roads to Berenice. Other Buildings in Egypt. The Temple at Cyzicus. - - - 354

CHAPTER XXIII

Buildings of Hadrian in Athens and in other Cities of Greece. Buildings of Herodes Atticus. - - - - - - 360

CHAPTER XXIV

Hadrian's Buildings in Italy. His Villa at Tivoli. - - - 366

CHAPTER XXV

The City of Rome in Hadrian's Time. Buildings of the Emperor in Rome. Completion of the Forum of Trajan. The Temple of Venus and Rome. Hadrian's Tomb. - - - 373

BIBLIOGRAPHY. - - - - - - - - - - 382

INDEX. - - - - - - - - - - 403

INTRODUCTION.

THOSE who are familiar with the late Ferdinand Gregorovius' essay on Hadrian, will not think any apology necessary for this translation into English of an eminently readable, and, on the whole, adequate account of one of the most interesting personages in ancient history. Gregorovius, though not a historian of the first order, was an accomplished man of letters, and a genuine lover of Rome and of things Roman. Moreover, his book still possesses the claim to attention urged by the author himself in his preface to the edition of 1883. Hadrian has not yet "found another biographer either in Germany or abroad," and even to the educated public he is a far less familiar figure than many men of infinitely less importance in history.

Gregorovius would have been the last to claim for his essay that it said the final word on Hadrian, and it must be confessed that his work is not all equally good. He is at his best in the chapters which describe the general culture, the literary, philosophic, and artistic movements of the day. He is weakest when dealing with the political history, and with the many technicalities of Roman administration. Here his grasp of the situation is less sure, and his use of technical terms not always correct.

But I am writing a brief introduction, not a review, and I will content myself with one more criticism, which indeed applies to other accounts of Hadrian besides that which is now in question. Gregorovius reproduces with much skill and fidelity the most familiar aspects of the emperor, as the restless traveller, the indefatigable connoisseur and collector, the patron of learning and the arts. We are allowed to see, too, that he was an administrator of ubiquitous activity, with whose name a number of changes in the machinery and methods of government are associated. What we miss is some account of the master-idea which shaped Hadrian's policy, and gave unity to a career and a character full of apparent inconsistencies.

The omission is due partly to the nature of our evidence. Until comparatively recent times students of Hadrian were forced to rely mainly on the rather meagre literary tradition preserved in the biography of Spartianus, in the excerpts from Dion Cassius, and in Aurelius Victor. It is only within the last twenty or thirty years that the " ceaseless researches of science " have not merely produced new evidence, but in doing so have rendered intelligible much that was before difficult to understand. One result has been to place in our hands the clue to Hadrian's policy as ruler of the empire, and to enable us to gauge more correctly the direction of his aims and the importance of his achievements.

Hadrian has unquestionably suffered in general reputation by the fate which placed him betweeen two such commanding figures as Trajan and Marcus Aurelius. By the side of the former, Hadrian appeared timid and commonplace. As Trajan became the ideal Roman soldier, Hadrian was represented as the peace-loving scholar who, in tastes and pursuits, was more Greek than Roman. Yet Hadrian was every inch a soldier, deeply versed in both the theory and the practice of the art of war ; and if he was a lover of Greeks and Greek civilization, he was also an admirer of old Roman writers and fashions. On the other hand, Marcus Aurelius justly ranks above him as a man, and holds a place in literature, and in the history of human thought, to which Hadrian has no claim.

But viewed as a statesman, as the ruler of a great empire, Hadrian stands higher than either Trajan or Marcus. He is more truly representative of his time, and he left a deeper mark upon it. Above all, it was he and not they who shaped the policy of the empire, and shaped it in accordance with ideas which, if not new, were first clearly conceived and effectively carried out by him.

For Hadrian's policy was not the result of a scholar's love of peace, or of cosmopolitan tastes, or even of mere restlessness. It was directed by one dominant idea, the influence of which is everywhere traceable. This master idea was, to use a modern expression, the imperial idea (*Reichsidee*)—the conception of the empire, as a single well-compacted state, internally homogeneous, and standing out in clear relief against surrounding barbarism. The realization of this conception was the object for which Hadrian laboured. If he refused to follow Trajan in his forward policy, it was not from timidity, or, as Gregorovius seems to think, from a scholarly love of peace and quiet. Indeed, as I have hinted, the contrast so often drawn between Trajan the man of war and Hadrian the man of peace, the Romulus and Numa of the second century, is somewhat misleading. Hadrian was anxious for peace, not in order to secure leisure for peaceful pursuits, but because the empire needed it, and he abandoned a policy of conquest, in the conviction that the empire had reached its natural limits, and required not expansion but consolidation.

In this belief he set himself to give the empire, what it had only imperfectly possessed before, definite and well-marked frontiers. The lines of demarcation which thus "separated the barbarians" from Roman territory he protected by a system of frontier defences, which was no doubt developed by his successors, but the idea and plan of which were unquestionably his; and to hold these defences he maintained a frontier force, the efficiency of which was his constant care. We are too apt, in thinking of Hadrian's travels, to picture them only as the restless wanderings of a connoisseur from one famous site to another in the peaceful provinces of the interior, and to forget how large a portion of his time was spent, not in Athens or Smyrna, but in reviewing the troops and inspecting the stations along the whole line of the imperial frontier.

This frontier policy of precise delimitation and vigilant defence, he supplemented within the empire by a policy of consolidation. When Hadrian assumed the command, the old theory of the empire as a federation of distinct communities in alliances with, and under the protectorate of

Rome, was rapidly losing ground.   The differences in race and language, in habits of life, and modes of thought, which had formerly justified and even necessitated it, were fast disappearing.   The titles and distinctions which had once implied not only a desire for political independence, but a partial possession of it were becoming mere phrases. Even the " freedom " of a free community could be ridiculed with impunity by a popular orator, and the native state, with its native ruler, was, except in a few outlying corners of the empire, a thing of the past.   The idea of a single Roman state was in the air, and Hadrian gave effect to it with singular skill and perseverance.   His cosmopolitanism was in reality imperialism, and sprung from his desire to stamp everything with the imperial mark, and to utilize everything for the benefit of the empire.   He was a Phil-Hellenist, not merely from sentiment, but from the conviction that Latins, Greeks, and even barbarians had all something to contribute to the common service.   The man who appointed the Greek Arrian to the command of Roman legions, and of a Roman frontier province, was noted equally for his careful study of old Roman tactics and for his liberal adoption of barbarian movements.

In other departments of his administration the influence of this dominant idea of imperial unity are as plainly seen.   He was liberal in granting the Roman franchise. He encouraged the diffusion over the empire of municipalities modelled on the Roman pattern. The imperial civil service was developed and enlarged, and the old distinction, once so earnestly maintained between the public service of the state and the private service of Caesar, is scarcely heard of after the reign of Hadrian.

Between the time of Augustus and that of Diocletian there was no emperor who so correctly appreciated the needs of the empire, or who carried into practice with equal consistency a deliberate and comprehensive policy.

HENRY PELHAM.

FIRST BOOK

POLITICAL HISTORY

CHAPTER I

An Ancient Portrait of Hadrian

A ROMAN historian of the second half of the fourth century has drawn the following picture of the Emperor Hadrian :

"Aelius Hadrianus was of Italian origin. His father, who bore the same name, was a cousin of Trajan, and was born at Adria in Picenum, the place which gave its name to the Adriatic Sea. He reigned twenty-two years. He was so thoroughly familiar with Greek literature that he was called 'the little Greek.' He had completely adopted the studies, the manner of life, the language, and the whole culture of the Athenians. He was a singer and musician, a physician, a geometrician, a painter, and a sculptor in bronze and marble, almost a second Polycletus and Euphranor. He was accomplished in all these arts. A *bel esprit* of so brilliant a character has not often been seen among men. His memory was prodigious. Places, actions, soldiers, absentees even, he knew them all by name. His endurance was superhuman. He travelled on foot through all the provinces, outstripping his attendants. He restored the cities in the empire and increased their importance. Smiths, carpenters, masons, architects, and all kinds of workmen, he divided into cohorts like legions, for the purpose of building fortresses and beautifying the cities. He was never the same: a many-sided man, a born ruler in vice as well as in virtue. He ruled his inclinations by a certain ingenuity. He artfully concealed the envy, ill-humour, extravagance, and audacious egotism of his nature, and feigned moderation, affability

A

and benignity, while hiding the thirst for fame with which he was consumed. No one was so ready to challenge or to answer others, either in jest or earnest. He instantly capped verse with verse, witty sallies with others as witty, as if he had prepared them beforehand. He obtained peace from many kings by secret favours, and openly boasted that, by his inactivity, he had gained more than others by war.

"He gave the offices of the state and of the court, and even of the army, the form which still obtains at the present day, with the slight exception of the changes introduced by Constantine. He lived 62 years. His end was distressing. Racked by terrible pains in all his limbs, he often besought his most faithful servants to put him to death. He was sedulously watched by those dearest to him, in order that he might not commit suicide."

I have placed this portrait at the beginning like a copper-plate engraving. It is ascribed to Aurelius Victor. It is clumsy and inadequate, but not without life, and it is at all events the only condensed portrait of the emperor which has come down to us from ancient times.[1] On the whole this sketch conveys the average verdict of Roman posterity on Hadrian, and but shortly after his death the most opposite opinions of him prevailed. His biographer Spartianus, who wrote in the time of Diocletian, has knit together both views without expressing his own opinion. His *Life of Hadrian* is the main authority for the history of this emperor, together with the extracts which the Byzantine monk Xiphilinus made in the eleventh century from the historical works of Dion Cassius.

There are traits in the emperor's character concerning which there is no doubt: his Greek culture, his versatility, his Proteus-like nature, his thirst for knowledge, his enthusiasm for art; then come his restless love of travelling, and his wisdom in the administration of the empire.

The modern view of history is, that the reign of Hadrian was the beginning of an age which has been named after

---

[1] Aurelius Victor, *Epitome* 14. I have omitted but little, and nothing that is essential to Hadrian. This part of the epitome is not original, but probably borrowed from Marius Maximus.—Teuffel, *Geschichte der röm. Liter.* 5th ed., p. 967 *sq.* (§ 414).

the Antonines, whom he had chosen to be his successors. It has been extolled as the happiest period of the Roman empire, if not of the world. It shines more brightly from the union of Greek and Roman culture, which it diffused throughout the peaceful empire, than from the contrast it presents to the dark shadows that surround it. As we look back we see the dark shadow of the excessive tyranny of the Caesars of the first century,—as we look at the succeeding age, we see the shadow of the barbarians by whom Rome is to be destroyed.

After the time of Nerva, despots had disappeared from the throne of the Caesars. Their mad outbreaks had shaken the foundations of Roman society and the structure of the state, but Roman virtus is re-established by the help of Stoic philosophy, and the Roman empire attains an overwhelming force, whose brilliancy conceals the chronic internal disease from which it dies a lingering death. After the death of Trajan, thirty legions, stationed on the borders of the empire, secure the peace of the world. The provinces have become accustomed to the dominion of Rome. Their cities are once more flourishing, and are adorned with the beauty of Greek art. The sciences awake in a renaissance of Hellenism, and the Christian religion comes more prominently forward. A spirit of humanity is diffused throughout the world that was changing so rapidly. Civil legislation becomes more philosophic and more humane. The privileges of the aristocracy disappear. The people, the slaves, and the poor, become objects for the care of the government. The barriers of the old theory of life fall before the morality of the Stoic. The conception of the nation widens in the Roman empire into the conception of humanity. The provinces in which Octavianus had erected the altar of the genius of Rome as symbol of their subjection, demand their equal rights with this terrible Rome, which had conquered and enslaved them by force of arms. The Roman empire is a confederation of peoples whose culture is fostered by the majestic flow of the two languages of the world. Like the nations, the ancient systems of thought and religion are fused in one cosmopolitan union. But a union of this kind is the cause of a restless uncertainty in many minds, making them more of a prey than ever to the delusions of mystery and the gloom of superstition. So glaring are the contradictions in this world-wide civilization of the empire, that this period between Antiquity and Christianity may be called a Roman-Hellenic middle age.

Hadrian in himself also unites two natures. He is both Roman and Greek. His artistic soul delights in the ideals of beauty of the ancient world. He wishes to restore them as far as it is possible for art to do so. At the same time, as a Roman, he reforms the institutions of the monarchy,—the government, the army, and the law. He lays the foundations of a state that will suit an altered society. The empire under him reaches the zenith of its greatness, and he revels, as a comprehensive mind would, in the fulness of its culture. Conquests he does not seek. He gives the provinces acquired by Trajan back to the Parthians. Wars he does not wage. Mars rests unconcerned amid his preparations, and yet he never appeared more formidable to the enemies of Rome.[1]

Hadrian's task is to keep the Roman empire together as a powerful monarchy, and to adorn it with knowledge, humanity, and beauty. On his coins are the words, "Golden age" and "Enricher of the world,"—flatteries of the senate not destitute of truth. He himself is the mirror of his time in good and evil, in virtue and vice. His enigmatic personality is of more human interest and is more attractive as a study, than that of the philosophic Antonines. He directed the current of his time, and impressed it less with his powerful will, than with his genial, though often eccentric and theatrical, temperament.

Hadrian was the first to bring both halves of the ancient world, Greece and Rome, into closer intellectual contact. Their fusion was impossible, but their universal connection in the second century was a factor of vital importance in the growth of the Christian idea. Antiquity made room for this idea, while it had itself become ripe for death. But it cast a halo of departing glory under this gifted sophist on the throne of the Caesars. Hadrian it was who restored Athens, and finished the temple of the Olympian Zeus, which had

---

[1] Dion Cassius, lxix.: τήν τε γὰρ παρασκευὴν αὐτοῦ ὁρῶντες—οὐδὲν ἐνεόχμωσαν.

been begun by Pisistratus.   He it was who made Greek
oratory blossom afresh, and who called upon the arts to
adorn the world with their richest beauty.   When the artistic
fire, which he had kindled on the altar of the genius of
Hellas, was extinguished, the world became flat and insipid.   It
was first Stoic, then Christian.   Hadrian, however, accomplished the apotheosis of antiquity.

CHAPTER II

Circumstances in the Life of Hadrian until the Accession of Trajan

THE ancestors of Publius Aelius Hadrianus are said to have left Hadria to settle at Italica in Spain, in the time of the Scipios. Scipio had founded this city of the province of Baetica in the second Punic war, and Augustus first made it into a municipium. It flourished greatly, and became an important place. It gave two famous men to the empire, Trajan and Hadrian. Its ruins are still to be seen at Santiponce, a short distance from Seville. Hadrian's ancestors lived there in comfortable circumstances. They belonged to the Roman tribe Sergia.[1]

Hadrian was born on the 24th January, 76 A.D., in Rome, when Vespasian was emperor. His father was P. Aelius Hadrianus Afer, a distinguished man of senatorial rank, and a cousin of Trajan. His mother, Domitia Paulina, came from Gades, the modern Cadiz. Of his brothers and sisters, none are known by name except Paulina, who married L. Julius Ursus Servianus.

In his tenth year Hadrian lost his father, and became a ward of the knight Caelius Attianus, and of the ex-praetor Trajan. In this way, the fact of relationship and guardianship brought him into close connection with the fortunes of a future emperor. The boy was educated in the schools of Rome. His brilliantly gifted mind was

---

[1] Inscriptions of the Aelii, *Corp. Inscr. Latin.* ii., 1130, 1138, 1139. The famous inscription on the base of the statue of Hadrian in the theatre of Athens records him as belonging to the Tribus Sergia. Henzen, *Annali dell' Inst.*, 1862, p. 139. *C. I. L.* iii., part I., 550.

TRAJANUS.
Avus Imp. Traj.

M. ULPIUS TRAJANUS.
Pater Imp. Traj.

ULPIA = AELIUS HADRIANUS MARILLENUS.
Avus Imp. Hadr.

M. ULPIUS TRAJANUS.
Imp.
= POMPEIA PLOTINA.

MARCIANA
= C. MATIDIUS PATRUINUS.

P. AELIUS HADRIANUS AFER.
Pater Imp. Hadr.
= DOMITIA PAULINA.

MATIDIA I.
= C. VIBIUS SABINUS.

PAULINA.
= L. JULIUS URSUS SERVIANUS.

MATIDIA II.

SABINA = P. AELIUS HADRIANUS.
Imp.

especially attracted by Greek literature, and, in its favour, he neglected the Latin tongue. The nickname of " Little Grecian" was given to him. Whether he studied in Athens as well, is uncertain and improbable; for in his fifteenth year he went home to Spain, where he took service in the army.[1] His guardian, Trajan, soon recalled him to Rome, not only because he had given himself up immoderately to the pleasures of the chase, but chiefly, no doubt, on account of his extravagance and dissipation.

The chase was one of his greatest passions. As a vigorous pedestrian, as well as a hunter, he found few to equal him. Even when emperor, he would kill lions from the saddle. He had an accident while hunting, and broke his collar-bone and one of his ribs.[2]

The passions of youth did not destroy Hadrian's ardent thirst for knowledge. This he could gratify in Rome, the home of all learning. Here he studied among learned men and poets; here he painted and carved in the studios of artists. With no branch of knowledge did he remain unacquainted.[3] A young man glowing with life, a well-informed companion, he must have been much sought after in the best circles of Rome, and must especially have won the favour of the highly cultivated ladies of Trajan's house,—Marciana, Plotina, and Matidia.

But the happy times of the Flavian Emperors, Vespasian and Titus, passed by, and the appearance of a brutal despot, Domitian, once more cast a gloom over the Roman world. It was then that Hadrian learned to abhor tyranny, as under this oppression he began his career of office, every step of which he painfully mounted. He first became judge in the year 93 A.D., over a court for private cases, and he subsequently filled some other offices of small importance; then he became tribune of the IInd legion Adjutrix, which had been raised by Vespasian, and which was probably stationed in Britain at the time.[4]

[1] Spart. *Vita*, c. 2.   [2] Spart. c. 26.

[3] Dion Cassius, lxix. 3: καὶ γὰρ ἔπλασσε καὶ ἔγραφε καὶ οὐδὲν ὅ τι οὐκ εἰρηνικὸν καὶ πολεμικὸν καὶ βασιλικὸν καὶ ἰδιωτικὸν εἰδέναι ἔλεγεν.

[4] Henzen, *Annali dell' Inst.*, 1862, p. 145.

Domitian perished on the 18th September 96 A.D. by the daggers of conspirators, who raised the noble senator, Cocceius Nerva to the throne. A new age began for mankind. Imperial lawsuits were stopped, prisons were opened, and exiles were recalled. Things once irreconcileable, sovereignty and freedom, were, in the opinion of Tacitus, blended by Nerva.[1] A god then inspired this emperor, who was oppressed both by the Praetorians and the populace of Rome, to perform the only great act of his reign : he adopted Trajan. At the same time the lucky star of Hadrian became visible above the horizon.

He was then military tribune in the Vth legion Macedonica in Lower Moesia. From there he was sent (97 A.D.) to convey the congratulations of the army of the Danube to Trajan, who was governing Upper Germany as consular legate. Trajan kept him near his own person as tribune to the XXIInd legion. The emperor-designate seems to have assumed the government of the whole of Germany, while Servianus, Hadrian's brother-in-law, became legate in Upper Germany in his place.[2]

Meanwhile Nerva died on the 27th January 98 A.D., and the first provincial was now to mount the throne of the empire. He was a citizen of that Spanish Italica, which was Hadrian's birthplace. Hadrian hurried to Cologne, where Trajan was at the time, in order to be the first to bring him the great news. But his brother-in-law did his best to detain him on his journey, taking secret means to make his carriage break down ; whereupon Hadrian, who was a good runner, quickly resolved to continue his journey on foot to Cologne, and overtook the messengers sent by his brother-in-law. Servianus was a serious man, to whom the versatility of his brother-in-law was not congenial. He immediately laid before the new emperor the not inconsiderable list of debts of the young spendthrift.[3] He was probably ambitious and envious of the

---

[1] Tacitus, *Agricola*, c. 3.

[2] Henzen, *Annali dell' Inst.*, 1862, p. 147 ; Joh. Dierauer, *Beitraege zu einer krit. Gesch. Trajan's*, vol. i., p. 29 ; Pliny (*Ep.* viii. 23) calls Servianus "exactissimus vir."

[3] Qui et sumptibus et aere alieno ejus prodito Traiani odium in eum movit—Spart. c. 2.

favour shown by Trajan to Hadrian. But one day in old age, he was to atone for his ambition by death.

Hadrian only gained Trajan's goodwill slowly, and was indebted chiefly for it to the empress, who had at that time been calumniated in a scandalous manner. Apart even from the formal praise of her in Pliny's *Panegyricus*, there is everything to show that Pompeia Plotina was a woman of true nobility. When she first entered the palace of the Caesars as empress, she turned round on the steps, and, addressing the populace, said : " May I be the same when I leave this palace, as I am to-day when I enter it." As empress she deserved no reproach.[1] The strength of her character can be seen to-day in busts, which show a face of earnest and almost unapproachable gravity.

The new emperor remained for some time at his important post in Germany, and, only in the second half of the year 99 A.D., did he come to Rome, accompanied probably by his cousin. It soon became clear that Hadrian knew how to overcome his adversaries, and to gain the confidence of Trajan. For, about the year 100 A.D., persuaded by Plotina and her friend Sura, Trajan gave him to wife Sabina, grand-child of his sister Marciana, whose daughter Matidia had married L. Vibius Sabinus. In this way Hadrian became doubly related to Trajan.[2] We are not told that Sabina ever shared her husband's intellectual tastes, and he appears not to have been fond of her. She must at the time of her marriage have been very young.[3]

---

[1] Dion Cassius, lxviii. 5. Yet elsewhere (lxix. 1 and 10) he speaks in a scandalous manner of the favours shown by Plotina to Hadrian, ἐξ ἐρωτικῆς φιλίας.—Pliny, *Paneg.*, c. 83.

[2] See the genealogical table in Dierauer and in J. Centerwall, *Spart. vita Hadriani comment. illustrata* in *Upsala Universitets-Arsskrift*, Ups. 1869, vol. i., p. 27.

[3] Mommsen (*Abhandl. der Berl. Akadem.*, 1863. *Grabrede des Kaiser's Hadrian auf die ältere Matidia*, p. 483) remarks, in the genealogical table on Sabina, that she was born at the latest in 88 A.D.

CHAPTER III

Circumstances in the Life of Hadrian during the Reign of Trajan

IN Rome Hadrian had now every opportunity of satisfying
his thirst for knowledge. A new life had begun since Nerva
had removed the load of despotism from the empire.
Tacitus greeted the change with joy.[1] The letters of the
younger Pliny to his friends tell us of the number of cultivated men in Rome, and of the energy which was displayed
in every department of knowledge. Among Hadrian's personal friends were the last famous authors of Latin literature,
who were giving up the field to the Greeks, Juvenal and
Martial, Statius and Silius Italicus, the last, it appears, being
a fellow-citizen from Italica. The great Tacitus, after the
death of his step-father Agricola in 93 A.D., was again living
in Rome, busy with the completion of his literary works,
and it was here that he wrote his *Germania* in the year
98 A.D. He probably survived Hadrian's ascent of the
throne, and it is natural to suppose that Hadrian would early
seek the friendship of such a man.[2]

Whenever Hadrian was in Rome he frequented the society
of the foremost men of intellect, such as Caninius Rufus,
Augurinus, Spurinna, Calpurnius Piso, Sossius Senecio, and
Arrius Antoninus. He made friends with the historian
Suetonius, and with the Poet Florus. He listened to the

[1] Tacitus, *Agricola*, c. 3: Nunc demum redit animus: et quamquam,
primo statim beatissimī saeculi ortu, Nerva Caesar res olim dissociabiles
miscuerit principatum ac libertatem....

[2] The death of Tacitus is placed between 117 A.D. and 120 A.D. Teuffel,
Geschichte der röm. Liter. p. 765.

orators Quintilian, a Spaniard by birth, and Dion Chrysostom, who, banished by Domitian, returned to Rome as a friend of Nerva and then of Trajan, and died there in 117 A.D. He also became acquainted with the noble Plutarch, when the latter gave lectures in Rome in the time of Domitian.

Art attracted Hadrian as much as literature, and under the rule of Trajan it blossomed into fresh life. He was an enthusiast for art from his youth, and subsequently he took a warm interest in the magnificent schemes of Trajan, which were executed by the architect Apollodorus, a Greek from Damascus. An anecdote has been preserved that one day Hadrian interrupted a conversation between this great man and the Emperor Trajan over a building plan, and that the architect ironically said to him " Go and paint pumpkins, for you understand nothing of these things."[1] This anecdote throws a light not only on the artistic tastes of Hadrian, who was then painting still life, but on his familiarity with Trajan's building schemes, and on the professional pride of Apollodorus, the Bramante or Michael-Angelo of his time.

In the year 101 A.D. the office of quaestor was bestowed upon Hadrian. This was a step upwards in his career, as well as in the favour of Trajan ; for he now became attached to the person of the emperor, whose speeches he had to read to the senate. As his Spanish accent was laughed at, he took great pains to improve it, and soon made himself perfect in the Latin tongue.[2] This happy youthful time, full of work and enjoyment, came to an end for Hadrian in this same year (101 A.D.), when Trajan entered upon a new period in his reign, a period of wars and conquests. The Dacians from whom he had refused to take the tribute accepted by Domitian, made inroads into the Roman territory, and Trajan set out from Rome to chastise them. Hadrian accompanied him in the first war, distinguishing himself so much that he twice received military marks of honour.[3]

---

[1] Dion Cassius, lxix. 4.

[2] Spart. *Vita*, c. 3 : cum orationem imperatoris in senatu agrestius pronuntians rissus esset, usque ad summam peritiam et facundiam Latinis operam dedit. Dion Cassius, lxix. 3 : φύσει δὲ φιλόλογος ἐν ἑκατέρᾳ τῇ γλώσσῃ.

[3] The inscription on the Athenian pediment calls him " Comes Expedi-

On his return to Rome after this victorious expedition he was made curator of the acts of the senate, then tribune of the people in 105 A.D. He held this last office for a few months only, as he was obliged to accompany the emperor in the second Dacian war, where he commanded as legate the Ist legion Minervia.[1] The expedition ended with the conquest of Dacia, whose courageous king Decebalus, committed suicide. Hadrian had led his legion with bravery and ability, and had probably shown a talent for command, which had hardly been expected of him.[2]

In token of his satisfaction Trajan sent him a diamond ring which he himself had received from Nerva on his adoption, and this mark of distinction gave to the favourite the first well-founded hope of a brilliant future.

While still absent at the war he was made praetor, and in that capacity, on his return from the Danube, he gave games to the people at the emperor's expense, in 106 A.D., while the emperor himself celebrated his Dacian triumph, with an expenditure that recalled the times of Domitian. The festivities, which lasted for one hundred and twenty-three days, during which eleven thousand wild animals were hunted, and ten thousand gladiators bled in the arena, must have given Hadrian food for reflection. It was an example that, as emperor, he never imitated.

Trajan immediately appointed him praetorian legate of Lower Pannonia. He was thus to govern a great province, and to give proof that he was qualified for the highest offices of state. This he did to the complete satisfaction of the emperor, for he kept the Sarmatians in check, and gained so much reputation by his military discipline and severity towards the procurators, that in 108 A.D., he received the dignity of the consulship.[3]

---

tionis Dacicae" with which it connects the quaestorship. For this *cursus honorum* see the *Comment.* of Henzen, who takes the relation of Hadrian to the emperor to be that of an adjutant; also Mommsen, *C.I.L.* iii., n. 550.

[1] Borghesi, *Œuvres*, ii. 202, and the Athenian inscription. For the second Dacian war see La Berge, *Essai sur la règne de Trajan*, p. 48 *sq.*

[2] Spart. c. 3: quando quidem multa egregia ejus facta claruerunt.

[3] With M. Trebatius Priscus, only as *suffectus*. The inscription of the Fasti Feriar. Latinar. *C.I.L.* vi., 2016, fixes the date for the year 108 A.D.

After this he was looked upon as the probable successor to the childless Trajan, who already appears to have thought of adopting him.[1] On the death of his patron, L. Licinius Sura, adjutant-general of the emperor, which occurred at this time, the office was bestowed upon Hadrian. Trajan gave him many proofs of his confidence, the empress Plotina favoured him, and powerful friends, such as the senators Sosius Papus and Plotorius Nepos, the knight Livianus and his former guardian Attianus, endeavoured to promote his advancement. But he had many enemies, among whom were Celsus, Nigrinus, Palma, and Lusius Quietus, famous statesmen and generals of Trajan. Hadrian had pursued the usual civil and military career which led to the highest offices of state; in the field he had won respect, he had commanded a legion with distinction, and he had governed a troublesome province with wisdom. It was a great age in which Hadrian's qualities as a ruler were developed, just as the sovereign whom Hadrian served, and whose actions he had the opportunity of narrowly observing, was a great man. Hadrian was surrounded by a crowd of distinguished men, whom Trajan's reign had called forth.

The empty régime of mad self-interest which the caprice of despots had substituted for statecraft, had been swept away by the strong current of political feeling which this ruler had awakened. The spirit of Rome again made itself felt triumphantly through the world as in the days of Julius Caesar and Octavianus. Rome shone by the fame of her arms over foreign nations, but her strength was accompanied by the spirit of a wise government which embraced the world, while the freedom of the citizen was preserved. Never had the sway of Rome extended farther; Trajan had subjugated the Sarmatian Danube, had destroyed the empire of Decebalus, and had turned Dacia into a province. In the East he had conquered lands that were the home of fable as far as the Red Sea, and had added Arabia as a province to the empire. Captive barbarian princes again adorned the Roman triumphs. Their heavy marble statues

See also: Josef Klein, *Fasti Consulares inde a Caesaris nece usque ad imperium Diocletiani*.

[1] Wilhelm Henzen, *Annali dell' Inst.* 1862, p. 158. Spart. c.¶3.

with faces full of sullen defiance even now recall to us in Rome the days of Trajan.[1]   Thousands of artists displayed the new splendour of the monarchy by magnificent buildings. In the year 1 1 3 A.D., the triumphal column was unveiled in the Forum of Trajan, the inimitable pattern for the imitation of ambitious conquerors down to the latest posterity.

It is doubtful if Hadrian ever ardently desired the laurels of the conqueror.   He had other ideals.   Had the choice been his between the fame of Homer and Achilles, he would have chosen the former.   The honour which he had just received from the people of Athens he will have valued quite as highly as a triumph.   For the respect that he commanded as probable successor to the throne, even outside Rome, and the popularity that he enjoyed among the Greeks as a Philhellene, is shown by the fact that the city of Athens elected him archon in the year 1 1 2 A.D.   A statue in his honour was at once erected in the theatre of Dionysus.   Its pedestal, with inscriptions both in Greek and Latin, is still preserved, and it is to this record that we are indebted for the most accurate information as to the political career of Hadrian up to the time of his consulate.[2]

[1] The bust of Decebalus was found in the year 1855 near the Forum of Trajan, and was transfered to the Museum at St. Petersburg.—Wilhelm Froehner, *La Colonne Trajane*, Paris, 1865, p. 5.

[2] From a fragment of the *Mirabilia* of Phlegon, c. 25 (*Phlegontis Trall. Opusc.*, ed. Franz), it appears that 112 A.D. was the year of Hadrian's archonship.   Keil, *Griech. Inschr. Philol. Suppl.* ii. 593, 594.

CHAPTER IV

Hadrian accompanies the Emperor in the Parthian War. Rising of the Jews. Lusius Quietus. Death of Trajan and Adoption of Hadrian

HADRIAN accompanied the emperor in the Parthian war, from which Trajan was not to return. He was his legate on the staff, and this distinction also he owed to Plotina's good-will.[1] Thirst for fame, and ambition to appear the greatest king in the world, had taken possession of the hitherto moderate Trajan, and had impelled him to the most daring enterprises. He proposed to solve the eastern question by driving the powerful Parthians, who had stepped into the place of the Persians, beyond the Tigris, and by taking possession of the highways of commerce to India. It was a war of Greek and Roman culture against time-worn Asia, a renaissance of the ideas of Alexander the Great; but the East was the undoing of Trajan.

Perhaps this expedition that excited such general interest at the time, was the only one which inspired the Philhellene Hadrian with a feeling of romance. The emperor set out from Italy in October 113 A.D.[2] When, in the spring of 114 A.D., he brought votive offerings from the spoils of the Dacians to Zeus Casius at Antioch, which he had appointed as the meeting-place of the army, Hadrian wrote some Greek

[1] Spart. c. 4: cujus studio etiam legatus expeditionis parthicae tempore destinatus est.

[2] Greek Anthology: *Epigrammatum Anthologia Palatina*, ed. F. Duebner, vi. 332 and note p. 267. The votive offerings were two goblets and a gilded buffalo-horn.

verses, wherein he called upon the god to give the emperor the victory over the Achaemenidae, so that he might unite the spoils of the Arsacids with those of the Getae.

After the conquest of Armenia and Mesopotamia in the year 115 A.D., Trajan spent the winter again in Antioch, and during his residence the city was destroyed by an earthquake on 13th December 115 A.D. The countries of the Euphrates were subjugated by brilliant victories. He pressed forward to Babylon, captured Seleucia on the Tigris, and Ctesiphon, the second city of importance in Parthia, sailed down the river into the Persian Gulf, and here abandoned the most fascinating of all dreams to western conquerors,—the conquest of India. Sixteen hundred years were to pass away after Trajan's time, before this magic land was conquered and enslaved by bold and rapacious adventurers from the shores of distant Britain.

On Trajan's return to Babylon in the winter of 116 A.D., his wonderful good fortune deserted him. The peoples whom he had conquered in the districts watered by the two rivers, took up arms in his rear.[1] The flame of this insurrection was kindled by the Jews, who had for some time been settled in Mesopotamia and Babylonia, partly under their own princes, but vassals of the Parthians, —as in Gordyene and Adiabene on the Tigris, where the Izati ruled, a dynasty which had been converted to Judaism—in Osroëne, Naarda, and Nisibis, and as far as Arabia. Since the days of the Ptolemies Jews swarmed in Egypt and Greece, as well as in the island of Cyprus, after Augustus had allowed Herod to rent the copper mines which were to be found there. In all these countries the Jews rose, intoxicated with the hopes of a Messiah, and encouraged to fight the Roman oppressor by the favourable opportunity of the Parthian war. Their hatred against the destroyers of Jerusalem converted them into raging cannibals.

The province of Cyrene, which had already survived one Jewish storm in the time of Vespasian, was deluged with the blood of the Greeks, and turned into a desert. The insurgents were led by a brave man called Lucuas. Even

---

[1] Dion Cassius, lxviii. 29 : πάντα τὰ ἑαλωκότα ἐταράχθη καὶ ἀπέστη.

in Egypt the army of the procurator Lupus, defeated by the rebels, had to withdraw to Alexandria, which at this juncture was destroyed by fire. Trajan was obliged to send Marcius Turbo, one of Hadrian's best friends, to Egypt, with some troops. The brave general crushed the rebellion of the Jews with great difficulty and with frightful severity, and then sailed for Cyprus, where the Hebrews had also risen under their leader Artemion, and had nearly become masters of the island. They had even destroyed the city of Salamis, and it is reported, though it is scarcely credible, that 240,000 Greeks and Romans were killed in this uprising. Turbo, however, suppressed the rebellion here also, and from that time the entry of every Jew into Cyprus was punished with death.[1]

It does not appear that Hadrian took any part in these Jewish wars; it is more likely that he remained by the emperor's side at his post as adjutant-general.[2] At this time Trajan commissioned his boldest general, Lusius Quietus, to subjugate the Jews in the countries of the Euphrates. This formidable warrior was one of the chiefs of Berber, or Moorish race in Africa, who were under the protection of Rome, and whose services the Imperial Government endeavoured to secure by means of money and marks of favour. For this purpose there was one special procurator in *Mauretania Caesariensis* with the title *ad curam gentium*.[3] The Berber prince was completely Romanized, as his name shows; he was burning with ambition to distinguish himself under the banner of the emperor. Rejected at first by the Romans with contempt, he had led his Moorish cavalry as

---

[1] Eusebius, *Hist. Eccl.* iv. 2, and in the *Chronicle*. Dion Cassius, lxviii. 32. Orosius, vii. 12. Gregory, called Bar Hebraeus, *Chronicon*, ed. Bruns und Kirsch, p. 54. 18th and 19th year of Trajan.

[2] Jost, *Allgemein. Gesch. des Israel. Volks*, ii. 111, and Milman, *History of the Jews*, ii.[3] 421, are wrong in asserting that Hadrian fought against the rebels in Cyprus in 116 A.D.

[3] Renier, *Inscr. rom. de l'Algérie*, 4033. Henzen, *C.I.L.* vi. 378a. Jung, *Die roman. Landschaften d. röm. Reiches*, p. 101. Quietus, like Abdel-Kader, was originally a petty chief in his own country, τῶν Μαύρων ἄρχων (Dion Cassius, lxviii. 32) and allied with the Romans. Themistius, ed. Dindorf, *Orat.* 16, 205, calls him ἐξ ἀδόξου καὶ ἀπῳκισμένης ἐσχατιᾶς (Μαυρετανίας).

auxiliaries to Trajan in the Dacian expedition, and had distinguished himself by deeds of valour. It is supposed that he is depicted on the bas-relief of Trajan's column with his savage warriors.[1]

Lusius Quietus carried out his commission in Mesopotamia with African cruelty. He retook Nisibis and Edessa which he destroyed, slaughtering the Jews in thousands. On this account the Rabbinical writers have given the name of Quietus to the whole of Trajan's Jewish war, and indeed have extended it to the country of Judaea itself.[2] For, after the rising in the country of the Euphrates had been put down, Trajan sent the same general to Palestine, not indeed as procurator, but with the full power of a proconsular legate. This mark of distinction given to the Moorish adventurer, who had been elected *Consul suffectus*, seems to have aroused the jealousy of Hadrian.[3]

The mission of Quietus to Palestine, in the beginning of the year 117 A.D., was connected with the measures taken by the emperor for the suppression of the revolt in Egypt and Mesopotamia. For Palestine was the historical and ideal centre of the whole Jewish race, and Jerusalem was the object of their rising in the East, the ultimate aim of which could only be the restoration of the temple and the deliverance of Israel from the yoke of the Romans. It was highly probable that in Judaea the High priest and his Sanhedrin had woven the threads of the rebellion of the Jewish people. When Trajan commenced the Parthian war, he probably summoned a portion of the troops from the fortresses of Palestine, and so denuded the land. This appears to have been the case with the Xth legion Fretensis, which had been stationed there since the time of Titus.[4]

---

[1] Froehner, *La Colonne Trajane*, p. 14, 21, and *planches* 86, 88. On him Borghesi, *Œuvres*, i. viii. 500 *sq.*

[2] "Polemos Schel Quitos"—Graetz, *Geschichte der Juden*, 1866, iv. 132 and note 24. Volkmar, *Judith*, p. 41 *sq.*, especially p. 83 *sq.*

[3] Dion Cassius, lxviii. 32, says of Quietus: ὥστε ἐς τοὺς ἐστρατηγηκότας (propraetorian legate) ἐσγραφῆναι καὶ ὑπατεῦσαι τῆς τε Παλαιστίνης ἄρξαι· ἐξ ὧν που καὶ τὰ μάλιστα ἐφθονήθη καὶ ἐμισήθη καὶ ἀπώλετο. Eusebius, *Hist. Eccl.* iv. 2: Ἰουδαίων ἡγεμών.

[4] Gruter, 367, 6: Inscription on A. Atinius, TRIB . MIL . LEG . X . FRET . A . DIVO . TRAJANO . EXPED . PARTHICA . DONIS . DONATUS.

No trustworthy historian speaks of an actual insurrection at that time in Judaea ; but Spartianus implies the rebellious feeling of the heavily oppressed country, and the despatch of Quietus, the destroying angel of the Jews in Mesopotamia, to Palestine, proves that there was more than a mere inclination to rebel in the province.[1] The Moorish prince came to Judaea to preserve this important key between the countries of the Euphrates and Egypt, and he certainly came with troops. He had brought back the Xth legion, or that part of it which had been withdrawn from the Parthian war, and he commanded it as legate.

Meanwhile Trajan had returned to the Euphrates. Shattered by failure, repulsed from the rock fortress Atra (in which stood a famous temple of the Sun), ill from disappointment and fatigue, despairing of the East, whose conquest on the farther side of the Euphrates now appeared impossible to the Romans, the emperor began his homeward journey to Italy in the spring of 117 A.D. He left Hadrian in Antioch, handing over to him, as legate, the supreme command in Syria and of the Eastern army, and sailed towards the West.[2] His condition however compelled him to land at Cilicia ; and he took to his bed at Selinus (the modern Selinti) in the beginning of August, and he never rose from it again.

The death of Trajan in Asia, after so many heroic struggles amid such bold and fantastic projects, reminds us of Alexander, and, like Alexander, he had appointed no successor. His most famous generals were still fighting against the insurgents, and no one knew the intentions of the emperor. Priscus, Palma, Quietus, or even Hadrian himself could draw their swords if any one of them were sure of the vote of the legions. It was a critical moment. The empire might easily again fall into anarchy, as it did after the death of Nero. It seems strange that Trajan had not long before prevented the possibility of such a catastrophe, as Nerva had done with such a happy result. When he thought over the names of his great men, he

---

[1] Spart. *Vita*, c. 5 : Aegyptus seditionibus urgebatur, Lycia (the reading probably is Lybia) denique ac Palaestina rebelles animos efferebant.

[2] Dion Cassius, lxviii. 33.

must have been convinced that his own relation ought to be his successor. He was aware that Hadrian had a powerful party at court, and had a firmer footing than any other aspirant to the crown. Did he still waver in his resolution to adopt Hadrian, whose incalculable character probably did not inspire him with confidence? He had scarcely been fond of him, even though by the act of placing power in his hands, he had shown that he felt no other choice was open to him. He had exiled Laberius Maximus and Frugi Crassus, enemies of Hadrian, and he had withdrawn his favour from Palma and Celsus, while he had conferred the greatest distinction upon Hadrian, giving him the complete command of Syria, and of the army. Perhaps he dallied with the adoption, because he wished to carry it into effect at Rome by an act of the senate. However, his illness overtook him, and the dying emperor gave way at Selinus to the representations of the Empress Plotina, of the elder Matidia and of Attianus, who were at his side, and Hadrian was virtually adopted.

Trajan died on the 7th or 8th August, 117 A.D. On the 9th Hadrian received at Antioch a deed of adoption, and on the 11th of the same month, the death of the emperor was made public.

At once the report was spread that a trick had been played at Selinus. Dion Cassius maintains that Hadrian was not adopted by Trajan, but that he owed the fortune which he fraudulently obtained, to Attianus and to the love of Plotina.[1] He says he heard from his father, Apronianus, who became prefect of Cilicia long after the death of Trajan, that the death of the emperor was purposely concealed until the document had been framed and made public. Spartianus, too, mentions a rumour that Plotina, after the death of the emperor, substituted a person who, feigning the voice of a dying man, pronounced the adoption of Hadrian.[2] Whether the document was forged,[3] whether the empress lent herself to a deception unworthy of her,

[1] Dion Cassius, lxix. 1, Eutrop. viii. 6.   [2] Spart. c. 4.

[3] Gibbon, La Berge, Dierauer, and others maintain the fictitious adoption. I however agree with the contrary reasons advanced by Centerwall (*Spart. vita Hadriani comment. illustrata* in *Upsula Univ.-*

is a doubtful question ; but the most credible view will always be, that Trajan in his last hours agreed to the adoption of his cousin.

As Hadrian received the document on the 9th of August, this day is the birthday of his adoption. Not until the 11th was the death of Trajan made known. This day is therefore the *dies imperii*, the day of the year of his ascent to the throne. The legions which he commanded as legate of Syria, then the most important province of the empire, at once hailed him Imperator in Antioch, and he gave them a double donative which might appear either as an acknowledgment of his gratification or as evidence of his insecurity.[1]

At the same time Hadrian despatched a most respectful letter to the senate, excusing himself for having assumed the imperial title merely on the acclamation of the army, on the ground that the empire could not remain without an emperor. He asked that the choice of the army should be confirmed.[2] As a matter of fact it was immaterial in the eye of the law, whether the imperial dignity was bestowed by the army or by the senate.[3]

As the ashes of Trajan, escorted by the widowed empress, by Matidia Augusta and Attianus, were to be embarked at Selinus, Hadrian went to that port. The ship of mourning set sail, and he returned to Antioch. Here he remained for several months that he might put in order the disturbed affairs of the East.

Arsskr., Ups. 1869, i., pp. 52-59), and Duruy (*History of Rome*, v., pp. 3 and 4). Haakh (Hadr. in Pauly, *R.E.*) thinks that Trajan entertained the idea of adoption, and Merivale, vii. 412, that Plotina carried it out. Adoption-coins, Eckhel, *Doctrina Numorum*, vi., p. 475 *sq.*, Cohen, *Description des Monnaies*, ii., p. 110, n. 51 *sq.*

[1] Hadrian at once adopted the titles of Trajan, and accordingly called himself *Germanicus Dacicus Parthicus.*—Eckhel, vi., p. 518. Later he dropped these titles.

[2] Dion Cassius, lxix. 2.   [3] Mommsen, *Röm. Staatsrecht*, ii.[3] 790.

CHAPTER V

Hadrian gives up the lately acquired Provinces of Trajan. State of Judaea. Fall of Lusius Quietus

ROME had now an emperor, related to Trajan, the "best" of princes, by ties of natural, though not of intellectual kinship. Hitherto Hadrian had not made himself prominent in the state as a great personality. The whole period from Nerva to the last of the Antonines was such that it was no longer possible for a man to seize dominion by force, as, fortunately for the empire, adoption was the means to the throne, and the brilliancy of the imperial power over-shadowed every other personality. Hadrian had passed through his political career with honour, but without special distinction. Laurels such as Trajan's generals had gained, did not adorn his brow. He was known as one of the cleverest men in Rome, highly cultivated, with an unmistakable leaning towards Hellenism, adapted, apparently, more to enjoy than to govern the world. What characteristics this "Greek" on the throne of the Caesars might disclose, were known to no one, but it was quite clear that the new emperor was not the man to carry out the imperial idea of Trajan, sword in hand. From the first hour of his reign he turned away from it. He showed that his inclinations lay in another direction, and that his wish was to develop the inner life of the empire apart from wars and conquests, making it more secure within the limits protected by the legions—limits not to be extended.

There was no desire in Hadrian's nature for imperial greatness. If he had carried on the boundless conquests of his predecessors, he would have begun his reign with endless

wars, and would have exhausted the already impoverished
treasury of the empire, only to relinquish the fame to the
ambitious generals of Trajan.   Already in Antioch he
sketched the programme of his policy of peace.   He disdained to enter upon the oriental inheritance of his predecessor.   He resolved to give up the newly acquired but
untenable provinces on the other side of the Euphrates.
This determination to abandon the great designs of Trajan
was inevitable under the circumstances.[1]   For Trajan himself
had been forced to learn that distant countries were easier
to conquer than to maintain; he had experienced their
defection, and when Hadrian took the reins of government
the Moors, the Sarmatians, and the Britons were in rebellion,
and Palestine, Cyprus, and Cyrene had to be pacified.
Nevertheless, Hadrian's renunciation was a daring one, as
it must have appeared un-Roman.   It affronted the war-
party, in whose opinion the empire could only maintain its
supremacy in the world by extension.   It embittered the
generals and officers of Trajan, who expected honours and
wealth from the prosecution of the war in the East, and who
now saw the eagles of Rome turning homewards as if they
had been vanquished.   Thus Hadrian showed himself in
the commencement of his reign a man of prudent and
independent mind.[2]   But the dissatisfaction of his opponents
is displayed in the judgments of later Roman historians,
who ascribe Hadrian's relinquishment of the conquests of
his predecessor to vulgar envy of his greatness.[3]   But had
not Augustus recognized the expediency, after many military
conquests, of seeking the welfare of the empire only by
concentrating its possessions?   Had he not voluntarily

[1] This necessity is referred to by Spart. c. 5 : Hadrian followed the
example of Cato, qui Macedonas liberos pronunciavit, quia tueri non
poterant.

[2] This is also Ranke's opinion.   *Weltgeschichte*, iii. 285.

[3] Eutrop. viii. c. 6 : Qui Trajani gloriae invidens statim provincias tres
reliquit, quas Trajanus addiderat.   The *Chron. Heiron.* following Eutropius says "Hadrianus Trajani invidens gloria," etc.   Dion makes no
mention whatever of this incident.   Fronto (ed. Rom. 1846) *Principia
Historiae*, p. 226, merely says "Hadrianus provincias manu Trajani captas
omittere maluit, quam retinere."

relinquished the province of Great Armenia in favour of the son of Artavasdes?[1]

Hadrian made the Euphrates the boundary of the Roman Empire in Asia, giving up Armenia, Mesopotamia, and Assyria, and, after making an agreement with the Parthians, he withdrew his legions from their country. Chosroes he recognized as king of the Parthians. Parthamaspates, the Arsacid who had been forced upon the country as prince, but who had been already expelled by Chosroes, he compensated by giving him the dominion over other districts. For he was ever anxious to secure the Roman influence in the countries of the Euphrates. On the other side of the river too, several kings seem to have acknowledged the supreme power of the emperor.[2]

Of all the conquests of Trajan, Hadrian only kept Arabia-Petraea. This new province, on account of its situation on the borders of Syria and Judaea, on the Red Sea, and its proximity to Egypt, was of great military and commercial importance.

The rising of the Jewish people had been already crushed by the generals of Trajan in Egypt and Cyprus. In Palestine however the agitation was not over, and here Lusius Quietus ruled as governor with great severity. The attempt has been made to prove from the Talmud and the Book of Judith, that Quietus actually waged war against the rebels in Judaea. For that wonderful book, which records the glorification of the Jewish nation and its final conquest over the enemies of Israel, is said, though no proof can be adduced, to have originated in the time of Hadrian. Nineveh is supposed to represent Antioch, Judith Judaea, and Holofernes the cruel Quietus.[3]

---

[1] Mon. Ancyr. *C.I.L.* iii. 2, p. 782.

[2] Amongst the coins of the Mesopotamian princes of Edessa there is one of Abgarus with the head of Hadrian.—Mionnet, v., p. 613.

[3] Volkmar warmly asserts the historical relations of the book of Judith with the Jewish war of Trajan and the fall of Quietus. By the Polemos Schel Quitos he understands the war in Judaea. His Jewish sources are Midrasch on Genesis, Bereschit Rabba, c. 64, the Chronicle of the Seder olam Rabba, which is said to have been edited shortly after the war. He is followed by Graetz (*Gesch. d. Juden*, 1866, iv. 132 and note iv.) Schuerer, *Lehrbuch der neuesten Zeitgesch.* p. 354. A. Hausrath, *Neut. Zeitung*, iii.

The Talmudic authorities, which are quite untrustworthy, maintain that Quietus certainly conquered Judaea, but that the new emperor put a stop to his ravages there, whereupon the Jews laid down their arms, though only on condition of being allowed to rebuild the Temple. There are no facts, however, to vouch for the accuracy of this rabbinical fable which speaks of so great a concession on the part of the emperor to the Jews, even while they were still armed. Only Hadrian's love of peace is not to be doubted. It is possible that messengers from the Sanhedrin sought him in Antioch, to lay before him the complaints and the wishes of their people. But that he went himself in person to Jerusalem is not credible, for he had neither time to do so, nor, after the conclusion of peace with the Parthians, was Judaea of sufficient political importance to call Hadrian away from all his pressing affairs.[1]

Lusius Quietus, however, he removed from Palestine. Dion Cassius and Spartianus have pointed out that this favourite of Trajan was the object of his hatred, and we can easily believe that this powerful man would not, in any case, have hastened to recognize the proclamation of Hadrian as emperor. Hadrian took away from him, as it appears, at the very commencement of his reign, the government of Judaea, and not only the command of the Roman troops who were there, but of his own Moorish warriors, whom he had taken with him.[2] He banished

---

374 sq. J. Derenbourg (*Essai sur l'Hist. et la Géogr. de la Palestine*, i. part, p. 402 sq.) entirely denies the war of Trajan and Hadrian in Judaea. So does Renan, *Les Évangiles*, p. 507.

[1] Duerr (*Die Reisen des Kaisers Hadrian*, p. 16) endeavours to prove this first visit in Judaea, as also Pagi (*Critica in Baron.* p. 121) from a very confused passage in Epiphanius (*De mensuris*, c. 14). And yet he allows Hadrian but two and a half months for his sojourn in Antioch until his departure for Illyricum. And not less untenable is his conjecture that Hadrian then visited Alexandria. Zoega wrongly asserts the presence of the emperor there for the first time before 130 A.D. Eckhel, iv., p. 41 sq.; vi., p. 489 sq. No conclusion as to Hadrian's visit to Alexandria, which Pagi has placed in 119 A.D., can be drawn from coins, as they bear no date.

[2] Spart. c. 5: L. Quietum sublatis gentibus Mauris, quos regebat, quia suspectus imperio fuerat, exarmavit Marcio Turbone Judaeis

him from Palestine. He probably sent him to Rome, to answer for himself before the senate, as, according to Spartianus, he was suspected of ambitious designs upon the throne. But to Mauretania, which had risen in insurrection, Hadrian sent Marcius Turbo as prefect, the conqueror of the Jews in Egypt, a man of proved military fidelity and of untiring energy.[1] It is not known to what new governor Hadrian gave the place of Quietus in Palestine.[2]

The fall of the hated Moorish prince, who was steeped in the blood of Israel, was looked upon by the Jews, though perhaps erroneously, as an earnest of the goodwill of the new emperor; while his withdrawal, contrary to imperial tradition, from the policy of Trajan, revived their hopes of a Messiah. They rejoiced; the bloody conquests of Quietus in Mesopotamia had been fought uselessly, for they saw their brethren there, freed from the yoke of the "tyrant Trajan," after Hadrian had given up possession of the country. The destroyer of the Jews had been banished, and soon indeed they heard of his ignominious death. They instituted a festival in memory of the deliverance of Israel.[3] That they looked upon Hadrian in the beginning of his reign with hope and sympathy, and expected from him an improvement in the fortunes of Judaea, is indicated by passages in the Sibylline books, where the poet, probably an Alexandrian Jew, glorifies the successor of Trajan,[4] the noble ruler who takes his name

compressis ad deprimendum tumultum Mauretaniae destinato, post haec Antiochia degressus est ad inspiciendas reliquias Trajani.

[1] Eckhel, vi., p. 498, and others (Notes to Dion. in ed. of Sturz, vi. 640) wrongly suppose that Hadrian sent Quietus as regent to Mauretania.

[2] Marquardt (*Röm. Staatsverwaltung*, i.[2] 420) places Q. Pompeius Falco, a friend of the young Pliny, as legate of Judaea, between Quietus and the later Rufus. Yet he was still legate there under Trajan about 109 A.D. Henzen, 5451 (with restitution of Borghesi, iv. 125) Mommsen in *Hermes*, iii. 51, and in Index nominum to Keil's *Ep. Plin.*, Borghesi, viii. 365. Waddington, *Fastes des Prov. asiatiques*, p. 203.

[3] "Jom Trajanus"—Volkmar, *Judith*, p. 40 *sq.*

[4] *Orac. Sibyll.*, ed. Alexander, v., lines 247-285, 414-434. Graetz, iv. 138. Hausrath, iii. 307 *sq.* Volkmar, *Judith*, page 104 *sq.* Renan (*L'Église chrétienne*, p. 13) asserts, with good reason, that these prophecies were written already in Hadrian's lifetime.

from a Sea; with him a new age of happiness for Israel and Jerusalem is to begin.

The Talmudists maintain that Hadrian really promised the Jews to allow them to rebuild their Temple as a national sanctuary, and to restore the city which Titus had destroyed. We can understand how this saying arose among the Jews; but it is quite inconceivable that a Roman emperor should make such a promise to despised Jewish rebels, for this would have been tantamount to the acknowledgment of the Jews as a nation, which for political reasons Rome had destroyed. It was Hadrian who finally obliterated the stronghold of Judaism, by founding the Roman colony Aelia Capitolina on the ruins of Jerusalem. This was perhaps even a project of Trajan.[1] It certainly must be considered in connection with the last rebellion of the Jews in the East, and with the resolve of Hadrian to surrender the Parthian conquests. Jerusalem had been the strongest of all the fortresses of Syria. Titus had destroyed it, and Hadrian was the first to feel that this destruction was a mistake. As soon as he had withdrawn the boundaries of the empire to this side of the Euphrates, retaining only Arabia of Trajan's new provinces, he must have thought of building strong places between the Euphrates and the Red Sea, to serve as a support to the Roman army against the Parthians, the Bedawin of Arabia, and the Jews, and, at the same time, as emporiums of commerce. The renewed prosperity of the cities of Heliopolis (Baalbek), Damascus, Palmyra, Bostra, Gerasa, and others in the Trachonitis and in the country beyond the Jordan, did, as a matter of fact, begin in the time of Hadrian. It is unnecessary to mention of what importance the situation of Jerusalem was on the elevated plateau commanding the passes to the Phoenician Sea, the valley of the Jordan, the Dead Sea, and the caravan routes of Arabia. Hadrian therefore followed the plan of restoring Jerusalem as a Roman colony, but it was late in his reign before he carried it out.

At Antioch, the emperor received from Rome the letters of congratulation of the senate, who not only granted him divine honours in memory of his adopted father, for which

[1] Ewald, *Geschichte d. Volkes Israel*, vii. 361.

he had asked, but awarded him also the Parthian triumph in the place of Trajan.   This he declined.[1]

The aristocratic opposition which had become powerful in the service of Trajan might become dangerous to the new sovereign.   It seemed therefore advisable to his friends to encounter it at once.   Attianus had already advised him at Selinus to make suspicious enemies harmless ; and, as such, had pointed out to him Bebius Macer the prefect of the city, Laberius Maximus, and Frugi Crassus.[2]   But Hadrian showed himself nobler than his followers, and he did not accept the advice.   Attianus, and Similis, one of the most honourable men of his time, were made prefects of the Praetorium.

---

[1] Spart. c. 6.

[2] Spart. c. 5.   Yet Crassus was afterwards assassinated by a servile procurator.

CHAPTER VI

*Return of Hadrian to Rome by way of Illyricum.
War with the Roxolani. Arrangement of affairs
in Pannonia and Dacia. Conspiracy and Execution
of the Four Consulars. Arrival of Hadrian in
Rome in August* 118 A.D.

AFTER Hadrian had established peace in the East, and
had appointed L. Catilius Severus legate of Syria, he left
Antioch to return to Italy.[1] Spartianus says that he came
home by way of Illyria. This name primarily denoted the
eastern shores of the Adriatic Sea, but since the time of
Trajan it had been applied to the large tract of country
bordering the Danube as far as Macedonia, Moesia, Pannonia,
Dalmatia, Dacia, and even Raetia and Noricum.[2] These
provinces received a special share of Hadrian's attention
because he had served as a tribune in Moesia, governed
Pannonia as legate, and fought in Dacia by the side of
Trajan.

The time of his departure from Syria cannot correctly be
ascertained. It is, however, certain that a whole year elapsed
between his assumption of the imperial power and his
arrival in Rome. This interval lends colour to the supposi-

---

[1] The coins in Eckhel, vi., pp. 475, 476, probably refer to the settlement of
the East : Oriens, Concordia, Justitia, Pax. For Catilius Severus,
a friend of the younger Pliny, and his proconsulship in Asia during the
years 117 to 119 A.D., see Waddington, *Fastes des Provinces asiatiques*,
p. 134.

[2] Marquardt, *Röm. Staatsver.* i. 295. Jung, *Die roman. Landschaften
d. röm. Reiches*, p. 333.

tion that the emperor undertook an expedition against the
Sarmatians and Roxolani on his return journey from Syria.[1]
If this is correct, Hadrian, after sending on his troops in
advance to Moesia, penetrated through the Hellespont and
the Bosporus into the countries of the Danube, and, on the
conclusion of the expedition, he sailed from one of the ports
of Illyria to Brundusium.

Moesia, an imperial province divided into two districts,
which were separated by the Danube from Dacia, and by the
Haemus from Thrace, was of no small importance to the
empire, as the frontier on the Black Sea, where the turbulent
tribes of Sarmatia sought to advance from the Dnieper to
the mouths of the Danube. It stretched from the time of
Nero beyond Tyras, the colony of Miletus, to the lands of
the kings of the Bosporus, against whose attacks the rest of
the free Greek states on the northern shore of the Black Sea
could only be protected by the neighbouring Roman troops
In Troesmis the Vth legion Macedonica protected the
mouth of the Danube, while in Tomi and Odessus (Varna) a
small fleet of warships was stationed.

The Roxolani had at that time made common cause with
the Jazyges to invade the provinces of Moesia and Dacia,
and Hadrian therefore felt himself compelled to undertake
an expedition against them. But it did not come to a serious
war ; the emperor seems indeed to have so terrified the
barbarians by the mere sight of his powerful army and of their

---

[1] This is the view taken by Flemmer (*De itiner. et reb. gestis Adriani*,
p. 2) with which Duerr, *Die Reisen des Kaisers Hadrian*, p. 16, concurs.
It contradicts the statement of Spartianus (c. 5), who does not connect
this campaign with the return to Rome over Illyricum. Eusebius, who
places the Sarmatian war in Hadrian's fourth year, is of less weight, for
his Roman chronology is useless. The chronology of Spartianus is also
much confused. The connection of events makes Duerr's view acceptable.
The conjectured presence of Hadrian in Juliopolis on the 12th November
117 A.D., cannot however be proved from a letter of the emperor to the
youth of Pergamum (Curtius, *Hermes*, vii. 37, 38), as the geographical
position of the place is doubtful, and the iteration figure of the Tribunicia
potestas is missing. When Duerr (p. 24) concludes from the sacrifices
which the Arvals offered also to Victoria in honour of the *adventus* of
the emperor, that this has reference to the victory over the Roxolani, he
forgets that the senate had offered Hadrian the Parthian triumph of Trajan.

military dexterity—he made the Batavian cavalry swim armed across the Danube—that they submitted and accepted him as arbitrator in their quarrels.[1] The principle which Hadrian always adopted in his dealings with the barbarian princes was to subdue them by negotiation rather than by force. He satisfied their demands where he recognized they were just, and for some time the Roman Empire had submitted to subsidize such princes. The king of the Roxolani, Rasparaganus, one of these chieftains in the pay of Rome, had complained that his subsidies had been diminished; Hadrian granted him the continuation of the payment, but he made him harmless for the future. The Sarmatian king was obliged to beg for the honour of being taken into the *Gens Aelia*, and from thenceforth he seems to have lived as a pensioner of the Roman state with his whole family in banishment at Pola in Istria.[2]

Hadrian strengthened the Roman stations in Lower Moesia, but it is uncertain whether he did this in 118 A.D. or later. Coins and inscriptions refer to the activity of the emperor there.[3] Under his rule Moesia was separated from Dalmatia and made into a separate administrative area.[4]

The emperor was also engaged in arranging matters in Pannonia and Dacia on the other side of the Danube. He summoned Marcius Turbo from Mauretania, giving to him the temporary government of this consular province and raising him to the dignity of a prefect of Egypt in order to

[1] Dion Cassius, lxix. 6. *C.I.L.* iii., n. 3676: Inscription relating to a warrior of the Batavian cohort, who swam the Danube.

[2] Inscription from Pola, *C.I.L.* v. pt. 1, 32 : P . AELIO . RASPARAGANO . REGI . ROXOLANORUM, and 33 : his son Aelius Peregrinus, who is not called *rex*. Here Roxolani and Sarmati are used indiscriminately.

[3] ADVENTUI . AUG . MOESIAE . S . C.—EXERC . MOESIACUS, Eckhel, vi., p. 499. A coin of Hadrian with Aeliana Pincensia, Eckhel, vi., p. 447, refers to *metalla* in Moesia. Inscript. at Tomi, the metropolis of Moesia inferior : *C.I.L.* iii. 765, add. p. 997. Troesmis (Iglitza) became under Hadrian a garrison town, Renier, *Rev. Arch.* xii. 414, *C.I.L.* iii. 2, n. 6166. Nicopolis is called Adrianopolis, Mionnet, i., p. 359. Mommsen, *Eph. ep.* iii. 234. Viminacium bears the name of Aelium, *C.I.L.* iii., p. 264.

[4] Henri Cons (*La Prov. rom. de Dalmatie*, 1882, p. 267) gives as his authorities for this *C.I.L.* iii. 2829 ; *C.I.L.* iii. 4115, 2828 ; Inscription in honour of Hadrian at Burnum in 118 A.D.

increase his authority.[1] Hadrian divided Dacia, it is uncertain when, into two districts (*inferior* and *superior*) giving
it a praetorian legate.[2] And yet the wish has been attributed
to him to give up this province, the most important of all
Trajan's conquests, and to return to the old frontier of the
Danube. It is said that he was only induced to retain it
by the representations of his friends, who urged that the
Roman colonists who had been settled there by his predecessor in great numbers, would inevitably fall a sacrifice to
the fury of the barbarians.[3]

But a glance at this country which had been so quickly
Romanized, and was now garrisoned by several legions,
would have sufficed to convince Hadrian that this Danubian
province must remain Roman, a bulwark of the empire and
of Italy in particular. It is, therefore, incredible that he
demolished the upper part of the great bridge built across
the Danube by Trajan at Turnu Severin and Orsova, the
admired work of the architect Apollodorus, merely to restrain
the barbarians from incursions into the countries on the
right bank of the stream.[4]

The work of colonizing the large territory of the
Danube was eagerly pushed forward in Hadrian's reign, as
is proved by the monuments found there. Trajan's colony
of Ulpia Sarmizegetusa (of which the ruins are to be seen
to-day near Vasarhely in Transylvania), the principal city of
Dacia and the seat of the worship of Augustus, erected a
statue to the Emperor Hadrian, the inscription on which
commemorates his second consulate (118 A.D.).[5]

---

[1] Spart. c. 6, 7, Inscription in honour of Turbo at Sarmizegetusa, *C.I.L.*
iii., n. 1461.

[2] In 129 A.D. Plautius Caesianus appears as legate in Dacia inferior
C.I.L. iii., n. 876. Marquardt, *Röm. Staatsverw.* i. 309.

[3] Eutrop. viii. c. 6.

[4] Dion Cassius, lxviii. 13. The bridge of twenty stone pillars was 150
feet high and 60 wide. J. Aschbach on Trajan's stone bridge over the
Danube in *Mittheilungen d. k. k. Central Commission d. Erforschung
und Erhaltung v. Baudenkmale*, Wien 1858, iii. 197 *sq*. Even Aschbach
still believed in the absurd story that Hadrian destroyed this bridge too
from his envy of Trajan. Duruy, v., rightly doubts its destruction.

[5] *C.I.L.* iii., n. 1445, 1446. The legate of Hadrian, Cn. Papirius
Aelianus, built an aqueduct there (132, 133 A.D.). A Hadrianic inscription

While he was still occupied in the countries of the Danube, a conspiracy was formed against his throne and his life. Disappointed ambition induced some of the most important men in Rome to attempt the overthrow of Trajan's successor by a revolution, which, if it had succeeded, would have robbed the world of the happy age of the Antonines. The chief of these malcontents were the consuls Lusius Quietus, Publius Celsus, Avidius Nigrinus, and Cornelius Palma, the distinguished conqueror of the province of Arabia. They represented the military and political school of Trajan, whose principles were slighted by the new emperor, whom they looked upon as an upstart without any military reputation, and a favourite of women. These great men, who had been rivals of Hadrian, were justified by their services in forming ambitious hopes. Even if Trajan had never thought of appointing the Moorish adventurer Quietus to succeed him in the empire, he had made the audacious man of such importance that Hadrian feared him, and banished him.[1] Nigrinus, particularly, had been pointed out as a possible successor to Trajan. He had governed Achaia as proconsul in the last years of the emperor.[2] His daughter had married Ceionius Commodus, who was to become, as Aelius Verus, the adopted son of Hadrian, and the father of the emperor Lucius Verus.[3]

Not one of these great men stood at the head of refractory legions; not one had the praetorians on their side, nor the

from Sarmizegetusa with the sentence "cujus virtute Dacia imperio addita felix est" is considered genuine by Zumpt, *Rhein. Mus.* 1843, p. 257, in opposition to Eckhel, vi., p. 494, and Mommsen, who consider it false. Coins with EXERCIT. DAC. and DACIA, Eckhel, vi., p. 494. Duerr considers, p. 19, that the settlement of Roman colonies at Drobeta (*C.I.L.* iii. 1581) Nicopolis, and Viminacium, was made by Hadrian. At this time the Legio XIII. Gemina was quartered at Heviz in Dacia, *C.I.L.* iii., n. 953. In many cities of Dacia the name Aelius occurs among distinguished citizens.—Jung, *Die roman. Landsch.* p. 397.

[1] Panegyric on Quietus in Ammianus Marcellinus, ed. Gronov., p. 619 and in Themistius, *Orat.* 16, p. 205 (Dindorf).

[2] A Delphian inscription, C. Wescher, *Étude sur le Monum. bilingue de Delphes*, Paris, 1868, p. 23 *sq.*, speaks of him as propraetorian legate.

[3] Spart. c. 7 is therefore wrong in saying of Nigrinus that Hadrian had intended him to be his successor.

senate, which, on the contrary, had been won over by the promises and flatteries of Hadrian.   As all the actual facts of their opposition remain unknown to us, it seems at this distance of time to have been both feeble and foolish.   It almost appears as if the emperor's friends had dignified the murmurs of discontent with the name of a state conspiracy. It was said that Hadrian was to be killed when hunting, or while he was offering sacrifice, and that the plan was betrayed.   The obsequious senate hastened to give the emperor a proof of its submission by causing the unfortunate men to be seized and immediately put to death.   Palma was executed in Tarracina, Celsus in Baiae, Quietus at some unknown place on his journey, and Nigrinus in Faventia. The different localities mentioned as the places of their execution do not support the theory of conspiracy, unless indeed we suppose that the consulars were taken separately in their flight, or that each was surprised where he happened to be at the time.[1]

When Hadrian heard of these events he could thank the senate for sparing him the responsibility of the execution, or, at any rate, for giving him the opportunity of a disclaimer. In his autobiography, which has perished, he is said to have maintained that the senate acted contrary to his wishes in putting these great men to death.[2]   This may possibly be true, for in Trajan's time one senator only had been condemned, and he had been condemned by the senate without the knowledge of the emperor.[3]   Hadrian expressly ascribed the crime to the counsels of the prefect Attianus.[4]   But whether this advice was given to the senate or to himself, remains doubtful.   Spartianus expresses no opinion upon it, while Dion Cassius makes it clear that he does not consider the emperor innocent.   The most powerful of his adversaries had been removed by his zealous friends, and this bloody act was a warning to the rest.   Otherwise cruelty was not in Hadrian's nature.   Until his latter days, when some great men again fell victims to his suspicions, he was the most humane of princes.

---

[1] Spart. c. 7.   Dion Cassius, lxix. 2.
[2] Spart. c. 7: Invito Hadriano, ut ipse in vita sua dicit occisi sunt.
[3] Eutrop. viii. 4.
[4] Spart. c. 9: Quorum quidem necem in Attiani consilia refundebat.

Great discontent prevailed in Rome. The most prominent men of Trajan's court, four consulars, had been put to death without a trial. In spite of the complaisance of the senate, the aristocracy must have felt deeply injured, and must have dreaded the return of the reign of terror of Domitian. For this reason Hadrian hurried to Rome to dispel the unfavourable opinion which had been formed of him. He had thought, even in Illyria, of propitiating the Roman people by presents: three gold pieces were given to each man, and greater benefits were still to flow, to wipe out the blood that had been shed. Hadrian entered Rome on the 7th or 8th of August 118 A.D.[1]

[1] The date of Hadrian's arrival in Rome is fixed by the *Acta Arvalia*, which record that the Arvals assembled in the temple of Concordia, coopted the Emperor Hadrian in place of Trajan into their brotherhood, and offered sacrifices in honour of his arrival. Henzen, *Acta Arvalia*, p. cliii. *sq.*; *C.I.L.* vi., p. 536 *sq.* As consuls L. Pomp. Bassus, and L . . . inius B(arbar)us. Proof of the date in Duerr., p. 21 *sq.*, Eckhel vi., p. 476. Gold and silver coins of arrival struck by the Senate representing head of Hadrian crowned with laurel, Rome sitting on a breast-plate and shield, grasping the hand of the emperor. Cohen, ii.², p. 113, n. 91 : IMP.CAESAR.TRAJANUS.HADRIANUS.AUG.—ADVENTUS.AUG. PONT.MAX.TR.POT.COS.II.S.C. The proper consuls for the first half of the year 118 A.D. were, Hadrianus *iterum* and Cn. Pedanius Fuscus Salinator, stepson of Domitia Paulina, sister of Hadrian and wife of Servianus. See Borghesi, ii., p. 212. L. Pompeius Bassus and his colleague were *suffecti*.

CHAPTER VII

Hadrian's first acts in Rome. The great Remission of Debt. Third Consulate of the Emperor. Fall of Attianus. Marcius Turbo becomes Prefect. Death of Matidia Augusta. The Palilia of the year 121 A.D.

THE capital received Trajan's successor with imperial honours, and he hurried to the senate to wash away the stains from his purple robe, asserting his innocence of the death of the consulars. He swore never to sanction the punishment of a senator without the concurrence of the whole body.[1] A similar promise had been given previously by Nerva and Trajan, and might be looked upon as a kind of treaty with the senate, whose freedom and existence depended on the caprice of the emperor. Hadrian next celebrated the memory of his father by adoption with brilliant festivities. He had gracefully declined the Parthian triumph which had been voted to him. The triumphal procession was abandoned; but on the car of victory the statue of his great predecessor was placed, crowned with laurel.[2]

It was probably on this occasion that the ashes of Trajan were solemnly laid in the pedestal of the great triumphal column in the Forum of Trajan, and that the dead emperor was placed among the gods.[3] Hadrian himself had demanded

[1] In senatu quoque excussatis quae facta erant juravit, se numquam senatorem nisi ex senatus sententia puniturum.—Spart. c. 7.

[2] Medal TRIUMPHUS . PARTHICUS, struck after the death of Trajan. Cohen, ii.², p. 78, n. 585.

[3] Cohen, ii.², p. 87, n. 658.   DIVO . TRAJANO . PARTH . AUG . PATRI. A phoenix.

this from the senate, and it was a request not easy to refuse, as the same honour had been granted to Nerva at the wish of Trajan. And Trajan had been really loved. The senate offered Hadrian the title of *pater patriae*, but the emperor again declined it. This title, which was first bestowed upon Cicero, was already a customary attribute of the emperors, but after the example of Augustus, they generally pretended at first to refuse, before they accepted, a distinction which theoretically, was the highest honour in the state, but which in reality was so often nothing but a mockery. Tiberius too had declined the title, and Trajan had only taken it after refusing it.[1] Despite Hadrian's refusal, there are coins and records of the early years of his reign which give him this title, either because it was used after the first decree of the senate, or else because it was looked upon as a matter of course.[2] Hadrian first assumed the title of *pater patriae* and his wife Sabina that of Augusta in the year 128 A.D.[3]

In order to conquer the affections of the people as if by storm, the emperor, after his arrival, showered free gifts upon Rome and the empire with a prodigality which until then had been unheard of. Following the example of Trajan, he had already wholly remitted to Italy, and in part to the provinces, the gifts of homage (*aurum coronarium*), which the cities and provinces were accustomed to make to the emperors on their accession.[4] Now, however, he

---

[1] Suetonius, *Tiber.* c. 68. Tacitus, *Annal.* i. 72. Pliny, *Paneg.* 21. Pertinax was shrewd enough to have himself called *pater patriae* the first day of his reign. Julius Capitolinus, *Pertinax*, c. 5.

[2] The *Acta Arvalia* give Hadrian the title already before his arrival in Rome, the 3rd January 118 A.D.; and there again on the 7th January 122 A.D. Henzen, cli. clxiii. Some coins of Hadrian's first consulate bear the letters *P.P.* On the coins of the second (118 A.D.) the title is altogether wanting. The coins of the third (119 A.D.) and last of his consulates sometimes bear the title, sometimes omit it. Eckhel also remarks that the title on inscriptions never stands before Trib. Pot. xii., and shows from two Alexandrian coins that Hadrian assumed the title A.U.C. 881.

[3] Duerr, p. 28 *sq.*

[4] On the *aurum coronarium*, Gellius, v. 6. Lipsius, *De magn. Rom.* ii. c. 51. Casaubon on Spart. c. 6. Antoninus Pius also remitted the *aurum coronarium*, Capitolinus, c. 4.

astonished the empire by a magnificent remission of debt. He remitted, so Spartianus says, an immense sum which was due to the fiscus from private debtors in Rome and Italy, and also large sums in the provinces, after burning the bonds in the Forum of the deified Trajan in order to ensure absolute security to every one. Dion Cassius says: "As soon as he came to Rome he forgave all debts to the fiscus and the aerarium, which had been due for sixteen years."[1] Inscriptions have immortalized this famous action, and coins have been stamped to commemorate it, which represent a lictor, a staff in his left hand, and in his right a torch, with which he is burning a bundle of bonds which lie on the ground; before him stand three figures, one with raised hand.[2] There is a similar representation on a marble relief that was excavated from the forum in Rome a few years since.

The amount of the debt remitted would be in our money about nine millions sterling, and generosity on this scale, though not of this kind, was unexampled.[3] It proves how heavy the burden of taxation had become through Trajan's wars. The question is,—Whom did this remission benefit? Spartianus clearly speaks only of the imperial treasury, and is ambiguous about the provinces, so that it is doubtful whether he means the imperial provinces only, or all the provinces in the empire. Dion connects the remission with both treasuries, the fiscus and the aerarium, and accordingly concludes that the latter was at the disposal of the emperor, and no longer exclusively at the disposal of the senate. But the Roman inscription, which speaks throughout only of the fiscus, contradicts such an interpretation. It cannot

---

[1] Spart. c. 7. Dion Cassius, lxix. 8. The *Chronicon* of Eusebius under the second consulate of Hadrian : ᾿Αδριανὸς χρεῶν ὀφειλὰς τῶν ὑπ᾿ αὐτὸν πόλεων καὶ πολιτῶν τῷ δημοσίῳ λόγῳ ἀνηκούσας ἀπέκοψε.

[2] Inscription from the Forum of Trajan (copied by Anonymus of Einsiedeln), *C.I.L.* vi., n. 967. A fragmentary inscription of Hadrian, likewise from the Forum of Trajan, in the basement of the Capitol. museum apparently refers to the same remission. The coins in question, Eckhel, vi., p. 472. Cohen, ii., p. 208, n. 1210 *sq.*: RELIQUA . VETERA . HS . NOVIES . MILL . ABOLITA . S . C.

[3] Augustus had already remitted debts. Suetonius, *Aug.* c. 32.

therefore be proved that Hadrian's liberality extended to both treasuries.[1]

The great remission of debt embraced the arrears of sixteen years. Marcus Aurelius later on extended this favour to a further forty-six years.[2] Whether this financial amnesty of Hadrian led to a revision of arrears, every fifteen years, and so laid the foundation of the system of indictions of the time of Constantine, is uncertain.[3]

The date of this remission is undoubtedly the year 118 A.D., for this is shown by the inscription which records the second consulate of the emperor with that of Fuscus Salinator.[4] Evidently this act of grace was connected with the festivities in honour of Trajan, as the bones were burnt in his Forum.

Hadrian, no doubt, performed other acts of generosity at the same time, giving money to the people, and insignia to the senators according to their rank, and relieving the provinces from the cost of the imperial post.

He remained for more than two years in Rome. After he had held his second consulate in 118 A.D. with Cn. Pedanius Fuscus Salinator, he took the consular dignity again in the following year for the third time with the Stoic philosopher, Q. Junius Rusticus, at all events for four months

Hieronymus says only "reliqua tributorum Urbis relaxavit," but Eusebius speaks of cities and citizens in general who were subject to the emperor. Scaliger (*Animadv. in Chronol. Eusebii*, p. 193) understands merely "urbes Provinciar. Caesaris." Spanheim (*De Praest. et Usu Num. Diss.* ix. 812) explains this "reliqua" as "publica et fiscalia debita." Tillemont makes a distinction between "a thrésor du prince et thrésor public du prince," and confesses his uncertainty (*Not. sur l'Emp. Adr.* 2, 3, 892 sq.). Centerwall (*ibid.* p. 66) thinks that the remission refers to both treasuries; whereas O. Hirschfeld (*Unters. auf d. Geb. der röm. Verwaltungsgesch.* i. 1876, p. 12) believes that the remission refers only to the fiscus. Peter (*Gesch. Roms*, iii. 2-174) separates the remission of the debts of the fiscus for Italy from those of the arrears of taxes for the provinces, and explains the passage in Spartianus accordingly. He assumes 94-114 A.D. as the period.

[2] Dion Cassius, lxxi. 32.

[3] Mommsen (*Röm. Staatsrecht*, ii., p. 616) asserts it. Noris (*Annus et Ep. Syromaced.*, page 174) denies it, as the remission comprised sixteen years.

[4] Coins which testify to the remission in the third consulate of Hadrian are simply repetitions of this liberality. Occo, ed. Biragus, 170.

until the end of April. It almost looks as if he despised the consulship, for he never afterwards took this office. All his later years are designated by the third consulate, and Hadrian still suffers from this caprice, as it has obscured, and made the chronological record of the acts of his reign almost impossible from the year 119 A.D., especially as the indication of the *Potestas Tribunicia* is generally missing on his coins and inscriptions. This was the only power which Hadrian retained, and which had to be renewed on the day of adoption.[1]

On his birthday, the 24th January 119 A.D., Hadrian celebrated gladiatorial games in the amphitheatre, and threw gifts into the circus. He took great pains to secure the goodwill of the people.[2] He was to be seen administering justice in the courts of the praetors and consuls, in the palace, in the Forum, in the Pantheon. He aimed only at being a servant of the people, as he told the senate. A woman with a petition once placed herself in his way, to whom he said, " I have no time now"; "Then be emperor no longer," cried the woman, and Hadrian turned round and granted her request.[3] He left nothing undone which could secure him the approval both of small and great. He cared nothing for show. He was never attended by a brilliant escort. He was accessible to all, he accepted invitations readily, and visited senators and knights like a private gentleman. He was amiable to persons of inferior rank, and he rebuked those who would deprive him of this " enjoyment of humanity" by reminding him of his imperial dignity.[4] In the palace, where he did not allow the freedmen to exercise any authority, he was temperate, but cheerful when at table with his friends. He liked to be surrounded by

[1] According to his epitaph twenty-two times. From this it has been supposed that Hadrian transferred the renewal of the *potestas tribunicia* to the 1st of January. Aschbach, *Die Consulate der r. Kaiser*, p. 71, according to Borghesi, *Giorn. Arcad.* cx., and letter to Henzen in Orelli, 5459. But it seems that it was not renewed at New Year, but on the 10th of December : Mommsen, *Rom. Staatsrecht*, ii. 799 *sq.* See also Duerr, *Die Reisen des Kaiser Hadrian*, p. 19, note 58.

[2] Plebis jactantissimus amator.—Spart. c. 17.

[3] Dion Cassius, lxix. 6.—A similar anecdote is related of Trajan, and referred to by Dante, *Purg.* cant. x.   [4] Spart. c. 20.

learned men and artists. He made the historian Suetonius
his secretary.

His brother-in-law Servianus should have been his best
friend, but this seems by no means to have been the case,
for he remains in the background during the whole of
Hadrian's reign. He appears nowhere among the statesmen
of the emperor, although in 134 A.D. he was made consul
for the third time. Attianus fell into disgrace. Hadrian had
made him, his old guardian, and Similis, prefects, and had
given both men the highest power in the state and in his
cabinet. Attianus had been his first confidant, and to his
exertions he in great measure owed his adoption. It was
Attianus who suggested the violent removal of the consulars.
He had now however become inconvenient to the emperor,[1]
who sacrificed him, not so much because he was afraid of
seeing him become as great as Sejanus, but to make a show
of atonement for the executions. The fall of his first minister
was however so gentle, that it could not have been regarded
as serious. If the account of Spartianus is correct, Hadrian
certainly wished to put him to death, but in the end he only
compelled him to resign his office as prefect. As compen-
sation he left him the consular rank and the dignity of
senator, which he considered the greatest distinction of all.[2]

The successor of Attianus in the prefecture was Marcius
Turbo, a general of the old Roman type. There is a
story that when Hadrian once urged him to take rest, he
replied in the words of Vespasian : "A prefect of the praetorium must die standing." Similis too, the second prefect of
the guard, resigned his post. Of the house of the Sulpicii,
he was one of the purest characters in Rome at that time.
He seems to have been imbued with the old republican
spirit, which made it impossible for him to endure an imperial
court for any length of time. He had been unwilling to
accept office, and laid it down again with great joy to retire
to his estate in the country. There he spent seven peaceful
years. On his tomb he ordered these stoical words to be
written, " Here lies Similis, who existed for so many years

[1] Cum Attiani, praefecti sui et quondam tutoris, potentiam ferre non
posset.—Spart. c. 9.
[2] Nihil se amplius habere, quod in eum conferri posset.—Spart. c. 8.

and lived seven."[1]   His successor in the prefecture was
Septicius Clarus, a friend of the younger Pliny.[2]

Immediately after the fall of these favourites, Hadrian
made a journey into Campania or Southern Italy, where
he loaded all the cities with benefits.[3]

Directly afterwards his mother-in-law, Matidia Augusta,
died. He paid the highest honours to her remains, and
the senate consecrated her. At her burial in the end of
December 119 A.D., gladiatorial games were given, and
the emperor himself delivered a funeral oration, in which
he praised her beauty, her kindness of heart, and gentleness.
A fragment of this oration was found at Tivoli.[4]

Spartianus has given the completion of the obsequies of
Matidia as the date for Hadrian's departure into Gaul, i.e.
for the beginning of his first great journey; but from the
coins it appears that the emperor was still in Rome on the
21st of April 121 A.D.[5] These gold and copper coins represent on one side the head of Hadrian crowned with laurel,
on the other side the figure of a woman seated, holding in
her right hand a wheel, in her left three obelisks or cones.
The legend denotes the circus games which had been established in the year 874 A.U.C., on the anniversary of the
foundation of the city (the Palilia).[6] The old Roman
shepherds' festival of the god of shepherds, Pales, on the
21st of April, had been long looked upon as the foundation
day of Rome; but that Hadrian was the first to celebrate
the Palilia as the birthday festival of the genius of Rome,
and distinguish them by this official name, cannot exactly

[1] Dion Cassius, lxix. 19.—On Similis, Borghesi, Œuvres, iii. 127.
[2] Spart. c. 8 and 9. These events fall at the end of 118, or certainly in
the year 119. On Sept. Clarus, see Pliny, Ep. i. 115; vii. 28; viii. 1.
[3] Spart. c. 9: Summotis his a praefectura, quibus debebat imperium,
Campaniam petit.
[4] Mommsen, Abhandl. der Berliner Acad. 1863, p. 483 sq. The Acta
Arvalia record the consecration of Matidia on the 23rd December 119
A.D.—Henzen, clviii. Consecration coins: Eckhel, vi., p. 471.
[5] Duerr, p. 25 sq.
[6] Eckhel, vi., p. 501. Cohen ii.[2], p. 118, n. 162. ANN . DCCCLXXIIII . NAT .
URBIS . P . CIR . CON. Mommsen (C.I.L. i., p. 391) reads "Natali Urbis
Parilibus Circenses Constituti." Cohen, though uncertain, reads
"(primum?) circenses constituti." Foy-Vaillant reads "Populo."

be proved.[1]   In any case the emperor reorganized this festival, for these coins relate clearly to new circus games ordered by him in celebration of the festival of the city on the 21st of April 121 A.D., and there is much in favour of the theory, though it cannot be proved, that on this day the foundation stone of the temple of Rome and Venus was laid by Hadrian.[2]   It is also noteworthy that the coins do not precisely indicate that Hadrian must have been present in Rome on that day.

[1] Duerr, p. 26, asserts this, according to Athenaeus 8, 361, who says that since the erection of Hadrian's temple of Fortuna urbis, the festival formerly known as Parilia was called Romana.   See Eckhel, vi., p. 502. Preller, *Röm. Myth.* ii.[3] 356.

[2] Flemmer, p. 14 *sq.*, rightly lays stress on the fact that the coin does not mention the laying of the foundation stone of the temple, whereas there are coins that distinctly refer to the temple.—Eckhel, vi., p. 510.

CHAPTER VIII

General Remarks on Hadrian's Journeys.   Coins which commemorate them

HADRIAN had spent his first years in Rome in laying the foundations of his policy and of the government of the empire.   His throne stood firm.   He had won the senate by respecting its rights, the people and the army by his liberality ; and the great number of distinguished statesmen whom the time of Trajan had produced, and with some of whom he was acquainted, aided him in his task of government.   Now, however, he was anxious to learn the condition of the provinces of the empire from personal observation, and he made long journeys through them.

Augustus, too, had spent some eleven years away from Italy, and had visited every country of the empire, with the exception of Africa and Sardinia; but Hadrian made his journeys on a definite plan.[1]   They are a unique phenomenon in the history of all ancient and modern princes.   Neither wars nor conquests urged him into distant countries, like his predecessor Trajan, whom the old Roman principle of the extension of the empire had carried to the gates of India.   Hadrian on the contrary dared to keep the temple of Janus closed, and to declare the Roman empire stationary within the limits fixed by himself.[2]

[1] Suetonius, *Aug.* c. 47 : nec est, ut opinor, provincia, excepta dum taxat Africa et Sardinia, quam non adierit.

[2] This is probably represented by the coin of TELLUS . STABILITA, Cohen, ii., p. 225, n. 1429 *sq.*   A woman reclining on the ground, supported by a basket of fruit, and carrying the globe ; sometimes she holds in her left hand a vine branch.

Was not this empire which embraced the whole
civilized world wide enough to satisfy the ambition of
Caesar? and could not in future the strength of the state
be spent in its preservation and well-being?

The journeys of Hadrian are the more remarkable, as
they portray the Roman emperor in quite a new relation to
the Orbis Romanus. The gigantic geographical works of
Strabo and Pliny had spread a knowledge of the world in
Greek and Latin literature; Hadrian made it a personal
task and business for the sovereign. Hitherto the city of
Rome alone had represented the world, and the provinces
had merely been utilized by the Caesars as supplies for the
all-devouring capital. Hadrian was the first to look upon
the empire as a whole, and upon all its parts as equal
among themselves, equal even to Rome.

He passes through the countries, carrying blessings and
peace with him, from the borders of Caledonia to the shores
of the Red Sea, from the columns of Hercules on the
Mediterranean to the oasis of Palmyra in the desert of Syria.
New cities arise at his nod, and ancient cities are restored.
Many are called after him *Hadriana* and *Aelia.* He appears
everywhere ordering and creating, and everywhere he leaves
benefits behind him. By his own age he was probably
compared to the wandering Hercules, and from the same
feeling he was called the new Dionysus.[1] Apart from his
deep love of Hellenism, his nature was touched by the
distinguishing characteristic of the men of the Renaissance
of the fifteenth century, by the ardent desire to know
everything worth knowing, and to unveil all mysteries.
Spartianus says that he was so fond of travel that he wished
to see everything that he had heard about the places of the
earth, with his own eyes, and Tertullian has called him
the inquirer into all curiosities.[2] The passion to know
foreign countries and people, the thirst for knowledge of a
restless mind, drove the emperor of Rome from land to
land, and the consciousness that this large and beautiful
world through which he wandered, belonged to him as its

[1] Eckhel, vi., p. 504, coin with HERC. GADIT. More in Flemmer,
p. 35. Of Hadrian as new Dionysus later.

[2] Curiositatum omnium explorator.—Tertullian, *adv. Gentes,* c. 5.

ruler, must have filled him with an almost divine satisfaction.

With the feelings of a modern traveller, Hadrian ascends high mountains to enjoy the sunrise and the view over land and sea. He sails up the mysterious Nile, and revels in the wonders of the days of the Pharaohs. Like a sentimental traveller, he writes his name on the statue of Memnon. He goes into ecstasies over the monuments of famous historical cities in Hellas and Asia. He restores their temples. He visits the graves of the heroes in Ilium, of Pompey in Pelusium, of Miltiades and Epaminondas, and even of Alcibiades in Melissa. In Trebizond he allows his statue to be erected on the spot where Xenophon and the remnant of the Ten Thousand had again reached the sea. He is initiated in the Eleusinian mysteries. He observes with a fine irony the customs and religions of nations, and he discusses questions of grammar and philosophy with the learned men of Athens, Smyrna, and Alexandria. But it is the same traveller too who reviews, with the eye of a Roman commander, the legions on the frontiers of the empire ; he builds gigantic walls and fortresses, and restores the relaxed discipline of the troops.

Dion, indeed, has looked at the objects of Hadrian's journeys merely from a military point of view when he says: " The emperor travelled from one province to another, visited countries and cities, castles and fortresses, of which he built some at a more convenient place, some he allowed to fall into ruins, while others he strengthened. He directed his attention, not only to military concerns generally—to arms, engines, trenches, walls, and fortifications—but also to the smallest details, and to the character of every soldier and officer. He braced and strengthened manners that had become effeminate, he exercised the army in every kind of combat, alternately bestowing praise and blame, and teaching every man his duty." [1]

Orders of the day and coins with the legend *Exercitus* and *Disciplina* prove his care in these matters, while there are none in existence of the warlike Trajan. The military organization of the empire was certainly the first condition

---

[1] Dion Cassius, lxix. 9.

of its existence, and just because Hadrian did not wish to wage war, he secured peace by his careful development of the Roman army.[1]   He visited the camps of the legions on many frontiers, and established firm lines around the Roman territory at the most dangerous points, in order to protect civilization from the inroads of the barbarians.   Rome was never safer from these incursions than during the peaceful reign of Hadrian.   He improved the military system, and his regulations lasted until the time of Constantine.

But Hadrian inquired into all other branches of government in the provinces.   He makes the ubiquity of the prince a new principle of the monarchy, whose first officer he wishes to be considered.   The *Disciplina Augusti* becomes under him a conception of government which is not applied to the army alone.   It means Roman culture stamped in permanent form by the laws of the monarchy, and the practice of a wise government.   When this discipline declines, Rome too will fall.

Everywhere Hadrian sets up his tribunal as a judge. Bad administrators and governors he punishes with severity. His sharp eyes are not to be deceived.   The fortunes of his subjects were never put before him in painted colours.   He regulates the finances of the provinces; he gives constitutions to the cities, and founds colonies; he builds streets and harbours; he promotes arts and science, trade and agriculture.   The personal inclinations of the man, combined with the serious duty of the ruler, made him that great traveller in the imperial purple, the wonder of his own age and of posterity.

Hadrian by his Spartan simplicity afforded the Roman satirists, who ridiculed the effeminate luxury of fashionable travellers, no opportunity for sarcasm.[2]   He travelled without state and with few followers.[3]   On his marches he faced the hardships of every climate, always with head uncovered, on horseback or on foot, but never in a carriage.   He often

---

[1] Hadrian took over thirty legions from Trajan. Of these he lost the leg. IX. in Britain, and in Judaea the leg. XXII. Deiotariana. Pfitzner, *Gesch. der röm. Kaiserlegionen*, 1881, p. 94 *sq.*; "Bestand der 28 Legionen," p. 97.

[2] Verses of Florus: Ego nolo Caesar esse,
Ambulare per Britannos, etc

[3] Dion Cassius, lxix. 10.

marched miles in front of his attendants, armed like a Roman footsoldier, in order, like Trajan, to set his soldiers an example. In camp he shared their fare. A Roman historian has ventured to say of him that he travelled through all the provinces of the Roman world on foot.[1]

The friends of a Roman emperor, who were usually called his "attendants" (*comites*), never deserved their name better than under him. A few are known to us as his travelling companions, such as Antinous and Verus.[2] On the Nile his wife Sabina accompanied him with her court. He took his secretary with him, perhaps on one occasion the historian Suetonius. Instead of cohorts of soldiers (only a small number of the praetorians served as his guard) he was accompanied by crowds of engineers and artisans, whom he employed on his buildings.

He treated the provinces with as much affection as Rome; distinguishing indeed Athens, the capital of intellect, more than Rome, the capital of power. He never levied contributions upon the countries through which he travelled, as Nero and his rapacious followers had formerly plundered Hellas. He entered the countries of the empire as unassumingly as a private gentleman, and quitted them as an imperial benefactor. What happiness it must have been for him to receive, and at the same time deserve, the homage of old and famous cities! As Homer says of Odysseus, so might Hadrian boast of himself, that he had learnt to know many cities and customs of men. Dion says of him: "He visited more cities than any other ruler, and to all he was benevolent; he gave them aqueducts and harbours, corn and gold, buildings and honours of many kinds."[3]

In our time of steamboats and railways, the traveller Hadrian who fearlessly, but with unheard-of difficulty, penetrated into the most untrodden parts of the world, offers a strange spectacle. Kings of the present time might envy this emperor of Rome; and if another proof is wanting that this age belongs to the happiest period of humanity, it may

[1] Aurel. Victor, *Epit.* 14. Eutrop. viii. 7.

[2] A *T. Caesernius, comes in oriente* of Hadrian, in Renier, *Inscr. rom. de l'Algérie*, n. 1817.

[3] Dion Cassius, lxix. 5.

D

be found in the fact that it produced as its ruler the great traveller Hadrian.

He doubtless made notes of what he heard and saw, and used them later in his *Memoirs*. Unfortunately they are lost; only one letter of Hadrian, written from Egypt to his brother-in-law Servianus, has been preserved, and it shows how keen were his powers of observation. His view of the world and of mankind would have been more instructive to us than the whole declamatory literature of the Sophists of that time. As the journeys of Hadrian were in themselves the greatest evidence of Hadrian's activity as a ruler, the loss of correct information about them is greatly to be regretted. The statements of Spartianus, and the extracts of Xiphilinus from Dion Cassius present only a number of confused notes, and this lack of information cannot be adequately supplied by such records as we possess referring to the journeys of the emperor. These records are inscriptions from the cities and provinces, and above all, numerous coins which were struck in memory of his visit and residence.

Among the coins are some which have no local allusion, but simply wish the emperor a prosperous journey. They represent a ship sailing, with Hadrian seated, the figure of a god accompanying him; dolphins and sea monsters play around the boat, and on the sail is written "Good luck to Augustus."[1] The coins in gold, silver, and copper from twenty-five provinces form a priceless collection of local monuments, which in this way have never been historically repeated. The most numerous are those which commemorate the arrival (*adventus*) of the emperor in a province, and those which honour him as restorer (*restitutor*) of a country or of a city.[2] It is noticeable that no exception is made in the case of Italy, but that it is on the same footing with the other provinces.[3]

[1] FELICITATI . AUG. Cohen, ii., p. 161, n. 651 *sq.*

[2] ADVENTUI . AUG . ALEXANDRIAE . ASIAE . BRITANNIAE . HISPANIAE . JUDAEAE, etc.—RESTITUTORI . ACHAJAE . AFRICAE . GALLIAE, etc.—Foy-Vaillant, *Numismata*, i. 60 *sq.*, and passim in the works on coinage. The classification of the travelling coins, according to Eckhel, vi. 475 *sq.*, in Greppo, *Mémoire sur les Voyages de l'Emp. Hadrien*, c. 2.

[3] ADVENTUI . AUG . ITALIAE, or merely AD . AUG . S . C.—FORTUNAE . REDUCI ; ITALIA . FELIX (with cornucopia and lance); RESTITUTORI . ITALIAE.

The coins of arrival depict on the reverse side the emperor before the figure of a woman who represents the genius of the province ; she sacrifices before an altar, or she offers her hand to the emperor.   The genius sometimes represents a divinity of the country, like Isis and Serapis in Alexandria.[1] Rome too had many opportunities of recording the return of Hadrian.   But on the coins which refer to such an event, the name of Rome is always wanting ; the genius of the city is depicted, seated on armour and offering her hand to the emperor, or Hadrian is on horseback, followed by two warriors, while Rome helmeted offers him a branch ; behind are the seven hills, and below the god Tiber.[2]

On the coins of restoration Hadrian is represented standing upright in the act of raising a woman who kneels before him.[3]   So extremely numerous were the restorations which this emperor carried out that they were commemorated on coins which designated him "Restorer" or "Saviour of the world," a designation which would appear a grand expression of the Roman consciousness of sovereign dominion, were it not at the same time a proof of the slavish flattery of the people to their despots.   For Nero had already caused himself to be described on coins as " Saviour of the world."[4] The earth is represented as a noble woman, on her head a mural crown, on her lap a globe, the emperor raising her from an attitude of humility.[5]   A coin with the beautiful legend, "Golden age," has the same signification ; a half-clad genius stands within a circle, which he touches with his right hand, while in his left he holds a globe, upon which is seated a phoenix.[6]   These remarkable coins at all events teach us that the age of Hadrian was conscious of its good fortune under the blessings of peace.   In the same way

[1] Cohen, ii., p. 108, n. 18.

[2] ADVENTUI . AUG . P . M . P . P.   Foy-Vaillant, iii. 115.

[3] So Achaia, Cohen, ii., p. 209, n. 1214.   Judaea, n. 547, yet without the epithet *Restitutori*.   Eckhel, vi. 446.

[4] Eckhel, vi. 278: τῷ σωτῆρι τῆς οἰκουμένης.   There is also a coin of Augustus with SALUS . GENERIS . HUMANI.   Eckhel, vi., p. 108.

[5] RESTITUTORI . ORBIS . TERRARUM, Cohen, ii., p. 214, n. 1285.   TELLUS . STABIL., p. 225, n. 1435.   The earth with cornucopia, in front, the globe and four children, the seasons.   Similarly, n. 1436, TEMPORUM . FELICITAS.

[6] SAEC . AUR . P . M . TRIB . P . COS . III.   Foy-Vaillant, ii. 148.

the coins which record the benevolence of Hadrian are magnificently summed up in one which terms him " Enricher of
the world." [1]

The number of places which the emperor visited and
loaded with benefits, is shown by the coins struck in his
honour by the different cities, even if they seldom record
particular facts. [2]   In addition come the number of those
which refer to the reviews of troops in particular provinces ;
the emperor is seated on horseback in front of the soldiers, or
he is speaking to them from a stage. [3]

But the drawback generally to any chronological use that
can be made of Hadrian's coins is, that they do not belong
to the year in which the emperor visited the particular provinces ; indeed, they are chiefly of later date, and were even
struck in Rome by the senate.   The number of times that
he had held the tribunitian power is nearly always wanting ;
the coins are distinguished only by the third consulate of the
emperor (in 119 A.D.), and as Hadrian did not fill this office
again, the third consulate lasted until his death, and it
becomes impossible to fix the year.

The journeys of Hadrian can only be fixed as epochs, and
the particular year can seldom be given.   All attempts to do
this by the help of records and of scanty historical information
have been unsuccessful from the time of Scaliger and Pagi,
from Tillemont and Eckhel until our own day. [4]

---

[1] LOCUPLETATORI . ORBIS . TERRARUM.   Cohen, ii., p. 185, n. 950.

[2] Compiled by Foy-Vaillant, *Numismata alia Imperator—in coloniis,
municipiis—Hadrianus*, p. 153 *sq.*

[3] EXERCITUS, with the name of the province.   DISCIPLINA . AUG. and
DECURSIO.   Eckhel, vi., p. 503.   Cohen, ii., n. 553 *sq.*, 589 *sq.*

[4] The journeys of Hadrian have principally been commented on by J.
M. Flemmer, *Comment. de itincrib. et reb. gestis Hadriani Imp.*, Havniae,
1836 ; J. G. H. Greppo, *Mémoire sur les Voyages de l'Emp. Hadrien*, Paris,
1842 ; and also by J. Duerr, *Die Reisen des Kaisers Hadrian.*   This
monograph has been most carefully compiled from the documentary
material, which has been considerably enlarged during late years, and is
therefore a valuable contribution to the history of this period.   I hope it
may be the precursor of a complete work on the state of the empire
under Hadrian.

CHAPTER IX

*Hadrian's Journeys into Gaul and Germany as far as
the Danubian Provinces. The Condition of these
Countries*

IN the year 120 or 121 A.D., Hadrian left Rome to start on
his first great imperial journey in the west of Europe. Of the
two divisions of the empire, the western provinces, with the
exception of Italy and Spain, had only become Roman
under Julius Caesar, and consequently were an acquisition
of the monarchy. These countries of the Celts, Sarmatians,
and Germans, from the Alps to the Danube, and from Gaul
to Britain, which were looked upon by the Romans as
barbarous and without history of their own, were not calculated to excite the emperor's desire for travel, either by
the beauty of their scenery or by the importance of their
cities. He was in the first instance, therefore, impelled to
visit them by his duties and aims as a sovereign. Hadrian
perceived that the fortunes of Rome were not to be established in the East, to which Trajan had shown so great a
partiality, but in the western countries of the Germans and
Celts. History indeed, had shown the Romans that the
duration of their empire depended not on the events which
happened on the distant Euphrates, but on what took place
on the Danube and the Rhine. There lay the Achilles'
tendon of Rome close to Italy, and Britain itself was considered the furthest Roman bulwark for the purpose of
preventing the Celts and Germans from crossing the sea in
their thirst for conquest.

Hadrian went first into Gaul ; by which road, or whether

accompanied by his wife Sabina, we do not know. For Spartianus dismisses this Gallic journey with a few words. Coins record the arrival of the emperor.[1] He probably landed at Massilia. This famous colony of the Phocaeans was still a free city allied to Rome, entirely Greek in constitution and culture. It shone by its schools of science, and flourished by its extensive Mediterranean trade. That Hadrian sailed on the Rhone seems to be proved by an inscription made by the sailors of this river.[2]

Gaul, already a rich and flourishing country, consisted at this time of four provinces: Narbonensis, which was governed by the senate, and Aquitania, Lugdunensis and Belgica, which were ruled by the emperor's praetorian legates. Lugdunum (Lyons) was the capital of these three last provinces, and there stood the altar of Rome and of Augustus, the symbol of the Roman empire and the Roman power, to which the subject nations were obliged to pay divine honour.[3] There on the 1st August the Gallic diet annually assembled. Other cities had greatly developed, such as Narbonne, Nismes, Arles, Bordeaux, and Toulouse. Lutetia (Paris), where Julius Caesar had once assembled a council of the Gauls, was already a thriving place of trade.[4] The whole country as far as Trèves was so highly civilized by Roman culture, that later on, after the fall of the empire, it formed the nucleus of new Europe.

We do not know what improvements Hadrian made in this well regulated province; the title of "Restorer," which is given to him on the coins, may refer to the Latin right which he bestowed upon the province Narbonensis and upon other parts of Gaul.[5]

---

[1] Eckhel, vi. 494.

[2] HADRIANO . AUG . P . M . TR . POT . III . COS . III . N(AUTAE). RHODANICI . PRINCIPI . INDULGENTISSIMO, from Tournon. Flemmer, p. 12. Greppo, p. 85.

[3] According to Strabo, 192, the altar contained the names of sixty tribes, and each was represented by a monument.

[4] The name Παρίσιοι is already known to Strabo (194).

[5] Zumpt, Comm. Ep. i., c. 6, p. 410, enumerates the following cities as having received new rights from Hadrian : Aquae Sextiae, Avenio, Cabellio, Nemausus, Tolosa, Acusium, Mantuna, Reii, Ruscino, Apta Julia.

From there he went to Germany. Tacitus was the first to revive the interest of Rome in this country, which was plunged, for the most part, in gloom and obscurity, though its people were full of vigour and were ardent for liberty. The emperors had always been aware of the danger which threatened the empire from this quarter. Caesar had conquered the banks of the Rhine in order to protect Gaul. Augustus wished to be master of Germany as far as the Elbe, and to make it into a proper province, but his plan was not carried out, and the consequence of the defeat of Varus was that Rome lost most of her fortresses east of the Rhine, until Domitian again pushed forward the boundary.

The Roman territory on the Rhine was then divided into the districts *Germania superior* and *inferior*, which were governed by consular legates. In Upper Germany the strong city Mayence (Moguntiacum) was the capital, and the seat of the military governor. Other places, like Worms (Borbetomagus), Spire (Spira), Strasburg (Argentoratum), and Augusta Rauracorum (Basel) flourished greatly.[1] Eastwards from the Rhine and northwards from the Danube, Upper Germany included the countries which had been civilized by Roman colonists (decumates), whose development in the time of the emperors is proved by inscriptions and ruins from Baden to Tübingen and the Odenwald.[2] Trajan had made roads there, and had built forts, his most important work being Baden-Baden.[3] The district of Helvetia belonged also to Upper Germany, and here too Roman civilization flourished, protected by the *limes* or boundary dyke.[4]

Lower Germany, the Batavian country on the Lower Rhine, however scarcely stretched beyond the river in the time of Hadrian. Its capital, the former town of the Ubii, was Colonia Agrippina (Cologne), where an altar of Augustus,

---

[1] Strasburg, first mentioned by Ptolemy, became the junction of the roads which led from Pannonia, Raetia, and Italy into eastern and northern Gaul.—Mannert, ii. 1, p. 227.

[2] Ukert, iii. 1, p. 267 *sq.*, 286 *sq.* The expression *Decumates agri* is only found in Tacitus, *Germ.* 32.

[3] Francke, *Gesch. Trajans*, p. 59.

[4] Mommsen, *Die Schweiz in römischer Zeit*, p. 11.

the *Ara Ubiorum*, reminded the subject Germans east of the Rhine, that they were vassals of Rome and of the divine emperor.

The origin and government of these two Germanic provinces has not yet been satisfactorily explained. Until the time of Constantine they seem to have had no separate administration, but to have been great military districts under the command of the legates of the army, who were stationed at Mayence and Cologne, while as belonging to Gaul they were governed by the procurator of the province Belgica.[1]

Hadrian marched through the Roman district of Germania and visited the fixed quarters of the legions and the colonies. Spartianus has devoted a whole chapter to this journey of the emperor, but does little more than remark on the pains he took about the discipline of the army. From the time of Octavius the choicest troops of Rome were stationed in both Germanies, first eight legions and then fewer.[2] Hadrian found the military discipline relaxed, and he removed everything from the camps which could enervate the soldiers. He was thoughtful about their surroundings, he visited their hospitals, and cared for their welfare; but he punished desertion severely, and forbade the abuse of the sale of leave by the officers. He acted in the same way in all the other provinces. We have general orders of his, and a list of military diplomas, in which he gave citizenship and the right

[1] On this opinion (which rests on Strabo, Pliny, and Ptolemy), advanced by Fechter and renewed by Mommsen, see O. Hirschfeld, *Die Verwaltung der Rheingrenze in der ersten 3 Jahrhunderten der röm. Kaiserzeit*, p. 434 *sq.* Marquardt (*Röm. Staatsv.* i. 273) credits the Emperor Tiberius (17 A.D.) with the organization of the two Germanies as military provinces, which however stood to Gallia in the same relation as later Numidia to Africa, inasmuch as they belonged to the administration of the *legatus Belgicae.* See also E. Huebner, *Der röm. Grenzwall in Germanien*, p. 41. The military commanders there were called in the first century, *legatus exerc. superioris* or *inferioris*, but already in the second, *legatus pro praetore Germaniae sup.* or *inf.*, and *leg. imp. Cesaris Antonini Aug. Pii, pro praet. German. superioris et exercitus in ea tendentis.*—Jung., *Rom. Landsch.*, p. 195 *sq.*

[2] Pfitzner, p. 136, mentions for the years 107-120 A.D., in Germania superior, the legio VIII. Aug., XXII. Primigenia; in Germ. inferior, I. Minervia, VI. Victrix, XXX. Ulpia.

of connubium to soldiers who had served their time.[1]   A warrior prince without war, he was beloved by the army, and he never had to fear a rising among the legions.

He paid attention also to the finances of the German countries. His coins bear simply the name of *Germania* and *Exercitus Germanicus*.   The country is represented as a woman with spear and shield.   On the coins of the army the emperor appears on horseback addressing the soldiers.[2] There are, however, no coins of arrival and restoration for Germany, and this deficiency supports the opinion, though it may not quite establish it, that *Germania superior* and *inferior* did not constitute a separate administrative area, but were assigned to Belgium.

There is no historical evidence for the theory, though there are good reasons for supposing that the continuation of the *limes* begun by Domitian, was the work of Trajan and Hadrian.   These gigantic lines of fortification, sixty miles in length, whose remains are now called "Walls of the devil," or Pfahlgraben, enclose the *Agri decumates* from Kehlheim on the Danube across the Maine as far as the confluence of the Lahn and the Rhine.   They secured the safety of both Germanies and of northern Raetia as boundaries of the Roman empire against the irruption of the free Germans from the east.   As Hadrian caused a similar wall to be built in Britain, we may venture to ascribe the completion of the German wall to him, particularly as Spartian speaks of more lines of this kind in Hadrian's time.[3]

In consequence of these strong barriers the German frontier long remained quiet.   Not until the Antonines did the Catti, and then the Marcomanni rise again.   Hadrian's

---

[1] To the veterans he gave the right over the *peculium castrense*, to dispose by will of the fortunes they had earned during service. Inst. lib. ii., Tit. xii. Renier *Recueil de Diplomes militaires*, Paris 1876. PRIVILEGIA. MILITUM, etc., *C.I.L.* iii. 2, p. 834 *sq.*

[2] Eckhel, vi. 494.

[3] Spart. c. 12.   C. Arnd, *Der Pfahlgraben nach den neuesten Forschungen*, 1861, and the literature concerning it, in E. Huebner, *Der röm. Grenzwall in Germanien.*   According to him, Hadrian separated the two Germanies from Gallia in consequence of this *limes*.   See also O. Hirschfeld, *Die Verwaltung der Rheingrenze*, etc.

travels in Germany were generally beneficial to the Rhine-land, and they were the first means since the days of Tacitus of diffusing fresh information about this central part of Europe. But on the other side of the *limes* lay the unconquered *Germania magna* of Ptolemy, with its tribes which were scarcely known by name. According to the account of Spartianus, Hadrian gave a king to one of these races, and he goes on to say that the Roman rule prevailed over the land, but at the same time the empire submitted to pay subsidies to the princes of the barbarians. But this could only have been on the borders of the Roman territory, as the interior of Germany remained closed to the Romans. The deepest obscurity shrouded the forest-covered countries as far as the Oder and Vistula, whose people bear unknown names in the map of Ptolemy, while the places which the distinguished geographer marked do not indicate cities but districts.[1]

In Hadrian's time the strength of the German people, of the Goths, the Vandals, the Lombards, and the Saxons lay dormant in impenetrable countries, which remained undisturbed by Roman influence even when it was greatest and most formidable. Not even a Tacitus could have foreseen the future of this savage wilderness. Gaul, on the other side of the Rhine, became rich by its proximity to the sea, by more favourable natural conditions, and by the early enjoyment of Roman civilization ; Germany, on this side of the stream, remained condemned to poverty, and to a longer period of barbarity, but it preserved its powerful primitive speech and its racial character. It appears first in the history of the world after its migratory tribes had destroyed the Roman empire. It first adopted Roman civilization through the medium of Christian Rome, and revived the name of the universal empire when the high priest of Christianity erected his throne on the ruins of the imperial power. The Reformation of the Church would not have been begun or would not have been carried out, if the whole of Germany had, like Gaul and Spain, become a Roman province.

During his first residence in Germany, which was of some duration, Hadrian probably visited the provinces of Raetia

[1] Kiepert, *Lehrbuch der alten Geographie*, i. 465.

and Noricum, and even Pannonia.[1] Of these partially Celtic countries of the Danube, which Claudius had first set in order, Raetia and the "kingdom" of Noricum were governed by imperial procurators, without much display of troops, while Pannonia was under a consular legate of the emperor, and was of the highest military importance, as an eastern bulwark between the Danube and the Alps. On this account it was strongly fortified. In Upper Pannonia it was of importance to strengthen the line of the Danube. This was done at Mursa, not far from the junction of the Danube with the Drave, and this place (the Esseg of to-day) was made by Hadrian into the colony Aelia Mursa; further on Aelium Aquincum (Alt-Ofen), which was a municipium from the time of Hadrian, was also fortified. Still further up, Brigetio, Aelium Carnuntum, and Vindobona, the forerunner of Vienna, where the xth legion Gemina lay, protected the Danube.[2] In Upper Pannonia Hadrian seems to have subdued the district from Noviodunum to the Alpine country of the Carni above Aquileia, to have united it with Italy, and to have bestowed citizenship upon it.[3]

The emperor returned from the Danube to the Rhine. As a Forum Adriani in the neighbourhood of Lugdunum Batavorum is called after him, it is probable that he then went from the lower Rhine to Britain by sea.[4]

[1] Flemmer and Duerr very rightly think so because no more suitable time can be found for it. See the coins mentioned by Flemmer, p. 17 sq.: EXER . NORICUS . RHAETICUS, and in Duerr, p. 35, the cities favoured or built by Hadrian: Aelia Ovilava, Cetium, Vindobona, Carnuntum, Brigetio, Aquincum, Solva, Abudiacum.—Augusta Vindelicorum (Augsburg, a *vicus* founded by Augustus, in Ptolemy an *oppidum*) was no colony, but was created a city by Hadrian, and adopted the name Aelia, *C.I.L.* iii. 2, p. 711. Zumpt denies the colony Juvavum (Salzburg) ascribed to Hadrian, *Comment. Ep.* i. 417. See also Mommsen, *C.I.L.* iii. 2, p. 669.

[2] MURSENSES . CONDITORI . SUO, *C.I.L.* iii., n. 3279. Aelia Mursa, iii., p. 423. Aquincum, p. 439. According to Mommsen, *Die römischen Lagerstädte*, p. 323, it is probable that Hadrian granted municipal rights to *Canabae* of the three great camps on the middle Danube, Carnuntum (Petronell), Aquincum, and Viminiacum (Costolat).

[3] *C.I.L.* iii., n. 3915, inscription in honour of Hadrian of the Aelii Carni Cives Romani ; see also Mommsen's notes, p. 498.

[4] Greppo, p. 71, assumes this from the Tabula Peutingeriana. See also Flemmer, p. 19. Duerr, p. 36.

CHAPTER X

*Hadrian in Britain. He goes through Gaul to Spain
and to Mauretania*

BRITAIN had not long been brought under the dominion of
Rome. Julius Caesar was the first Roman general who had
entered the country. The conquest of the island was afterwards attempted by Claudius in 43 A.D., and the colony
of Camalodunum founded. His successors continued the
undertaking. The names of Paulinus Suetonius, Cerealis,
and Agricola are conspicuous in these bold and difficult
expeditions, which resulted in the subjection of Britain as
far as the Clyde. Agricola built a strong wall between the
Firths of Forth and Clyde, and this line, stretching between
the Glasgow and Edinburgh of to-day, was the most northerly
limit which the Romans reached in Scotland. Nerva and
even Trajan appear to have given up the war of conquest on
the further side of Northumberland. Under Trajan, York
(Eburacum) the former capital of the warlike Brigantes,
became the capital of the province, the seat of the governor,
and the place where all the Roman roads met.

Late in the time of Trajan, and in the early days of
Hadrian's reign, the people of the Brigantes were in vio-
lent insurrection, and the Romans suffered serious losses.[1]
Hadrian, therefore, sent troops to Britain under M. Maenius
Agrippa and T. Pontius Sabinus.[2] The IXth legion, which

---

[1] Spart. c. 5: Britanni teneri sub romana ditione non poterant. Fronto,
de bello Parthico, p. 144: Quid? avo vestro Hadriano imperium obtinente
quantum militum a . . . Britannis caesum.

[2] The inscription in Henzen-Orelli, 804, speaks of Agrippa as "electum
a Divo Hadriano et missum in exped. Britannicam tribun. cohortis I.

was stationed at York, had been cut to pieces in the war, so that it had to be replaced by the VIth Victrix from Castra Vetera on the Lower Rhine.[1]   The insurrection, however, must have been quelled before Hadrian reached the island, for there is nothing to prove his own active share in the war.[2]   Coins exist which record the arrival of the emperor in Britain, and his reviews of the troops there, but his coins of restoration are wanting for this country as well as for Germany.[3]

As he was convinced that the country could not be held as far as Agricola's boundary wall, he decided to build another further south, and to separate Roman civilization from the wild Caledonians by an impassable barrier.   For this division no better line could be found than that between Carlisle and Newcastle from sea to sea.   The Wall of the Picts, the remains of Hadrian's gigantic work, the counterpart to the *limes* in Germany, is still standing.   This wonderful system of forts was begun in 122 A.D.   Inscrip-

Hispanor. equitatae." Subsequently he is "praefectus classis Britanniae et procur. prov. Brit." See in reference to him *C.I.L.* vii., n. 379-382. Sabinus probably was sent to Britain in the beginning of Hadrian's reign. *Bull. d. Inst.* 1851, p. 136. He conducted cavalry to Britain of leg. VII. Gemina, VIII. Augusta, XXII. Primigenia. Henzen, 5456. Pfitzner, p. 92, 246. Huebner (*Hermes*, 1881, 547).

[1] Huebner, *C.I.L.*, vii., n. 241, according to Borghesi, iv. 115, and in *Hermes*, 1881, p. 546. Henzen, 3186.

[2] The verses of Florus :

Ego nolo Caesar esse
Ambulare per Britannos,

have, according to Huebner (*C.I.L.*, p. 100), reference to the expedition of Hadrian to Britain, which is, however, a misconception of the term *ambulare*. Florus thinks only of the barren countries in general, and therefore chooses Britain as *ultima Thule*. Eutrop. 8, 3, says of Hadrian : "Pacem omni tempore imperii sui habuit" and once only did he wage war by means of a legate. Pfitzner, p. 91, believes that the war in Britain was the only one which Hadrian carried on personally, but he does not prove it. The inscription 806 in Orelli, where Hadrian is called *Britannicus*, is not genuine. It goes without saying, that the expedition coins (in Cohen, ii., n. 589-593), where Hadrian is represented seated on horseback, with or without lance, are no proof of his presence at a war.

[3] Eckhel, vi. 493, ADVENTUI. AUG. BRIT. EXERC. BRITANNICUS. *C.I.L.*, vii., n. 498, mutilated inscription from the military station Segedunum, apparently a laudatory address of Hadrian to the army in Britain.

tions prove that the work was carried on under Hadrian by the legate Aulus Platorius Nepos of the IInd legion ; but the VIth Victrix and the XXth Valeria Victrix were also engaged in it.[1]

The wall was eighty Roman or sixteen geographical miles in length, and stretched from the south-westerly corner of the Solway to the mouth of the Tyne without forming a straight line.[2]   The fortification consisted of an inner or southerly earthen wall with ditches, and an outer northerly stone wall with numerous towers and about eighty small forts. Between the earthen and the stone walls, and supported by them, were seventeen large towers, or fortified camps, united by a paved military road running from sea to sea.   One of these, *pons Aelius*, the nearest to the eastern sea, where a bridge goes over the Tyne, proves by its name that it was founded by Hadrian.   The name was repeated later in Rome in the famous bridge which led to the tomb of the emperor.[3]

After an attempt on the part of Antoninus Pius to return to the Scottish line of Agricola, the wall of Hadrian was maintained as a boundary by Septimius Severus.   Under its protection the civilization of Rome was developed in Britain with growing success, and Juvenal was able to flatter the Romans with the idea that the Britons were actually on the point of keeping a public orator in their pay.[4]   Hadrian

---

[1] *C.I.L.* vii., n. 660-663, 713, and Huebner, *ibid.*, p. 100. Platorius Nepos was still legate in Britain in 124 A.D.   Renier, *Rec. d. dipl. milit.*, n. 25, of 18 October 124 A.D.   Before him it was probably Q. Pompeius Falco, Waddington, *Fastes des Prov. Asiat.*, p. 203.   Under Hadrian there were three legions stationed in Britain : II. Augusta, VI. Victrix, XX. Valeria. Pfitzner, p. 97.

[2] Mannert, ii., p. 67 *sq.*, 119 *sq.*

[3] The seventeen towers (their names in the *Notitia*) have been compiled by Huebner (*Jahrb. f. Alterthumsk.*) from groups of inscriptions. All names are originally British, with the exception of *pons Aelius* and *Petrianae* (so called from a cohort). In the ruins of the tower Proclitia many coins were found of which some were of Hadrian and Sabina, but none of emperors before his time. See J. C. Bruce in *Comment. Philol.*, Berlin, 1877, p. 739.   On the wall itself, Bruce, *The Roman Wall*, etc., 3rd ed., London, 1877.—Huebner, *Deutsche Rundschau*, 1878, Heft 7.

[4] Juvenal, xv. 112.

revived two military colonies, Glevum and Eburacum.[1]
Londinium, destroyed in 61 A.D., was restored.[2] The
Romans stamped the seal of history on the wonderful island,
little dreaming that a time would come when, after the
fusion of Celts, Latins, and Germans, a commercial power
would be developed more important than Carthage, and
an empire greater in extent and population than that of
Rome.

It was in Britain that several distinguished men, among
whom Spartianus only mentions the prefect of the praetorium,
Septicius Clarus and Suetonius, fell into disgrace with the
emperor. He had found out that they had entered into
more confidential relations with his wife than befitted the
honour of his house, and he deprived them of their offices.[3]
These events have not been sufficiently explained. Was the
empress with him in Britain? Or had she remained in
Rome, and had the information reached him thence? While
Hadrian was on his journeys, his spies took care that he
knew all that went on in the capital and elsewhere, that was
worth knowing. He had probably arranged a system
approaching to our telegraph and newspaper offices, and his
correspondents were in reality agents of the secret police.
They were called *frumentarii*. These formidable men were
to be found in every city of the empire. Antoninus Pius
was the first to do away with them.[4]

From Britain Hadrian returned to Gaul, and here he built
at Nismes a temple in honour of Augusta Plotina.[5] The

[1] Zumpt, *Comm. Ep.* i. 415.

[2] Tacitus, *Annal.* xiv. 33 : Londinium—cognomento quidem coloniae
non insigne, sed copia negotiatorum et commeatuum maxime celebre.

[3] Spart. c. 11.

[4] The term *frumentarii* is thus explained by Salmasius in the note to
Spart. c. 11,—they were couriers who appeared with the postal organization introduced by Augustus, and also arranged for the provisioning
of the troops with corn. Quotations from Aristides, *Or.* ix., and Epictet.
Diss. iv. 13, 5, Friedlaender, *Darstellungen aus der Sittengesch. Roms*, i.,
5th ed., 381 *sq.* Nompère de Champagny, *Les Antonins*, ii. 185, con-
gratulates the Roman empire of that time on the absence of an organized
system of police like our own governments, yet even under the Antonines
no free expression on political matters was possible.

[5] Dion Cassius, lxix. 10.

empress-widow must therefore have been dead by this time. Plotina had made his fortune, and he did not forget it, honouring her as his mother as long as she lived. He wrote an elegy in her memory, and at his wish she was consecrated by the senate.[1]

Afterwards the emperor went to Spain, his native land.[2] This great country, full of flourishing cities (Pliny had already enumerated four hundred), was as completely Romanized in the time of Hadrian as the south of Gaul, and was, in fact, more Roman than Rome. Vespasian had already bestowed Latin rights upon it. For a century Spain had taken a high place in the civilized Roman world; to Rome it had given two emperors, and men of genius like Seneca, Lucan, Martial, Columella, and the orator Quintilian. The Spanish countries were divided into the provinces *Hispania citerior*, with its capital Tarraco, *Hispania ulterior*, or Baetica, with its capital Corduba, and Lusitania with its capital Emerita. Of these provinces the second was under the dominion of the senate. One legion only, the VIIth Gemina, had been stationed since the time of Vespasian in the peaceful country.

The emperor spent the winter in Tarraco. Here he escaped from the attack of a mad slave who sprang upon him with a drawn sword, and he was humane enough to hand over the lunatic, not to the hangman, but to the physician. He convoked the diet of the province for the object of raising troops, to which the Italian colonists and other communities objected, as they were greatly impoverished. The nucleus of such a diet (*concilia*) was the altar of Augustus, with the worship of the deified emperors. Baetica also possessed a concilium; a rescript of Hadrian to it still exists.[3] He restored the temple of the deified Augustus at

---

[1] Consecration coins in Eckhel, vi. 466, DIVIS. PARENTIBUS. In the collection of sentences and letters of Hadrian, by Dositheus (saec. 3), there is one to Hadrian's mother (§ 15), probably Plotina. He invites her to dine with him, as it is his birthday; Sabina, he says, is gone into the country. Boecking, *Corp. Juris R. Antejust.*, 212.

[2] Eckhel, vi. 495: "Hispania, mulier sedens juxta rupem d. ramum, pro pedibus cuniculus" (symbol of Spain).
　　　　　EXERCITUS. HISPANICUS. RESTITUTORI. HISP.

[3] Dig. 47, 14, 1, *De abigeis puniendis.* On the state of Spain, J. Jung, *Die rom. Landschaften d. röm. Reichs*, p. 18 *sq.*

Tarraco, which Tiberius had built to replace the altar of Augustus. The Tarraconese were remarkable for their slavish submission to the empire. They were the first to introduce the worship of Augustus in the West. They erected so many statues in honour of the Emperor Hadrian, that later on a special official had to be appointed by the province to attend to them.[1] Hadrian does not appear to have visited his birthplace Italica, but he loaded it with many benefits, and promoted the wish expressed by it to the senate to be raised from a colonia to a municipium.[2]

Where the emperor went from Spain, whether he returned to Rome and thence journeyed to the East, or whether he went straight from Tarraco to Mauretania cannot be ascertained, as all trustworthy information is wanting. We can only conjecture that from Spain he visited the neighbouring Mauretania.[3] This country, the present Morocco, the ancient kingdom of Juba, was the most westerly province of Rome in North Africa, and had been added to the empire by the Emperor Claudius. It was divided into Tingitana (Tangier) and Caesariensis (Algiers), and was governed by an imperial procurator or prefect, as, for instance, by Marcius Turbo in the beginning of Hadrian's reign. The indomitable inhabitants, the Mauri or Maurusii (the Berbers of to-day), fought incessantly against the dominion of the Romans, whose military power in the country consisted chiefly of auxiliaries of light cavalry. They also attempted to pass over to Spain in search of booty.

Hadrian was obliged to put down a rising of these tribes, which was probably connected with the fall of the former Moorish prince, Lusius Quietus. The suppression of this rebellion must have given the Romans some trouble, for the senate ordered festivals in gratitude for it.[4] The Mauretanian restoration coins of Hadrian perhaps refer to the

---

[1] "Ad statuas curandas Divi Hadriani," *C.I.L.* ii. 4230. A succession of mile-stones on the Via Tarraconensis at the time of Hadrian, *ibid.* 4735 *sq.*

[2] Gellius, xvi. 13. Dion Cassius, lxix. 10.

[3] Coins, ADVENTUI . AUG . MAURETANIAE.—EXERCITUS . MAURETANICUS.—RESTITUTORI . MAURITANIAE. Eckhel, vi. 498.

[4] Spart. c. 12: Motus Maurorum conpressit et a senatu supplicationes emeruit.

E

pacification of the country ; and the emperor certainly
restored the Roman colonies there, even if he did not increase
their number.[1]

But all accounts leave us in the dark ; we must therefore
accompany Hadrian on his first great journey to the East
without knowing whether he undertook it from Spain, or
from Africa, or from Rome, if indeed, as seems probable, he
had returned to the capital for a short visit.

[1] Zumpt (*Comm. Ep.* i. 421) ascribes to him, or to his successor,
Rusadir, Volubilis, Arsenaria, Bida, and other places mentioned in
the *Itinerarium Antonini.*

CHAPTER XI

Hadrian's first Journey to the East. The Countries on the Pontus. Ilium. Pergamum. Cyzicus. Rhodes

AFTER Hadrian had travelled through the West, he sailed in better spirits to the East of his empire, where in Antioch he had attained the sovereignty of the world. If in the West he had been occupied exclusively with the duties of a ruler, it may be imagined what enjoyment the East held out to him. Everything which could delight an inquiring mind was centred there; the records of humanity, the mysteries of different religions, the wonders of creation, and an existence still full of life and activity. Europe to-day is indisputably leader in the historical progress of the world, as she alone still preserves creative power. The world submits to be guided by her as the fountain of knowledge and of learning, and the West is indebted for this cosmopolitan greatness first to the Greeks, then to the Romans, and especially to the Eternal City. But in the middle of the second century, Europe was civilized only as far as the Roman power extended. Younger historically than the rest of the world, much less populous than Asia, barren of ideas after the fall of Greece, life flowed monotonously, devoid of the stimulus produced by the interchange of minds and nationalities. On the other hand, the Hellenic East was a school for Europe, whence, with the exception of Roman law, she derived her scientific and religious ideas, which were vital forces in many even of the practical forms of civilization. The centre too of the commerce of the world was still in Asia.

Hadrian now went through the countries of the East

where every coast and island was full of the classical recollections of antiquity, and where the re-awakened spirit of
Hellas offered him enthusiastic homage as its protector.

His first journey in the East must have been made
between the years 123 A.D. and 125 A.D. Spartianus has expressed this in a laconic line: "After this he sailed to Achaia
by Asia and the islands."[1]   By Asia the Romans understood
the province of *Asia proconsularis*, once the territory of the
kings of Pergamum. They had inherited it from Attalus III.
in the year 133 B.C., and had made it into a province.   It
comprised Mysia, Lydia, Phrygia and Caria, Pamphylia,
Pisidia, and Lycaonia.   For a long time Roman Asia had
lain politically dead ; but it was still full of cities of Ionians,
Dorians, and Aeolians, and of cities of the Alexandrian
period, which had preserved their Greek constitution.   There
were no Roman colonies except Parium, Alexandria Troas,
and Tralles.   Ephesus was the seat of the proconsul,
and in its neighbourhood many other cities flourished, whose
prosperity had increased with the long peace, and whose
beauty had been renewed by the renaissance of the arts.

Hadrian's first Asiatic journey must however have extended further, at all events from the Cilician frontier of
Syria to the Black Sea.

The coins which refer to this journey to the East generally
bear the legend, *Adventui Augusti Asiae*, and represent a
woman kneeling, whom Hadrian raises from the ground.[2]
The East is symbolized by a shining sun.[3]

Individual provinces, Bithynia, Cilicia, and Phrygia, recorded
the arrival of Hadrian or named him "Restorer." But neither
from them, nor from the coins and inscriptions of the cities,
can the length of his stay be ascertained, nor can we tell if
they in any way belong to his first journey to the East.
Inscriptions giving him the divine titles Olympius and
Panhellenius, refer to the later date when he had assumed
these titles.   Even in his absence any special event might
induce a community to pay him honour.

[1] Spart. c. 13.
[2] Cohen, ii., p. 109, n. 24.
[3] ORIENS.   Cohen, ii., p. 189, n. 1003-1005.   The sun-head (ORIENS. AUG.)
is the symbol of the East conquered by Trajan.   Eckhel, vi., p. 439.

We cannot therefore follow the emperor's first journey in Asia exactly, and can only say generally that, between 123 A.D. and 125 A.D., he travelled through Asia Minor to the Black Sea.

Trebizond is one of the furthest points visited by Hadrian, and Arrian, in his report of the circumnavigation of the Black Sea, remarks that he had been there.[1] Cerasus begins the list of imperial coins with him, and numerous medals with the likeness of Hadrian and Sabina have been preserved from Amisus.[2] We are not told if his wanderings extended to the Phasis. As it is certain that he was in Cappadocia, he will hardly have been satisfied with a visit to Mazaca, but will have visited the Roman border fortresses at Melitene on the Euphrates. The XIIth legion Fulminata was stationed there, while southwards at Samosata, the capital of Commagene, lay the Xth legion Flavia Firma, and northwards in Lesser Armenia the XVth legion Apollinaris at Satala.[3]

In the country of Pontus, the cities Amasia and Neocaesarea bore the name of Adriana; and from the time of Hadrian, Tyana in Cappadocia bore on its coins the title of an autonomous city. This and other circumstances prove the activity of the emperor in these countries.[4] The province of Cappadocia, which extended to the Black Sea, and which had been Roman since the days of Tiberius, was governed by consular legates, while Galatia, which Augustus had made into a province, with its capital Ancyra, was ruled by a praetorian legate. The extensive territory on the other side of the Sangarius, once the kingdom of Mithridates, seems to have been divided since the time of Trajan into these two

[1] Arrian, *Peripl. Pont. Euxin.* i.

[2] Greppo, p. 153.

[3] Marquardt, *Röm. Staatsverw.* i. 369, 400. The Hadrian coins EXERCITUS . PARTHICUS (the emperor stands on a stage addressing the soldiers) can only have reference to an inspection of troops on the Euphrates.

[4] Mionnet, Suppl. viii., p. 713. A mile-stone at Nicopolis in Cappadocia, in the year 129 A.D., points to making of roads, *C.I.L.* iii., add. n. 6057. The military coins EXER . CAPPADOCICUS represent Hadrian in the customary military activity.

districts.[1] The condition of the countries on the Upper Euphrates remains on the whole obscure. In the north of Cappadocia, Lesser Armenia formed the Roman boundary against Great Armenia, and further towards Colchis and the Caucasus the Albanians and Iberians were settled. From Melitene and Satala the Roman troops kept an eye on the movements of the Parthians, and the imperial government endeavoured to combine the heads of the tribes in the north-east of Asia in a defensive league. Hadrian sought to establish friendly relations with the Albanians and Iberians. He assembled a peace congress of barbarian princes, whom he won over by gifts. Some appeared, but others remained away in defiance, like the Iberian Pharasmanes.

He even restored to the Parthian king Chosroes his daughter whom Trajan had carried off into captivity.[2] But the pride of the Romans forbade him to restore to the king the golden throne of the Arsacids, the booty of the same emperor, which he had carried off from Ctesiphon. In consequence of the negociations with Chosroes, the Parthians . maintained peace during the whole of Hadrian's reign, and Great Armenia too remained tranquil under Arsacid princes, who were appointed and protected by Rome, though they did not pay tribute.[3]

Bithynia, which originally belonged to Pontus, and was subsequently converted by Augustus into an independent proconsular province, was particularly favoured by Hadrian. Like Pontus and Galatia, this province had a general assembly, which is mentioned on coins and inscriptions.[4]

[1] Perrot, *Galatia prov. Roman.*, p. 61.

[2] Schneiderwirth (*Die Parther*, p. 153) places this in the first journey of Hadrian more correctly than Longpérier (*Mém. sur la Chronologie des Rois parthes*, p. 143), who puts it in the last years of Hadrian. Spart. c. 12 says of Hadrian that he settled a (threatening) Parthian war by negociation, and (ch. 13) he mentions a congress of princes, and apparently places it in Hadrian's second Oriental journey. But is it possible that Hadrian should have delayed the settlement of such weighty matters so long?

[3] In Lesser Armenia the colony Sinis is ascribed to Hadrian, in Galatia Germa. Zumpt, *Comm. Ep.* i. 418.

[4] Perrot, *Inscr. inédites de la Mer noire (Rev. Arch.* 1874), p. 11.

Bithynian arrival and restoration coins of Hadrian exist.[1] Some cities assumed his name, like Cius, and Bithynium or Claudiopolis, the birthplace of his darling, the beautiful Antinous, and this circumstance explains the prodigality of his benefits to that country. He restored the capital Nicomedia, which had been destroyed by an earthquake, and also Nicaea.[2] Bithynia was a senatorial province, but Hadrian later converted it into an imperial province, giving the senate Pamphylia in exchange. We do not, however, possess any records of the date at which the emperor visited Bithynia.

He went west towards Mysia, and his first journey to Asia must have been the most convenient time for his visit to this country. The towns Sestus and Abydus paid him honour as their deliverer and founder, and Parium, a colony founded by Caesar, was called Hadriana.[3] In the mountain district of Olympus he founded the cities Hadriani and Hadrianotherae.[4] Hadrian also visited Ilium. It was afterwards said that he disparaged Homer, but how could the Philhellene have neglected to honour the tombs of heroes that had outlasted centuries?

Novum Ilium, inhabited by Aeolian Greeks, lay in the centre of the plain of Troy, one of the most charming districts in Asia Minor; opposite was the island Tenedos, behind it was Lemnos the island of Philoctetes, and Imbros, and the gloomy mountains of Samothrace rising from the sea. The situation of Ilium was considered by the ancients identical with that of the Troy of Homer, except by a few sceptical philologists. The people of Ilium were shrewd enough to maintain that the city of Priam had never quite disappeared, but had again been occupied by the Trojans after the departure of the Greeks. A small temple of Athene on the Pergamos or Mount of the Citadel was looked upon as the original

---

[1] In an inscription with the thirteenth tribunate of Hadrian (129 A.D.), Apamea in Bithynia dedicates a Balineum Hadrianum : Ephem. Epigr. C.I.L. ii., n. 349.

[2] *Chron. Paschale*, 254.

[3] Sestus, *C.I.A.* iii. 484 ; Abydus, 472 ; Parium, n. 1746 in Le Bas-Waddington. HADRIANO . CONDITORI, *C.I.L.* iii., n. 374.

[4] Mionnet, ii., p. 428, 433 ; *Suppl.* v. 38, 49.

temple of the tutelar goddess, from which the palladium stolen by Diomed had been brought to Rome.[1]   So sacred did the Romans consider it, that it formed one of the eight temples in the empire in favour of whose divinities Roman law permitted testamentary dispositions.[2]

Xerxes had in former days offered sacrifices to Athene in Ilium, and Alexander the Great had done the same.   To this enthusiast for Homer the Ilians showed even the arms of their heroes and the lyre of Paris.   After the victory on the Granicus, Alexander made votive offerings to the temple of Athene; he pronounced the place free and autonomous, and promised to make it into an important city.   Lysimachus afterwards enlarged and surrounded it with walls.   Antiochus, too, piously honoured the legends of Ilium, and finally the Romans looked with feigned enthusiasm on this new Ilium as the cradle of their world-wide power.   Pliny called it the source of all fame.[3]   Fimbria indeed, Sulla's antagonist, destroyed the city, but Julius Caesar restored it, and his successors, the Caesars, enlarged its territory.   The Ilians themselves did not forget, when they sent envoys to the emperor, to remind him that Troy was the mother of Rome.[4]

Troy was immortal in the memory of mankind, and that this is so to-day is proved by the enthusiasm which the discoveries of Schliemann have excited.   Like the Greeks and Romans, he sought the site of ancient Troy in New Ilium, and the latter he found in Hissarlik.   For New Ilium had also disappeared, and we are as doubtful about its position as the Greeks were about that of Troy.[5]

When Hadrian visited New Ilium in 124 or 125 A.D., he doubted as little as the emperor before him, or as Arrian, Appian, and the sophist Aristides, as Pausanias and Plutarch afterwards, that this was the site of the sacred Troy,

---

[1] Strabo, 593 *sq.*

[2] Jovem Tarpejum, Apollinem Didymaeum, Martem in Gallia, Minervam Iliensem, Herculem Gaditanum, Dianam Ephesiam, Matrem Deorum Sipelensem (Smyrna) Coelestem Salmensem Carthaginis. Ulp. *Fr.* xxii. 6.

[3] Pliny, *Hist. Nat.* v. 33.

[4] Tacitus, *Annal.* iv. 55 : parentem urbis Romae Trojam.

[5] Mannert, vi. 3, 497.

although of the city of Priam, according to the testimony of the sceptical Strabo, not one stone remained. Philostratus relates that the emperor gave fresh burial to the bones of Ajax in the Ajanteum. This we may suppose refers to a celebration of funeral rites,[1] and an inscription from New Ilium, with no special meaning, makes mention of Hadrian.[2] Ilian coins of Hadrian are in existence which represent Aeneas as a fugitive carrying his father on his back, and leading young Ascanius by the hand; underneath is depicted the Roman she-wolf.[3]

Another place in the Troad still bore the ancient name at this period, namely, the Roman colony Alexandria Troas, to the south of New Ilium. It was originally called Sigia, then Antigonia, because king Antigonus had enlarged it, until finally it received the name of Alexandria Troas from Lysimachus, in honour of Alexander. The Romans also honoured it, and Caesar, when he contemplated a change in his royal residence, is said to have hesitated between it and Novum Ilium.[4] Constantine too, before he decided upon Byzantium, wished to make the capital of the empire in the Trojan country. Alexandria Troas was also visited by Hadrian, and experienced his favour. He caused an aqueduct to be built there by Herodes Atticus, of which the imposing remains are still to be seen in the village of Eskistambul. Byzantine remains prove the existence of this place until the end of the Middle Ages.[5] St. Paul, the apostle of that new religion whose written records were to supplant Homer and his gods, was once in this city of Troas on his first missionary journey. From Troas he sailed to Samothrace, and thence to Macedonia.[6]

---

[1] Philostr. *Heroica*, ed. Kayser, ii. 137.

[2] *C.I.L.* iii. 1, n. 466 : Trib. Pot. VIII. (124/125 A.D.).

[3] Schliemann, *Ilios*, p. 720. The imperial coins, of copper only, with the inscriptions of Hector the Ilian, Priamus the Ilian, are properly considered by Schliemann as sufficient evidence for the identity of this place with Troy.

[4] Suetonius, *Caes.* c. 79 : Quia etiam varia fama percrebuit, migraturum Alexandream vel Ilium.

[5] Mannert, vi. 3, 474. Schliemann, *Ilios*, p. 67.

[6] *Acts of the Apostles*, c. 16, v. 8, 11.

In Mysia, Hadrian visited Pergamum, the famous seat of the Attalids, and now a flourishing city, a possession which first directed Roman efforts to the acquisition of the province of Asia. There he could admire the Acropolis with the magnificent temple of Athene Polias and the sanctuaries of Asclepius and Augustus. He could look at the theatres, the gymnasia, and the basilicas, with which the highly cultured kings after Lysimachus and Eumenes had adorned the city, and could admire the marble groups of gods and giants surrounding the great altar of Attalus, still resplendent with unimpaired beauty. More than seventeen centuries after Hadrian's visit, these statues were to be disinterred from the ruins and placed in the capital of the new German empire.[1] That Hadrian conferred benefits upon Pergamum may be conjectured from a statue which the people and council of the city erected to him in his seventh tribunate.[2]

The city of Cyzicus, the ancient colony of Miletus and ally of the king of Pergamum, on the isthmus in the Propontis, opposite the island Proconnesus, was treated by the emperor with special favour. She had lost her freedom under Tiberius in the year 24 A.D., but flourished again in the time of Hadrian by her commerce and industry, by the beauty of her monuments, especially the temples of Cybele, of Adrastea and Proserpine. Later on Hadrian built a marvellous temple there. He granted to the city the honour coveted by so many other communities in Asia, of celebrating the worship of the Roman gods and of the emperor with festival games called Neocoria, and from that time Cyzicus adopted the name of Philosebastos and Adriane.[3]

It cannot be doubted that Hadrian on the same journey visited Smyrna, Sardis, Miletus, Ephesus, and Halicarnassus, as well as other famous cities of Asia Minor, which have

---

[1] *The Excavations at Pergamum*, 1880-1881, Report by A. Conze, Humann and Bohn in *Jahrbuch der Königl. Preuss. Kunstsammlung*, iii. 1, 1882. In the Augusteum at Pergamum there have been found fragments of statues of Trajan and Hadrian.

[2] Le Bas-Waddington, iii. 1, n. 1721.

[3] J. H. Krause, *Neokoros*, p. 36. J. Marquardt, *Cyzikus und sein Gebiet*, p. 84. An inscription calls Hadrian σωτὴρ καὶ κτίστης, *Rev. Arch.* N.S. xxxii., p. 268, in Duerr, *Anhang*, n. 69.

recorded his name in coins and inscriptions.   As Spartianus states that he journeyed to Achaia by Asia and the islands, it must have been Rhodes, Cos, Chios, the fertile Lesbos with the beautiful Mitylene, Lemnos, and Samothrace, which he visited.   The ancient mysteries in Samothrace, into which Philip and Olympias once allowed themselves to be initiated, were still so much honoured that they must have excited Hadrian's curiosity.   The council and people of Samothrace erected a statue in his honour, the inscription on which has been found in the ruins of the Doric temple of marble, but it does not prove that Hadrian visited this island.[1]   Inscriptions and coins make his presence in Crete probable.[2]   But his visit to Rhodes he himself has proved in a letter to Ephesus, found a few years ago as a marble inscription, in which he tells the archons and the council of the city that he had sailed from Ephesus to Rhodes.[3]

Rhodes the magnificent, dedicated to the sun, great at one time by her naval power, and famous throughout the world for her schools of orators and sculptors, had decayed after the civil wars in Caesar's time, but Strabo still ventured to give her the preference over all other cities. Only a short time before Hadrian, Dion Chrysostom had spoken of her as the richest Greek city, and even after Hadrian's time Lucian could say of her that her beauty was

---

[1] The inscription records the 16th tribunate of Hadrian (132 A.D.), *Arch. Unters. auf Samothrake* by A. Conze, Hauser und Niemann, 1875, p. 36, *sq.*   There has also been found an inscription in honour of Hadrian from Maroneia, which calls him σωτήρ.   Further, a Latin inscription with the consuls of the year 124 A.D., from which it is supposed that Hadrian was presented with the highest magisterial office (*rex*) in Samothrace.

[2] *C.I.G.* ii. 427.   Inscriptions from Lyttos, and Cretan coins in Mionnet, ii., p. 260.   A beautiful statue of an emperor resembling Hadrian was found at Hierapytna in Crete, and stands in the museum at Constantinople. *Gazette Archéol.* vi. 1880, 52 *sq.*

[3] Wood, *Discoveries at Ephesus*, App. 5: "Inscriptions from the Odeum," n. 1.   Hadrian recommends to the city council the Ephesian citizen, L. Erastus, who frequently travels on the seas, and has already met him, the emperor, twice : τὸ πρῶτον εἰς 'Ρόδον ἀπὸ τῆς 'Εφέσου κομιζόμεν(ῳ), νῦν δὲ ἀπὸ 'Ελευσῖνος πρὸς ὑμᾶς ἀφικομένῳ.   The date of the letter in which Hadrian calls himself Pater Patr. δημαρ. ἐξουσ. τὸ γ΄, in Wood has been correctly emended by Duerr (*Nachtrag*, p. 124) ιγ (Trib. Pot. XIII., *i.e.* 129 A.D.).

worthy of the sun-god.[1]　Her situation on the eastern
promontory of the island, opposite the steep rocky coast of
Caria, her arsenals, harbours, and high walls, her streets,
temples, and porticos, her innumerable pictures and works
of art in marble and copper, which even Nero had not
plundered, formed a delightful combination of grace, splendour, and strength, before the great earthquake destroyed
the city in the time of Antoninus Pius.[2]　Although Vespasian
had deprived her of the last vestige of autonomy, Rhodes
must still have been flourishing in the time of Hadrian.　The
story related by a later Byzantine, that the emperor restored
the famous Colossus, which three hundred years before had
been destroyed by an earthquake, is certainly a fable.[3]

[1] Strabo, 652.　Dion Chrys., ed. Dindorf, *Orat.* xxxi., p. 363.　Lucian,
Amores, c. 8 : ἡ πόλις Ἡλίου πρέπον ἔχουσα τῷ θεῷ τὸ κάλλος.

[2] Pausanias, viii. 43, 4.　Aristides, *Orat.* 43.　Dion Chrys. xxi.

[3] Malalas, 279.

CHAPTER XII

Hadrian's Residence in Athens, and in other Cities of Greece. Return of the Emperor to Rome by way of Sicily

THERE was no country which could equal Hellas in its attraction for Hadrian. It was the treasure-house of the highest ideals of antiquity, and on this account it was still visited, as in the time of Cicero, by cultivated men from all parts of the empire. Greece was certainly no longer full of prosperous cities, like Asia Minor, but was already in Strabo's time so decayed that it was looked upon merely with the interest of the antiquary.[1] Its population had decreased to such an extent that, according to the statement of Plutarch, it could scarcely furnish 3000 hoplites, the number that Megara had once sent to the battle of Plataea. In Peloponnesus the number of cities had dwindled down to little more than about sixty, of which Sparta and Argos alone were of any importance, and in the time of Pausanias there were many deserted places even in Phocis, Boeotia, Attica, and Achaia. Thousands of Greeks from Old Hellas, as well as from the Hellenic countries, lived homeless in the provinces of the West. The world had become their country. This wholesale dispersion of the Greeks in the Roman empire is a parallel, but also a contrast to the fate of the Jews after their conquest by Pompey and Titus. Their home when in exile was not the civilised world, but the synagogue.

In spite of the extinction of all political life, many free cities, with their monuments, still existed in Hellas, and Pau-

[1] Curtius, *Peloponnesos*, 3, Abschn. i. 79.

sanias, who visited Greece a generation after Hadrian and noted its ruins with sorrowful affection, could derive consolation from the fact that the famous old countries and cities still preserved their constitutions, their diets, courts of justice and magistrates, and indeed their festival games.

Achaia, as Greece was called by the Romans, suffered from the caprices of her rulers, but on the whole benefited by their pious regard. They did not disturb ancient systems. Augustus had made Greece, like Macedonia, into a senatorial province, having for its capital New Corinth. Tiberius, however, took away the government from the senate, as it was costly, oppressive, tyrannical, and burdensome to the Greeks. He even united Hellas and Macedonia with Moesia.[1] Claudius however gave both provinces back to the senate.[2]

Greece had been the classical stage for the vanity of Nero who, like Caligula, plundered the treasures of Greek art with shameless rapacity. He travelled through Greece like a comedian and an athlete, but an actor even in his remorse, he avoided Athens as the sanctuary of the avenging Eumenides, and he did not visit Sparta, from his dislike to the legislation of Lycurgus. He deluged Hellas with blood, but to reward the flatteries of the Greeks, as well as to produce a theatrical effect, he proclaimed the freedom of the Hellenes at the Isthmian games, as once Flaminius had done. Soon afterwards the parsimonious Vespasian took away this freedom, which related only to taxation, and gave Achaia back to the government of the senate.[3] The Flavian dynasty revived with the provincial government the financial oppression of Greece, and it was of no practical benefit to the Athenians that Domitian in the year 93 A.D. assumed the dignity of their archon Eponymus.[4] Hadrian received the same honour in the year 112 A.D. when still a private individual. Two years later, Trajan visited Athens. The Panhellenes erected the statue of this just emperor at Olympia.

The Greeks overwhelmed their rulers with shameless

[1] Tacitus, *Annals*, i. 80.
[2] Finlay, *History of Greece*, p. 54.
[3] Pausanias, *Achaica*, xvii. 4.
[4] Philostr. *Vita Apollonii*, viii. 16. Hertzberg, *Gesch. Griechenl. unter der Herrschaft der Römer*, ii. 137.

honours. The deification of the emperor had become the religion of the land, after the days of Caesar and Antony. The temples of Caesar and Augustus stood in the chief square of Sparta;[1] and on the Acropolis of Athens stood the temple of the genius of Rome and Augustus. As the free Athenians erected an altar to Pity, their slavish posterity might have paid a similar honour to Flattery. The love of freedom was extinguished in Hellas; the country had resigned itself to its destiny, Rome, but a deep gulf separated Romans and Greeks from one another. Rome looked with contempt on the degenerate grandsons of Miltiades and Leonidas, while the Greeks, as aristocrats of mind and culture, felt themselves superior to the Romans. The Romanizing of Achaia made slow progress, for the spirit of Greece survived in its mighty literature, in its undying memories, and in the perpetual self-esteem of the Hellenic communities. Only a few commercial cities, Patras, Corinth, and Nicopolis on the peninsula of Actium, made an exception as Roman colonies in Hellas. In Corinth, Pausanias found no descendants of the old inhabitants.[2]

The Corinthians adopted Roman customs, and even their bloody gladiatorial games, but when the Athenians wished to follow their example, the philosopher Demonax rose and said, " Let the altar of Pity first be overthrown."[3]

And now Hadrian had come, and the Greeks received him gladly as their " saviour and founder." No previous emperor of Rome had been in such close touch with them, and changeable though he was, he remained faithful to his Greek sympathies. More lavishly here in Greece than in any other part of the empire, did he bestow the blessings of his liberality. With Hadrian there began for Athens an after-summer of its former splendour, a last renaissance, not of the republican life of the state, but of science and literature. It was more fully developed under the Antonines, and continued, though with many interruptions, during the ever deepening decay of Greece, until the extinction of Hellenism under Justinian.

It is unknown at what port the emperor landed. There

[1] Pausanias, *Laconica*, xi. 4.   [2] Pausanias, *Corinthiaca*, i. 2.
[3] Lucian, *Demonax* 57.

are no coins to record Hadrian's arrival in Achaia ; we have only coins of restoration.[1]   Neither from them, nor from the coins of the colony of Corinth, which record his arrival, can any precise date be fixed.[2]   No Athenian coin of the emperor's arrival has been found.   In the inscriptions, his visits to Athens are merely mentioned, and though his first residence is reckoned an era of the city, no precise date can be fixed for his first or second visit.[3]   We can only learn from these inscriptions that the new era of Hadrian did not occur before the year 124-125 A.D., and that the emperor could not have come to Athens before September 124 A.D.[4]   We may conclude that he arrived in the autumn of the year 125 A.D., to make a stay of some duration.[5]

He found satisfaction here for all his ideal aspirations. In the charming pastoral scene, framed by the sea, Hymettus, Pentelicus, and Parnes, he could rest from his labours, and admire the sublime works of antiquity, whose eternal youth and beauty, in Plutarch's opinion, had defied the powers of time.   They were still standing uninjured.   Pausanias, afterward, was astonished by the temples, the academies and gymnasia, the porticos and squares, the citadel of Athens filled with votive offerings, pictures, and statues; and even Lucian, when in his youth he saw Athens for the first time, was amazed at the beauty and magnificence of the city, and at the number of its inhabitants.[6]   In Athens, Hadrian could

---

[1] Eckhel, vi., p. 487.   Cohen, ii., p. 209, n. 1214 *sq.*

[2] COL . L . JUL . COR . ADVENT . AUG., with a trireme, Greppo, p. 119. Coins of arrival from Patras are missing.

[3] The formula is ἀπὸ τῆς Ἀδριανοῦ (πρώτης) εἰς Ἀθήνας ἐπιδημίας.   The era is counted from the first arrival, not from the archon-year 112 A.D.   Dumont, *Fastes éponymiques*, p. 27.   The five inscriptions (*Corp. Inscr. Atticar.* iii. 1, 735, 69a add., 1107, 1023, 1120) give the three years (twice), the 4th, 15th, 27th year.

[4] Dittenberger, *Hadrian's erste Anwesenheit in Athen*, in *Hermes*, 1873, p. 225.   This article was occasioned by Hirschfeld's *Catalogo de' Pritani ateniensi*, in *Bull. Inst.* 1872, p. 118 *sq.*

[5] According to Corsini (*Fasti Attici*, ii. 403), in the month Boedromion (about September), because the Athenians moved, in honour of Hadrian, the beginning of the year from the month Hekatombaion to the month Boedromion.

[6] Lucian, *Skythes*, c. 9.

be an artist among artists, and he could dispute, in the halls
of the academy under the plane trees on the Cephisus, with
philosophers who called themselves followers of the divine
Plato.   In Athens, wisdom and simplicity were taught, as
Lucian says in his *Nigrinus*, where he draws a contrast
between her classic peace and the din of Rome, with her
ostentatious slavery, her formalities and her banquets, her
sycophants, her poisoners, legacy-hunters, and false friends.[1]
In the patriarchal figure of the philosopher Demonax,
Lucian has drawn a picture of the happiness of a life of
Athenian simplicity, and this sage may have been a man of
thirty-five when Hadrian came to Athens.   The emperor
was here transformed into a Greek sophist, and dreamer
over the beauties of antiquity.   Steeped in poetry and
sentiment, they are still a powerful attraction to every
cultivated man who, in this place full of consecrated gifts,
has communion with the gods, the heroes, and the sages of
Attica, as he wanders among the ruins of their temples.

But the laconic style of Hadrian's biographers forbids us
to see much of this prince, this most ardent lover of the
Muses, in his intercourse with the Athenians.[2]   Spartianus
sums up the events of his first visit there in these words:
"After the example of Hercules and Philip, he took part in
the Eleusinian mysteries; he made many presents to the
Athenians, and presided as Agonothetes."[3]

Hadrian was, without doubt, initiated into the mysteries
of Demeter on his first visit to Athens.[4]   Augustus also had
been allowed to share in these rites, and later, Marcus
Aurelius and Alexander Severus.[5]   The ruler of Rome and
of the world, attired as a Greek, did not disdain to fill the

---

[1] Lucian, *Nigrinus*, 14 *sq.*

[2] Athenaeus, viii. 361, 3, calls the Emperor Hadrian παντ' ἄριστος καὶ
μουσικώτατος βασιλεύς.

[3] Spart. c. 13.

[4] Spart. c. 13.   Dion Cassius, lxix. 11.   Euseb. *Chron.*, ed. Schoene, ii.
166 *sq.*: ἐχείμασεν εἰς Ἀθήνας μυηθεὶς τὰ Ἐλευσίνια.   It is probable that this
initiation still consisted of two parts, and that therefore Hadrian passed
in the second and greater rite on his second journey.   Flemmer, p. 38.
Hertzberg, i. 314.

[5] Leake, *Topogr. Athens*, pp. xxi., xxv.

F

office of umpire at the games of the great Dionysia. As it
was the duty of the archon to preside at these festivals,
Hadrian must have been a second time archon of the
Athenians.[1] The Dionysia were celebrated from the 8th to
the 12th Elaphebolion (end of March to beginning of April);
consequently in the spring of 126 A.D., Hadrian was still in
Athens. The Athenians were delighted to see the emperor
seated in the theatre of the great Attic poets, gravely
awarding the prizes; but we do not know what pieces were
then given; they were probably comedies of Menander,
for the plays of Sophocles and Aristophanes were hardly
any longer put on the stage, and there was no living poet
who was able to write a respectable play.

In gratitude for this honour paid to the Attic theatre, or
in recognition of its restoration by Hadrian, the Athenians
determined to erect twelve statues in honour of the emperor,
one for each phyle of the city, to be placed in the passage
of the auditorium. The statue which had been erected to
him as archon in 112 A.D. made the number thirteen.[2]

During his first sojourn in Athens, Hadrian seems to have
determined to rebuild the temple of the Olympian Zeus, and
to have made other plans for important buildings. He
reformed the Athenian constitution on the basis of the old
republican system. The nature of the improvement, however,
is unknown.[3] His care for the material welfare of the city,
whose harbours had lain desolate, and whose trade and
industry had decayed ever since the time of Sulla, is still
to be seen from an inscription on the gate of the hall of the

---

[1] Ahrens (*De Athenar. statu.* p. 15). Dion Cassius, lxix. 16, relates
Hadrian's participation in the Dionysia in connection with the completion
or consecration of the Olympieum, which took place during a later visit
of the emperor, but Spartianus (c. 13) connects his Agonothesia with his
first sojourn in Athens.

[2] Some pediments of these statues have been found. The inscriptions
in *C.I.A.* iii. 1, n. 464 *sq.* Benndorf, *Beitraege zur Kenntniss des attisch.
Theatres*, in *Zeitschrift fuer oester. Gymnas.* 1875, p. 15 *sq.*

[3] Hieron. *Chron.* i. 45 : Atheniensibus leges petentibus ex Draconis et
Solonis reliquorumque libris jura componit. This sounds rather strange;
see Hertzberg, ii. 317.

new agora, which records a regulation of Hadrian about the sale of oil.[1]

It is incredible that the emperor should have spent a year in Athens, until the time of his departure from Achaia in the summer of 126 A.D., without travelling through the countries of ancient Greece. They certainly sent their deputies to Athens to present both petitions and invitations. There are not, however, many inscriptions of the existing Greek cities which mention Hadrian as their benefactor and restorer, nor do they help us to determine the date of his visit. He probably visited in person places such as Corinth, Argos, Mantinea, Nemea, where he erected buildings, and gave votive offerings to the temples.[2] On Argive coins he is glorified as " Founder."[3]

Sparta has recorded his arrival in an inscription.[4] This city was now the most important in Peloponnesus.[5] She had preserved her old customs; the gerusia was still in existence, and the Spartan year was always called after one of the five ephors, just as the Athenian year was called after one of the archons. Pausanias found the historical monuments in Sparta uninjured, the market-place, with the government buildings, and the Persian stoa, the bronze house of Athene on the citadel, and numerous temples, tombs, and works of art.[6]

In Mantinea, Hadrian restored the tomb of Epaminondas, and furnished it with an inscription.[7] And can we believe that the emperor, who enlarged the temple of Zeus in Athens, and then assumed the name of " the Olympian," never visited Olympia, which was resplendent with his games and sanctuaries? No inscriptions prove it, but the want of them can only be accidental.

[1] *C.I.G.* i. 355 and *C.I.A.* iii. 1, n. 38. Gold and grain distributions by Hadrian for Athens. Dion Cassius, lxix. 16.

[2] See further on, under buildings of Hadrian.

[3] Mionnet, *Suppl.* iv., p. 240, n. 28.

[4] *C.I.G.* 1241. Other inscriptions from Sparta, *C.I.G.* 1308, 1309, 1312 (here σωτῆρος Ὀλυμπίου); Le Bas-Foucart, *Laconie*, n. 193 (Σεβαστῷ σωτῆρι); see Duerr, *Anhang*, 113 *sq.*

[5] Curtius, *Peloponnes.* ii. 226.   [6] Pausanias, *Laconica*, xi.

[7] Pausanias, *Arcadica*, xi. 8.

Corinth, the most splendid city of Greece, the Roman colony Julia of the Great Caesar, was favoured and adorned by Hadrian. It possessed very few objects of antiquity worth seeing, for most of its public buildings had sprung up since the time of Caesar, among them being a temple of Octavia, the sister of Augustus.[1]

At Thespiae, Hadrian made a votive offering of the skin of a bear, his own booty in the chase, with verses composed by himself.[2] It was from Thespiae that Caligula stole that wonderful work of art, the Eros of Praxiteles. Claudius restored it to the city, but it was again carried off by Nero, and only a copy, made by the Athenian Menodorus, stood in the temple when Pausanias visited it.[3]

And did Hadrian not see Thebes as well? The city of Pindar had indeed so completely disappeared in the time of Pausanias that only the citadel was inhabited.[4] The whole country of Boeotia was ruined and many of her cities lay desolate. Plutarch had given fame to the small Chaeronea, but this noble man, whom Hadrian honoured and made procurator of Greece, died about the year 120 A.D. One of the most important Boeotian cities must at that time have been Lebadea; for the oracle of Trophonius, which was still much consulted, gave life to it by attracting many visitors. It is not known if Hadrian consulted the oracle, but his curiosity would have made him inquire into this ancient mystery.

He consulted the oracle at Delphi, either personally or by representatives, as to the fatherland of Homer. The Amphictyons erected a statue to him there.[5] This league was still in existence, and its council at the time of Pausanias consisted of thirty members, furnished by Nicopolis, Macedonia and Thessaly, Boeotia and Phocis, Doris, Locris,

[1] Pausanias, *Corinthiaca*, ii. 6.

[2] Kaibel, *Epigr. graeca*, n. 811. The city of Thespiae erected a statue to Hadrian as its εὐεργέτης καὶ κτίστης, still without the title of Olympius. *C.I.G.* i. 1614.

[3] Pausanias, *Boeotica*, xxvii. 4.

[4] Two inscriptions from Thebes (Duerr, *Anhang*, n. 93, 94) are of later date, as they give Hadrian the title Olympius.

[5] *C.I.G.* 1713: τὸ κοινὸν τῶν Ἀμφικτυόνων, still without the title of Olympius.

Euboea, Argos, Sicyon and Corinth, Megara and Athens.[1]
Nero had robbed the sanctuary of Apollo of five hundred
bronze statues, and had confiscated the possessions of the
temple.   The decline of Delphi was irreparable, for the
Pythian oracle had lost its authority.   Pausanias does not
once speak of its activity in his time.   He found the ancient
treasure-houses empty, but in his long description of the
Delphian wonders he enumerated many old votive offerings
within the sacred precincts.   Of the temples, one lay in
ruins, another had no statues left in it, but the third still
contained the images of several Roman emperors.   Among
these the statue erected in honour of Hadrian may have
been found.[2]

Hadrian visited the Augustan Actia Nicopolis in Epirus,
for the coins of this city represent him on board ship, and
bear the legend, " Appearance of the emperor."[3]   From there
he may have visited Dodona.[4]   That he saw the vale of
Tempe in Thessaly cannot be doubted, for he named a
pleasure ground at his villa at Tivoli after it.   But we do not
know if his journeys in Northern Greece, Epirus, Thessaly,
Macedonia, and Thrace, where he founded Adrianopolis,
were performed during his first sojourn in Hellas, or not.
His arrival in Macedonia and Thrace is recorded by coins.[5]
After a residence of about three years in the East, and in

[1] Pausanias, *Phocica*, viii. 3.

[2] Pausanias, *Phocica*, viii. 4 : τῶν ἐν Ῥώμῃ βασιλευσάντων—οὐ πολλῶν τινῶν
εἰκόνας.   In the treasure-house of the Corinthians, Plutarch found nothing
but the bronze palm : *Moralia*, ed. Wittenbach, ii. 438.

[3] Greppo, p. 114.   Hadrian coins from Nicopolis are numerous;
Mionnet, *Suppl.* iii., p. 378 *sq.*

[4] An inscription, *C.I.G.* 1822, gives Hadrian the surname Dodonaius.
See Greppo, p. 115.

[5] ADVENTUI . AUG . MACEDONIAE . RESTITUTORI . MACEDONIAE.
Eckhel, vi., p. 498.   ADVENTUI . AUG . THRACIAE.   Cohen, ii.[2], p. 112,
n. 77.   Greppo, p. 111, enumerates the Thracian cities, whose emperor-
coins begin with H : Bizya, Mesembria, Peutalia, Trajanopolis, and
Coela on the Chersonnese.   Coela called itself Aelium Municip.—
Mionnet, *Suppl.* ii., p. 526.   Flemmer, p. 89, believes that Hadrian
visited these countries during his sojourn in Athens (according to him
876-879 or 880 A.U.C.) in the year 879 A.U.C. = 126 A.D., whereas Duerr,
p. 56, places the visit to northern Greece in the time before his arrival
in Athens, in the late autumn of 124 A.D. to the autumn of 125 A.D.

the Hellenic countries, Hadrian returned to Rome by way of Sicily.[1]   There he made the ascent of Etna to see the sun rise, which, as people then liked to believe, displayed the colours of the rainbow.[2]   On this journey he visited also the famous cities of Messana, Tauromenium, Catana, Syracuse, and Thermae.   They were Roman colonies, and in addition there were sixty-three communities on the island, which were nearly all endowed with Latin rights.[3]

If the want of records, which is perhaps only accidental, as to the relations of Hadrian with Sicily, permits us to draw any inference, it is that he did not treat this treasure-house of Rome, as Strabo called the island, with great generosity. Only one coin of the senate speaks of him generally as the restorer of Sicily; the emperor raises the kneeling figure of a woman, who is crowned with ears of corn, and who holds ears of corn also in her hand.[4]

Hadrian returned to Rome either in the end of 126 A.D., or in the beginning of the following year.

[1] ADVENTUI . AUG . SICILIAE.   Eckhel, vi., p. 500.
[2] Spart. c. 13.
[3] Pliny, *H.N.* iii. 14.
[4] Eckhel, vi., p. 500.   A coin of Hadrian in Foy-Vaillant, with the head of Medusa (?) and a sea monster above it, bearing the legend SICILIA S.C., is declared doubtful by Eckhel.   Zumpt, *Comm. Ep.* i. 409, believes that Hadrian endowed the cities Lilybaeum and Panormus with the rights of colonies, and ascribes to him the colonies Uselis and Cornus in Sardinia.

CHAPTER XIII

Hadrian in Rome. The Title Pater Patriae. The Emperor goes to Africa. Condition of this Province. Carthage. Lambaesis

THE peaceful condition of Rome during the long absence of the emperor, proved that the monarchy stood firm on the foundations of the excellent government which had been handed down to Hadrian by his predecessor, and which he himself had improved. His throne was not only protected by praetorian guards and by the army, but by the wisdom and justice of his sway. The balance of power between emperor, senate, and army had never perhaps been more perfect. Nothing astounds us more than the picture of this powerful, highly disciplined army of the empire. The legions which Trajan had accustomed to the glories of war had become peaceful guardians of the frontiers, working hard and uncomplainingly at walls and fortifications, and submitting to the strict discipline which the emperor enforced.

Hadrian returned to Rome even more Greek than he had been before, and this no doubt displeased many Romans of the school of Trajan. He had been so much attracted by the charms of Athens that he introduced Greek customs, and even the Eleusinian mysteries, into Rome. His court assumed more and more a Hellenic character. He was surrounded by Greek sophists and sages; his favourite was a Bithynian youth named Antinous, from Claudiopolis, with whom he had become acquainted in Asia Minor, and had brought to Rome. Hadrian founded an academy in Rome, probably after he came back, to which he gave the name of Athenaeum.[1]

His return gave the senate a fresh opportunity of meeting him with proofs of their respect. The statement that they made the proposal that he should at last assume the title Pater Patriae is therefore very likely correct,[2] and this it appears Hadrian did on the day of the dedication of the magnificent temple of Rome and Venus, a festival which could not be more suitably celebrated than on the anniversary of the foundation of the city, the 21st of April. The year in which it took place, and in which Hadrian assumed the title, his wife Sabina taking that of Augusta, is unknown, but was probably earlier than 128 or 127 A.D.[3]

The emperor remained some time longer in Rome, but he was always planning fresh journeys. This ceaseless travelling affected even his biographers. Spartianus writes like a courier; after mentioning Hadrian's return to Rome from Sicily, he says, almost breathlessly, "From here he went to Africa," and then he adds, as if frightened, "Never did a prince travel so quickly through so many countries."[4] This same unrest seems even now to affect every biographer of the emperor, all the more so as he is compelled to make use of the fragmentary information of Spartianus and of Dion, and to travel with them over land and sea in hopeless haste. Spartianus, however, has in this instance allowed the emperor too short a stay in Rome.

Hadrian visited Africa for the first time in the summer of 128 A.D. His visit to this province occurs between the first and second journey to the East. Spartianus mentions it twice, and ends with this remark, "Rain, which had been wanting for five years, fell at his arrival in Africa, and on that account the emperor was beloved by the Africans."[5] It was not the first or the last time that the flattery of

---

[1] On his introduction of Hellenism into Rome, consult Aurelius Victor, *Epit.* 14.

[2] Flemmer, p. 44, reasons so.

[3] See the clear explanation in Duerr, p. 28 *sq.*

[4] Spart. c. 13: Nec quisquam principum tantum terrarum tam celeriter peragravit.

[5] Spart. c. 22.

subjects connected the occurrences of nature with the appearance of a prince.   The people of Africa had, however, better grounds for honouring the emperor when he visited them. In the year 128 A.D. he travelled through Numidia, and set to rights the military organization of the country.

The province of Africa, with which Numidia was united until the time of Septimius Severus, stretched from the borders of Mauretania as far as Cyrenaica and the great Syrtis.[1]   It was a fertile district, one of the most important granaries for Rome, containing more than three hundred flourishing cities.   It produced valuable fruits, wild animals for the arena, ivory, yellow marble (*giallo antico*) for the emperor's magnificent buildings, and beautiful fabrics.   In no province were there so many imperial domains as in Africa, the land of the great *latifundia*.   The emperors made the most of these latifundia, and Trajan in particular provided his family with estates there.   The unsatisfactory relations of the small farmers or colonists to the occupiers of the large estates were mitigated by Hadrian's humane regulations.[2]

Africa, like Asia, was a senatorial province of the first rank, governed by a proconsul, but from the time of Caligula a legate appointed by the emperor held an independent command over the IIIrd legion Augusta, which Octavian had transferred thither.[3]   The Romanizing of the country had progressed rapidly, even though the Punic language and character still remained, mingled with the ancient worship of Moloch and Astarte.   Carthage was the centre of this Phoenician religion ; for there stood the temple of Juno Caelestis, or Astarte, the sacred Queen of Heaven, to whom great honour was paid, not only in Africa, but, since the third Punic war, in Rome as well.[4]

[1] The Roman provinces in Africa were Africa and Numidia, the two Mauretanias, Crete and Cyrenaica, and Egypt.

[2] *Bull. d. Corresp. africaine algér.* 1882, fasc. ii. 62.   On the state of affairs there, Boissière, *L'Algérie romaine* ; Jung, *Rom. Landsch.* p. 194 ; L. Friedlaender, *Das röm. Africa*, in *Deutsche Rundschau*, Heft. 4 und 5, 1883.

[3] Legatus Augusti propraetore legionis : Marquardt, *Röm. Staatsverw.* I[2], p. 468.   Arnold, *Rom. Prov. Admin.* p. 108.

[4] Preller, *R. Mythol.*, Juno Caelestis.

Roman colonies were more plentiful in Africa than else-where. Hadrian himself increased their number, for from him Utica, Zama, and Thaenae received colonial rights.[1] Carthage, the residence of the proconsul, took the name of Hadrianopolis.[2] This is a proof that the emperor showed it especial favour, and adorned it with monuments. The New Carthage of the Romans, the foundation of Caesar, had already in the time of Augustus resumed her ancient position in Africa. She was the second city in the West, the third in the whole empire for size, beauty, and population, in which she was only surpassed by Rome and Alexandria; an emporium of commerce, with perhaps a million inhabit-ants, magnificent streets, splendid temples, theatres, and villas, and with her incomparable harbour, which, as in the days of Hamilcar, was alive with the ships of sea-faring nations. Carthage, indeed, was able to maintain her position until the time of the Vandals, as the seat of the finest Latin civilization, and she was the birthplace of famous men like Appuleius and Tertullian, Cyprian, Lactantius, and Augustine. Latin studies flourished throughout Africa as far as Numidia. Hadrian's great jurist, Salvius Julianus, was an African from Hadrumetum, and the orator Fronto came from Cirta, the capital of Numidia.

A great military road, starting from Lambaesis, protected the whole district of Numidia from the depredations of the Bedawin on the south. In the year 123 A.D., Hadrian had al-ready caused a road to be made by the IIIrd legion Augusta, under the command of his legate, P. Metilius Secundus, between Carthage and Theveste, a place in Numidia only a few miles to the east of Lambaesis.[3] The same legion was stationed at Lambaesis under the successor of Secundus, the legate Q. Fabius Catullinus, who, after giving up the com-

[1] Zumpt, *Comm. Ep.* i. 421 *C.I.L.* vi., n. 1686: COLONI. COLONIAE. AELIA. HADRIANAE. AUG. ZAMAE. REGIAE. COLON. AELIAE. AUGUST. MERCURIALIS. THAENITANA, n. 1685, and Gruter, 363: COL. JULIA. AELIA. HADRIANA. AUGUSTA. UTIKENSIS. Janssen, *Inscr. musei Lugduno-Batavi*, p. 80; in Duerr, p. 40.

[2] Spart. c. 20.

[3] Inscription on a milestone; Guerin, *Voyages archéol. dans la Régence de Tunis*, ii. 75. *C.I.L.* viii., n. 10049.

mand of his African legion on 1st of January 130 A.D., had held the consulship with M. Antonius Asper.[1]

Hadrian inspected the legion, and this review is recorded in an inscription on marble which gives the emperor's speech to the troops, and his favourable testimony to their military zeal under the leadership of Catullinus. The date of the order of the day was about the end of June, or the middle of July 128 A.D.[2]

Lambaesis, whose ruins are to be found at Djebel Aures, is one of the most remarkable examples of the activity of the Roman legionaries, for the city owed its origin to the camp of the IIIrd legion, whose entrenchments are still to be seen. This legion remained there for a long time, and indeed it appears to have been in Numidia as late as the year 400 A.D.[3]

We cannot ascertain how far Hadrian's journey in Africa extended. The province owed to him the foundation of several municipia and colonies, which assumed the name of Aelia.[4] He had a road made from Cirta to Rusicade by the legate of the IIIrd legion, C. Julius Major, seemingly after his own departure from Africa.[5] He probably then

---

[1] The legates of the legio III. Aug. held the command for three years, and were then promoted to a consulship. Henzen, *Diploma militare d'Adriano*, in *Annali d. Inst.* 1857, p. 20. Wilmanns, *Die röm. Lagerstaedte Africas* (*Comment. Philol.* Berlin, 1877), p. 209, calculates, according to Henzen, the duration of the command of Catullinus from the middle of 126 A.D. to the middle of 129 A.D.

[2] See the inscription found by Renier in Wilmanns (*Die röm. Lagerstaedte*) and *C.I.L.* viii., n. 2532.

[3] Dedicatory inscriptions to Hadrian by veterans of this legion at Lambaesis, under P. Cassius Secundus and Q. Fabius Catullinus, in Renier, *Inscr. rom. de l'Algérie*, n. 1 *sq.* On Lambaesis, Boissière, *L'Algérie romaine*, p. 333 *sq.* From the *Canabae*, originally settlements of veterans and merchants, a city arose under Marcus Aurelius. Unfortunately, the French have, since 1844, used this ancient station as a quarry, and thus destroyed it.

[4] Duerr, p. 40 *sq.*, has recorded the relations of Hadrian to Aelia near Thysdrus, to Aelium, Colonia Aelia Banasa, Aelium Choba, etc.

[5] EX . AUCTOR . IMP . CAES . HADRIANI . AUG . PONTES . VIAE . NOVAE . RUSICADENSIS . . . Renier, *Inscr. rom. de l'Algérie*, n. 2296; n. 3842, inscription from Quiza and Arsennaria.

planted colonies in Libya, which had been devastated by the rebellion of the Jews, while in Cyrenaica he founded the city of Hadriana or Hadrianopolis.[1]

[1] It is mentioned in the *Itinerar. Anton.* and in the Tabula Peutingeriana. The coin RESTITUTORI LIBYAE is doubtful, according to Eckhel, vi., p. 497.

CHAPTER XIV

Second Journey to the East. Hadrian in Athens and Eleusis. Journey to Asia. Ephesus. Smyrna. Sardis

FROM Africa Hadrian returned to Rome to begin his second great journey to the East, by way of Athens to Asia Minor, Syria, and Egypt.[1] The Romans might well be astonished at the restlessness of their emperor, who seemed to look upon the capital of the empire as only a temporary dwelling place, and to prefer foreign provinces, especially Greece, to Italy. He sailed for Athens either at the end of 128 A.D., or at the beginning of the following year.

If the information of Spartianus is correct, his presence was required there for the dedication of the buildings begun by him, and now completed ; but that the dedication of the great temple of Zeus took place then, or that so many of Hadrian's buildings in Athens could have been finished simultaneously, admits of reasonable doubt.[2] The Athenians must have been transported with delight at the speedy return of the emperor. Having reckoned his first arrival as an epoch in the calendar, they will have celebrated his second

---

[1] Spart. c. 13 : Denique, cum post Africam Romam redisset, statim ad orientem profectus per Athenas iter fecit—but who vouches for the chronological accuracy of this *statim?* Duerr, p. 32, concludes from Ulpian, *Dig.* 5, 3, 20, 6, that Hadrian was in Rome in the first half of March 129 A.D., as the S.C. Juventianum was passed on a motion by Hadrian in writing on the 14th of March.

[2] Spartian's sentence presupposes this : Atque opera, quae apud Athenienses coeperat, dedicavit, ut Jovis Olympii aedem et aram sibi.

visit with extraordinary honours. It was then, apparently, that they added to the twelve Attic tribes a thirteenth, giving it the name Hadrianis.[1] To the emperor, if he were sufficiently familiar with the past history of Athens, the honour must have appeared a doubtful one. For it was the same honour which Antigonus and Demetrius had formerly received from the Athenians, and had afterwards been obliged to surrender to the kings Attalus of Pergamum and Ptolemy of Egypt.[2]

Unfortunately, we are very much in the dark as to the indebtedness of Greece to this emperor, with regard to the improvement in the conditions of its municipal and national economy; for the list of inscriptions and coins of the cities, praising him as their benefactor and founder, conveys no definite information. In spite of all the glitter of new temples, festivals, and games, Greece remained politically a ruin, never to be reanimated by a vigorous national life.

From Athens Hadrian revisited the most important cities in Greece. Sparta celebrated his second visit by games, and extolled him as her deliverer.[3] An inscription from Mantinea, according to which the grammateus of this city dedicated to him a statue and a temple, is probably of this date.[4] Megara created a new tribe, Hadrianis, in honour of the emperor.[5] Inscriptions from Corinth, Thespiae, Coronea, and from Phocis and some of the islands, leave it uncertain as to the period to which they belong.[6] Before Hadrian journeyed further from Athens into Asia, he was again in Eleusis, and he there probably received the second

---

[1] The phyle Hadrianis is frequently mentioned in inscriptions, which have been collected by Hertzberg, ii. 343 *sq.* Dittenberger, *Die attischen Phylen* (in *Hermes*, 1875, ix. 386, 397). Hermann, *Jahrbuch d. griech. Staatsalterthümer*, 5. Auflage, § 176. In consequence of the thirteenth phyle, the council of Athens was again reduced to 500.

[2] Pausanias, i. 5, 5.

[3] *C.I.G.* n. 1308 *sq.*

[4] Le Bas-Foucart, Sect. vi. *Arcadie*, n. 352 *g.*

[5] *C.I.G.* n. 1072.

[6] Passim in Boeckh, *C.I.G.* Thespiae 1614, Coronea 1615, Mitylene 2177, Andros 2349 m. (add. vol. ii.), Aegina 332, Thera 2454.

and final initiation.[1]	The council of this city erected a
statue to the priestess of Demeter, on the base of which
she has commemorated both the emperor and herself in
verse.	"I have celebrated the mysteries," so says this
noble priestess, "not to the honour of the Dioscuri, nor to
Asclepius, nor to Heracles, but to Hadrian, the sovereign of
the world, the ruler over innumerable mortals, the bestower
of inexhaustible benefits upon every city, and especially
upon the city of Cecrops."[2]

Hadrian was able to celebrate the festival of the month
Boedromion at Eleusis;[3] he then went, about the autumn of
129 A.D., to Ephesus by sea.[4]	It was his second visit to
the city of Artemis.

Ephesus, one of the great centres of commerce between
Asia, Greece, and Egypt, was still so flourishing at this time
that she could venture to call herself "the first and greatest
metropolis of Asia."[5]	She was also the seat of the Roman
proconsul.	Other cities of the province, such as Pergamum,
Sardis, Cyzicus, and Smyrna, cast envious glances upon their
fortunate rival.	They disputed her precedence, particularly
in the right of presiding at the festal union and provincial
diet of Asia (τὸ κοινὸν ᾿Ασίας).	The provincial games were
celebrated in every city, but the Panionian games, which
were connected with the festival of the great Artemis, were
held only in Ephesus.[6]

[1] The initiation consisted of two parts. ἐποπτεύειν, the word which
Eusebius and Dion use of Hadrian's Eleusinian initiation, means, to
receive the last and highest degree.	Cp. Salmasius on the 13th chapter
of Spartianus.

[2] Ἄσπετον ὃς πάσαις πλοῦτον κατέχευε πόλεσσιν, ᾿Αδριανὸν κλεινῆς δ᾽ ἔξοχα
Κεκροπίης.	C.I.G. i., n. 434.

[3] On the Eleusian festivals, from 14 to 25 Boedromion, see the table
in A. Mommsen, Heortologie, p. 268.

[4] He says so himself, in the letter to the Ephesians referred to previously
(Wood, Discov. of Ephes. n. 1).	The date is Trib. Pot. XIII. (129 A.D.).
The inscription was found by Wood in the great theatre, and is now in
London.

[5] πρώτη καὶ μεγίστη μητρόπολις τῆς ᾿Ασίας, in inscriptions in Wood, Discov.
Appendix.	The πρώτη and μητρόπολις were also claimed by other cities
of Asia.

[6] Hadrian himself was honoured as Panionius.	Inscription from
Ephesus, Curtius in Hermes, iv. 1, p. 182.

Ever since the Romans had inherited this city from Attalus of Pergamum, they had looked upon it as a jewel of their empire. All the emperors showed it favour. It was one of the fourteen cities of Asia Minor, which Tiberius restored after the terrible earthquake. On the base of the statue which the cities dedicated to him, the genius of Ephesus is depicted with three ears of corn, a pomegranate and a poppy in her hand, symbols of the fertility of the district.[1] Claudius and Nero, Vespasian and Trajan, and finally Hadrian himself, adorned the city with so many buildings that the ruins to-day of temples and theatres, of stadia, gymnasia, baths, and aqueducts, lying scattered over hills and valleys, belong almost entirely to the Roman period.[2]

Near the slopes of the hills of Coressus and Prion, on which the magnificent remains of the city walls still show the strength of the old fortifications, lay Ephesus, stretched out in a wide plain watered by the Cenchrius and the Cayster "rich in swans." The charm of this landscape surpasses even the beauty of the plain of Sardis through which the Hermus flows. The city was connected with the sea, that was some miles distant, by artificial harbours. The riches of nature, the influence of Lydia and Persia, and the intoxicating sensuousness of the worship of Artemis, had conspired to make the people of Ephesus the most luxurious of Ionia. Their city was the paradise of the pleasures, the vices and the mysteries of the East. It was full of musicians, comedians and dancers, priests, magicians and astrologers. Their superstitious arts were famous throughout the world; the Ephesian symbols of the girdle and wreath of the many-breasted Diana were even worn in Rome as amulets, and the sentimental tales of fiction, for which no more suitable scene than Ephesus could be found, were eagerly read throughout the empire.

The city owed its world-wide fame to the temple of

[1] This pedestal stands in the museum of Naples. A similar representation on Ephesian coins, Mionnet, *Suppl.* vi., n. 880. Edward Falkener, *Ephesus and the Temple of Diana*, 1862, ii. 291.

[2] Wood, p. 11. Under Antoninus a great part of the city near the Odeum was rebuilt. See, in addition to Wood and Falkener, also E. Guhl, *Ephesiaca*, 1843; Hyde Clarke, *Ephesus*, 1862.

Artemis, a masterpiece of Ionic architecture.   Seven times
was it destroyed and rebuilt,[1] and finally, on the night that
Alexander the Great was born, it was utterly demolished by
the torch of a madman.   This temple, the work of Chersiphron, was the largest of antiquity, 425 feet long and
220 feet broad, supported by columns 60 feet in height.[2]
Dinocrates, the gifted architect of Alexander, at once began
a magnificent new building, apparently on the same scale,[3]
and this Hadrian found when he came to Ephesus.   Of its
one hundred and twenty-seven pillars, thirty-six were adorned
on the base with figures larger than life in relievo.[4]   The
artists of Greece had vied with each other, both before
and after the time of Alexander, to adorn the sanctuary of
Diana with beautiful works of art.   Phidias and Polycletus,
Praxiteles and Myron worked for it ; Lysippus had placed
there the statue of Alexander; and the great painters, Parrhasius (an Ephesian by birth), Euphranor, Zeuxis and
Apelles, produced their noblest paintings for this temple.[5]
Though, in the course of time, many works of art may have
disappeared, the Artemisium was still, in the age of Hadrian,
a richer museum than the temple of Apollo at Delphi.   It
served at the same time as the common treasure-house for
all Asia, wherein cities and private individuals deposited
their gold.

The priesthood of Artemis had at one time authority, in the
name of the goddess, to govern the city and its neighbourhood.[6]   Alexander, and subsequently Mithridates and Mark
Antony, to please the priests, had largely increased the extent
of the temple precincts, which were intended to serve as an
asylum.   Augustus judiciously modified their extent, and

[1] Pliny, *H.N.* xvi. 79, 1.

[2] Strabo, 640.

[3] Of this temple Callimachus, *Hymn to Diana*, v. 249, says : τοῦ δ' οὔτι
θεώτερον ὄψεται ἠώς, οὐδ' ἀφνειότερον.

[4] Pliny, *H.N.* xxxvi. 21 (columnae celatae) : see explanations to map of
city of Ephesus by F. Adler, *Abhandl. der Akad. d. Wissensch. zu Berlin,*
1873, 34 *sq.*

[5] Guhl, *Ephesiaca*, p. 186 *sq.*   Falkener, p. 305.

[6] On their power and policy consult Curtius, *Beitraege zur Gesch. und
Topogr. Kleinasiens*, Berlin, 1873.

surrounded them with a wall.[1]   But the emperor respected
the privileges of the temple, and Hadrian especially seems to
have been well disposed to Diana of the Ephesians.   The
fact that Ephesus was the seat of the proconsul must have
tended to spread Roman and imperial worship, which was in
no way antagonistic to the policy of the priesthood of the
temple.   Servility to the emperor seems to have flourished
nowhere so much as in this city, and Ephesus probably was
the real birthplace of this degrading emperor-worship.[2]
Ephesian coins connect Hadrian even with the great
goddess Artemis, who is depicted upon them standing in
her temple or between two stags, as she is represented in
the well-known statue in Naples.[3]   The second Neocoria of
the city is recorded on coins and inscriptions in honour of
the emperor.[4]   After Hadrian had assumed the surname
Olympius, his Olympian games were celebrated there.   A
sanctuary of the deified emperor, belonging to the whole
province of Asia, stood there under the authority of the
high priest, the Asiarch, who presided over the games.[5]   The
priests of the Artemisium dedicated statues to Hadrian and
his consort, worshipping them as gods after their death,
equally with Diana.[6]

[1] Strabo, 641.   Augustus built the peribolus in the year 6 B.C.   Wood
found the Augustan inscriptions on the corner of it, and they led him to
the site of the temple.   The Artemisium was destroyed by the Goths
about one hundred and forty years after the visit of Hadrian, when
Gallienus was emperor (260-268 A.D.).   Its position had become so utterly
effaced that it took Wood six years until he found it in the spring of 1870.
A big swampy pit, grown over with rush and jungle, and a dust heap of
lime with a few remains of the temple are all that is left of the once
glorious Artemisium.   Close by stands the magnificent mosque of Selim,
which was built from stones of the temple.

[2] Krause, *Neokoros*.   Preller, *R. Mythologie*, "Kaisercultus," 425.
Smyrna, however, claims to have been the first to erect a templum urbis
Romae.   Tacitus, *Ann.* iv. 56.

[3] Mionnet, *Suppl.* vi., p. 136, n. 381 *sq.*

[4] *C.I.A.* iii. pt. I., n. 485.   *C.I.G.* 2965.   [5] *C.I.L.* iii. 246 *sq.*

[6] Ephesian inscriptions in honour of Hadrian, compiled by Duerr,
Anhang, n. 27 *sq.*   Inscriptions to Sabina, *C.I.G.* n. 2964-66.   N. 2965
was erected when Aurelius Fulvus Antoninus, subsequently the emperor
Anton. Pius, was proconsul of Asia (before 135 A.D.).   Wood, *App.* n. 3.
C.I.L. iii., n. 6070 *a*, inscription on a statue erected by the bule in Ephesus

If the emperor had looked deeper into the fantastic world of Ephesus, he would have discerned a quiet but well organized community, who called themselves Christians, living side by side with the worshippers of the ancient goddess, with her choruses of maidens clad in purple, and her swarms of effeminate priests in the temple. Into this fertile soil of Asiatic fanaticism the seed of the Gospel had early fallen, and had flourished vigorously. From the neighbourhood of the temple of Artemis the disciples of the new religion of the world had promulgated their doctrine through Asia Minor. In Ephesus the Apostle Paul had preached for three years, and probably the Apostle John had lived there. The fourth gospel originated here, and this very city of Diana, which "manifested to Asia and the world the service of God," was a centre of life for the gospel, and a school for Christian dogma.[1]

From Ephesus Hadrian revisited many other cities in Asia. Smyrna, the queen of the Ionian Sea, appears to have attracted him the most. Above the city stood the legendary seat of the Tantalids, the gloomy mountain Sipylus, where the rocky image of the weeping Niobe is still to be seen ; at her feet lay the gulf covered with ships, while the smooth plains that stretched for miles showed a continuous line of orchards.

Smyrna boasted that she had been founded by Tantalus, or by Theseus, or by the Amazons ; above all, she plumed herself upon being the birthplace of Homer. The statue of the poet stood in a magnificent building, the Homereum, and received as much honour as Cybele, the mother of the gods, in her famous temple. The great city vied with Ephesus in calling herself the first and most splendid city of Asia in beauty and size, metropolis of Asia, three times Neocorus of the Augusti, and glory of Ionia.[2] Her

to the younger Matidia, sister of Diva Sabina. The oldest inscription of Hadrian of which we know is a decree of the emperor of 27th September 120 A.D., in the form of a letter to the gerusia of the city, whose envoys presented it to Cornelius Priscus, proconsul of Asia. Curtius, *Inschriften aus Ephesus*, in *Hermes*, iv. 1, 178.

[1] Renan, *St. Paul*, p. 333 *sq.*; *L'Eglise chrétienne*, p. 46.

[2] *C.I.G.* n. 3191, 3202, and some other inscriptions.

splendour must have been great, if we may credit the enthusiastic description of Aristides, when he speaks of the charm of her scenery, her baths, theatres and porticos, her many gymnasia and temples. He described Smyrna, after she had been destroyed by an earthquake in the time of Marcus Aurelius, as the picture of the earth, the theatre of Greece, the creation of nymphs and Graces.[1]

The city was rich from its trade by sea and caravan, and it was also an important seat of philosophy. The celebrated Polemon, a friend of Hadrian, lived there. To please him, Hadrian loaded Smyrna with favours.[2] The grateful Smyrniots erected a temple to the emperor, and afterwards celebrated the Olympia of Hadrian with special magnificence.[3] Smyrna even assumed the surname Adriana.[4]

In the interior of Lydia, near the slopes of Sipylus and Tmolus, where the Hermus flows through a great plain, lay a number of ancient cities which had been made famous as scenes of the contest for the supremacy in Asia, first between the kings of Lydia and Persia, and subsequently between the Seleucids and the Romans. The most considerable were Magnesia (near Mount Sipylus, where the Scipios had broken the power of king Antiochus), Sardis and Philadelphia. Sardis was still rich and powerful in the time of Hadrian. The old royal citadel was still in existence on its steep rocky height, at whose foot, on the bank of the golden Pactolus, stood the temple of Cybele, her priesthood always at variance with the priesthood of

[1] *Or.* xx. monody on Smyrna. Strabo (646) had already called her καλλίστη τῶν πασῶν: Lucian, Εἰκόνες, 960, ἡ καλλίστη τῶν Ἰωνικῶν πόλεων.

[2] Philostr. *Vita Soph.* ii., p. 43 (ed. Kayser). The Smyrniot inscription. C.I.G. 3148 records the benefactions of Hadrian, received through Polemon, the second Neocoria, the atelia, festival games, the appointment of theologoi and hymnodoi, great sums of money, and buildings. Coins struck in honour of Hadrian by Polemon : Mionnet, iii., p. 227 ; *Suppl.* vi., p. 340.

[3] C.I.G. n. 3174 : Ὀλυμπίῳ σωτῆρι καὶ κτίστῃ. N. 3175 is an inscription from the time of Antoninus Pius, according to which Hadrian had issued regulations to the Smyrniots with respect to these Olympia. Smyrniot coins of Hadrian with the figure of Jupiter and two temples, Mionnet, iii., p. 227 *sq.*

[4] Mionnet, iii., p. 205. Eckhel, ii. 544.

Diana of the Ephesians. On the other side of the Hermus, between the river and the sea of Gyges, were situated the burial-places of the Lydian kings, with their innumerable tumuli as well preserved as when they were described by Herodotus.[1]

Sardis received the first Neocoria from Hadrian.[2] An inscription of this city, which relates to a decree of Trajan about quinquennial games, calls Hadrian the new Dionysus.[3] In this ancient city of Croesus, as in the other cities of Lydia, the Christian community was already very large, and soon after Hadrian's time Bishop Melito became famous as the apologist of Christianity, and compiler of the canonical writings of the Old Testament.

There are inscriptions from other cities in Lydia and Caria, such as Colophon and Magnesia on the Meander, from Thyatira, from Tralles and Miletus, which mention the benefactions of Hadrian.[4] The once magnificent Miletus, decayed since the time of Alexander the Great, still existed with its harbour. It claimed to be the metropolis of Ionia, but the preservation of its fame was due only to the ancient oracle temple of Apollo Didymeus. Milesian inscriptions connect Hadrian with this god, and with the Pythian Artemis.[5] Phrygia has Hadrianic coins

[1] When, in the spring of 1882, I visited Sardis, Mr. Dennis was busy excavating some tumuli. The Sardian Acropolis is in danger of falling before long from the rocky summit.

[2] Krause, *Neokoros*, p. 53.

[3] Perhaps this decree was issued by Hadrian himself, see Boeckh's note in *C.I.G.* n. 3455.

[4] Colophon: *C.I.G.* n. 3036. Magnesia: Mionnet, iii. 148. The inscription of the Magnetes, *C.I.G.* n. 2910, mentions extraordinary presents received from Hadrian. The inscription of Tralles, *C.I.G.* n. 2927, says that the strategus Aulus Fabricius Priscianus Charmosynos provisioned the city, by order of Hadrian, with 60,000 modii of grain from Egypt. Tralles and Miletus called Hadrian their founder. Mionnet, *Suppl.* vii., p. 470; vi., p. 274. The cities Philomelium and Stratonicea assumed the name Adriane. In Thyatira mention is made of an Adrianeum. *C.I.G.* 3491.

[5] Ἀπόλλωνι Διδυμεῖ καὶ Αὐτοκράτορι Ἀδριανῷ.—*C.I.G.* 2863, 2866, 2877. The attribute Olympius shows that they were placed subsequent to its acceptance. *C.I.G.* 339: ἡ μητρόπολις, τῆς Ἰωνίας Μιλησίων πόλις, erects a monument to Hadrian in the Olympieum of Athens.

of arrival and restoration. Inscriptions are preserved, especially from Aezani, which record that Hadrian fixed the boundaries which had been disputed for ages between this community and the temple of Zeus.[1]

He spent the winter of 129-130 A.D. in Ephesus or in Smyrna. From there he could visit Lycia, the wonderful land of Sarpedon, whose league of cities with an independent constitution had existed down to the time of Vespasian. For it was Vespasian who first deprived Lycia of her autonomy, and united the district with Pamphylia as a Roman province. The Greek character had developed there in manners, customs and language, and also in art, as may be seen from the monuments and tombs.[2]

The most important cities of Lycia were Xanthus with its famous temple and oracle of Apollo, Patara, Telmessus, Tlos, Phaselis, Pinara, Myra and Olympus. Inscriptions from the port of Phaselis record the arrival of Hadrian, but his visit there seems to have taken place after his return from Egypt.[3]

He then visited many harbours and cities in Pisidia and Pamphylia, such as Olbia and Perge, Aspendus, Side and Cibyra.[4]

[1] Le Bas-Wadd. n. 860, under Avidius Quietus, proconsul of Asia.

[2] The interest in this country has been revived by the Austrian expedition in the year 1882. *Vorlaeuf Bericht ueber zwei oesterr. archaeolog. Expeditionen nach Kleinasien*, von Otto Benndorf, Wien, 1883. *Eine Reise durch das Land des Sarpedon*, von Alex. v. Warsberg, *Oesterr. Rundschau*, 1883.

[3] Phaselis: *C.I.G.* n. 4336, 4337, and add. p. 1157: statues erected ὑπὲρ τῆς ἐπιβάσεως αὐτοῦ, by the Acalassenians and Corydalles. Two others, 4334, 4335, have the Trib. Pot. XV. For these Duerr gives, p. 160, the year 130 A.D., and fixes that time for the visit of Hadrian to Lycia. But as the 22nd of March 129 A.D. is given for Hadrian's 13th Trib. Pot. (*C.I.L.* iii., pt. ii. p. 1111, Mommsen's table), the 14th will still fall in the spring of 130 A.D. and the 15th only in the spring of 131 A.D. Statues might have been erected even in the emperor's absence. Olympus in Lycia erected one to him with the inscription, πατρὶ πατρίδος σωτῆρι τοῦ κόσμου, without the addition of Olympius: Le Bas-Wadd. n. 1342. In Myra grain magazines of Hadrian are mentioned, *C.I.L.* iii., n. 232 (in ruinis Myrorum ad ostia fluvii Andraki).

[4] An inscription from Cibyra calls him εὐεργέτην καὶ σωτῆρα τοῦ κόσμου: *C.I.G.* 4380—most likely the same Cibyra which erected a monument

In Cilicia, the cities of Tarsus, Adane, Aegae and Mops-vestia could not have assumed the name Adriana without special reason. As this coast lying between Pamphylia and Syria seems to have been a separate province since the time of Hadrian governed by a propraetorian legate, it is clear that the emperor reorganized it.[1]

Hadrian then went into Syria.

at Puteoli in honour of Hadrian after his death. *C.I.G.* 5852. There were, however, two cities of this name in Pisidia or Cabalia, and in Pamphylia.

[1] Marquardt, *Röm Staatsv.* i., p. 388. ADVENT . AUG . CILICIAE. Cohen, ii., p. 109, n. 29. Tarsus records the first Neocoria under Hadrian. Krause, *Neokoros*, p. 80.

CHAPTER XV

Hadrian in Syria. Antioch. Phoenicia. Heliopolis. Damascus. Palmyra

SYRIA, which had been Roman since the time of Pompey, was the most important of all the provinces of the empire in Asia; it was garrisoned by several legions, and was governed by a consular legate appointed by the emperor. After Judaea had been separated from it in the year 70 A.D., this great territory, originally full of ancient Semitic, and, from the time of Alexander, of Greek culture, comprised northern Syria, Phoenicia and Chalcidene with the eastern districts of Auranitis and Trachonitis. As Commagene was also under the rule of the legate of Syria, the whole province stretched from Cappadocia and Cilicia to the Euphrates, between the Arabian desert, its barrier against the Bedawin, and the Phoenician sea past Palmyra, Damascus and the Lebanon down to the borders of Palestine.

Numerous cities, Greek in constitution, chiefly foundations of the Seleucids, or ancient seats of the Phoenicians and Aramaeans, were then flourishing by their maritime intercourse, by the caravan traffic with Persia and India, and by their trade in the fabrics of the East. The ruling population was Greek, and was based on the down-trodden Aramaic and Phoenician nationalities, which, to the east of Damascus, mingled with the Arabs. The native Semites found themselves in the same relation to the Greeks and Romans, as the Carthaginians in Africa, and with equal vitality the worship of Baal and Melkart, Adonis and Astarte—a worship which in antiquity rivalled that of the Egyptians—continued to exist.

The capital of Syria, the seat of the Roman government, was the free, autonomous city of Antioch on the Orontes, which Seleucus Nicator had founded in honour of his father Antiochus. She called herself " the Great," and was, in fact, one of the most populous and beautiful cities of the Roman empire.[1]

She shone by her wealth and magnificence, and by the luxury of her festivals, which were celebrated in the groves of Daphne, hard by the Seleucid temple of Apollo.

It was in Antioch that Hadrian had once been legate of Syria. His adoption by Trajan had been conferred upon him in the royal palace on the island of Orontes, the residence of the Roman governor, and the first months of his reign had been spent there. We do not know whether he had visited Antioch again before his second journey to the East. His visit in the year 130 A.D. cannot be doubted, although there are no records to confirm it, inscriptions and coins of Antioch being strangely wanting. There are not even Syrian coins of the arrival of Hadrian, only those marked *Exercitus Syriacus*.[2]

The luxury of the Syrians infected the Roman army, and nowhere had Hadrian so much trouble as in Antioch with the discipline of the troops. They were refractory and corrupted by every vice. Insurrections often took place, even under Marcus Aurelius, when the strict Avidius Cassius, afterwards himself a rebel, was their commander.[3] The citizens of Antioch, like the Alexandrians, were mischievous, satirical and frivolous. Even the emperor Julian suffered from their faults, and revenged himself upon them by his *Misopogon*.

Hadrian, too, must have had disagreeable experiences of

---

[1] Strabo, 750.   [2] Eckhel, vi., p. 501.

[3] Fronto, *Princip. Histor.*, p. 227 : Corruptissimi vero omnium Syriatici milites. *Ad Verum Imp.*, p. 133 : Antiochiae adsidue plaudere histrionibus consueti, saepius in nemore vicinae ganeae quam sub signis habiti. Thus, says Fronto, Verus received the Syrian army. The discipline of Hadrian had therefore borne no fruit. The Roman troops in Syria were distributed among many garrisons. In the beginning of the first century of the empire, four legions were quartered there : VI. Ferrata, X. Fretensis, III. Gallica, XII. Fulminata. Marquardt, *Röm. Staatsv.* i. 427.

the character of this people, for Spartianus tells us that Antioch became so hateful to him that he wished to separate Syria from Phoenicia, in order that the city might not be called the metropolis of so large a district.[1] However, he must have had more serious reasons for this project to divide Syria than his discontent with the populace of the capital of the province. He did not carry it out, for Syria was first actually divided by Septimius Severus in the year 198 A.D.[2] Indeed Hadrian's dislike for Antioch may be doubted, or it may have been only a transitory feeling; for a later Byzantine writer asserts that the emperor built a theatre there, a temple for the nymphs of Daphne, baths and aqueducts, and dedicated them solemnly on the 23rd of June.[3]

Hadrian went up Mount Casius, in the vicinity of Antioch, in order to see the sun rise, and to offer sacrifices in the sanctuary of Zeus, where, in former times, he had accompanied Trajan when he had brought votive offerings from the spoils of the Dacian war.[4] A storm broke, and both victim and priest were struck by lightning. With this anecdote, Spartianus dismisses the subject, without saying anything about the actions of Hadrian in Syria, or without mentioning the names of many other cities, particularly the famous old cities of Phoenicia, which he visited. Hadrian must then have gone southwards along the coast by Laodicea, Aradus and Tripolis to Byblus and Berytus. The Seleucid Laodicea commemorated his gifts by an inscription on a statue which the city erected to him in the Olympieum at Athens.[5] From Berytus, too, there is a

[1] Spart. c. 14.

[2] Marquardt, *Röm. Staatsv.* i. 423. E. Bormann, *De Syriae Prov. Rom. partibus*, p. 16 *sq.* Septimius Severus seems to have placed Antioch under Laodicea, nevertheless the city maintained her rank until the time of the Arabs. Herodian, iii. *in Sever.*, p. 523. Suidas, *V. Sever.*, p. 869. Eckhel, iii. 317.

[3] Malalas, 278 (ed. Migne).

[4] According to Pliny, *H.N.* v. 18, 3, one could see the sun from Casius already about the fourth night watch, and, so to say, observe day and night at the same time.

[5] *C.I.A.* iii., pt. 1. 479. She calls herself Julia Laodicea, and ἱερά, ἄσυλος, αὐτόνομος, and friendly ally of the Roman people.

dedicatory inscription in honour of Hadrian.[1]   This noble
seaport at the foot of the Lebanon, the present Beyrout, bore
the name of Julia Augusta Felix Berytus, after its colonization by Augustus.   The key to the district of the Lebanon,
its fine situation and safe harbour have preserved it through
all the storms of time, and make it even to-day one of the
most flourishing cities of Syria.

From Berytus Hadrian could proceed to Tyre and Sidon.
These remarkable cities, parents of so many Phoenician
colonies, which long before the time of the Greeks had
thrown open the seas to all nations, and had made themselves masters of the commerce of the world, were now
merely the ruins of their former days, but in spite of their
decay they were still large and splendid places.   Trade and
navigation, especially the silk manufacture and the purple
fishery, maintained their prosperity.   They had retained
some degree of liberty from the days of the Seleucids, and
even under the Romans.   Strabo spoke of both cities as
brilliant in antiquity and in his own time ; he praised their
situation on their famous harbours, of which Tyre had
preserved both—the Egyptian and the Sidonian—while the
dam of Alexander still connected the island with the main-
land.[2]   Tyre had borne the title of metropolis for a long
time, and seems to have generally maintained her precedence
among the cities of Phoenicia.[3]   She first became a colony
with Latin rights in the time of Septimius Severus.   She
was the chief seat of the worship of Melkart, or the
Phoenician Heracles, who had a famous temple there.[4]   At
the same time, one of the earliest and most important of the
Christian communities of Syria arose at Tyre.

No precise information has come down to us of the
presence of Hadrian in Tyre and Sidon.   Nor have we any
accurate account of his journey to Heliopolis or Baalbek, in

---

[1] *C.I.L.* iii. 165.   Coin : Astarte in a temple, with the horn of plenty, in
Foy-Vaillant, p. 153.   Mionnet, v. 340.

[2] Strabo, 756 *sq.*   Prutz, *Aus Phoenizien*, p. 182 *sq.*

[3] According to Suidas (Paulus Tyrius) Hadrian conferred this title upon
her, whereas Tyre had held it already since 94 A.D.   Bormann, p. 17.

[4] Lucian, *Dea Syria*, c. 3.   In Sidon stood the temple of Astarte, and
Byblus was the principal seat of the Adonis worship.

Coele-Syria, or to Damascus and Palmyra. But the emperor must have visited these cities from Berytus (Beyrout).

Heliopolis, whose foundation was ascribed by the Arabians to Solomon, was one of the most ancient cities in Syria, for its colossal square buildings on the Acropolis point to a very early period of Syrian strength and architecture.[1] It did not then possess the magnificent temple whose ruins to-day are one of the wonders of the East. Strabo, indeed, only mentions it casually in connection with Chalcis in Coele-Syria. Augustus restored it, but did not make it into a colony. On its coins, which exist from the time of Hadrian to Gallienus, it is called Colonia Julia Augusta Felix Heliopolitana, but whether Hadrian first bestowed the right of a colony upon it is doubtful.[2] In any case the emperor may have erected many buildings there, although the monumental splendour of the city of Baal belongs to the time of his successors. Antoninus Pius is said to have commenced the buildings of the great temple of Zeus.[3]

From Heliopolis a caravan road ran over the Anti-Lebanon to Damascus, the paradise of the Syrian desert. This famous city, one of the most ancient in the East, was, even in the time of David, the seat of a Syrian principality. It maintained its position through all the storms in the history of Asia, under the government of the Assyrians, Babylonians and Persians, and became, after Alexander, the residence of the Seleucids, before they made Antioch the capital of their beautiful empire. Greek culture penetrated into Damascus. Greeks, Jews, Syrians and Arabians composed the inhabitants of this flourishing city, which was the crowded emporium of commerce between the countries of the Euphrates, Arabia, Egypt and Phoenicia. In the year 64 B.C., Pompey conquered it for the Romans,

---

[1] Ritter, *Erdkunde*, viii. 2. Abtheil., p. 229.

[2] These names, *C.I.L.* iii., n. 202, at the time of Sept. Severus. Zumpt, *Comm. Ep.* i. 418, asserts that Hadrian fortified Heliopolis about 132 A.D., because of the Jewish war, and raised it to a colony. See also Marquardt, *Röm. Staatsv.* i. 428. But Moinnet (v., p. 298) has a coin of Nerva with COL. JULIA HEL., and the symbol of a husbandman with two rams.

[3] Malalas, ed. Bonn, 280.

but it did not then become incorporated with the empire, for tributary kings reigned there, and for some time it was in the possession of Herod the Great, when he was governor of Coele-Syria.   Damascus first became a Roman city of the province of Syria after Cornelius Palma had broken the power of the kings of Arabia.

The numerous channels of the Chrysorrhoas (Baradá), which flow with considerable force from the Anti-Lebanon, early converted the desert round Damascus into a luxuri-antly fertile plain, and even to-day the gardens, which stretch for miles around, are looked upon by the Bedawin as the Eden of the world.   On the coins, the city is depicted as a woman with a mural crown on her head, seated on a rock overhanging the river, holding in her left hand a fish, in her right a cornucopia.[1] We know nothing at all of what Hadrian did for Damascus.   He seems to have made it a metropolis.[2] We hear nothing of his buildings there.   The gigantic temple of the sun, whose ruins now stand near the great mosque, and over a por-tion of the bazaar, belongs probably to the time of Aurelian. In Damascus Paul was converted, and a numerous Christian community existed there, as in Ephesus, from that time.

Close to the eastern borders of the Syrian desert was the oasis of Palmyra, the halting-place for the caravan traffic of India and Mesopotamia.   A great road ran here from the Euphrates to Phoenicia, meeting the roads which reached Palmyra from Thapsacus, Babylon and the Persian Gulf.[3]

Palmyra was the ancient Tadmor of the Arabians, which Solomon is said to have founded as a meeting-place for the caravans close to the Syrian desert.   From the Seleucids the city had received a thoroughly Greek culture.   It was afterwards a constant subject of dispute between the great powers of Rome and Parthia, until at last it was taken possession of by Trajan, who united it with Syria.[4]

An inscription records the visit of Hadrian to this mar-

---

[1] Eckhel, iii. 331.   Mionnet, v., p. 287.

[2] Marquardt, *Röm. Staatsv.* i. 430.   According to Noris, *Epoch. Syro-maced.*, p. 76, he added it to Phoenicia.   But all this is doubtful.

[3] Movers, *Phoenizien*, iii. 1, 292.   [4] Pliny, *H.N.* v. 21, 3.

vellous city, and at the same time vouches for the emperor's previous visit to Baalbek and Damascus, for he could only have reached Palmyra by this route. The Greek inscription was erected by the council and people of Palmyra to a citizen, Males Agrippa, who, at the time of the emperor's arrival, was secretary for the second time to the community, and who had deserved well from his fellow citizens and from strangers by the games he had given, and the sacrifices he had offered in the temple, as well as by his hospitable reception of the Roman troops.[1]

Hadrian was again in Palmyra, either in 130 A.D., on his journey through Syria to Egypt, or later, on his return thence to Syria. He probably granted both Italian and colonial rights to the city, for in his honour it assumed the name Adriana.[2]

His particular attention must have been directed to the military roads leading to the country of the Euphrates and to Bostra, and these he probably strengthened by forts. In the neighbourhood of Palmyra, the ruins of a temple bear the name of Hadrian, in whose honour it was built.[3]

The glory of Palmyra began, as did that of Bostra, Petra and Baalbek, in the time of Hadrian and the Antonines, and reached its height in the third century, under the rule of Odenathus and of the great Zenobia. Aurelian then destroyed this noble city in the year 273 A.D.

From Syria and Phoenicia Hadrian went, in 130 A.D., to Judaea, and we follow him here with great interest, as the land was soon to become the theatre of terrible events.

---

[1] *C.I.G.* 4482. Le Bas-Wadd. 2585. Vogüé, *Syrie centrale, Inscr. sémitiques*, Paris, 1868, p. 19, n. 16. . . . ἐπιδημία θεοῦ Ἀδριανοῦ. The inscription must have been placed soon after Hadrian's visit. Waddington concludes, from the Palmyrenian text, the 442nd year of the Seleucid era, which began on the 1st October 130 A.D. Vogüé places the inscription in the year 131 A.D.

[2] *C.I.G.* n. 4482, 6015, Ἀδριανὴ Πάλμυρα. Steph. Byz. (*Ethnikon*), under Palmyra, says expressly that the Palmyrenians Ἀδριανοπολῖται μετωνομάσθησαν ἐπικτισθείσης τῆς πολέως ἀπὸ τοῦ αὐτοκράτορος. This is confirmed by *C.I.G.* 6015, where a Palmyrenian, Heliodorus, calls himself Adrianos. In Renier (*Inscr. de l'Algérie*, n. 1638) a Zabdiol Hadrianus is mentioned, veteran of the *numerus Palmyrenorum* in Numidia.

[3] Vogüé, *Inscr. Aram.*, p. 50: ὑπὲρ σωτηρίας . . . Ἀδριανοῦ.

CHAPTER XVI

Hadrian in Judaea. Condition of Jerusalem. Foundation of the Colony Aelia Capitolina. Hadrian in Arabia. Bostra. Petra. The Country of Peraea. Gaza. Pelusium

JUDAEA, or Palestine, had been separated from Syria after the war of destruction under Titus, and formed a separate province, under a praetorian legate who resided in Caesarea Palestina.[1]   This city, with Emmaus Nicopolis, both veteran colonies of Vespasian, had recently been destroyed by an earthquake in the year 129 A.D.   The Jewish inhabitants who still remained, lived on in poverty among the ruins, as the Arabian inhabitants of the country do to-day under the Turkish pasha.   All the intellectual strength of the Jews had taken refuge in the schools of the Rabbis at Jamnia, a city by the sea, between Joppa and Ashdod. Inspired prophets, at whose head stood the Rabbi Akiba, kept alive the hopes of a Messiah.

When Hadrian came to Judaea, he saw no signs, deeply disturbed as the country was within, of an approaching outbreak, but he received only tokens of submission.   In memory of his visit, coins were struck by the senate, which do not indeed call him the benefactor or restorer of Judaea, but which bear the usual symbol of restoration, a woman kneeling, whom the emperor raises from the ground, while children, probably the genii of the district of Palestine,

[1] Henzen (Note 3 in *Borghesi*, iv. 160) believes that the name Palaestina for Judaea was introduced by Hadrian.   See *Bullet. d. Inst.* 1848, p. 127. Ptolemy, v, c. 15, has both names, Παλαιστίνη ἡ Ἰουδαία Συρία.

come to meet him with palms of peace.[1] There is no authentic record of Hadrian's arrival among the ruins of Jerusalem.

The fame of the old capital of the Jews was so great in the West, that Pliny had called it the most renowned city, not only of Judaea, but of the East.[2] But the city of the Asmoneans and of Herod had been destroyed by the Romans, and had not been rebuilt. Hadrian found it still lying in ruins, even if no longer in the condition in which Titus had left it. The destruction inflicted by this conqueror of Judaea was not quite complete. Josephus relates that Titus had spared the Herodian towers of Phasaelus, Hippicus and Mariamne, near the west wall, the one to be used as a garrison for the Roman camp, the other to serve as a witness to posterity of the strength of the city which had been subdued by the Roman forces.[3] Moreover, all the monumental buildings could not have been razed to the ground. A path, which still exists round the walls of the Harâm-es-Scherif, plainly shows important remains of the time of Herod, if not of the time of Solomon. The gigantic square stones at the wailing place of the Jews are still looked upon as the original blocks of the temple.[4] In the fourth century, so little did Eusebius believe in the total destruction of Jerusalem, that he actually maintained that Titus had only demolished half the city, and that the rest had been destroyed by Hadrian.[5]

[1] ADVENTUI . AUG . JUDAEAE . S . C. Eckhel, vi. 495. F. Madden, *Coins of the Jews* (in *Internat. Numis. Orientalia*, 1881, ii., p. 231, where the dates of the same author's Jewish coinage, p. 212, n. 5, are corrected) gives two arrival coins : Hadrian before a woman, Judaea, with a palm branch and a box, between them a burning altar, and at her side a child with a palm branch ; Hadrian before the figure of Judaea, two children with branches meeting him.

[2] Hierosolyma longe clarissima urbium Orientis non Judaeae modo. Pliny, *H.N.* v. 15, 1.

[3] Josephus, *Bell.* vii. 1, 1.

[4] That Titus did not completely destroy Jerusalem is proved by De Saulcy, *Les derniers Jours de Jérusalem*, Paris, 1806, p. 425 *sq.*; Sepp, *Jerusal. und das heil. Land*, i.², p. 100 *sq.*

[5] Eus. *Dem. Evang.* vi., n. 18. Ancient traditions assert that the Christian church on Zion (the *coenaculum*) and seven synagogues were

That a part of Jerusalem was still inhabited, is proved mainly by the fact that Titus, after his departure, ordered the Xth legion Fretensis, which he himself had brought from the Euphrates to his father in Judaea, to occupy a camp on the west wall.[1] Although the ultimate fate of this legion is obscure, it is indisputable that it continued to serve as a garrison in Palestine, as it was a fixed principle of the Roman government to keep the same troops in the same province. Many legions were stationed in the same place for centuries, until the decay of the empire.[2]

The Xth legion was in Judaea in Trajan's time, and from there it took part in the Parthian war.[3] In the year 130 A.D. Tineius Rufus commanded it as legate of Palestine, and Hadrian must then have reviewed it, or the part of it that was stationed in Jerusalem.[4]

Wherever legions were permanently quartered, a garrison town arose to supply the necessities of officers and men ; the Xth legion must therefore have given to the ruined houses

spared: Epiphan. *De pond. et mens*, c. 14. Basnage (*Hist. des Juifs*, xi. 255) thinks that remnants of the tribes of Judah and Benjamin still remained in Jerusalem after Titus, which is surely very doubtful.

[1] Joseph. vii. 1, 2, 3. On the legio X. Fretensis, Clermont-Ganneau in *Comptes rendues, Acad. d'Inscr.* 1872, p. 158 *sq.*

[2] The legio III. Gallica remained in Syria from the time of Augustus until the fifth century; the IIIrd Cyrenaica from Trajan to Arcadius in Arabia. Clermont-Ganneau, p. 162, gives two tile inscriptions of the Xth legion from Jerusalem, of unknown date, and a dedicatory inscription of their princeps, Sabinus.

[3] The inscription Henzen 5451 (restit. of Borghesi, iv. 125) gives Q. Pomp. Falco, the friend of the younger Pliny, as *Legat. Aug. pro pr. prov. Judaeae et legionis x. Fretensis.* He was legate there about 109 A.D. (Waddingt. *Fastes d. Prov. asiatiques*, p. 203), consul 112 A.D., proconsul of Asia 128 A.D. On him, Borghesi, viii. 365, and Mommsen, *Ind. nom.* to Keil's edition of the *Epistles* of Pliny.

[4] The coin (Eckhel, vi. 496) EXERCITUS JUDAICUS, may even have been struck after the Jewish war, and is not absolutely reliable. Not till late after Hadrian, was the Xth legion stationed in Aila on the Red Sea (Euseb. *Onomasticon* to Ἀιλαμ, and *Notitia Dign.* c. 29). The southern part of Arabia had been added to Palestine as *Palaestina salutaris* or *tertia* at the end of the fourth century, or the beginning of the fifth. Kuhn, *Staedt. Verf.* ii. 360, 373 *sq.*

of Jerusalem more than the mere appearance of a town. The number of Jewish and Christian inhabitants had also gradually increased. The camp of the Roman troops on the west side, where the Herodian towers (the present Turkish citadel El Kalah) were used by them as fortress and capitol, might then be the foundation of a new colony, which Hadrian allowed to spring up on the ruins of the ancient city of David. The time of its origin is uncertain. The emperor had probably given orders, before his visit, for the foundation of the colony, but the rebuilding of Jerusalem was not finished either in the year 130 A.D. or for some years afterwards.

Hadrian included Jerusalem in the system of military roads and fortresses which he extended as far as Petra in Arabia. The former capital of the Jews, like Damascus and Palmyra in Syria, and like Ptolemais, Nicopolis, and Caesarea in Palestine, was, as a Roman colony, to take a new position in the East. As the emperor endeavoured to be present wherever anything important was to be done in the empire, he doubtless examined the plan of the new Jerusalem on the spot, and issued his instructions accordingly. Greek and Roman engineers must have superintended the building of the colony, and the work itself was carried out by the xth legion and by the forced labour of the people of the country. The conversion of the city of Jehovah into a heathen colony, after 130 A.D., was carried on with such energy that two years later it was the occasion of the last outbreak of the Jews against the Romans.[1]

---

[1] If we are to believe Epiphanius (*De pond. et mens*, c. 19) and the Talmudists, Hadrian ordered the rebuilding of Jerusalem already in 117 A.D. from Antioch, entrusting it to the famous proselyte, Acylas of Sinope, whom Epiphanius makes even a brother-in-law (πενθερίδης) of Hadrian. The Alexandrine Chronicle places the foundation of the Aelia Capitolina in the year 119 A.D. Ewald, vii. 362, even believes that the building had been already begun by Quietus before the death of Trajan. Renan (*L'Egl. chrét.*, p. 26) assumes without reason the year 122 A.D.; Tobler (*Topogr. Jerusal.* i. 133) the year 126 A.D., as also Ritter, *Erdk.* xvi. 1, 301. Kuhn (*Die staedt. Verf.* ii. 357) agrees, with some qualification, to the date of the Alexandrine Chronicle. Muenter (*Der Judenkrieg*) is more cautious, and merely assumes that the rebuilding had been begun before the outbreak of Hadrian's Jewish war. Graetz also seems to incline to the year 130 A.D.

In the opinion of the Talmudists, who maintain that Hadrian, at the commencement of his reign, had promised the restoration of the temple to the insurgent Jews, the emperor was guilty of a breach of faith, and they attribute his change of mind to the influence of the Samaritans and the Christianized Jews.[1]   This, however, is erroneous, for Hadrian could never have sacrificed his political principles to the Messianic hopes of the Jews.   While the barbaric provinces of the empire were already almost Romanized in the West, while in the East Hellenism had penetrated into Arabia, and had, since the time of Herod the Great, also taken root all around Judaea, Judaea itself was the only country that opposed its national feeling to the power of Rome.   To overcome this opposition, and to Romanize Palestine, was the aim of the imperial government, particularly after the frightful rebellion of the Jews under Trajan.   The desire of the Hebrews to rebuild their national sanctuary, was a perpetual protest against the doom brought upon them by the Romans; and a Byzantine historian has indeed spoken of this hope, or design, as the ground of the bitterness which the emperor Hadrian showed towards them.[2]   By the conversion of Jerusalem into a Roman colony, national Judaism in Palestine was for ever extinguished.

We know nothing more of the residence of Hadrian in these countries.   He seems to have favoured some cities there, those especially in which a mixed population of Jews, Greeks and Syrians were settled.   Thus Sepphoris or Diocesarea in Galilee called itself Hadriana; the people in Tiberias built an Adrianeum; and there are coins of the Roman colony Caesarea in Samaria, which refer to the benefactions of Hadrian.[3]

From Judaea he went to Roman Arabia.   Coins record his arrival there; the emperor stretches out his hand to the

[1] Graetz, iv. 140.   Derenbourg, *Essai sur l'Hist. et la Géogr. de la Palestine*, p. 414.   Volkmar, *Judith*, 108.

[2] Cedrenus, ed. Bekker, i. 437.

[3] Coins from Tiberias and Caesarea in Mionnet, v., p. 483 *sq.*   One from Tiberias shows Jupiter in a temple with four pillars in front, perhaps the Adrianeum, which under Constantine became a church.   Greppo, p. 185.   Noris, *Epoch. Syrom.*, pp. 469, 471.

figure of a woman near an altar of sacrifice; he as restorer raises kneeling Arabia, who holds a branch, probably of myrrh in her hand, while a camel stands by her side.[1]

The province called Arabia by the Romans was the country of the Edomites, an extensive district, which stretched in the south and east of Palestine from Damascus and the Hauran, down past Petra to the northern border of the Red Sea.[2]   It had been conquered by Cornelius Palma, and Trajan had made it into an imperial province in 105 A.D.   Roman civilization found its way into the volcanic countries of the Hauran and the Trachonitis, and, further south, into the districts of Arabia, where at the present time deserted cities with ruined temples and strange burial-places astonish the traveller.   Even though the Sabaean Arabians from Jemen have erected buildings of stone there, the temples of Busan, Kanawât, Suwêda, Hebrân, and Bostra bear witness to the fact that, after the conquest by Trajan, Roman art made its way into the country, following Greek culture, and that the Romans in Arabia made use of the Greek tongue,[3] which long previously, under the Seleucids, had found a home in those parts.

The capital of the province was Bostra, situated in a fertile oasis to the south of the Hauran, at that time a flourishing centre of trade for Arabian and Greek merchants.   The caravan road, which was protected by military posts, connected it with Palmyra, and extended to the Persian Gulf, while on the eastern borders, garrisons, of which the most remote was Nemâra, were stationed to protect the country

---

[1] ADVENTUI . AUG . ARABIAE—RESTITUTORI . ARABIAE . S . C.   Eckhel, vi. 492.

[2] Bunbury, *History of Ancient Geogr.* ii. 506.

[3] Among 600 inscriptions collected by Wetzstein, there are 10 old Semitic as against 260 Nabataean, and against 300 Greek and Latin. The Auranitis, Batanea, and Trachonitis belonged to Syria; they were first united with Arabia by Diocletian.   Marquardt, *Röm Staatsv.*, i. 423. Wetzstein, *Reisebericht ueber den Hauran und die Trachonen,* 1868. Vogüé, *Syrie centrale, Architecture civile et religieuse.*   An inscription from Zerbire in the Trachonitis mentions, among the sons of the Semite Garmos, a Hadrianos.   Le Bas-Wadd. vi. 2513.   Kaibel, *Epigr. graeca,* n. 454.   Hadrianic coins from Gaba in the Trachonitis, Mionnet, v. 317.

against the Bedawin races of Arabia. Bostra was called
Nova Trajana, because the Emperor Trajan had rebuilt it,
and it also assumed the name Adriana.[1] It was rich and
powerful from its trade with Arabia and Persia as late as
the days of Constantine. Petra, lying to the south, the
ancient capital of the Nabataean kings, whose rule had
formerly extended to Damascus, was its rival. Arabia
Petraea takes its name from the city of Petra. The ruins
of cemeteries and temples here prove the existence of a
high state of civilization under the rule of the Romans.
Like Palmyra in the north, Petra was the emporium of commerce in the south with Arabia, India and China. Caravans
brought spices, precious stuffs and silks, oils and ointments
from Forat on the Persian Gulf; while from the harbour of
Elath, on the Red Sea, the great road of commerce ran
through Petra to Gaza, by which the wares of Persia and
Arabia were forwarded to Phoenicia.[2]

Petra must have owed much to the emperor; its name on
the coins, of which the first were struck in his reign, was
Adriana Petra Metropolis, and he seems to have granted
more privileges to it than to Bostra.[3] He there reviewed the
IIIrd legion Cyrenaica, which afterwards had its fixed
quarters at Bostra.[4]

Westwards from the north of the province of Arabia lay
Peraea, in the country across the Jordan, where, by the side
of the Dead Sea, the Elamite caravan road ran to Damascus.
In this district were important autonomous cities, completely
Greek in constitution and culture, such as Pella, Gerasa,
Gadara, Philadelphia (Rabbath Hammon or Hammân). Of
the latter place, which Ptolemy Philadelphus II. of Egypt

---

[1] On a coin of Commodus; Mionnet, *Suppl.* viii. 389. The Bostrian
era began with the year 106 A.D. Bostra became a Roman military
station under Alexander Severus. Wetzstein, *Reiseber.*, p. 111.

[2] Vogüé, *Syrie centrale, Arch.*, p. 12. Movers, iii. 1, 291.

[3] Ἀδριανὴ Πέτρα (γαίης Ἀραβίης) μητρόπολις. Eckhel, iii. 504. Mionnet, v.
587. De Saulcy, *Num. de la Terre Sainte*, p. 351. *C.I.G.* 4667, 5366[b],
add. p. 1242 (instead of Ἀδραηνῶν read Ἀδριανῶν Πετραίων). On the
province in general, Laborde et Linant, *Voyage dans l'Arabie Petrée*,
Paris, 1830.

[4] Marquardt, i. 431.

had once rebuilt, Hadrianic coins are extant.[1] We cannot, however, follow the emperor further on his journeys through these countries. He went to Egypt. In order to reach Pelusium, he may have travelled from Petra to the harbour of Aila or Elath on the Red Sea, then through the Sinaitic Peninsula to Arsinoe (Suez), and further to the Pelusian mouths of the Nile; or he may have struck the road at Gaza, the last place in Canaan, where two great caravan roads from Elath met.[2]

Gaza was, after Ascalon, the most important city on the Philistine coast, where the ancient Greek communities preserved their autonomy, and where there were no Roman colonies.[3] From a coin which exists, it is probable that Hadrian visited this city, and that his arrival formed an epoch in its history.[4]

Spartianus mentions the first route for this journey of the emperor into Egypt; Dion seems to have assumed that he took the other.[5] Both, however, are unanimous that the first Egyptian city of importance which Hadrian visited was Pelusium. This important harbour, situated between Egypt, Arabia and Palestine, still flourished by its commerce, and maintained its position even as late as the Crusades.[6] The hill Casius was in its neighbourhood, where there was a temple of Jupiter, and the grave of Pompey.[7] The grave was in a grove of trees, which had been planted by Caesar

---

[1] Τύχη Φιλαδελφέων, Mionnet, v. 332. Hadrianic coin from Gerasa, *ibid.* v. 329.

This road to Gaza mentioned by Pliny, *H.N.* vi. 32, 3.

[3] Stark, *Gaza und die philistaeische Kueste*, 1852, p. 514.

[4] On the probable visit of Hadrian to Gaza and the era there, Eckhel, iii. 453. Noris, *Ep. Syrom.*, p. 332. De Saulcy (*Num. de la Terre Sainte*, p. 215), from the Hadrian coin of the third year of the era, infers the year 128 A.D.(?) for the date of his visit. According to the Alexandrian Chronicle, Hadrian established festival games in Gaza.

[5] Spart. c. 14: Peragrata Arabia Pelusium . . . venit. Dion lxix. 11: διὰ δὲ τῆς Ἰουδαίας . . . ἐς Αἴγυπτον παριών. Hadrian, however, would have touched Arabia from Judaea in any case, as Ostracine, east of Pelusium, was already considered the boundary of Arabia. Immediately behind, on the lake Sirbon, were the borders of Idumaea and Palestine. Pliny, *H.N.* v. 14, 1.

[6] Lumbroso, *L'Egitto*, p. 56.   [7] Strabo, 760.

and dedicated to Nemesis, but the Jewish rebels had destroyed it in the time of Trajan.[1]   The tomb itself was buried in the sand, and the statues dedicated to Pompey lay overthrown on the ground.   Hadrian restored the Mausoleum, and wrote verses in honour of the illustrious dead.[2]

From the Pelusian mouths of the Nile, which was at that time still completely navigable, the emperor went to Alexandria.

[1] Appian *Bell.* civ. ii. 90.

[2] Dion Cassius, lxix. 11.   The verses which Hadrian is said to have dedicated to Pompey (λέγεται), and which are found in the *Anthol. Gr.* are cited by Appian, ii. 86, without naming Hadrian as their author.

CHAPTER XVII

Hadrian in Egypt. Condition of the Country. Alexandria. Letter of Hadrian to Servianus. Influence of Egypt and Alexandria on the West

EGYPT, whose civilization was the most ancient in the world, at this time merely indicated the province, fertilized by the Nile, which supplied Rome with corn. From the time of Augustus it had been an appanage of the emperor, so jealously watched that no senator or knight was allowed to go thither without his permission. A Roman pasha, a prefect of the equestrian order, governed or misgoverned the unhappy land as viceroy, from Alexandria.[1]

The province was divided into the districts of Upper Egypt or the Thebais, Middle Egypt or Heptanomis, and the Delta, and these again were divided into forty-six Nomes. The Roman roads ran through Egypt as far as Hierasycaminus, in the Ethiopian country of Dodecaschoenus, beyond the first cataract.

After a history of several thousand years under native dynasties, the people of the Pharaohs lost their independence for ever, first to the Persians, then to the Greeks, and finally to the Romans. This fate of foreign dominion

---

[1] Rhammius Martialis is mentioned as the first prefect (Eparchos) under Hadrian, in the year 118 A.D., *C.I.G.* 4713, and Letronne, *Inscr. de l'Egypte*, i. 513, n. 16. His predecessor as prefect, in the last years of Trajan, was M. Turbo. On the 19th February 122 A.D., Haterius Nepos is mentioned. Memnon's inscription, *ibid.* ii. 430. The population is said to have been about eight millions; to-day, over six millions. Marquardt, *Röm. Staatsv.* i. 439.

has continued until the present time, for Egypt, on account
of its situation, is doomed to belong not to a single nation,
but to the world.   From the time of Alexander the Great
it was a land belonging to everybody, the prey of foreign
adventurers, as it still is to-day.   Years of slavery had deprived the inhabitants of all public spirit, so that the ancient
cities, even the Greek cities, with the exception perhaps of
Ptolemais and Naucratis, had lost their liberty as communities, and were governed by Roman officials without the
concurrence of a Senate.   Even Alexandria no longer
possessed any municipal constitution, and her only distinction as the capital of Egypt was that an imperial judge
administered justice there.

The emperors established their government of Egypt on
the foundation laid by the Ptolemies.   They were their
successors, the divinely honoured kings of the country, and,
like them, they allowed the old religious customs and the
priesthood to remain.   But the inhabitants, who were ground
down by taxation, had no longer any political rights, they
lived like the pariahs or helots enslaved by the Greeks and
Romans.   Their condition was like that of the fellah of the
present day.   The Romans despised the Egyptians, each and
all, not only the natives, but the Hellenes and Jews, who,
since the time of Alexander the Great, had settled in the
country in great numbers.   Their gloomy superstition, their
licentiousness, and their disunion made the Romans consider
them unfit for the rights of citizens.   In their opinion, coercive
measures were the only means of holding this turbulent
population in check.[1]   And yet two legions, the XXIInd
Dejotariana and the IInd Trajana, sufficed to maintain the
peace of the province.[2]

With the exception of tumults, such as the discovery of

[1] See the remarkable opinion of Tacitus, *Hist.* i. 11 : Aegyptum copi-
asque, quibus coercetur, iam inde a divo Augusto Equites Romani
obtinent, loco regum.   Ita visum expedire provinciam aditu difficilem,
annonae fecundam, superstitione ac lascivia discordem et mobilem,
insciam legum, ignaram magistratuum domi retinere.

[2] In the time of Antoninus Pius, only the IInd Trajana was in Egypt,
as the XXIInd Dejotariana had perished in the Jewish war of Hadrian.
Pfitzner, p. 226.

Apis had caused shortly before Hadrian's arrival, the country remained quiet for a long time; and only in Trajan's last years did a fanatical rebellion take place on the part of the Jewish inhabitants, in conjunction with the rising in Asia.

The whole strength of Egypt was concentrated entirely in Alexandria. In the year 130 A.D., this city was still the same harbour of the world which Strabo had described in the time of Augustus.[1] In size it was second only to Rome.[2] Dion Chrysostom, who had accompanied Vespasian there, said it was the most remarkable of all the remarkable sights in the world.[3] Her situation made her mistress of the Red Sea, the Indian Ocean, and the Mediterranean, and market for a hundred nations of the earth. Her commercial and industrial prosperity was not surpassed by any other city, and she was at once the treasure-house of Egyptian mystery and of Greek knowledge. Trading vessels from every coast filled the large harbour, and in the warehouses, products from the tropics were stored, which caravans brought from Arsinoe, Myus Hormus and Berenice.

The splendour of her buildings was not unworthy of the importance of Alexandria. The Serapeum in the quarter of the city called Rhacotis, the ancient royal fortress in Bruchium, the Museum with its colonnades and its large library, the Caesareum, the famous street Canobus, the gymnasia, theatres, hippodrome, temples and innumerable works of art of ancient and modern times, formed a whole of such dazzling beauty that in the age of the Antonines, Aristides could say that the large and fine city of Alexandria was the jewel of the Roman empire, which it

---

[1] The arrival of Hadrian in Alexandria falls into the Alexandrian 15th year of the emperor (from 29th of Aug. 130 A.D. to 29th of Aug. 131 A.D.) Eckhel, iv. 64; vi. 489 *sq*.: Alexandria, with its African helmet, kisses the emperor's hands—Alexandria salutes the emperor, who enters on a quadriga—Hadrian is seated on board a ship. Cohen, ii. n. 58. Hadrian and Sabina hold the hands of Isis and Serapis. The numerous Alexandrian coins in Zoega, *Num. Aeg.*, n. 296 *sq*.

[2] Aristides, *Orat.* xiv. 363.

[3] Dion Chrys. (Dind.) *Orat.* xxxii. 412 *sq*. Other references in Lumbroso, *L'Egitto*, c. xii.

adorned as a necklace or bracelet adorns a woman of fashion. The divine worship of Alexander still existed, and Hadrian, who had visited the tomb of Pompey, would not omit to pay honour to the Sema, where the immortal founder of the city lay buried in a great sarcophagus under a glass canopy, the canopy of gold belonging to Ptolemy Lagus having been carried off by the covetous Auletes.[1]

Alexandria was laid waste in the last insurrection of the Jews, and Hadrian caused this damage to be repaired in the early years of his reign, when he also seems to have sent colonies into the ravaged provinces of Cyrene.[2] As the oldest cities of the Pharaohs lay for the most part in ruins, Alexandria had no longer a rival in Egypt. The deafening crowd in the city, composed of the mixture of religions and races from three parts of the world, the feverish struggle for existence, the intoxicating life of Africa and Asia, the remarkable spirit of cosmopolitan Hellenism, which had here taken up its abode, the frivolity, love of pleasure, and vice of the people, astonished even the Romans and the Greeks. Dion Chrysostom, in his speech to the Alexandrians, has drawn in strong characters the dark side to his praise of the splendour of their city. "I have praised," so he said to them, "your sea and land, your harbours and monuments, but not yourselves"; and he goes on to paint the people as devoid of all seriousness, steeped in every vice, delighting in nothing but the theatre and the circus. The corruption of morals, the quarrelsome

---

[1] Strabo, 794. The tomb was visited before him by Caesar and Augustus; after him by Septimius Severus and Caracalla, who there deposited his imperial insignia. According to Dion Cassius, lxxv. 13, Severus placed the sacred books of the Egyptian priests, which had been collected by him, into the tomb, and then locked it to the people, in order that nobody might further see the corpse of Alexander nor read these books. In Clarke (*The Tomb of Alexander*, 1805, p. 58 *sq.*), the further fate of the Sema, where the Ptolemies also were buried.

[2] On this account perhaps the coin in Eckhel, vi. 497, RESTITUTORI. AUG. LYBIAE. Hieron. in Euseb. *Chron.*, ed. Schoene, p. 165: Hadr. Alexandriam a Romanis subversam publicis instauravit expensis. The Armenian translation has *a Judaeis*. In any case this *subversio* is an exaggeration, yet Zoega (*Num. Aeg.*, p. 101) wrongly substituted in the passage in Eusebius, Hierosolyma for Alexandria.

and ribald spirit of the Alexandrians, was everywhere notorious.[1]   Hadrian too has drawn their character in the following letter to his brother-in-law :

" I am now become fully acquainted with that Egypt which you extol so highly. I have found the people vain, fickle, and shifting with every breath of opinion. Those who worship Serapis are in fact Christians ; and they who call themselves Christian bishops are actually worshippers of Serapis. There is no chief of a Jewish synagogue, no Samaritan, no Christian bishop, who is not an astrologer, a fortune teller and a conjuror. The patriarch himself, when he comes to Egypt, is compelled by one party to worship Serapis, by the other, Christ.[2] It is a rebellious, good-for-nothing, slanderous people. The city is rich in treasures and resources. No one sits idle. There are workers here in glass, there in paper, and there in linen. All these busy men seem to carry on some trade. Even those who are tormented by gout and sciatica find something to do. They have but one God (alluding to their idolatry of lucre)—him Christians, Jews, and Gentiles worship all alike.[3] It is lamentable that this city has a bad character, for its size and importance make it worthy to be the capital of Egypt. I have given these people everything they asked for. I have confirmed all their ancient privileges, and added new, which they could not help acknowledging in my presence. But no sooner had I turned my back than they lavished every kind of insult on my son Verus and my friend Antinous.[1] I wish them no worse than that they should feed on their own chickens, and how foully they hatch them I am ashamed to say. I sent you three coloured cups, which the priest of the temple consecrated for me, as special votive offerings for you and my sister. You may drink from them

[1] They suffered heavily for their insolence under Caracalla. Herodian, iv. 98 *sq.* Dion Cassius, 77, 22. Their character has been drawn by Ammian. Marcell. xxii., c. 18. Other references by Lumbroso, c. 13, *Carattere degli Allessandrini.*

[2] Probably the patriarch of the Jews. Tillemont, *Adrien*, p. 409.

[3] Unus illis est deus—instead of *unus*, *nummus* ought to be read, according to Lehrs. Friedlaender, ii. 5, 138.

[4] In the text *Antonio*, for which *Antinoo* should be read.

on feast days, but see that our African friend does not use them too much."[1]

There is no sufficient ground for considering this letter a forgery, although several things in it appear as if they could hardly have been said by Hadrian.[2]   But even if the letter were not genuine, it is a description of ancient life in Alexandria, the great workshop of magic mystery, of theosophy, and of Christian as well as of heathen philosophy. Yet Greek science still flourished here, producing at this time the astronomer, Claudius Ptolemy.   Side by side with it there grew up an eccentric and fantastic school of thought among Greeks, Jews and Christians.   It was a mixture of Monotheism and Pantheism.   The ideas of Asia and Greece here met together, and formed the doctrine of the Gnostics, of which the Egyptian mysteries were the foundation, and among the Gnostics there were Christians to be found who were said to worship Serapis.   The Jews formed a large part of the population of Alexandria.   To them belonged two of the five quarters of the city.   Their rich community was under the government of a president or ethnarch.   The Platonic philosophy of Philo, in the first century after Christ, had arisen out of the union of the

---

[1] The translation is almost entirely borrowed from Merivale.

[2] Vopiscus has inserted the letter in the *vita Saturnini*, c. 8, and says that he took it from Phlegon's biography of Hadrian. According to its superscription (Had. Aug. Serviano consuli salutem) it is directed to Servianus when he was consul.   Now the fasti (Klein, *Fasti consulares*) name as consuls : Trebius Sergianus for the year 132 A.D., and L. Julius Ursus Servianus Cos. iii. for 134 A.D.   The superscription may have been made later, or the word *consuli* may have been added.   The greatest difficulty seems to lie in the words *filium meum Verum* ; for the adoption took place only in 136 A.D.   *Filius*, however, may be merely another expression for the favourite of Hadrian, and Verus was most likely already selected to be his successor.   He accompanied the emperor in Egypt. It is unnecessary for Greppo, p. 230, to assume a new journey of Hadrian to Egypt at the close of his career.   From the *nemo illic*, Casaubon concludes that the letter was written after Hadrian's departure from Egypt; or that he had at least left Alexandria, as he writes himself. I take the letter as genuine, even though, as the text shows, some passages have been interpolated.   I object less to the *filium meum* than to the repeated reference to the Christians of Alexandria, which cannot be Hadrianic.

Mosaic doctrine with Greek ideas. One thing there is which Hadrian's singular letter has overlooked, and that is, the powerful influence which the spirit of Alexandria exercised upon Rome and the West. This influence had made itself felt at once, as soon as Egypt became Roman, and it lasted for three hundred years. No foreign ruler after the Persian Cambyses, who had laid hands on the gods of the country, had been able to destroy their well-established power. The Lagidae, like the Romans, had acknowledged these gods, and had made them their own. While the Egyptians themselves succumbed to the dominion of the foreigner, their divinities from Memphis and Thebes made a conquest both of Greece and Rome. Isis, Osiris, the dog-headed Anubis, and Serapis changed into Zeus, had no such extent of power under Rameses the Great as they possessed in the first three centuries of the Roman empire. The knowledge of the priests of Egypt was the most ancient in the world, and they seemed therefore to be in possession of the records of mankind. In comparison with this priesthood, in which the same forms had been transmitted for hundreds of years, even the priesthood of Jehovah, of Melkart and Astarte in Syria, of Delphian Apollo, or of Zeus of Dodona, appeared as of yesterday. The mysteries of the Nile fascinated the minds of the West; scenes taken from Egyptian worship are still to be admired as paintings on the walls of Pompeii. Temples of Isis were to be found both there and in Herculaneum, in Campania and in Etruria: in Rome there was an Iseum and Serapeum, where Domitian celebrated the Egyptian mysteries.[1]

Soon after the time of the Antonines, the worship of these gods became a necessity for the Latin world. Merchants from Alexandria spread both the religion and the customs of Egypt as far as Gaul and Spain. Carpets, mosaics, images

[1] It was here that the famous Nile of the Braccio nuovo was found. Excavations in June 1883 brought to light a small obelisk, with hieroglyphic inscriptions, behind the Minerva. Already in the last days of the republic the worship of Isis had found entrance into Rome; Preller, *R. Mythol.*, Abschnitt Isis und Serapis. Even a region of Rome was called after the temple of Isis and Serapis which Caracalla built, namely, the III., as a temple of Isis was situated near to the Coliseum.

of the Sphinx, landscapes of the Nile, vessels and pearls of
Cleopatra, were eagerly sought after in the West, and even the
arrangement of Egyptian houses was a subject for imitation.
Soothsayers and conjurors, astronomers and physicians,
dancers and musicians, orators and learned men, poured out
in swarms from Alexandria over the western world, and these
influences were encouraged by Hadrian.[1]

The emperor, with his thirst for knowledge, took the
liveliest interest in Alexandrian learning, whose seat under
the rule of the Romans was still the Museum. He disputed
there with philologists and sophists, and must have had
plenty of opportunity to laugh at their pedantry. The
privileges mentioned in his letter refer partly to this famous
home of the Muses. But there must have been many other
benefits for which the Alexandrians had to thank him. They
rewarded him by malicious abuse, and by cringing flattery.
They raised statues and altars to him.[2] There are more
Alexandrian and Egyptian coins of Hadrian than of any
other emperor.[2]

[1] Lumbroso, *L'Egitto*. That the art of painting too was influenced by
Egypt, is shown by a curious passage in Petronius, *Satyricon*, c. 2 :
Pictura quoque non alium exitum fecit postquam Aegyptiorum audacia
tam magnae artis compendiariam invenit ; meaning probably the genre.

[2] Eckhel, iv. 64.

CHAPTER XVIII

Hadrian's Journey on the Nile. Heliopolis. Death of Antinous. Thebes. The Colossus of Memnon. Coptus. Myus Hormus. Mons Claudianus. Return to Alexandria

In order to become acquainted with the wonders of Egypt, Hadrian went up the Nile from Alexandria. It had long been the fashion. For the monuments of the gray past, and the banks of the most mysterious of rivers, exercised a mighty fascination over Greeks and Romans, just as they have attracted men of every nation since the expedition of Napoleon. Animal-worship unchanged through the centuries, this riddle of man's religion, must have greatly excited the curiosity of the foreigner. In this deification of animals lay the most profound expression of contempt that could be felt by the human mind, and the most malignant satire on the apotheosis of kings and emperors. For of what importance was the divinity of Sesostris, Alexander, Augustus or Hadrian in comparison with the divine majesty of the bull Apis, or of the sacred cats, dogs, peacocks, crocodiles and apes?

Egypt was even then a museum of the age of the Pharaohs, and of their mummy worship. The ancient cities were still full of curious buildings, strange sculptures, hieroglyphics and paintings, even though their glory had disappeared. Memphis and Heliopolis, Bubastis, Abydus, Sais and Tanis, and Thebes with its hundred gates, had long sunk into decay, though they were still inhabited.

The imperial travellers must have presented an unwonted

spectacle, as they sailed up the river in a fleet of dahabeahs.
The emperor would be accompanied by Egyptian men of
learning and science from the Museum, by priests and
astrologers. In his train were Verus and the beautiful
Antinous. The empress too was with him. She had
among the ladies of her court a Greek poetess, Julia Balbilla.
They landed wherever an object of curiosity presented
itself, and of these there were more than there are to-day.
They marvelled at the great pyramids, the colossal Sphinx,
and the sacred city of Memphis.

Memphis, the ancient capital of the Pharaohs, though
fallen into decay, was not yet buried in the sands of the
desert, and was still considered the second city of Egypt in
the time of Strabo. Under the Ptolemies, she had contributed
much of the material of her temples and palaces for the
building of Alexandria. The great citadel of the Pharaohs
had long been in ruins. But many noble monuments
such as the temple of Ptah, the pyramids, the cemeteries,
and the Serapeum, still existed with their ancient worship.
The city was still the principal seat of the Egyptian
hierarchy, and the home of Apis ; on that account the
Roman government had made it one of the strongest
military posts in Egypt, and here a legion was stationed.
Within the precincts of the Serapeum, Hadrian could gaze
at the white-browed Apis, whose discovery, shortly before
his arrival, had been the cause of great tumults among
the priests and the people, for the Alexandrians grudged
the possession of the bull to the people of Memphis, who
however triumphantly kept him. The emperor could
wander through the half-sunken avenues of sphinxes, where
the long row of embalmed divine animals reposed, each
one like a Pharaoh, in a gigantic granite sarcophagus.[1]
With less trouble than the traveller of to-day, Hadrian
could admire the tomb of Ti, rich in sculptures, the

[1] A Hadrianic coin from Memphis has the Apis, Mionnet, v., p. 534.
To-day this Egyptian Serapeum lies buried beneath the sand. Mariette
discovered there bull-tombs of the eighteenth to the twenty-sixth dynasty.
Only those of the latter are now visible, beginning from Psammetichus.
At present (Summer 1883) Maspero has just excavated tombs of the
sixth dynasty.

monument to an Egyptian official of the fifth imperial dynasty. The sand of the desert has now overwhelmed palaces, statues of the gods, and nearly all the pyramids. Miserable Arab villages, like Sakkara, have planted themselves among the ruins of Memphis, and the traveller gazes with astonishment at the torso of the powerful Pharaoh, Rameses II., lying alone in a thick grove of palms, a last sign of the magnificence of the temple of Ptah, in front of which this colossal statue once stood.

Close to Memphis was Heliopolis, the city of the sun-god, with its ancient temple and school of Egyptian science. In Strabo's time it was a desert, but he was shown the houses of the priests, where Plato and Eudoxus are said to have studied divine mysteries for thirteen years.[1] In Heliopolis the god Râ was still worshipped under the form of the sacred animal Mnevis, a rival or companion of Apis. The barbarous Cambyses had partially destroyed the temples, and even the obelisks, which the Pharaohs had in the course of centuries erected to the sun-god, for nowhere in Egypt had there been so many as at Heliopolis and in Thebes. Hadrian, like Strabo, saw many of them lying on the ground, half-burnt. Two of the larger obelisks were missing, for Augustus had carried off the obelisk of Rameses III., in memory of his victory, to Rome, where he placed it in the Circus Maximus. It now stands in the Piazza del Popolo. The other, Caligula set up in the circus of the Vatican, and it still adorns the Piazza of St. Peter. The largest of all, that of Totmes IV., Constantine carried off, and Constantius placed it in the Circus Maximus. It stands now in front of the Lateran. At the present time, one solitary obelisk alone remains standing on the site, now green with cornfields, of the ancient Heliopolis, and this is considered the oldest of them all, having been erected by Usortesen I. in the twelfth dynasty. Its hieroglyphics have been covered over by wasps' nests.

Proceeding up the Nile, the distinguished travellers came to Besa, a place on the right bank of the river, opposite Hermopolis, where a strange event took place in the death of Hadrian's favourite. Antinous, a young Greek Adonis

[1] Strabo, 806.

from Claudiopolis, had degraded himself so far as to become the emperor's Ganymede.   Hadrian loved him passionately. The emperor, indeed, was a thorough Greek in the vice of the East, a vice which even the great Trajan hardly condemned, and which was abominated by only a few noble men like Plutarch.   We do not know where the emperor met with this beautiful youth ; it might have been in his birthplace, Bithynia.   In Egypt he first became conspicuous as Hadrian's inseparable companion, which must have wounded Sabina deeply ; but the unhappy Augusta was relieved from his hateful presence at Besa, for there Antinous was drowned in the Nile.

His death was shrouded in mystery.   Was it an accident ? Was it a sacrifice ?   Hadrian's well-known humanity forbids the suspicion that he sacrificed his favourite in cold blood, as Tiberius sacrificed the beautiful Hypatus at Capri.   Did the enthusiastic youth offer himself voluntarily to the angel of death in order to save the life of the emperor ?   Did the Egyptian priests read in the stars some threatened evil to Hadrian, which was only to be averted by the sacrifice of what was dearest to him ?   Such a fancy would be in accord with the superstition of the time, with the country, and with the mysterious Nile.   It would agree, too, with the leaning to astrology of the emperor himself.   Did Antinous feel convinced as he plunged into the waters of the Nile that he would rise again as a god ?   Hadrian asserts in his memoirs that his favourite fell by accident into the Nile ; but it has not been believed.[1]   The divine honours which he bestowed on the dead permit us to conjecture that they were a reward for the freely given sacrifice, and that on whatever terms the sacrifice was made, this reward was an acknowledgment to the world at large of a

[1] Spart., c. 14, leaves the question undecided.   Dion Cassius, lxix. 11, takes it as true that Antinous sacrificed himself ; for Hadrian, who practised the magic arts, needed for his purpose a soul that would voluntarily sacrifice itself.   He says : εἶτ᾽ οὖν ἐς τὸν Νεῖλον ἐκπεσών, ὡς Ἀδριανὸς γράφει, εἴτε ἱερουργηθείς, ὡς ἡ ἀλήθεια ἔχει.   But in his opinion the sacrifice was voluntary.   Aurelius Victor (Ep. 14) inclines to the belief that Antinous sacrificed himself, in order to lengthen the life of the emperor.

noble deed inspired by heroic self-abnegation. We should like to think that the victim disappeared in the Nile without Hadrian's knowledge.

Hadrian bewailed Antinous with unmeasured grief, and with "womanish tears."[1] Now he was Achilles by the corpse of Patroclus, now Alexander by the funeral pile of Hephaestion. With great pomp he had the youth buried in Besa—a scene on the Nile of the most refined fantasy, in which the sorrowing emperor of Rome and the smiling Augusta, with their respective courts, were the actors. This, the most extraordinary episode of any journey on the Nile, gave a new god to the paganism which was fast disappearing, and its last ideal figure to ancient art. Probably during the funeral obsequies sharp-sighted courtiers could discern the star of Antinous in the heavens, and Hadrian then saw it for himself. The star remains. Its position is in the Milky Way between the Eagle and the Zodiac, for astronomers have preserved the fabled divinity of Antinous. In Egypt, that land of mystery and wonder, life could be a poem even in the garish day of the Roman empire under Hadrian.

The death of the young Bithynian seems to have occurred in October 130 A.D.[2] After the emperor had given orders to found a splendid city at Besa in honour of his friend, he continued his voyage up the Nile. For in October 130 A.D. the imperial party were at the ruins of Thebes.

Thebes, the most ancient city in Egypt and perhaps in the world, had been eclipsed by Memphis in earlier centuries, and then was destroyed by Cambyses. After the time of the Ptolemies, it was called Diospolis, and was succeeded as capital of the Thebaid by Ptolemais. It had fallen to pieces even in the time of Strabo.[3] On both sides

---

[1] Antinoum suum, dum per Nilum navigat, quem muliebriter flevit. Spart. c. 14.

[2] It is obvious that the death of Antinous occurred at this time. According to the Alexandrian Chronicle 254, Antinoe was founded on 30th October, from which Duerr, p. 64, infers that this day is the date of Antinous' death. The year 130 A.D. follows with certainty from the Memnon inscriptions, of which more later on.

[3] Κωμηδὸν συνοικεῖται, c. 816. Diospolis was the proper Thebes, or the

of the Nile, it presented similar groups of gigantic temples and palaces, of pylons and royal tombs, as are to be seen scattered about to-day in Luxor, Karnak, Medinet Habu, Der el-Bahri, and Koorneh.

In the time of Hadrian, the Rameseum, as the grave of Osymandias was called, the wonderful building erected by Rameses II., must still have existed in great masses on the western bank of the Nile. These gates, temples, arcades and courts, these splendid halls, the granite walls of which were covered with sculptures, seem to have materially influenced the art of the empire. A reflection of them is to be seen in the Forum of Trajan, where the central point was also the royal tomb.[1]

The greatest wonder among the graves and temples of Thebes was the Memnonium. Two bare monolithic colossi of the Pharaoh Amenhoteph III., of the eighteenth dynasty (about 1500 B.C.), hewn from the yellow sandstone, rose majestically in front of his temple. In the year 27 B.C. an earthquake had thrown down the upper half of one, and a current of air at sunrise awoke in the crevices of the statue that melancholy tone, which the Greeks declared was the morning greeting of the Ethiopian Memnon, who was killed by Achilles before Troy, to his mother Eos. Round about lay the remains of wonderful temples, which the same king had dedicated to Ammon.[2] From the time of Nero, travellers had been in the habit of carving their names on the legs of the colossus, and science has to thank a widely diffused vanity for a most wonderful collection of inscriptions. Since the time of Pococke, learned men have transcribed the inscriptions. They belong chiefly to the time of Hadrian, ten namely occurring before 130 A.D., seventeen

city of Ammon. The entire western part on the left bank was the Memnonia. R. O. Mueller, *Osymandias und sein Grabpalast*, in *Encycl. von Ersch. u. Gruber*, p. 260.

[1] Froehner (*La Colonne Trajane*, p. 49) finds that these analogies in the description of the Rameseum by Diodor. i. 45, and the column of Trajan, are an imitation of the Panium of Alexandria.

[2] Strabo, 816, is the first to mention the sound, which he himself had heard. Then Philostr. (*Apollon.* 6, 4). Pliny (*H.N.* 36, 58) is the first to speak of the colossus as Memnon. It was restored by Septimius Severus, when the tones ceased.

in this year, and in the later years of the emperor. He
and the empress both had their names cut upon it in Greek.
She was accompanied by the poetess Julia Balbilla, who
maintained that she was descended from a Syrian king
Antiochus, and who enjoyed so great a reputation that,
later on, the city of Tauromenium erected a statue to her as
a pattern of virtue, modesty and wisdom.[1] The imperial visit
to Memnon gave the Greek poetess an opportunity which
she had long sought, for the display of her talent. We
can still read the verses in the Aeolian dialect with which
she repeatedly haunted the melancholy Memnon. But the
god did not condescend to allow his lament to be heard;
the lady of the court was astonished that he dared to be
silent, when the illustrious Augusta was anxious to hear
him, and she even threatened him with the emperor's wrath.
The threat succeeded, for Memnon uttered his sound several
times in honour of Augustus. Balbilla fortunately has
recorded in an inscription that she heard the god, with the
"dear queen" Sabina, in the 15th year of Hadrian's reign,
on the 24th and 25th of the month Athyr. In this way
we know that the date of the emperor's visit to the Memnonium was the 20th and 21st November 130 A.D.[2]

Below Thebes lay Coptus, a great emporium of Indian
and Arabian goods. They were brought there by caravans,
on high roads which connected the city with the ports of
Myus Hormus and Berenice, and were then sent down the
Nile by boat to Alexandria.[3] A third port for Indian trade
was Arsinoe, on the Heroopolitic gulf of the Red Sea, where
the famous canal of the Nile, begun by Necho, repaired by
Darius, completed by Ptolemy Philadelphus, and finally

[1] *C.I.G.* n. 5904.

[2] Letronne, *La Statue vocale de Memnon*, Paris, 1833, p. 152 *sq*. The
verses of Balbilla referring to Hadrian, with the inscription: Ἰουλίας
Βαλβίλλης, ὅτε ἤκουσε τοῦ Μέμνονος ὁ σεβαστὸς Ἀδριανός. Referring to Sabina,
with the date, p. 162, p. 165, inscription on Sabina: Σαβεῖνα σεβαστὴ
αὐτοκράτορος Καίσαρος σεβαστοῦ ἐντὸς ὥρας Α, Μέμνονος δὶς ἤκουσε. *C.I.G.* 4925 *sq*.
Kaibel, *Epigr. graeca ex lapidib. conlecta*, Berlin, 1878, n. 988 *sq*. See
also the remarks of Puchstein, *Epigr. gr. in Egypto reperta*, Strassburg, 1880, pp. 16-30.

[3] Pliny, vi. 26, 7, gives the stations from Coptus to Berenice. Near
Coptus there were famous smaragdus mines.

restored by Trajan, stretched from Bubastis in the Delta through the Bitter Lakes to the sea. The Nile canal, whose recent reconstruction after the lapse of centuries, in our own time, has been an event of world-wide historical interest, was still used in the time of Hadrian, and probably as late as Septimius Severus, as a high road for commerce.[1]

From Coptus the emperor could go to Myus Hormus, the nearest mart for the Indian trade, which under the rule of Rome had become of great magnitude. Strabo was astonished that one hundred and twenty ships sailed thence annually to India, while in the time of the Ptolemies only a few would have attempted the voyage direct. How great must have been the increase a century later, in the number of ships going to India, to satisfy the demands occasioned by the height of luxury which Rome had reached.[2] A good many years after Strabo, a Greek wrote the Periplus of the Erythraean Sea, which the elder Pliny makes use of. This writing, the work probably of a well-educated captain, describes the coasting trade along the Red Sea through the straits of Bab-el-Mandeb, then much frequented by vessels, to Ceylon and India as far as the Ganges. It affords proof of the most active Indian trade being carried on by Arabians and Greeks, and of the closest connection between Egypt and Arabia.[3]

On the way to Myus Hormus lay Mons Claudianus, where inexhaustible quarries of porphyry and granite had been used for building purposes since the time of the Emperor Claudius. In the middle of the desert, which has overwhelmed the cities of ancient Egypt and the Roman ports and roads by the Red Sea, some Roman stations were discovered in the year 1822 at Jebel Fateereh and Jebel Dokhan. Quarries of porphyry were found at these stations, close to some remains of two unfinished temples, whose Greek inscriptions record that they were dedicated

[1] Humboldt, *Kosmos*, ii. 204. Trajan had, before the year 109 A.D., not only restored the canal from Bubastis to Arsinoe, but had also caused a branch canal to be made to Babylon (Cairo). Dierauer in *Buedinger*, i., p. 131.

[2] Strabo, 118. On the voyages to India, Friedlaender, ii. 59 *sq.*

[3] B. Fabricius, *Der Periplus des erythraeischen Meeres*, Leipzig, 1883.

on the 23rd April 118 A.D., not only to Jupiter Serapis, by the prefect of Egypt, Rhammius Martialis, and by Epaphroditus, the slave of the emperor and tenant of the mine, but also to the welfare and prosperity of Hadrian and his house, as well as to his success in all his undertakings.[1]   These inscriptions show that the porphyry quarries were managed as imperial property, by a procurator.   There were two Roman settlements in the neighbourhood, which were protected from the depredations of the Arabs by the cohort of light cavalry, Flavia Ciliciorum.[2]

Mines (*metalla*) were the Siberia for criminals in the Roman empire, and to be sentenced to them for life was considered the severest of all punishments, next to the punishment of death.[3]   Thousands of unhappy men, and in the time of Diocletian, many Christians, languished under the burning sun of the desert in those porphyry quarries, where they hewed and prepared the costly stone for the palaces of Rome.   If Hadrian visited Mons Claudianus, the sight of the sufferings of the men condemned to work there, might have suggested the decree by which he mitigated the lot of those among them who belonged to the class of free men.[4]

But the visit of the emperor to Myus Hormus and Berenice is only a conjecture, as is the theory that he extended his voyage up the Nile from Thebes to Syene and Philae. There are coins which refer to this Nile journey, representing the river god, sometimes surrounded by children ; he leans upon a sphinx, and holds in his right hand a cornucopia, in his left a reed.[5]

In the Libyan desert, Hadrian had an opportunity of gratifying his passion for the chase, when he had the good

---

[1] Letronne, *Inscr. de l'Egypte*, i. 153, and there the chapter on Mons Claudianus, p. 136 *sq.*   *C.I.G.* 4713.

[2] The cohors I. Flavia Ciliciorum (or Cilicum) equitata appears at the time of Antoninus Pius in an inscription at Syene (Assuan). *C.I.L.* iii. 2, add. 6025, p. 968.

[3] Dig. 48, 19, 28.

[4] Dig. *ibid.*

[5] HADRIANUS . AUG . COS . III . P . P.—NILUS, Cohen, ii., p. 187, n. 982 *sq.*

fortune to kill a lion.[1]   The poet Pancrates celebrated this heroic deed in verse, at the same time ingeniously showing the emperor a lotus as red as a rose, which had sprouted from the blood of the lion.   With still greater diplomacy he gave this lotus the name of Antinoe.[2]   Instead of laughing at the childish imitation of the Ajax flower, Hadrian rewarded the discoverer with a post in the Museum at Alexandria, and the effigies of the deified youth bore the lotus wreath.[3]

The emperor returned, we may suppose, to Alexandria ; but we do not know how long he remained in Egypt.   He left the country in order to go into Syria, either at the end of the year 131 A.D., or in the beginning of the following year.[4]   We have no record of the road which he took, nor of the causes which made him decide to return to Syria.

[1] A coin VIRTUTI . AUGUSTI represents him on horseback, throwing the lance at a lion.   Cohen, ii., p. 228, n. 1471.   Other coins with VIRTUTI . AUGUSTI refer to his hunts.

[2] This lotus was perhaps the Red Sea rose, *Nymphea nelumbo*, described by Herodotus, ii. 92.   Maspero, *Gesch. der morgenland. Voelker im Alterthum*, p. 8.

[3] Athen. *Deipn.* xv., c. 7.

[4] That he went to Syria is clear from the passage in Dion Cassius, lxix. 22, where it is said that the Jews were preparing for a rebellion, παρόντος μὲν ἔν τε τῇ Αἰγύπτῳ καὶ αὖθις ἐν τῇ Συρίᾳ τοῦ Ἀδριανοῦ ἡσύχαζον.

CHAPTER XIX

Hadrian returns from Egypt to Syria.   He revisits Athens.   Dedication of the Olympieum.   Hadrian's Divine Honours

AN insurrection was at that time fermenting in Palestine. If Hadrian had been made aware of its disturbed state, and went to Syria on that account, the Jews knew how to deceive him by their apparent tranquillity.   This, at least, is a fact, that the Jews, burning for rebellion, awaited his departure for the West to take up arms.   This last journey of Hadrian's is shrouded in obscurity.   He disappears from our sight from the time when, on the 21st November 130 A.D., we saw him in Egyptian Thebes, until the 5th May 134 A.D., on which day his presence in Rome is recorded.   We merely know from Dion Cassius, that Hadrian went from Egypt into Syria, and then further West.

Where did he stay in Syria? where did he go from there? and in what place did the information of the rebellion of the Jews in Palestine reach him?   We do not know, but we may conjecture that it was in Athens.   The latest writer on Hadrian's journeys has attempted to prove that the emperor was only twice in Athens, in the years 125 A.D. and 126 A.D., and finally in 129 A.D.   He therefore makes him stay from the end of the year 131 A.D., or from the beginning of 132 A.D., when he went from Egypt into Syria, entirely at the seat of war in Judaea.[1]   But this theory has no facts to support it.   Besides, how can it be believed that so great a Philhellene as Hadrian should

[1] Duerr, p. 42.

only twice have visited the city which he loved so passionately, and which he adorned with so many magnificent
buildings?[1]   As he was returning from Egypt through Syria
to the West, Athens would lie almost on his way.   Why
should he then have omitted to visit the city?   There is
also evidence which makes it probable that Hadrian was
again in Athens in the year 132 A.D.   In this year the
Greek cities put up statues in honour of the emperor in
the Olympieum, which was done in their name with great
ceremony by their representatives.[2]   Was this accidental
or arbitrary? or was it not rather pre-arranged at the
emperor's last visit to Athens (in 129 A.D.)?   And was
not a great Olympian festival fixed to coincide with the
expected return of the emperor to Athens?   We may
therefore assume that in the year 132 A.D. the temple of
the Olympian Zeus was finished and dedicated by Hadrian.[3]

The Athenians had seen no such festival for centuries.
Amid the decay of paganism, the whole pomp of the
ancient worship of the gods and the faded glory of the
Athenian constitution were once more revived.   It was at
the same time a national Greek festival, for in the finished

[1] Keil (*Philol.* ii. 1863, p. 546) assumes four visits of Hadrian to Athens,
112 A.D., 125 A.D., before and after the Egyptian journey, 130 A.D., and
lastly 132 A.D.   See also Ahrens, *De Athenar. statu. politico*, p. 15.

[2] The list of the respective inscriptions (*C.I.A.* iii. 1) begins with that
of the Col. Julia Augusta Diensium per legatum C. Memmium Lycium ;
TRIB . POT . XVI . COS . III . P.P. OLYMPIO is recorded, that is, the year
132 A.D.   No date is given for the other titles, but it is safe to assume
that the rest of this list belong to the same time ; nam hoc communi
consensu et uno tempore factum esse veri simile est (Dittenberger).

[3] Flemmer, p. 53, finds that there are one hundred and thirty different
opinions as to the time of dedication.   Duerr assumes, with others, the
autumn of 129 A.D.   L. Renier also (note to Le Bas-Foucart, *Inscr.
grecques*, ii. partie Megaride, explication to n. 49, p. 34) tries on weak
grounds to prove from Spartianus the year 129 A.D. or beginning of 130 A.D.
Franz (*Elem. Epigr. Gr.*, p. 286) declares himself for 132 A.D., in accordance with the dedicatory inscription from Sebastopolis (*C.I.A.* iii. 1,
n. 483) with Olympiad I., which falls on Olymp. 227, 3, 885 A.U.C., 132 A.D.
See in addition Corsini, *Fasti Attici*, ii. 105.   Keil, *ibid.*, supports Franz.
Lenormant (*Rech. arch. à Eleusis, R. d. Inscr.*, p. 179) assumes as dedication year 135 A.D., but he is silent on Hadrian's journeys after his return to Rome in 134 A.D.

and splendid temple of Zeus, Hadrian had made a new
religious centre for the whole of Hellas.   The Greek cities
far and near sent their representatives, who were commissioned to place the statues erected in honour of the
emperor in the Olympieum.   A list of inscriptions has
been preserved from the cities of Abydos, Aegina, Amphipolis, Anemurium, Thasos, Cyzicus, Smyrna, Laodicea,
Sebastopolis, Miletus, Ephesus, Dium, Cyprus, Pales, Pompeiopolis, Sestos, and others from ancient Greece will not have
been missing.[1]   It was not an Athenian, but the most
celebrated Sophist of that time, Polemon of Smyrna, who
had the honour of delivering the Olympian dedicatory
speech.   The emperor gave the people festivals, which
lasted all day.   It was then that he ordered a great
hunt in the stadium at Athens, in which a thousand wild
animals were killed.   The principal thing, however, that he
did was the new institution of the Olympian games.

These quinquennial Olympian games, or Adriana Olympia,
were in future celebrated not only in Athens, but in other
cities of the empire, especially in Ephesus, Cyzicus, and
Smyrna.   A new reckoning of Olympiads was instituted.[2]
The emperor now assumed, no doubt after a formal resolution of the assembled Greeks, the title of Olympian, or of
the Olympian Zeus, and in the Greek cities he received
the honour of the Olympian god as benefactor, founder
and restorer of the communities, as well as of the inhabited
world.[3]

[1] *C.I.A.*, *ibid.*   At this time it was still usual for Greek cities abroad to
erect, through their representatives, statues of honour to men of special
merit, in the grove of Polias on the Acropolis ; as, for instance, the
Gytheates to Herodes Atticus, and Tripolis to L. Aemilius Juncus, the
corrector of the free towns of Achaia, who was also consul in the year
127 A.D.   Wachsmuth (*Stadt Athen.* i. 69) infers from this that Athens'
new position was at least appreciated.

[2] On these games, Flemmer, p. 78 *sq.*, *C.I.A.*, n. 129 ; Henzen, *Annali
d. Inst.* 1865, p. 96 ; Curtius, *Hermes*, iv. 1, 182.   The enumeration of the
Olympia in various cities in Krause, *Olympia*, Abschnitt ii., p. 203 *sq.*

[3] Διὶ Ὀλυμπίῳ, Colophon, *C.I.G.*, n. 3036 ; Jovi Olympio, Le Bas-Wadd.
iii. 1, n. 1764 (Parium) ; n. 1570 (Priapus).   Θεὸς Ὀλύμπιος (*Nicomedia*,
Mionnet, ii. 468).   Often Ὀλυμπίῳ σωτῆρι καὶ κτίστῃ.   Smyrna, *C.I.G.*, n.
3174 ; Pergamum, n. 3547 ; Andros, n. 2349, m. add. vol. ii. ; Miletus, n.

Spartianus tells us that, in addition to the Olympieum,. Hadrian dedicated other buildings in Athens which had been begun by him, and among them the temple of the Panhellenic Zeus.[1]   The dedication of this temple was accompanied by the institution of a new national festival of the Panhellenia, with games at stated times to which all the Greek cities and colonies in future were to send their representatives, Athens being declared the first city of the Hellenes.   A parliament was to renew the old Achaean league.   This artificial revival of the past was, however, nothing but a pompous pretence.   The Greek nation was politically extinct, and at the Olympia as well as at the Panhellenia, the worship of the emperor alone was the real centre of Greek affairs.[2]   The Panhellenic games, whose president, or Agonothetes, was always the priest of the deified Hadrian, continued to exist, like the Olympic games,. for a long time after the death of the emperor.[3]

He was worshipped in the cities of Greece as Zeus Olympios, Panhellenios, Eleutherios, and Dodonaeos, as Zeus Ktistes and Soter, and Belaeos ; or simply as god, as in Sparta, Abae, Nicopolis, Thespiae, Coronea ; or as the Pythian Apollo and new Helios.[4]   He appears as a new

2863, 2866, 2877 ; Ephesus, n. 2963 b ; Aezani, n. 3832, 3833 ; Phaselis, n. 4334 ; Attalia, n. 4339 ; Cibyra, n. 4380 ; Isauria, n. 4382 ; Magnesia on the Maeander, *C.I.A.* iii. 480, etc. ; Metropolis in Lycia, Tarsus, Cyzicus,. Sebastopolis, etc.

[1] Dion Cassius, lxix. 10 ; Pausan. i. 18, 9.

[2] Hermann, *Griech. Staatsalt.* § 190. A Hellenodarch presided over this parliament ; Herodes Atticus seems to have been the first : Philostr., *Vita Soph.* ii. p. 58. A minister of finance was set over the treasury of the confederacy as Hellenotamias. Hertzberg, ii. 331.

[3] Inscription from Aezani in Phrygia, *C.I.G.* 3832, 3833, Le Bas-Waddington, iii. 1, n. 867 : ὁ ἄρχον τῶν Πανελλήνων καὶ ἱερεὺς θεοῦ Ἀδριανοῦ Πανελληνίου καὶ ἀγωνοθέτης τῶν μεγάλων Πανελληνίων.

[4] A Megarian inscription from the time of Julius Candidus, proconsul of Achaia, unites the titles of the gods Ὀλύμπιος, Πύθιος, Πανελλήνιος, *C.I.G.* n. 1072, Le Bas-Foucart, ii. *Megaride,* n. 49. As it has the δὶς αὐτοκράτορα, it falls in 135 or 136 A.D. The proconsulate of Candidus is fixed by Renier between 134 and 136 A.D., explicat. to n. 49, p. 34. Hadrian appears as new Helios, in Clazomenae, *Rev. Arch.* N.S. xxxii. 1876, p. 44 in Duerr, *Anh.* n. 38.

Dionysus at Aphrodisias in Caria, at Sardis, and even in a Greek inscription at Nismes.[1]

Thus was Hadrian placed on a level with the gods of Greece. If he was not dazzled by vanity he must have realized that he was only receiving the same honours from the miserable flattery of the Greeks which had been awarded to many despots before him, sharing these titles of divinity, as he did, with a Nero who had been raised to a level with Apollo and Heracles, and even with Zeus Eleutherios.[2] But Hadrian was vain enough to allow an altar to be set up to him in the Olympieum. Here and in the Eleusinian sanctuary he sat on the throne as Zeus, honour being also paid to his wife, for she was worshipped in Eleusis, as a new Demeter. But at the same time, and in the same place, altars were erected to Antinous as Iacchus,[3] so the unhappy Augusta was not freed from her rival even after his death.

There was hardly a Greek who felt the worthlessness of all these deifications. For since the time of the Diadochi the Hellenes were accustomed to honour with divine attributes, princes whom they feared, or whom they loved as benefactors. Deification was the only method of showing gratitude to their rulers which an enslaved people possessed. But Hadrian had behaved with such unexampled generosity to Athens, that in the opinion of Pausanias, he had restored prosperity to the city which had been plunged in misery by the wars of the Romans.[4]

[1] Le Bas-Wadd. iii. 1, n. 1619 (Aphrodisias), *C.I.G.* n. 3457 (Sardis), n. 6786 (Nemansus). Other deifications in Hertzberg, ii. 333.

[2] Eckhel, vi. p. 278.

[3] Lenormant, *Rech. Arch. à Eleusis*, p. 185. Sabina received in Eleusis a Hierophantes, *C.I.G.* n. 435. As new Demeter in Megara, *C.I.G.* n. 1073, Le Bas-Foucart, n. 50.

[4] Pausan. i. 20, 7. Compare this with the verses, already mentioned, of the Hierophantes of Eleusis on Hadrian, *C.I.G.* n. 434. According to Dion Cassius, lxix. 16, Hadrian presented the Athenians with the income of the isle of Cephallenia. As however Pales calls herself a free-town in the dedicatory inscription on the statue which she erected to the emperor in the Olympieum (*C.I.A.* n. 481), it is probable that not the whole of Cephallenia was presented to the Athenians. Flemmer, p. 59, and Bursian (*Geogr. Griech.* ii. 375) consider the presentation a formality.

CHAPTER XX

The rising of the Jews under Barcocheba

WHILE the exultant Greeks were building temples to the new Olympian Zeus, and the nations of the East and West were prostrating themselves in the dust before the majesty of the emperor, there was one people in the empire, who not only refused divine honours to Hadrian, but who rose in despair to defend the belief of their fathers in the one only God of heaven and earth, and to regain their freedom or to perish. This people was the Jewish nation in Palestine. Jerusalem demanded to be restored to its position in history as an equal of Athens and Rome. The days of Titus returned, and the fate of the sacred city was for ever sealed.

Dion has stated the reasons which drove the Jews of Palestine to revolt even under the rule of the peace-loving Hadrian. "As Hadrian built a city of his own, Aelia Capitolina, on the site of the ruined city of Jerusalem, and set up a temple to Zeus on the place where the temple of God had stood, a long and bloody war arose. For the Jews were furious that men of a strange race should settle in their city, and that foreign sanctuaries should be erected there."[1] According to this statement, the conversion of Jerusalem into a heathen city·was the cause of the war, while according to the view of Eusebius it was the result. This contradiction is explained by the fact that the Jewish rebellion interrupted the building of the city Aelia which was only finished after the war.

[1] Dion Cassius, lxix. 12.

Nothing but the deadly wound to their national pride could have driven the unhappy people to rebellion amid profound peace in the empire, and without the support of a strong power hostile to Rome, which the Parthians had offered to the Jews in the time of Trajan.[1] The progress of the building of Aelia explains the despair of the Jews. If Jerusalem were to remain in ruins, the sacred ruins would still define the historical centre of Israel around which the hopes of a Messiah might cling. But if a heathen city rose on its ashes, it would for ever hide the national sanctuary, whose restoration could never be expected. Foreign colonists with their idol-worship began to flock into the city, the square stones from the old temple were employed in profane buildings, and on Mount Moriah before the very eyes of the Jews, arose an idolatrous temple of Jupiter.

Had this Roman colony been founded in the first years of Hadrian's reign, it would either have been completed at the time of the rebellion, or strong walls and towers would have made the new city the object of the struggle between the Romans and the Jews. But so far from this being the case, it was not Jerusalem but Bether that was considered the seat of the war. The Jews did not wait until Aelia became an impregnable fortress, but they took up arms to prevent the building of the colony ; and Jerusalem devastated as it was, could have for them no strategical, but merely a moral importance.

Before the outbreak there were two pa/ ies in Judaea opposed to one another, the peaceful party and the fanatical party. Rabbi Joshua ben Chananja was at the head of the peaceful party. According to Talmudic authorities he had had personal interviews with Hadrian, particularly in Egypt, and it is said that he died after

---

[1] Spart., c. 14 ; moverunt ea tempestate et Judaei bellum, quod vetabantur mutilare genitalia. But such edicts of Hadrian, interdiction of worship, of circumcision, etc., were probably only promulgated at the close of the war, when Judaism was to be exterminated. Dodwell (*Diss. in Iren.* ii. § 31) makes too much of this passage of Spartianus, and likewise Münter, *Der Judenkrieg*, p. 36, Ewald, vii. 36, Madden, *Coins*, p. 231, Renan, *L'Eglise chrétienne*, p. 231. We must here accept Dion.

his return thence to Palestine.[1]   At the head of the fanatical
party stood the old Rabbi Akiba, who had seen the glory
of the temple before the time of Titus.   He was a
prominent member of the Sanhedrin, which, with its high
priest (Nasi or Prince) from the house of Hillel, had sat
in Jabne or Jamnia since the time of the Flavian dynasty.[2]
Akiba, one of the first compilers of the Mishna, was
considered the head of the spiritual regeneration of Judaism,
and was honoured by his people as a legendary second
Moses.   The rebellion seems to have originated chiefly
among the teachers of the law.   These dogmatists brooded
over the writings of the prophets, and their glowing fancy
imagined that Rome's great and fatal power might be
subdued by some Messianic miracle.

The Jews quietly made their preparations.   Following
an ancient Semitic custom, they hid stores of arms for
their defence among the rocks of limestone in which they
also made subterranean passages.[3]   As Jerusalem was in
ruins, which were being rebuilt, and was occupied by
part of the xth legion, Bether, a strong populous place,
whose situation cannot clearly be ascertained, became the
seat of the revolution.   It has been sought in the neighbourhood of Jerusalem or in the Castra Vetera near
Sepphoris.[4]   But the presence of Roman troops in Jerusalem,

---

[1] Derenbourg, p. 418, refers to the letter of Hadrian to Servianus,
wherein the Archisynagogus is spoken of.   See also Graetz, iv. 147.
Eisenmenger (Entdecktes Judenthum, 1711, ii. 931) cites from the Bere-
schith Rabba a conversation of Hadrian with this Rabbi, which however
is of very silly purport.

[2] Volkmar (Judith, p. 111) and others assert that they had emigrated
to Uscha in Galilee in the war of Quietus.

[3] Dion Cassius, lxix. 12.   Wetzstein (Reisebericht, p. 45) describes the
Troglodyte dwellings of the Hauran, and quotes Judges vi. 2 : "and the
hand of Midian prevailed against Israel; and because of the Midianites
the children of Israel made them the dens which are in the mountains,
and caves, and strongholds."

[4] So F. Lebrecht asserts (Bether, die fragliche Stadt im hadr-jüd.
Kriege, 1877).   Euseb. (H.E. iv. 6) places Bether in the neighbourhood of
Jerusalem.   Guerin (Judée ii. 388 sq.) somewhat westerly from Jerusalem,
as also Renan, L'Egl. chrét., p. 144 and Les Evangiles, p. 26.   Cassel
(Ersch und Gruber, iii. Ser. 27, Theil, p. 14) between Caesarea and

and the strong imperial leaning of that capital of Galilee, make both situations improbable.[1] The view of those who place Bether near the sea, four miles south of Caesarea, is probably more correct.

While Akiba was the spiritual leader of the insurrection, a man of determination appeared ready to act as general in the war. Talmudic legend has endowed the last national hero of Israel with the strength of Samson and the virtues of the Maccabees, and he is certainly of a better stamp than the robber and murderer whom the fathers of the Christian church have depicted.[2] This bold rebel opposed not only the Roman legions for more than two years, but won some bloody victories. Eusebius calls him Barcocheba, which means 'son of a star,' and was only his symbolic name ; for according to the Talmud he was called Barcosiba.

After the emperor had left Syria, the rebellion broke out about the year 132 A.D.[3] The few Roman garrisons in the country were either cut to pieces or besieged in their fortresses, and his first success made Barcocheba the hero of the rebellious nation. Fanatics saw in him the Messiah, who had at last really appeared. Akiba himself was so infatuated that he greeted him as the Messiah in the words of Scripture : " Cosiba is like a star that has appeared in Jacob." Only one sober-minded man, the Rabbi Jochannan ventured to call out : " Akiba, sooner will grass grow out of your chin, than the son of David appear." The Sanhedrin, however, acknowledged the leader

Diospolis. He is followed by Jost, *Gesch. des Judenthums*, p. 74. Graezt places Bether four miles south of Caesarea, as also Ewald, vii. 375, and as Levy, *Gesch. der jüd. Münzen*, p. 103, and Tobler, *Dritte Wander-ung nach Palaestina.* Sepp, *Jerus. und das heil. Land*, i. 647, seeks it two hours from Bethlehem. Adolf Neubauer, *La Géographie du Talmud*, 1868, between Jabne and Lydda, not far from Jerusalem.

[1] Sepphoris called itself Diocaesarea Adriana, whether before, or only after the war is doubtful. This city must have been inhabited by many Greeks and Syrians.

[2] Euseb., *H.E.* iv. 6 : Βαρχωχεβᾶς ὄνομα, ὅ δὴ ἀστέρα δηλοῖ, τὰ μὲν ἄλλα φονικὸς καὶ λῃστρικός τις ἀνήρ. For the legend about him, see Hieronymus *in Ruf.* ii. c. 8.

[3] Under the consulate of Augurinus and Severianus ; Eusebius and Hieronymus.

of the people as the man of promise, and an assembly of
the Jews confirmed him in his office as the temporal head
of Israel.

The legate in Palestine was, at that time, Tineius Rufus,
who vainly endeavoured to suppress the rebellion as it
blazed forth.[1]   He ravaged the country with fire and sword
and committed such atrocities that in the Jewish accounts
he is called Tyrannus Rufus.[2]   Meanwhile, a year sufficed
to give great strength to the rebellion.   The Jews received
their supplies by sea, and they were certainly in communication, if not with the Parthians, at all events with the
Bedawin of Arabia, and with their own countrymen in
Mesopotamia and Egypt.[3]   Their struggle assumed the
horrible character of a racial war.   The Jewish leader
repaid the inhumanity of Rufus by similar ferocity ; he
summoned the Christians of Palestine to join him, and on
their refusal he caused many of them to be put to death.[4]

In the scanty records that we possess of this desperate
Jewish war no other city except Bether is mentioned as
its theatre.   We hear nothing of Caesarea, of Lydda and
Nicopolis, where Roman garrisons were formerly stationed,
nothing of Joppa, Diocaesarea and Tiberias, nothing of
Machaerus and Massada, and of other fortresses near the
Dead Sea, whose names have been familiar from the time
of Titus.   Even Jerusalem is never mentioned.   It surely
must have been the endeavour of Barcocheba not only to
destroy the Roman colony, which was being built there,
but also solemnly to confirm the deliverance of Israel on
the most sacred spot of its history.   That this did happen,
and that a bold attempt was made by him to rebuild the

---

[1] Eusebius (*H.E.* iv. 6) calls him ἐπάρχων τῆς Ἰουδαίας.   Hieronymus
says : tenente provinciam Tinnio Rufo.   On the real name see Borghesi,
iv. 167, and the same, viii. 189, the *gens Tineia* was previously unknown.
But Borghesi is mistaken if he thinks that this T. Rufus was not legate
of Palestine till 136 A.D. with Severus.

[2] As a matter of fact there was a *gens Turrania*.   Sepulchral inscription
of C. Turranius Rufus on a *cippus* in the stanza del Fauno in the Capitol.

[3] This alliance is alluded to by Dion Cassius (lxix. 13).

[4] Justin., *Apol.* ii. 72.   Orosius, vii. 13.   *Chron. Euseb.* ed. Schoene,
p. 168 *sq.*

Temple, has been both maintained and disputed.[1] A temporary occupation of Jerusalem by the rebels might not have been impossible from the weakness of the Roman garrison. This is indeed probable from some coins which the Jewish leader caused to be struck after he became actually Nasi or Prince of Israel, and had probably been anointed king.[2] A number of shekels are ascribed to him. They bear either no date or are marked with the first and second year of the deliverance of Jerusalem or Israel.[3] If the list of undated coins belongs to the beginning of the insurrection, the others must belong to the time in which the Jews had confined their enemies to a few places and were themselves masters of the country. The most curious are those with the inscription " deliverance of Jerusalem "; the emblems on them—a palm branch in a crown of laurel, a bunch of grapes, two trumpets, a lyre, a vase and other symbols—are found on coins of the Asmoneans. Some have the design of a four-columned temple with the conventional figure of the beautiful gate and porch of Solomon's temple; in others a star shines over everything.[4] Most of the coins bear the name of Simon or Simeon,

---

[1] Deyling (*Aeliae Capitolinae Origenes*, 1743, p. 273). Muenter, Jost, Graetz, maintain the capture, although the Jewish authorities are silent upon it. So also Milman, *Hist. of the Jews*, ii. 431 ; Madden, *Coins*, etc. p. 134 ; De Saulcy, *Rech. sur la Num. Jud.*, p. 157 ; Cavedoni, *Biblische Numismatik*, p. 62 ; Ewald and Lebrecht. Cassel and Renan (*L'Eglise chrét.* in Appendix) deny it ; the latter thinks a temporary occupation of Jerusalem by the rebels possible.

[2] Eisenmenger, ii. 654. The book of Zemach David gives even a fabulous dynasty of Barcocheba lasting twenty-one years ; according to this Barcocheba is said to have died already under Domitian, and his son and grandson, Rufus and Romulus, to have carried on the war.

[3] All the coins of Barcocheba have been collected by De Saulcy, *Rech. sur la Num. Judaique*, Paris, 1854, p. 156, pl. xi.-xv. by Cel. Cavedoni, *Bibl. Numismatic*, transl. by A. von Werlhof, 2. Th., Hannov. 1856, p. 55 *sq.* where some new coins have been added to De Saulcy's collection ; by Madden, first in the *Hist. of Jewish Coinage*, then in the *Coins of the Jews* (Vol. ii. of the *Internat. Numismata Orientalia*, c. x., p. 230 *sq.*) See also M. A. Levy, *Gesch. der jüd. Münzen*, Leipzig, 1862, p. 93 *sq.*

[4] Madden, n. 19, 20, 37, 38. Cavedoni (p. 64) takes the four-columned building for the sacrarium of the synagogue, and not for the temple, which lay in ruins. The star refers to Barcocheba.

Prince of Israel, in a laurel wreath, from which it has been imagined that Barcocheba either bore this name originally or had assumed it from Simon Maccabeus, or from Simon Giora. But traces are to be found on these shekels of the names of Roman emperors in Greek and Latin characters as of Nero, Galba, Vespasian, Titus, Trajan (once indeed the head of Trajan) and this proves that old Roman drachmas from the coins of Antioch and Rome were merely re-stamped in the time of Barcocheba. The Asmonean symbols and the legends "deliverance of Jerusalem" and "deliverance of Israel" do not absolutely prove a new coinage, as the old Jewish die could have been used for them.[1] But even in this case the fact remains that coins of Barcocheba were issued, and that in them we possess witnesses of the last Jewish revolution, and of its earliest results.[2]

[1] For this re-stamping see Madden, de Saulcy, and Levy. Renan, *L'Eglise chrét.*, p. 547, believes that Barcocheba invariably made use of the coins of Simon Maccabeus, and that the re-stamped ones were coined in Bether.

[2] Cavedoni (p. 60) declares that the re-stamped coins prove by their style the time of Hadrian. Levy maintains that the legend "delivery of Jerusalem" proves nothing, as it may have been copied from older coins. He ascribes to Barcocheba only the re-stamped imperial coins; those with Simon, to Simon Giora. Cavedoni, however, thinks the coin bearing this legend proves the taking of the city, and as there are none in existence with the name of Jerusalem dating from the second year, the Jews must have been dislodged and driven to Bether during the first year. He proves that the Jerusalem Talmud mentions the Moneta Ben Cosibhae. Buxdorf, *Lex Talm.* p. 1029.

CHAPTER XXI

The Jewish war. Julius Severus assumes the command of the Roman army. The fall of Bether. The Destruction of Judaea

THE Romans at first looked upon the rising in Palestine as a contemptible tumult of the populace, until it grew into a real war, which began to be troublesome. The insurrection spread as far as Syria and Phoenicia, and threatened to excite all the Jews in the Diaspora and the hostile peoples in the East.[1] On this account Hadrian made the greatest efforts to subdue it. We do not know that he returned to Syria himself or that he repaired to the scene of action in order to place himself at the head of his army.[2] A stranger to the warlike passions of Trajan, he allowed the war in Judaea to be carried on by his legates.[3]

---

[1] Καὶ πάσης ὡς εἰπεῖν κινουμένης ἐπὶ τούτῳ τῆς οἰκουμένης, Dion Cassius, lxix. 13.

[2] This conclusion has been drawn from Dion Cassius, lxix. 14, where we are told that Hadrian, on account of the heavy losses of the Romans, omitted in his report to the senate the customary phrase " I and my army are well." But this omission shows rather that he was not with the army when he sent this report to the senate. Besides this, it follows from the connection in which Dion gives the above, that Hadrian sent this report to the senate not in the beginning, but at the end of the war, or about the beginning of 134 A.D.; for before the 5th May 134 A.D. he was again back in Rome.

[3] Lebrecht (p. 37) and Duerr assert the permanent presence of Hadrian in Palestine at the head of the army because this is maintained by all the Jewish, and several of the heathen authors, (Muenter, p. 83, Flemmer, p. 138). The former, however, are altogether uncritical, while the latter fable of a second destruction of Jerusalem by Hadrian. That

Unfortunately there is no Josephus to relate the last struggle of the Jews for their national existence. The events of the war, and the heroic actions of the despairing people, remain buried in obscurity. The account given by Dion is comprised in one page; Spartianus has disposed of the whole war in a single line, which proves with what contempt the Jewish struggle for freedom was looked upon by the Romans.[1] Both historians, or the authorities they quote, would surely have given more details if the emperor himself had been at the head of his army in the war. The descriptions of the Talmudic writers can only be looked upon as legends full of oriental exaggeration, and the narratives of two contemporaries, Antonius Julianus, and Ariston of Pella, have unfortunately been lost.[2] The severe defeats which the Romans endured are alluded to in a sentence of Fronto, who, long after the death of Hadrian, told the emperors Marcus Aurelius and Lucius Verus that they ought to bear their losses from the Parthians with equanimity, when they remembered how many Romans had been cut down by the Jews in the time of their grandfathers, and yet the empire had finally triumphed.[3]

Hadrian sent reinforcements to the sorely pressed Tineius Rufus. In addition to the xth legion Fretensis there were fighting in Judaea the IInd Trajana, the IIIrd Cyrenaica, which had been brought from Egypt and Arabia, and the IIIrd Gallica which was close at hand in Phoenicia.[4] The Syrian IVth legion Scythica, or a part of it, seems also to have been brought to Judaea. For in

Hadrian left the war to his legates is confirmed by Dion Cassius, lxix. 13, in these words: ἐπ' αὐτοὺς ἔπεμψεν.

[1] Spart. c. 13.

[2] Eusebius used Ariston; Minucius Felix and Gellius (Muenter, p. 12) mention Julianus. Even the memoirs of Hadrian by Phlegon seem to have treated the war but lightly, for a (mutilated) passage in Suidas (Phlegon) says: Philostorgios maintains, that Justus described the Jewish events much more accurately than Phlegon and Dion. Would Phlegon have been so inexact if Hadrian had carried on the war in person?

[3] *De bell. Parth.* at its beginning.

[4] On those legions, Pfitzner, pp. 228, 230. Orelli, 3571, according to whom a soldier of the IIIrd Gallica received marks of distinction in the Jewish war.

scriptions from Ancyra show that Publicius Marcellus, the governor of Syria at the time, left this province on account of the Jewish rebellion, and that Tiberius Julius Severus, legate of the IVth legion Scythica, was in power during the absence of the proconsul of Syria. According to these inscriptions Marcellus was sent to Judaea as general with troops of that legion.[1] Quintus Lollius Urbicius also received a command in this war.[2] Even some Gaetulian cavalry of the Xth legion Gemina, under S. Attius Senecio, were brought from Mauretania, and the VIIth Claudian legion from Moesia set up their military standard.[3]

As the Roman generals accomplished nothing, Hadrian at last sent the best captain of his time, Julius Severus, to Judaea.[4] He had been legate of Dacia, consul in the year 127 A.D., then legate of Lower Moesia, and finally governor of Britain, whence he was summoned to Palestine.[5] In the place of Rufus he took the chief command of the army, and became also governor of Judaea. Thereupon the war took a favourable turn for the Romans; for the numbers and desperation of the

[1] *C.I.G.* n. 4033, n. 4034, relating to inscriptions of Tiberius Severus. Borghesi, erroneously affirms, v. 412, that Marcellus fled from Syria: fuggito per la sollevazione dei Giudei. Dion Cassius has confounded Tiberius Jul. Severus with Sex. Jul. Severus. The former from Galatia was, according to the inscriptional *cursus honorum*, extraordinary legate in the province of Asia, then legate of the IVth Scythica, then deputy for Marcellus in Syria, then proconsul of Achaia. Waddington, *Mém. sur Aelius Aristides*, in *Mém. de l'Inst.*, xxvi. (1867), p. 214 *sq.*

[2] Renier, *Inscr. de l'Algérie*, n. 2319.

[3] *C.I.L.* vi., 3505. Pfitzner (p. 93) is of opinion that the XXIInd Dejotariana from Egypt also took part in the war, but that it was totally annihilated; the VIth Ferrata seems also to have fought in Judaea.

[4] Dion Cassius, lxix. 13. Inscription from Britain, *C.I.L.* vii., 275, with restitution of Borghesi, iv. 166.

[5] His name, S. Vinicius Faustinus C. Julius Severus. His *cursus honorum C.I.L.*, n. 2830 (Inscription from Cistagne in Dalmatia). His legation in Britain is there followed by *Leg. pr. pr. Judaeae, Leg. pr. pr. prov. Syriae.* The error of Mommsen (Borghesi, iv. 168, n. 1) that he was succeeded by Tineius Rufus in the command in Palestine, has been corrected by Marquardt, i. 420. The Jewish war broke out when Rufus was legate there.

rebels made Severus avoid pitched battles. He harassed
the enemy in petty warfare, cutting off their supplies and
breaking their strength. He succeeded in starving out
the Jewish garrisons. Fifty strongholds and 985 villages
are said to have fallen by degrees into his power, and
to have been destroyed by him.

If the unfortified city of Jerusalem came into Barcocheba's
possession, it was re-taken by the Romans without the
necessity of a siege. Greek and Roman authors certainly
speak not only of the siege, but also of the complete
destruction of Jerusalem in the time of Hadrian.[1] Rabbinical
tradition, which confuses the two wars under Titus and
Hadrian, merely asserts, like Jerome, that Tineius Rufus
ordered the plough to be driven over the site of the
temple.[2] Neither Dion nor Eusebius in his history of the
Church has a word to say about the conquest of Jerusalem.
Dion only relates the extraordinary anecdote that the
disastrous termination to the rebellion of the Jews had
already been foretold by the fall of Solomon's tomb. The
statements of fathers of the Church and chroniclers of later
days about a final destruction of the holy city, are to be
looked upon merely as a rhetorical repetition of her fate
under Titus. For it may reasonably be asked,—what was
there among the ruins of Jerusalem in Hadrian's time for

---

[1] Appian, living in Rome during the war, says, *de bello Syr.* c. 50,
Ιερουσαλημ ἦν—ὁ Οὐσπασιανὸς—κατέσκαψε, καὶ 'Αδριανὸς αὖθις ἐπ' ἐμοῦ. Then
Euseb., *Dem. Evang.* ii. c. 38 ; *Theophan.*, n. 9 ; *Chron.* ed. Schoene,
p. 168. *Chron. Suppl. e Syncello*, p. 226 : ἐπι 'Αδριανοῦ τελεία καὶ ἐσχάτη—
τῆς πόλεως ἅλωσις. In his *Hist. Eccl.*, Eusebius says nothing about it.
Hieron. *in Jer.* vi. c. 31, p. 877 : sub Adriano … io urbs Jerusalem subversa.
In Isaiam iii. c. 7 ; *in Ezech.* vii. 24 : sub Hadrian civitas aeterno igne
consumpta. *In Joel* 1, 4 ; *in Habac.* c. 2 ; *in Ephes.* c. 5. Chrysostom,
Oratio 3 *in Judaeos*, Francof. 1698, i. 431. *Chron. Paschale* for the year
119 A.D. Suidas, *Exc. in vita Adr.* 866. Passages also from the later
Byzantines in Deyling, p. 264. The only Jewish source which Muenter
uses is the Samaritan Book of Joshua. Renan, *l'Église chrétienne*, p.
543 *sq.*

[2] The Jewish passages in Muenter, p. 42. Templum aratum in
ignominia : Hieron. *in Zach.* c. 8. 18. 19. The legend originated
probably from the coin of the colony Aelia Capitolina which represented a
husbandman.

Barcocheba to destroy, even if it is true that he occupied the city?[1]

The Jews made their last stand in the fortress of Bether. Rabbinical legends contain the most exaggerated accounts of the population of this city and of the number of its synagogues, as well as of the heroic struggles for its defence. The length of the siege of Jerusalem under Vespasian and Titus is curiously transferred by them to the siege of Bether with much ingenuity. In this fortress Barcocheba remained some time, with the rest of the rebels, until famine and the siege engines of the Romans broke down their resistance. Bether was taken by Severus in the year 135 A.D. or 136 A.D., as the Rabbis say, on the same fatal 6th August on which Jerusalem fell for the third time before the sword of the enemy.[2]

In the ashes of Bether the last heroic struggle of the Jewish people ended. They alone, among all the nations subject to Rome had made the attempt, even in the time of the greatest military power of the empire, to regain their freedom. This attempt was, in face of the existing state of things in the world, an act of madness and despair; but even so, it does honour to the Jewish nation. As they were not adapted like the Hellenes, after the fall of their national state, to form a part of the Roman world, and to carry on a cosmopolitan existence, they were obliged, true to their character, to perish heroically among the ruins of Judaea.

Barcocheba's fate is unknown. More fortunate than Simon Giora, he seems to have found a soldier's death.

---

[1] Renan has demonstrated this exhaustively in *l'Église chrétienne*. The opinion of Muenter and others, *e.g.* De Saulcy (*Rech. sur la Num. Jud.*, p. 158), Champagny, *Les Antonins*, ii. 66, Schuerer, *Neutestam. Zeitgesch.*, p. 359, which asserts the siege and destruction of Jerusalem under Hadrian, may be dismissed. Scaliger, *Animado. in Euseb.*, p. 144, already considered this a myth, so also Pagi, and lastly the greatest explorer in Palestine, Robinson (*Bibl. Researches in Palestine*, ii. 6).

[2] Hieron. *in Zacch.* viii. 262, has borrowed this from the Talmudists, and confounds, as they have done, the two wars under Titus and Hadrian. He transfers the close of the war to the twentieth year of Hadrian. Euseb., *H.E.* iv. 5 (*Chron.* ed. Schoene, p. 168), places the fall of Bether in Hadrian's eighteenth year.

The rest of the rebels were slain, and thousands of Hebrews were carried off into captivity. The Romans sold them for the price of horses in the market by the terebinths of Hebron, the dwelling-place of Abraham. Those who were not sold here were offered at a low price in Gaza, or were dragged as slaves to Egypt and Rome.[1] Some scattered bands might have succeeded in fleeing to the deserts of Arabia and to Babylon.

The Talmudists may be forgiven their exaggerations when they say that streams of blood flowed through Judaea into the sea at Joppa, as even Dion Cassius places the number who fell by the sword in the war at 580,000, without counting those who died from hunger and plague. His figures are probably taken from official returns, or perhaps from the lost autobiography of Hadrian. The number of slain was boasted of before the senate, for laurel wreaths receive their value from the blood in which they are steeped. Palestine, a field strewn with dead bodies, became a desert waste. Jackals and hyaenas prowled through the devastated country and among the ruined cities.[2]

Hadrian's character for humanity suffered from the cruelties of the Jewish war, and he lost the feeling of happiness which he had hitherto enjoyed as he travelled peacefully through the world. He never saw Asia again. Necessity had made the patient, peace-loving emperor execute the most fearful judgment of history. He executed it as a Roman would, in cold blood, and we may venture to say that he had more justification than had Titus in his day. No man of feeling can refrain from pitying the fate of the Jewish people, but no thoughtful person can imagine that the victory of an Akiba and a Barcocheba would have promoted the historical development of Asia. The restoration of an independent Jewish state was inconceivable and impossible. It would have entirely destroyed the work of Rome in Syria, from the Euphrates to the Red Sea, and would have set up a narrow Semitic

[1] Hieron. *in Jer.* c. 31, *Zachar.* c. 2.
[2] Καὶ λύκοι, ὕαιναί τε πολλαὶ ἐς τὰς πόλεις αὐτῶν ἐσέπιπτον ὠρυομεναι. Dion, lxix. 14.

fanaticism and religious intolerance in the place of Greek
and Roman culture. The cosmopolitan idea of the Roman
empire had no such stubborn enemy as the Jews, and they
were therefore destroyed from political motives. Their
last heroic death-struggle appeared to the Romans and
Greeks merely as a crazy rebellion against the humane
government of Hadrian. Pausanias alludes once to this
Jewish war, saying: "Hadrian, who was emperor as late
as my time, honoured the gods highly, and cared intensely
for the happiness of all his subjects. He never waged
war from choice, but he put down the Hebrews in Syria
by force, as they had risen up against him."[1]

Hadrian would have disdained to accept triumphal
honours for the defeat of Judaea, even if he had won them
in person. He allowed no coins to be struck with the
inscription JUDAEA DEVICTA, as was done after the conquest
by Vespasian and Titus.[2] But he assumed the title of
Imperator for the second time, in consequence of the conclusion of the Jewish war.[3] No decorated army returned
from Palestine to Rome to proceed in triumph to the
Capitol through the arch of Titus, bearing a splendid booty.
What was there in Judaea for them to pillage? The

---

[1] Ἀδριανοῦ—τῶν ἀρχομένων ἐς εὐδαιμονίαν τὰ μέγιστα ἑκάστοις παρασχομένου· καὶ
ἐς μὲν πόλεμον οὐδένα ἑκούσιος κατέστη Ἑβραίους δὲ τοὺς ὑπὲρ Σύρων ἐχειρώσατο
ἀποστάντας. Renan, L'Église chrét., p. 213: Les fanatiques d'Israël combat-
taient pour la théocratie, pour la liberté de vexer les païens, d'exterminer
tout ce qui leur semblait le mal.

[2] It is very doubtful whether the coin EXER . JUDAICUS (Eckhel, vi. 496)
was struck in commemoration of the war as Graetz, iv. 169 supposes.
Froehner, Les Méd. de l'Emp. rom., p. 34, refers two medals of Hadrian
to the Jewish war; the first shows a Victoria on a biga, the second,
Roma seated on arms at the side of trophies, behind her a Victoria,
below Felix Roma. The hypothesis of Froehner falls to the ground, as in
the superscription the title Imp. II. is missing.

[3] Borghesi, viii. 580. In the military diploma (C.I.L. iii. 1, n. 35) of 15th
September, 134, the Imper. II. is missing. The war was therefore at that
time not ended. In n. 36, of 16th January, 138 A.D., the title is however
mentioned. This title was still given to Antoninus after the war in
Britain, although he was not present there. I pass over the inscription
relative to Hadrian as deliverer of the republic (in the Jewish war), and
boldly supplemented by Henzen, 5457.

generals who had been in command were rewarded.[1]   The emperor and the senate decreed triumphal distinctions to Julius Severus, the real conqueror of Judaea.[2]   The same general became governor of Syria, while Tiberius Severus, who had ruled the country as deputy for Marcellus, became legate of Bithynia.   This province, which had hitherto been proconsular, now became imperial, and the senate received Pamphylia in exchange.[3]

Whether Julius Severus continued to govern Judaea as legate of Syria, or whether the emperor gave a new ruler to this unhappy country, is uncertain.   Nothing more is heard of Tineius Rufus.

The adherents of Barcocheba were now frightfully persecuted ; members of the synagogue in Jamnia were executed, and Akiba himself suffered the painful death of a martyr.   Hadrian ordered the Jewish worship to be suppressed with the greatest severity, forbidding even the use of circumcision.   This edict drove the miserable remnant of the Jews under Hadrian's successor into rebellion, and Antoninus Pius felt himself obliged to repeal it.   The Jews however were forbidden to circumcise Gentiles, and they were not allowed to make proselytes.[4]

The last strength of Israel's manhood perished with

---

[1] So Q. Lollius Urbicius, Renier, *Inscriptions de l'Algérie*, n. 2319 : Legato imp. Had. in exped. Judaica, qua donatus est hasta pura, corona aurea ; n. 2320, his family.   As legate in Britain (140-143 A.D.) he built the wall of Antonius, *C.I.L.* vii., p. 192.   Henzen, 6501.   Kellermann, *Vigiles*, n. 247 : inscription in honour of C. Popilius, late legate of the legion X. Fretensis, tribune of the legion III. Cyrenaica, donato donis militarib. a. Divo Hadr. ob Judaicam expeditionem—Mommsen, *I.R.N.* 3542.   Granting of honours to C. Nummius Constans ob bellum Judaicum.

[2] *Cursus honor. C.I.L.* i, iii., n. 2830 : ornamenta triumphalia decrevit ob res in Judaea prospere gestas.   Perhaps Severus was the last who received these honours.   Before him they were received by Cornelius Palma.

[3] Dion Cassius, lxix. 14, *C.I.G.* 4033, 4034.   After his mission in Syria Tib. Severus became proconsul in Achaia, then corrector and curator in Bithynia.   Borghesi and Huebner (*Rhein. Mus.* xii. 1857, p. 58 *sq.*) have confounded him with Jul. Severus, who had nothing to do with Bithynia.   This has been corrected by Waddington, *Mém. sur Ael. Aristid.* in *Mém. de l'Inst.* xxvi. 1867, p. 227 *sq.*

[4] Dig. xlviii., Tit. 8. 1, 11, Tit. 2. 1, 3, § 3.

the distinguished families, the priests and teachers of the people. But the Christian communities too suffered from this persecution. Rejoicing as they did that their dogmatic view of the true Messiah had been proved by the downfall of the false one, they were nevertheless involved in the ruin of the rebels. During the war the Christian communities of Jerusalem are said to have sought an asylum in Decapolis on the other side of the Jordan.[1] There they suffered as much as the Jews from the vengeance of Rome. The terrors of this Jewish war and its painful consequences have been reflected in the synoptic gospels.[2] The Christian communities which had hitherto observed the Mosaic ritual now renounced it, in order that they might not share the fate of the Jews. For the first time they chose a bishop from among the uncircumcised, Marcus by name, and thus the last tie was severed which had connected the Christians of Palestine with the Jews.[3]

Hadrian unconsciously completed the service which Titus had rendered to the new religion. For only after Jerusalem had finally fallen as the capital of the Jews, and after the Jewish nation had been uprooted, could the Christian Church become cosmopolitan. Judaism itself certainly remained indestructible. The temple was replaced by the book of the law, the Mishna and the Talmud, which date from the time of Akiba. This renewal of theological work was the last national act of the people, who, scattered over the earth and afflicted with unspeakable sorrows, yet remained faithful to the God of their fathers; the only example in the world's history of a people who continued to exist without a country, and to whom their religion compensated for its loss.

[1] Graetz, iv. 182.

[2] Graetz, note 15 to Matth. 24. 15, Mark 13. 14, which has erroneously been applied to the time of Titus.

[3] Euseb., *H.E.* iv. 6, Sulpicius Severus, *H. Sacra*, ii. 31.

CHAPTER XXII

The Colony Aelia Capitolina

As Jerusalem still existed, even in its ruins, and as these could not be at once obliterated, it was determined that the former capital of Judaea should for ever lose its name and fame. All the Jews who had been living there and in the environs were driven out, and Roman veterans, Phoenicians and Syrians, were settled there as a new colony,[1] which the emperor called Aelia Capitolina. He dedicated it to himself, and to the Jupiter of the Capitol, by whom the Jehovah of the Hebrews had been overcome. This sanctuary would then take the place of the old temple on Moriah.[2] The victory of Jupiter over Jehovah was however only nominal, for in a Christian form the ancient God of the Jews conquered both Rome and the world.

The colony had been planned and begun before the Jewish war, and immediately after the war was ended the

---

[1] Eusebius, *H.E.* iv., c. 6, who, quoting from Ariston of Pella, says: the Roman colony was built because the city was completely depopulated after the expulsion of the Jews and the loss of the old inhabitants: ἐξ ἀλλοφύλου τε γένους συνοικισθείσης, ἡ μετέπειτα συστᾶσα Ῥωμαϊκὴ πολὶς τὴν ἐπωνυμίαν ἀμείψασα—Αἰλία προσαγορεύεται.

[2] It is called Capitolina in Dion, Ulpian, in the tabula Peutingeriana etc., and not Capitolia or Capitolias. Deyling has corrected the error of Harduin, that Domitian had already called Jerusalem Capitolias; this is a confusion with Capitolias in Coele-Syria. Sepp. i. 102, 179, asserts that that part of the city where the Xth legion was quartered, had been called Capitolias, and that the Aelia derived its name from it. Two editions of Ptolemy (Argentor. 1522, and by Victor Langlois, Paris, 1867), have indeed Capitolias; the Wilberg edition (1838) has Αἰλία Καπιτωλία.

new building was taken up again and vigorously carried on. Eusebius gives the 20th, Jerome the 21st year of Hadrian as the date of the (second) foundation of the Aelia, the colony must therefore have been consecrated in the year 136 A.D. or 137 A.D.[1]   Coins with the legend COLONIA . AELIA . CAPITOLINA . CONDITA commemorated this foundation.[2]

It is only a Christian legend that Hadrian entrusted the building of the new Jerusalem to the Greek Acylas from Sinope, who, at one time a Christian, was turned out of the community, and went over to Judaism.[3]   He made a reputation by translating the Bible into Greek.

If the Talmudists say that the emperor ploughed up the ground round Jerusalem in token of its degradation, and then built the new city, this fable is explained by the coins of the colony which bear the usual symbol of the husbandman, or by the Roman rite of making a circle with the plough-share round the city about to be founded.[4]

The colony was built on the site of the old city, but it had a diminished circumference.   For, as is admitted by all explorers in Palestine, the eastern slopes down to the brook Cedron, as well as mount Zion to the south,

---

[1] The *Chron. Paschale* erroneously gives 119 A.D. as the foundation year.   A distinction must be drawn between a first foundation and, after the interruption arising from the war, the second one, which Madden (*Hist. of Jew. Coinage*), p. 200, acknowledges as correct.   He places the first in the year 131 A.D., the last in 136 A.D.   The assumption that the new colony had been consecrated at the time of Hadrian's Vicennalia has some probability in its favour.   Deyling, p. 293.—De Saulcy, *Rech.*, p. 158.

[2] De Saulcy (*Num. de la T. S.*, p. 85), gives two such coins ; n. 1 represents a colonist with two bulls ; n. 2, as he believes, the genius of the colony in a tetrastyle.   The same in Madden, *Coins of the Jews*, p. 249. He wrongly considers the *aratum templum* the emblem of the colony. The figure n. 2, which is repeated in a coin of M. Aurelius and of L. Verus, is, according to him, either Jupiter or the city.   He places the colony-coins in the year 136 A.D.   De Saulcy in the year 137 A.D.

[3] This is related by Epiphanius of Eleutheropolis in Palestine, Bishop in Cyprus about 367 A.D., *de pond. et mens.* c. 14.   Curiously enough, he makes Acylas a brother-in-law (πενθερίδης) of Hadrian.   He is supported by *Chron. Paschale* for the year 132 A.D.

[4] Graetz, iv., n. 14, p. 451.

were outside the walls of Hadrian.[1] The Aelia established
the ground plan of the later Jerusalem, and it was the city
of Hadrian which Constantine and Helena found, when
they built their famous churches, and it was this Jerusalem, irrespective of the changes wrought by time, which
became the prey both of Arabs and Crusaders.

Hadrian had the new city divided into seven quarters,
over which he placed civil magistrates (Amphodarchs).
He built two market-places, a theatre for gladiatorial
combats, and other public buildings, many of which were
only finished after his time.[2] As a military colony was
required to be a strong place, it must have had a fort,
and this can only have stood on the site of the present
fortress of the Turks, namely the citadel of David by the
Jaffa gate, where the indestructible remains of Herod's towers
would certainly have been used by Hadrian for his fort.[3]

No spot could be more appropriate for the new temple
of the god of the Romans than the rocky plateau of Moriah,
supported by its gigantic walls. It had indeed been en-
cumbered since the days of Titus with masses of ruins
from the temple of Herod, but these gradually disappeared,
as the material was used for the building of the new city.
The temple of Jupiter had already been begun before the
war, for Dion states that its erection on the site of the
temple of Jehovah was one of the causes of the Jewish
rebellion.[4] Even in the fourth century, when Hadrian's

---

[1] Robinson, ii. 467. Sepp. i. 241 *sq.*

[2] These statements only in the *Chron. Pasch.* for the year 119 A.D. :
ἔκτισε τὰ δυὸ δημόσια καὶ τὸ θέατρον, τὸ Τρικάμαρον,—Τετράνυμφον—Δωδεκάπυλον
τὸ πρὶν ὀνομαζόμενον Ἀναβαθμοί, καὶ τὴν Κόδραν—ἑπτὰ ἄμφοδα.... Some expressions are obscure.

[3] Perhaps the citadel was the Dodecapylon. Robinson, ii. 454, places
the building of the citadel absolutely in the time of Hadrian.

[4] Eusebius and *Chron. Pasch.* do not mention the temple of Zeus, and
the fathers speak only of monuments of Zeus and of Hadrian on the site
of the temple. Hieron *in Isaiam* ii., c. 2 : Ubi quond. erat templum
Dei—ibi Adriani statua et Jovis idolum collocatum est. The equestrian
statue of Hadrian was still seen by Jerome "in ipso sancto sanctor loco"
(in Matth. c. 24, 15). But he also says (*ad Paulin. Ep.* 18), that a statue
of Zeus stood over the tomb of Christ. Joh. Chrysostom (*Adv. Judaeos,*
v. c. 11), speaks only in general of a statue of Hadrian in Jerusalem.

building no longer existed, the pilgrim of Bordeaux, and after him Jerome, saw on the site of the temple Hadrian's equestrian statue and the "perforated stone" (now *el Sachra*) which the sorrowing Jews were accustomed to anoint. Hadrian's temple can only have been of small dimensions, for it is not mentioned in the catalogue of the emperor's buildings in Jerusalem, which are enumerated in the Alexandrian chronicle. Coins of Aelia show a small round building with the figure of Zeus in the centre, standing either alone, or between Pallas and Hera, but it is doubtful whether the building is intended to represent the temple of Zeus.[1] As for the rest of the coins of the colony, they show, in addition to the image of Zeus, the image of Astarte, of Serapis (this latter more frequently after the time of Marcus Aurelius), of Apollo, of Dionysus, and the Dioscuri, thus proving that it was not the Capitoline Jupiter alone who was worshipped there.[2]

When Jerusalem again became the holy city of the Christians in the time of Constantine, the temple of Zeus was destroyed, with all the other sanctuaries of the gods. As the Christians found heathen temples and idols on the spot, which according to their belief was the site of Mount Calvary and of the sepulchre of Christ, they maintained that the Romans had intentionally profaned the holy places, and made them impossible to identify. Over the grave of our Saviour, they assert, stood a shrine of Astarte, or the Syrian Aphrodite; the same goddess was worshipped on Mount Calvary, and Thammus or Adonis in the grotto at Bethlehem.[3] In the marble image of a

---

[1] De Saulcy, *Numismatique de la Terre Sainte*, p. 85, n. 3. Madden, p. 250. Jupiter seated, at his sides Minerva and Juno, or perhaps the genius of the city.—Coin of M. Aurelius in Vogüé, *Le Temple de Jérusalem*, p. 62, a tetrastylon, in the centre Jupiter seated in a vaulted niche, around COL . AEL . CAP.

[2] Eckhel, iii., p. 1.

[3] Euseb. *Vit. Const.* iii. 26 (Aphrodite in the vault: he speaks, however, only of ἄθεοί τινες). Hieron., *ad Paulin.*, Ep. 58 (in crucis rupe statua Veneris; Adonis in Bethlehem). Socrates, *H.E.* i., c. 17 (Sepulchre of Christ, temple and figure of Aphrodite), likewise Sozomenus, *H.E.* ii., c. 1. Paulinus, *Ep.* xi., *ad Severum* (simulacrum Jovis in loco passionis; temple of Adonis in Bethlehem). Tobler, *Golgatha*, p. 50 *sq.*—Sepp,

boar on the gate leading to Bethlehem, Jerome, not without reason, saw an insult to the Jews, although this animal,
sacred to Ceres, was a military badge of the Romans.[1]

There are no remains of Hadrian's buildings in Jerusalem,
or none that can be identified as his, for it is only conjecture which ascribes to him the arch of *Ecce Homo*, the
splendid *Porta aurea*, the triple gate, the ruined columns
of the bazaar, or the foundations of the Damascus gate.[2]
There are no marble inscriptions in Jerusalem to give any
information now of this emperor or of the Aelia Capitolina,
while so many cities of the empire have afforded written
monuments for the learned to read.   Jerusalem has refused
this service ; for only one solitary imperial inscription
has been found there bearing the name of Antoninus Pius,
and this is of no value ; but a happy chance has brought
to light an authentic Greek inscription from the temple of
Herod, which refuses to the Gentiles entrance within the
sacred precincts on pain of death.[3]

It is certain that Hadrian ordered the Xth legion
Fretensis to stay in Aelia, and the VIth legion Ferrata
also remained behind as a garrison in Judaea.[4]   He forbade
the Jews to set foot in Jerusalem and in the surrounding
country, and this inhuman edict remained in force for
centuries ; but in the course of time the Jews were allowed
to come once a year, by bribing the Roman guards, to the
place of the temple, when they wept, on the anniversary
of its foundation, over the destruction of their city by Titus.

Jerusal. u. das heil.-Land i.,[2] p. 419, believes in an intentional dese-
cration by Hadrian and his successors ; but Robinson, ii. 73, Renan
and Tobler doubt the confused statements of the fathers.

[1] Hieron., *Chron.*   On the symbol Spannheim, *Hist. Christ*, saec. ii.,
p. 687.

[2] Robinson, i. 437.   Tobler, *Topogr.* i. 158.

[3] TITO . AELIO . HADRIANO . ANTONIO . AUG . PIO—P . P . PONTIF .
AUGUR (?) D . D., in Vogüé, *Le Temple*, pl. v., and from *C.I.L.* iii., n. 16.
The inscription has been inversely fixed to the south wall of the Harâm,
over the double gate, below the aksa ; Tobler, *Topagr.* i. 60.—The stēlē
with the Greek inscription was discovered by Clermont-Ganneau on the
Harâm wall, *Comptis rendus in Acad. d. Inscr.* 1872, p. 177.   It is now
in the Louvre, as the one solitary relic of the temple of Herod.

[4] Pfitzner, p. 188, 242.

The pilgrim of Bordeaux saw there the statue of Hadrian and the holy stone; the Jews anointed the stone with oil on that day, amid weeping and lamentation and rending of garments, and afterwards departed.[1] This striking commemoration, the oldest in history, is still repeated to-day at the wall of wailing in Jerusalem, though it has become a theatrical as much as an historical display of sorrow.[2]

Aelia Capitolina continued to be a heathen city until the days of Constantine.   The emperor Commodus must have derived some special benefit from it, for he gave it the name Commodiana.[3]

The name of Jerusalem did not certainly disappear after the time of Hadrian; it survived all the more in the memory of men, and the bishops especially made use of it, though it was replaced officially by the name Aelia.   This, indeed, continued for three hundred years to be the name for the city and bishopric of Jerusalem.[4]   It was still used officially in the year 637 A.D., for when the Caliph Omar took the holy city, he called it in the charter which he bestowed upon it, not Jerusalem, but Aelia.[5]

---

[1] *Itiner. Hierosol.*, ed. Wesseling, p. 591.   On the edict of Hadrian: Justin. *Apol.* ii. 84.   Tertull. *Adv. Jud.*, c 15, 16; *Apolog.*, c. 16. Celsus, *in Orig.* at the end, l. 8.   Gregor. Naz. *Orat.* 12, p. 202.   Sulp. Sever. ii. 45.   Euseb. *Dem.* ii., c. 38.   Hilar. *Psalm.* 58, p. 219.   Euseb. and Hieron. *Chron.*   Hieron. speaks touchingly about it, *Sophon*, c. ii.

[2] I witnessed it there in the Easter time of 1882.

[3] COL . AEL . CAPIT . AURELIA COMMODIANA PIA FELIX (De Saulcy, p. 94), first on coins under Caracalla.

[4] At the time when the Empress Eudocia visited Jerusalem, and even as late as the year 536 A.D., it is stated in the rolls of a synod at Jerusalem: In colonia Aelia metropoli sive Hierosolyma ; Harduin, *Concil.* ii. 1412 in Robinson, ii., p. 9.

[5] Tobler, *Golgatha*, p. 104.   In De Saulcy (p. 185, pl. 19), the first coin, struck in Jerusalem by the Arabian conqueror, with the inscription Aelia.

CHAPTER XXIII

The War with the Alani. Arrian's Periplus of the Black Sea

HADRIAN had returned to Rome before the Jewish war was over, for his presence there on the 5th May, 134 A.D., is proved by an inscription.[1] Towards the end of this war the Alani revolted, a tribe who lived between the Caucasus, the Caspian Sea, the river Cyrus and Iberia, and who were also called Massagetae. The Iberian king, Pharasmanes, had stirred them up to a predatory expedition, by which Armenia and Cappadocia were disturbed.

The Alani seem also to have penetrated into the country of the Parthians, for their king, Vologeses, appeased them by presents, while the Roman force, under the command of the governor of Cappadocia, Flavius Arrianus, reduced them to tranquillity.[2] The history of the dealings of this famous man with the Alani is lost. The writing called *The Order of Battle against the Alani*, which is added to the *Tactics* of Arrian, appears to have been a part of it; but it merely contains information about the composition of the Roman troops and their order of battle.[3] This motley army consisted of Celtic horsemen, infantry from the Bosporus,

---

[1] Greek letter of Hadrian to the congregation of the triumphantly crowned athletes who called themselves after Hercules. *C.I.G.* 5906, Latin in Gruter, 315 : Trib. Pot. xviii., Cos. iii., prid. iii.—Non Majar Romae.

[2] Dion Cassius, lxix. 15. Spart. c. 17. On these quarrels Schneiderwirth, *Die Parther*, p. 156.

[3] Ἔκταξις κατ' Ἀλανῶν, appended to the *Tactica*. Amstelodami, 1683, p. 98 *sq.*

Cyrenians, Numidians, Achaian cavalry, Armenians, men from Trebizond and Colchis, Getae and Italians, and the xiith and xvth legions. Xenophon, a Greek, whose name recalled famous times, was general of the whole army, and Valens, legate of the xvth legion, led the cavalry. After Arrian has described the order of battle in which the army was drawn up, he says that on the approach of the Scythians, who rode without armour on bare-backed horses, uttering a fearful war-cry, missiles were hurled, the infantry pressed forward, and the enemy took to flight. The whole war seems to have been of little importance.

Vologeses, king of Parthia, had moreover sent messengers to the senate to accuse Pharasmanes, and the barbaric chief of Iberia came to Rome with his wife and son to vindicate himself. He was received with hospitality. The emperor allowed him to offer sacrifice on the capitol, he increased his power, he even erected an equestrian statue of him in the temple of Bellona, and he delighted in the war dances of the Iberian nobles. This is the account of Dion, but Spartianus says that Hadrian wounded the pride of his vassal by ordering three hundred criminals in the arena to be clothed with the costly garments which the king had brought to the emperor as a present.

Flavius Arrian, a second Xenophon, possessed the full confidence of the emperor, who made him governor of the province of Cappadocia, where he remained as legate from about 131 A.D. to 137 A.D.[1] The result of this happy appointment was the *Periplus of the Black Sea*, a work which we possess in the form of a Greek letter addressed to Hadrian. For the emperor had commissioned his legate to sail round the coasts of the Black Sea in order to ascertain the condition of the Roman fortresses there, as well as all other particulars, and for this purpose Arrian drew up a report, written, unfor-

---

[1] He wrote his *Periplus of the Euxine* in 131 A.D. (Marquardt, *R. St.*; 368), his *Tactica* in 137 A.D., as he says there himself, in the 20th year of Hadrian. As late as 137 A.D. he is mentioned in an inscription from Sebastopolis as legate of Cappadocia (*Rev. Arch.* N.S. 1876, p. 199). He was succeeded as legate by L. Burbuleius Optatus Ligurianus, Borghesi iv. 158.

tunately, with the brevity of a soldier. But as an authentic geographical sketch it is of the greatest value.[1]

He began his voyage at Trebizond, the colony of Sinope. "Here," so he writes to the emperor, "we gazed with delight on the Black Sea from the same spot whence Xenophon, and you too, looked upon it."[2] Two rude altars stood there, but the Greek letters were defective and illegible, so Arrian ordered other altars to be erected of white marble, with a plain inscription. A statue of Hadrian stood there, too, with his right hand pointing to the sea. The people of Trebizond had probably erected it in memory of his visit. Arrian did not think the statue worthy of the emperor, so he begged him to send another to Trebizond, and also to replace the existing statue of Hermes, in the temple there, by a better one.

From Trebizond the voyage proceeded in an easterly direction towards the harbour Hyssus, where Arrian reviewed a cohort and twenty horse ;[3] then further on to the Pontic Athens, where a temple of Athene, a deserted fort, and a harbour were to be seen. From there he sailed to Apsarus, where five cohorts were stationed, who received their pay and were inspected. Arrian derives the name of the place from the death of Absyrtus, whose tomb was still to be seen.[4]

Then follows a list of all the rivers past which he sailed after leaving Trebizond. The distances are given in stadia from place to place, and from river to river. 1450 are reckoned from Trebizond to the Phasis. Arrian praises the water of this river on account of its lightness, clearness, and purity. It is said not to grow putrid if kept for ten years, but rather to improve. On the left of the mouth of the river stood the figure of Rhea, the goddess of the country, a

---

[1] Arrian also makes particular mention of letters in Latin which he sent to Hadrian, in addition to his Greek report. *Periplus*, p. 122.

[2] Xenophon, *Anabasis*, iv. 822 : καὶ ἦλθον ἐπὶ θάλατταν εἰς Τραπεζοῦντα πόλιν Ἑλληνίδα οἰκουμένην ἐν τῷ Εὐξείνῳ Πόντῳ Σινοπέων ἀποικίαν ἐν τῇ Κόλχων χώρᾳ.

[3] Ptolemy (v. 6, 5) enumerates Ischopolis, Cerasus, Pharnacia, Hyssi Portus, Trebizond.

[4] Ἄψορρος Ποταμός, in Ptolemy, *ibid.*

cymbal in her hand and lions under her seat. An anchor of the Argo was shown, but Arrian doubted its genuineness, as it was made of iron. On the other hand he placed more faith in some remains of a stone anchor which he saw. A fort stood on the Phasis, with a garrison of four hundred men—picked troops, under whose protection the merchants lived. Arrian ordered the harbour to be strengthened by a walled trench.[1]

The voyage proceeds to Sebastopolis or Dioscurias, formerly a colony of Miletus, the most northerly emporium for oriental goods, and the most important military station of the empire on this side. For the chain of Roman fortresses ended here, and behind lay the unconquered country of Caucasian tribes, of whom only a few acknowledged the supremacy of Rome. Sebastopolis was a flourishing market for the barbaric tribes, where, according to Strabo, seventy nations carried on their trade, and where a great slave market was held.[2] The city received favours from Hadrian, for it erected a statue to him in the Olympieum at Athens, and called him its benefactor.[3]

Then follows the list of peoples past whose shores Arrian sailed. Some paid tribute, others refused to pay it. Over many tribes Hadrian had appointed chiefs. The Colchians and Drilae are mentioned (both according to Xenophon) as neighbours to the people of Trebizond. The Drilae Arrian also calls Sanni.[4] He complains that they lead a predatory life, and molest the people of Trebizond. He thinks, with the help of the gods, they might be made to pay tribute, and if they refuse they ought to be put to death. The Machelones and the Heniochi, whose king is called Anchialus, are near neighbours to the Sanni.[5] Then follow the

[1] The citadel is called Phasis in the tabula Peutingeriana; by Ptolemy Sebastopolis. This geographer bounds Colchis on the north by Sarmatia, on the west by that part of the Euxine which stretches from the river Corax to the inner bay next to the Phasis. Then begins Armenia Minor and Iberia on the Caucasus.

[2] Strabo, xi. 498. To-day the Mingrelian place, Iskuriah.

[3] Σεβαστοπολειτν τῶῶν ἐν Πόντῳ ἡ βουλὴ καὶ ὁ δῆμος. C.I.G. 342.

[4] Ptolemy (v. 9, 20) alludes to a people, Σουρανοί, behind the Amazons and between the Hippian and Ceraunian mountains. Mannert, vi. 420, sq.

[5] Ptolem. (v. 9, 20) places the Heniochi in Sarmatia Asiatica between the Cercetae and the Suani.

Zydreti, subjects of Pharasmanes, then the Lazi, under king Malassus, who was set over them by Hadrian, and the Apsilae, to whom Trajan had given Julianus as a king. Close to these are the Abasgi (now Awchasi), whose king, Rhesmages, had been appointed by Hadrian. Similarly the Sanigri received their king Spadages from Hadrian. We may perceive the nature of the Roman power in these Caucasian districts, where the condition of the small and separate tribes has remained very much the same even until our own time. But the prosperity of the commercial cities which once flourished there has been destroyed by the Mongols and the Tartars. Russia, who, since the days of Peter the Great, has been in possession of nearly three sides of the Black Sea, carries on the work of colonization begun by the Greeks and Romans in these countries, but without their spirit ; and only in her warfare are we reminded of the days of Imperial Rome.

The river Apsarus is the extreme limit of the Euxine towards the east.[1] Arrian must thence have sailed northwards to the Singames, and then his course must have been along the left side of the Pontus to Sebastopol, whence he could see the range of the Caucasus, and its highest point Strobilus. He recalled to mind that it was there that Prometheus had been chained.

In the second part of the *Periplus* Arrian describes, too often only from imperfect information, the country on the banks of the Thracian Bosporus as far as Trebizond along the coasts of Bithynia, Paphlagonia, and the country of Pontus. The number of forts, harbours and commercial cities are an excellent proof of the state of civilization there while the north and north-eastern side of the Euxine were shrouded for Arrian, too, in the gloom of mystery and fable. We notice the most important places on this passage to Trebizond : Heraclea (Erakli), a·colony of Megara ; Sinope, a colony of Miletus ; Amisus, a colony of Athens ; Pharmacia (formerly Cerasus) and Trebizond, whose prosperity was largely due to Trajan. Arrian earnestly besought the emperor to build a harbour here.

The third and last line, which completes the circuit of the

---

[1] See the map of this *Periplus* in the edition of Nicol. Blancard.

Euxine, is the line from Sebastopolis to the Cimmerian, and
thence to the Thracian Bosporus, *i.e.* to Byzantium. The
death of Cotys II., the king of the Cimmerian Peninsula,
suggested this sketch of Arrian's.[1]   He wished to acquaint
the emperor with the geography of the Crimea. Subsequently the emperor gave the sovereignty of the Bosporus to
a son of Cotys, Roemetalces, who now called himself the
friend of the emperor and of the Romans, as was the habit
with other barbarian princes appointed by Rome.[2]   The
Bosporan kings had their likeness stamped on their coins in
addition to that of the emperor, and there are some in
existence of the time of Hadrian.[3]   The Cimmerian Bosporus,
however, never became a province under the rule of Rome.

From Sebastopolis the voyage is pursued along the coasts
of the present Mingrelia, Abasia and Circassia. Arrian
notices the people of the Zichi by the river Achaeus. They
too had received a king from Hadrian. The promontory of
Hercules, Vetus Lazica, Achaia Antiqua, the harbour of
Pagrae and Hieros Sindica, then the Cimmerian Bosporus,
and Panticapaeum are all mentioned.[4]   This city, now called
Kertsch, a colony of Miletus, was the most important place
in the Tauric Chersonesus, the residence of the Tauric
princes who were under the protection of Rome. The great
Mithridates died here. Arrian does not mention the Hyp-
hanis or river Kuban, which discharges itself opposite the
city. He places the Tanais (the Don), which separates
Europe from Asia, sixty stadia from Panticapaeum, and then
he makes it flow into the Black Sea from the Maeotis Palus
(the Sea of Azov, which, according to Arrian's estimate, com-
prises 9000 stadia).[5]   The way in which he speaks of it
proves that he never saw the Don, and it is most likely that
he allowed the whole excursion to be undertaken by some

---

[1] Cotys died in 131 A.D.   See *C.I.G.*, n. 2108 c, *sq.*

[2] Φιλόκαισαρ, φιλορώμαιος, the emperor himself he calls ἴδιον κτίστην. *C.I.G.*,
n. 2108 f, *sq.*

[3] Of Cotys and Roemetalces. The legend is Greek. Mionnet, ii., p.
372 ; *Suppl.* iv. 506 *sq.*   Under Constantine there still existed a Bosporan king—Sauromates.

[4] Ptolemy, iii. 6, 4 ; viii. 10, 4 : Παντικαπαία.

[5] Ptolemy (vii. 5, 6) has the correct estimate.

one else.   The important city Tanais (Azov), which even in
the Middle Ages still retained its trade with India, is not
mentioned.

From Panticapaeum the journey is continued to Theo-
dosia, formerly a colony of Miletus, which at that time was
abandoned.[1]   The city is now called Caffa, or Feodosia.
We may also mention Symbolon Portus (Balaclava).   It is
again remarkable that the promontory of Parthenion, with
its temple of Diana, and Kriu Metopon (Cape Merdwinoi),
known to Ptolemy, are not mentioned.   The Dead Sea
(Sinus Carcinites) is not spoken of by that name, but is
known as " not a large sea " at the lower end of the harbour
of Tamyrace.   The Greek colony Olbia, on the Borysthenes
(Dnieper) is mentioned.[2]   Then follows the harbour Odessus
(Odessa), 250 stadia further Istrianorum Portus, then Isia-
corum Portus, and Psilum at the   mouth of the Ister
(Danube).[3]   The mouths of the Hypanis (Bug) and the
Danastris (Dniester) are not mentioned.   Opposite to this
mouth of the Danube lies the island of Achilles, with an,
ancient temple of the hero, where sailors sacrifice goats to
him.[4]   Ancient votive offerings are to be found there, vases
rings, precious stones, with Greek and Latin inscriptions in
praise of Achilles and Patroclus.   Numerous sea birds make
themselves useful in the temple, which they clean with their
wings.   We cannot read without astonishment the wonderful
things narrated by a sensible man like Arrian, with the
greatest gravity.   Achilles was here a sea god for mariners,
to whom he spoke in oracles.   He appeared to them in
dreams or awake, but only on this island, while the Dioscuri
appeared everywhere.   Thetis gave the island to her son,
and he inhabited it.   Arrian obtained the whole of this information from hearsay, and he expressly says that it does
not appear incredible to him, as Achilles was such a great
hero.

[1] Arrian, *Per.* 132 : καὶ μνήμη ἐστιν αὐτῆς ἐν πολλοῖς γράμμασιν.

[2] Ptolemy, iii. 5, 28: Ὀλβία ἡ καὶ Βορυσθένης : cp. *Peripl. Anon.*, p. 9, in
Mannert, iv., p. 238.

[3] Ptolemy : Ὀρδησός or Ὀρδησσός, in European Sarmatia, not to be confounded with Odyssus or Odessus in Moesia inferior.

[4] Ptolemy iii. 10. 17 : Καὶ ἡ Ἀχιλλέως ἡ Λευκὴ νῆσος, also called Dromos
Achillis.

Four other mouths of the Danube follow after Psili Ostrum, then the cities Istria, Tomi, Callantra Portus,[1] Carorum Portus (the surrounding country is called Caria). We also notice Dionysopolis (Baldschick) in Lower Moesia, Odessus (Varna), the promontory of Haemus (K. Emineh), Mesembria (Missivria in Thrace), Apollonia (Sizeboli), Salmydessus (Midja), the fabulous Cyanae, the temple of Zeus Urios at the entrance of the Bosporus, the harbour of Daphne, and finally Byzantium.

The cities there were Greek. They had preserved their language and constitution under the Roman dominion, and to her alone they were indebted for protection from the incursions of the Scythians and Sarmatians. The most important communities among them, such as Istros, Tomi, Odessus, Mesembria and Apollonia, even formed a league of cities with a diet.[2]

---

[1] Ptolemy and Pliny speak of six, Strabo of seven mouths ; cf. Mannert, iv., p. 219.

[2] Κοινὸν τῆς πένταπόλεως or τῶν Ἑλλήνων : G. Perrot. *Inscr. inéd. de la mer noire, Rev. Arch.*, 1874, p. 22.

CHAPTER XXIV

Hadrian's last years in Rome. Death of Sabina Augusta. Adoption and Death of Aelius Verus.

AFTER the emperor had travelled through the length and breadth of his empire he found himself once more in the palace of the Caesars, wearied, aged and sad. He made additions to his villa at Tibur, and he built his tomb in Rome. The work of his life was accomplished. Increasing illness embittered his existence. The anxiety of appointing a successor to the empire weighed upon him : for like all the emperors before him except Vespasian, Hadrian had no natural heir.

It did not need a particularly jealous disposition to look with suspicion, or as Spartianus says, with hatred upon all, who, as possible inheritors of the throne were awaiting his death with ill-concealed eagerness.[1] Every ruler, who, like Hadrian, has played a long and distinguished part in the world, must be disturbed by painful thoughts as he approaches the end of his career. His nearest legitimate heirs were his brother-in-law Servianus, and the grandson of Servianus, Fuscus Salinator. The father of this young man, a consul and friend of Pliny, had married a daughter of Servianus and of Domitia Paulina, and of this marriage Fuscus was the offspring.[2] Astrologers had foretold that the young man would wear the purple, and this prediction may

---

[1] Spart. c. 23 : Omnes postremo, de quorum imperio cogitavit, quasi futuros imperatores detestavit.

[2] Pliny (*Ep*. vi. 26) to Servianus expressing his pleasure at this marriage. Borghesi, ii. 212. Hadrian even thought Servianus worthy of the throne, Dion Cassius, lxix. 17.

have been repeated to the emperor.   Other candidates for the throne were Platorius Nepos, once a favourite of Hadrian, and Terentius Gentianus, who was a favourite of the senate.

It does not transpire that Augusta Sabina took any part in the palace intrigues about the succession, as Trajan's wife had done before her.   She would scarcely have had time, for she died about the year 136 A.D.   Slander was active in ascribing her death to the hatred of the emperor, who was said to have made her take poison.[1]   Aurelius Victor gloomily narrates that Sabina was treated by her husband almost like a slave, and was at last obliged to put herself voluntarily to death ; that she had indeed publicly declared, that she would never have a son by Hadrian, as she knew he would inevitably be a curse to the human race.   As a similar saying is related of the father of Nero, the husband of Agrippina, this can only be considered a fable.   The commonplace biographers of Hadrian have even surpassed Tacitus and Suetonius in searching the chronicle of Roman scandal.[2]

We know nothing of Hadrian's domestic relations ; but to Sabina he seems not to have been much attached.[3]   The beautiful medals with the legend *Concordia Augusta* must have been a bitter satire on her married life.[4]   The emperor always paid honour to his wife in public, and so did the world by setting up altars to her by the side of those of the emperor.   She seems to have been enrolled among the gods by Antoninus Pius.[5]   Her memory, moreover, is preserved in the medals and inscriptions of Rome, as well as in those of the colonies.   Her portrait in numerous busts shows a distinguished but not pleasing face, with a massive and lofty forehead, a large nose, and lines of haughty sadness about

[1] Spart. c. 23 : Sabina uxor non sine fabula veneni dati ab Hadriano defuncta est.

[2] Duruy (iv. 409) defends Hadrian against Roman scandal regarding his conduct towards Sabina.

[3] In the collection of Dositheus, previously referred to, there is a letter of Hadrian's to his mother (Plotina) ; he invites her to dine with him as it is his birthday, and Sabina has gone into the country.   This betrays a mutual dislike.   Boecking, *Corp. Juris Rom. Antejust.* 212.

[4] Cohen, ii., p. 247, n. 2, *sq.*

[5] Consecration coins in Eckhel, vi. 522, Cohen, ii., n. 27.   The veiled Sabina holds a sceptre ; an eagle raises her.

the mouth, which seem to justify the epithet " morose " that was applied to her.[1] Sabina had probably been prominent as a woman of culture in Trajan's court circle, and naturally enjoyed the society of intellectual men. This displeased the suspicious Hadrian, who on one occasion dismissed Suetonius and others from the court. Meanwhile, in the silent marble alone the sorrowful face of this unhappy Augusta continues to live for us.

All the candidates for the throne were in the end greatly disconcerted by the emperor's choice. This fell upon Lucius Commodus Verus; and it must have been the more surprising as the man chosen was the son-in-law of that Nigrinus, whom the senate at the commencement of Hadrian's reign had ordered to be put to death for high treason. It almost looks as if the emperor wished to atone for a crime.

The declared heir to the throne was the son of Ceionius Commodus, whose consular race came from Etruria.[2] He became praetor in 130 A.D., and then (on 5th of December) his wife Domitia Lucilla bore him a son Lucius Verus, who afterwards became the inglorious colleague of Marcus Aurelius. His rare beauty and his charming manners procured him the favour of the emperor, whom he had been allowed to accompany on his voyage up the Nile. Evil interpretations were put upon this friendship by some who imagined that Verus was a second Antinous. His wit and conversation were brilliant, and he composed Latin and Greek verses as well as the emperor himself, who looked indulgently upon his excesses. The pleasure-loving Lucius Commodus was only carrying out the traditions of Hadrian and of Rome, when he confronted the Stoics with the maxims of Epicurus. He invented a pasty which Hadrian liked, and that was a merit as far as the emperor's kitchen went;[3] but another invention of his favourite must probably have met with less approval, namely, a specially artistic bed

[1] So she appears in the bust of alabaster in the Capitol, with a conspicuously high head-dress, with wreath of ears of corn and a diadem.

[2] Spart. *Helius*, c. 2 : Jul. Capitol., *Verus Imp.*, c. 1.

[3] Spart., *Helius*, c. 5, alleges that this pasty was called *pentafarmacum*, as it consisted of sow-udder and parts of pheasant, peacock, ham, and boar, contained in a crust of sugar.

hung with network curtains, on which Lucius, perfumed with Persian scents, was in the habit of reposing, Ovid's *Amores* in his hand. This to Hadrian, who had often slept like a common soldier, on the bare ground, would be very displeasing. Lucius masked his runners, whom he caused to run unmercifully, as winged cupids, giving them the names of the winds. The pedant Spartianus, in speaking about these excesses, remarks that though they were immoral, they were not dangerous to the state. They show clearly enough, however, that even the simplicity of Hadrian's court, and his efforts to improve the habits of the Romans, were not sufficient to eradicate the vices of society. Justin still pitied the children, who, in spite of Hadrian's prohibition, were openly sold to procurers in Rome, and Epictetus could satirize the women who devoured the Republic of Plato, as it taught them the happiness of a community of wives.[1] When the wife of Lucius Commodus complained of his intrigues, her husband quietly said : " Wife is a title of honour, and does not denote pleasure."[2] If Verus had been nothing but a libertine the choice would have done little credit to Hadrian's power of judgment. Either he saw in Verus qualities which made him worthy of the throne, or he was deceived in him. We may perhaps not be wrong in thinking that Hadrian was chiefly influenced by the striking and regal beauty of Verus.[3]

After Hadrian had determined to adopt Verus, the disappointed candidates endeavoured to interfere ; the choice, moreover, was repugnant to all the Romans.[4] As at the beginning, so at the end of his reign, Hadrian saw himself threatened by a conspiracy, and the feeling that after twenty years of wise government he could not carry out his wishes,

[1] Justin, *Apol.* ii. 70; Epictet. *Apophthegm.*, p. 427 (J. Stob. *Eclog. moral,* 131, 30).

[2] Spart. *Helius*, c. 5. He had several children by Lucilla, L. Aurelius Verus, who afterwards became emperor, and several daughters. Ceionia and Fabia are mentioned by name, and one of them was engaged to Marcus Aurelius, who however rejected her.

[3] Comptus, decorus. pulchritudinis regiae, oris venerandi,—Spart. *Helius,* c. 5.

[4] Invitis omnibus,—Spart. c. 23.

made him beside himself. The chiefs of the discontented party were his own brother-in-law and his brother-in-law's grandson Fuscus, the one an old man of ninety, the other a youth of seventeen. The emperor's rage was so uncontrollable that he did not spare even the old man. He ordered both the unfortunate men to be executed, or he compelled them to commit suicide. Hadrian was at that time at his villa at Tibur, where he lay ill and exhausted from loss of blood. From there he seems merely to have issued the sentence of death, for there is no account of a trial before the senate.[1]

Dion tells us that Servianus, before he died, called the gods to witness to his innocence, and implored them not to allow Hadrian himself to die when the time came for him ardently to desire death. As Servianus knew the state of mental torture the emperor was in, his curse seemed likely to be fulfilled. Paulina, the wife of Servianus, died before him. Hadrian did not show any public marks of respect to the memory of his sister, for which he has been reproached as wanting in affection.[2] For a long time he must have been on bad terms with his nearest relations.

Servianus and his young grandson were not the only men who fell victims to Hadrian's morbid derangement, for there were others whom he is said to have done away with, either publicly or secretly.[3] His secret police had plenty to do. The despot was latent in every Roman emperor, and there were traces of it in Hadrian's features. If only by force of contrast to the fine spirit of humanity by which he had been actuated throughout his life, these bloody sentences have left a deep impression on the memory of the world. Coming before us as bare facts only, we can neither explain nor palliate them. If his biographers are correct, Hadrian

[1] Spartianus (c. 23) only says : Tunc libere Servianum quasi adsectatorem imperii, quod servis regis coenam misisset, quod in sedili regio iuxta lectum posito sedisset, quod erectus ad stationes militum senex nonagenarius processisset, mori coegit. E. Knaut (*Hadrian als Regent und als Character*, Nordhausen, 1871), defends this and other of the emperor's actions, but shows too much predilection for him.

[2] Dion Cassius, lxix. 12.

[3] Spart. c. 23.

either ruined his best friends or put them to death, from his capricious ill-humour, and from his greatest fault, jealousy.[1] But when Marius Maximus asserts that Hadrian was naturally cruel, and did good only from fear of suffering the same fate as Domitian, it is more than absurd.[2]   Against this is the opinion of Dion, who says: "So far from being blood-thirsty, Hadrian punished persons who were hostile to him, merely by writing to their native cities that they had incurred his displeasure.[3]

The emperor adopted his heir to the throne in 136 A.D., probably on the 10th of August, the anniversary of his own accession.[4]   He gave him the name of Aelius, and the title of *Caesar*.   This Julian cognomen had hitherto been borne by all the members of the reigning imperial house, but Hadrian was the first to bestow it as a dignity upon his appointed successor.   Verus at the same time became second consul for 137 A.D., and tribune.   The emperor celebrated his adoption by games at the circus, and by costly presents to the people and the army.   In order that the new Caesar might show his practical capacity, and might carry

[1] Dion Cassius, lxix. 3: ὁ δὲ δὴ φθόνος αὐτοῦ δεινότατος.

[2] Spart. c. 20, and with it c. 15, where the ill-treated friends of Hadrian are enumerated : Attianus, Nepos, Septicius Clarus, Eudaemon, Polaenus, Marcellus, Heliodorus, Titianus, Umidius Quadratus, Catilius Severus, and Turbo.

[3] Dion Cassius, lxix. 23.   Nothing is more contradictory than the views expressed in Dion and Spartianus regarding the disposition of Hadrian. They judge from the sources before them.   Whatever there is in Dion in favour of Hadrian emanates probably from his autobiography.

[4] The Capitoline fasti call Aelius Verus *Caesar* only in his second consulate (137 A.D.) while during his first (136 A.D., with S. Vetulenus Civica Pompeianus) he is still officially called L. Ceionius Verus.   There can, therefore, be no question as to his adoption before 136 A.D.   An inscription in Gruter 874, 5, records these two as consuls on 19th of June, 136 A.D., without giving to L. Ceion. Commodus the title Aelius Caesar. On the other hand, there is an Alexandrian coin (Zoega tab. 9), showing that the adoption had taken place already on 29th of August.   Borghesi, viii. 457.   The adoption and nomination as Caesar has to be set down for August, 136 A.D.   This has lately been established, against Peter (*Röm. Gesch.* iii. 552 *sq.*) by J. Plew, *Marius Maximus als Quelle der Script. H. Aug.*, Strassburg, 1878.   The adoption coins in Foy-Vaillant, i. 164, Eckhel, vi. 525.

on his official career to the proconsulship, Hadrian entrusted him with the government of Pannonia, the same country in which the emperor himself had learnt the art of ruling. Verus went there first in the beginning of 137 A.D., as pro-consul, for the *tribunicia potestas* gave him the *imperium proconsulare* outside the city.[1] The inscription on a statue which Aelius Verus Caesar erected to his adopted father in Pannonia proves that he was still there in August.[2] Spartianus observes that he made only a moderate impression there by his qualities as a ruler.

Either the health of Verus was so much shattered that a longer residence in the Danubian countries would not have suited him, or the time of his mission had expired, as he returned to Rome before the end of 137 A.D., and here the emperor relinquished the government to him, retiring himself to his villa at Tivoli. The dissolute Verus, however, was seized by a fatal illness.[3] Hadrian saw the disappointment of his hopes, and sighed to think that he had leant on a tottering wall. He repented his imprudent choice, but it was only malicious calumny which said that he had adopted Verus because he foresaw his early death. Spartianus, who repeats this, quotes prophetic verses of Hadrian about Verus, and other sayings whose truth had been proved by magic and astrology.[4] The dying Caesar had prepared an eloquent speech to congratulate the emperor on 1st of January, and to thank him for his favours,

[1] Borghesi, *Ann. d. Inst.* 1855, p. 24; *Oeuv.* viii. 457. The Trib. Pot. and the second consulship is recorded on an Egyptian coin in Zoega, p. 161; a medal referring to the alimentation of Rome, in Froehner, *Les Med. de l'Emp. Röm.*, p. 45. The inscription of the city Cibyra, in Pisidia, which calls him her benefactor, *C.I.G.* 4380; that of Hadriani, Le Bas-Wadd. 1053 (Duerr, Anhang, 63).

[2] *C.I.L.* iii. 4336 from Javarin. His administration of Pannonia is recorded by a coin : PANNONIA. TR. POT. COS. II. S. C. Eckhel, vi. 526. Cohen, ii., p. 260, n. 24.

[3] A coin of L. Ael. Caesar, with Salus feeding the serpent, may refer to his illness. Cohen, ii., n. 43.

[4] It is doubtful whether the delicate health of Verus has any connection with Corinthian coins, which had been struck in memory of his adoption and nomination as Caesar, bearing the head of Aesculapius. Foy-Vaillant, i. 164.

when, for the good of the world, death snatched him away.[1]
A man like Verus would have suited the times of a Caligula
and Vitellius, but not an age which was influenced by the
Stoics.   Epicurus withdrew, leaving the path to the throne
open to Epictetus and his followers.   The memory of Verus
was kept alive for a time by the son who resembled him,
and who had the honour of being tolerated as a colleague
· by Marcus Aurelius.   Aelius Caesar, moreover, invented the
famous pasty, which survived him as his best memorial.
It became the favourite dish of the emperor Alexander
Severus.[2]

[1] Spart. *Hadr.*, c. 24, *Ael. Ver.*, c. 4.   The year 138 A.D. is fixed by *C.I.L.*
iii., n. 4366. (Javarin in Pannonia).
[2] Lampridius, *Alex. Sev.* c. 30.

CHAPTER XXV

Adoption of Antoninus. Death of the Emperor Hadrian

HADRIAN'S end was approaching. He summoned the principal senators, and poured out his heart in a melancholy speech on both kinds of succession, natural and appointed. He gave the preference to the latter; for the qualities of a son may be settled by nature which often produces feeble and irrational beings, while the judicious ruler can make the best choice. He thus had first appointed Verus, and now, fate having swept him off, he had found a ruler who combined all the qualities that could be desired. This was Aurelius Antoninus, a man who had never thought of the succession, but who, the emperor felt sure, would accept the offered dignity out of love to himself and the senate, however reluctant he might be to take it.[1]

As a matter of fact, the man of Hadrian's choice, a noble senator and a philosopher, did not covet the purple. Hadrian gave him time to consider whether he would accept his offer and the condition attached to it, namely, that he must himself adopt two young men, Marcus Annius Verus (called afterwards Antoninus), son of the brother of his wife, and Lucius Verus, son of the dead Aelius Verus Caesar. To this Aurelius Antoninus agreed, and the world owed two emperors, the ornaments of the Roman empire, Antoninus Pius and Marcus Aurelius, to Hadrian's wise choice. It was Hadrian's dying gift to humanity; and of his numerous benefits it was the greatest.

[1] Dion Cassius, lxix. 20.

For the rest, this new choice met with some opposition among those who were disappointed in their expectations, like L. Catilius Severus. He had been Hadrian's friend, his first successor in the supreme command in Syria (117-119 A.D.), then proconsul of Asia, and lastly, as it appears, prefect in Rome, in succession to Valerius Asiaticus.[1] Hadrian contented himself with removing him from office.

The new Caesar Antoninus belonged to the Aurelian family, and came from Nismes in Gaul. His house was rich in earnest and distinguished men. The tyranny of the Caesars had not been able to extinguish the virtues of ancient Rome in every family. In the race of the Antonines there was something of the nature of Cato, of Thrasea and Helvidius, a philosophic contemplation of the world deepening into melancholy. The maternal uncle of Aurelius, Arrius Antoninus, twice consul, was renowned for his excellent qualities, a holy man, as Capitolinus says, who commiserated Nerva when he ascended the throne. The parents of Antoninus were the consul Aurelius Fulvus, a melancholy and delicate man, and Arria Fadilla, who, after the death of her husband, married Julius Lupus. Antoninus himself was born on 19th of September, 86 A.D., at Lanuvium, and was brought up at Lorium. He filled the office of quaestor and praetor with distinction, and became consul in 120 A.D. Hadrian chose him as one of the four consulars to whom he entrusted the government of Italy, giving him the district in which he himself had the most property. Before the year 135 A.D., he was made proconsul in Asia, filling the office so well that he even surpassed the fame of his maternal uncle Arrius Antoninus, who had also been proconsul there. Pliny has marked him out for special praise.[2] After his return the emperor took Antoninus into the privy council, where Capitolinus tells us that he was always in favour of moderate measures. He must have been a man of fifty-two years of age with great experience in political matters, when Hadrian chose him for his successor.

[1] Waddington, *Fast. des Prov. Asiat.*, p. 134, 205.

[2] Pliny, iv. 3. On the proconsulate of Antoninus in Asia, see Waddington, *Fast. des Prov. Asiat.*, p. 205 *sq.* His successor there was L. Venuleius Apronianus.

Antoninus had married Annia Galeria Faustina, sister of Aelius Verus. She had borne him two sons, but as they were both dead, Hadrian adopted him only on the condition that he should adopt Marcus Annius Verus and Lucius Verus in the place of children. The former was the son of the praetor Annius Verus, and of Domitia Calvilla, and was a nephew of Faustina. Hadrian, who was fond of the boy, gave him the name Verissimus, on account of his love of truth. He was born on 26th of April, 121 A.D.

The new heir to the throne was adopted on 25th of February, 138 A.D., and assumed the name of T. Aelius Hadrianus Antoninus. After he had delivered his speech of thanks in the senate, the authority both of proconsul and tribune was bestowed upon him as co-regent and Caesar.[1]

The emperor meanwhile was tormented by cruel pains, as dropsy had now followed upon exhaustion. The last days of this once happy traveller through the world, the new Olympian Zeus, the distributer of blessings and benefits to his people, the ruler who had adorned the earth with works of beauty, were so terrible, that the dying Hadrian is one of the most striking examples of the vanity of all earthly things. He died daily, as Tiberius had done before him, without dying. Medicine and magic were alike of no avail. The physicians only provoked the sarcasm of the sufferer; he laughed satirically at their ignorance, and quoted the well-known saying, "many physicians are the death of the king."[2] He had not strength enough to kill himself, though he did not condemn suicide, and had once given the philosopher Euphrates permission to commit it. In his agony he begged for poison or for the stab of a dagger, promising

---

[1] Dion Cassius, lxix. 21. The proconsulate which the emperors from the time of Augustus, bestowed upon their adopted sons, did not, as Pagi (*Crit. in Baron*, p. 135) asserts, carry with it the title of Imperator for the Caesars. See Eckhel, viii., c. 2, p. 339, "De proconsulibus imperatoribus."

[2] Λέγων καὶ βοῶν τὸ δημῶδες, ὅτι πολλοὶ ἰατροὶ βασιλέα ἀπώλεσαν; Dion Cassius, lxix. 22. Epiphanius (*De Mensuris*, c. 14) asserts even that Hadrian wrote a satire on the physicians (ἐπιστόλην ὀνειδιστικήν). Dion (lxix. 17) speaks of a letter from Hadrian, in which he says how tormenting it is to wish to die, and yet not to die. It was Hamlet's lament in his famous monologue.

money and pardon. But no one ventured to lay hands on the emperor, and Antoninus kept watch over him. He prevailed so far on one of his favourite slaves, the Jazygian Mastor, that he promised to kill him. Hadrian showed the slave a place below the breast, where his physician Hermogenes had told him that a blow must be fatal. But Mastor ran away. A physician who had refused to administer poison to the emperor, killed himself. The superstition of the time surrounded Hadrian's melancholy death-bed with wonderful legends, for though incurable himself, he restored sight to the blind by merely touching them. This power of healing was in no way attributed to Hadrian's personal gifts, but was considered by the servile nation a proof of the divinity to which he had attained. Even in Vespasian's days the Alexandrians had brought the infirm and the blind to him to be healed.[1]

We do not know whether the unhappy man was in the palace of the Caesars, or in his villa at Tibur. He sought relief for his sufferings in the balmy air of Baiae, after he had resigned the reins of government to Antoninus ; but he soon summoned Antoninus to his side as he felt the near approach of death. In his last moments he uttered some Latin verses which have been preserved :

> "Soul of mine, pretty one, flitting one,
>   Guest and partner of my clay,
>   Whither wilt thou hie away ;
>   Pallid one, rigid one, naked one,
>   Never to play again, never to play ?"[2]

The verses are too like Hadrian not to be his. They illustrate the nature of this enigmatical man, who, with the darkness of death closing round him, still indulges in sarcasm.

[1] Tacit. *Hist.* iv. 81.

[2] The translation is from Merivale :

> "Animula, vagula, blandula :
>   Hospes comesque corporis,
>   Quae nunc abibis in loca ;
>   Pallidula, rigida, nudula,
>   Nec ut soles dabis jocos ?"
>   —Spart. c. 25.

Death released Hadrian on the 10th of July, 138 A.D., when he expired in the arms of one of the noblest of men, whom he had appointed to be his successor. Antoninus had the body of the dead man burnt, with great ceremony, in Cicero's villa at Puteoli, where the ashes remained until the hatred of the senate for his memory had subsided. For the senate had been greatly embittered by his last cruelties, Antoninus himself having been the means of saving many from persecution. The opposition of the old Romans had also been aroused, in whose eyes Hadrian's cosmopolitan tendencies must have seemed a departure from the traditions of the state. For had not the emperor been more of a Greek than a Roman? Had he not curtailed the privileges of Rome by making the provincials of equal rank with the citizens of Rome? The senate stood on its rights; it criticised the actions of the dead prince, and found that Hadrian, who had been declared Zeus by Greece in his lifetime, was not worthy after his death to be enrolled among the Roman divinities. The senate had the courage of its opinions, remembering that the apotheosis of the prince was a matter for it to decide, and that this had been refused to the murdered Domitian when the army demanded it.

This behaviour of the senate greatly disturbed the pious Antoninus. But by his prayers, his tears and complaints, he eventually succeeded in accomplishing the consecration of Hadrian by the senate,[1] and for this amiable action alone he deserved the epithet "pious." He had the ashes of Divus Hadrianus brought to Rome, where they were interred in the new mausoleum. Subsequently Antoninus dedicated a temple to him on the Forum of the Antonines, which he had built. He also erected a temple to the deified emperor in Cicero's villa at Puteoli,[2] appointing priests and flamens, who are mentioned in the inscriptions.[3] At Puteoli he founded in

---

[1] Dion Cassius, lxx. 1. Consecration coins in Eckhel, vi. 512.

[2] Its ruins are said to have been discovered not far from the amphitheatre in Puteoli: Mommsen on n. 2487, *I.R.N.*

[3] Flamen of Hadrian, Gruter, 446, 7. In Ostia, inscriptions from the theatre there, *Notizie degli scavi* (*Acad. d. Lincei*), 1880, p. 474, n. 5. Sodales (Hadrianales) frequent. In Gruter, 5, 3; 19, 3; 45, 9; 259, 3; 407, 1, 2; 412, 2; 457, 6; 467, 5; 1009, 9; 1090, 13; 1095, 1. Orelli,

his memory quinquennial games, called Pialia, or Eusebia. The emperor seems to have been especially honoured after his death in this place. Greeks erected monuments in his honour there, in compliance with a decree of the Philhellenes.[1]

It has been observed that the busts of Hadrian show a foreign, not a Roman face, possessing neither the Latin beauty of the Julian family, nor the mild gravity of the features of Trajan. It is more finely cut, but it is neither sympathetic nor intellectual. Artificially curled hair hangs over a brow, which cannot be called thoughtful, and the short beard which was said to have been worn to conceal a blemish, is rather a disfigurement, than an ornament to the face. Hadrian is said to have let it grow to conceal some scars. This marble face does not convey the impression of all that was contained in the character of this strange man. He was a mass of contradictions, which no single portrait could display. For on the one hand, we find his delight in the intellect of Greece, and in Eastern sensuality, his enthusiastic love for art, his sophistical versatility, his sound judgment, his statesmanship, his humanity and generosity. But there is also the darker side of his capricious temper, his inordinate vanity, his love of irony and of trifles, and his gloomy mysticism. Who could hope to reconcile these conflicting traits in one portrait? We cannot see his bust without asking who the distinguished man is, so conscious of his own power, with the questioning glance and the light observant smile playing round his mouth. It must be the likeness of one who has been sovereign in some sphere of life, and has ruled over the spirits of his age.

The emperor Julian, who knew how to draw the portraits of his predecessors with malicious wit, has summed up the character of Hadrian in his Olympic play of *The*

414, 2376. Hadrianic sodales were still in existence in 193 A.D. From the death of Hadrian dates the third sodalitas of the emperor worship. Marquardt, *R. St.* iii. 452.

[1] This appears from an inscription from the people of Cibyra, *C.I.G.* 5852. Eusebeia in Puteoli, *C.I.G.* 1068, 5810. *C.I.A.* iii. 1, n. 129; *I.R.N.*, n. 104. Inscription from Puteoli from the year 142 A.D.: ANTON . PIUS . CONSTITUTOR . CERTAMINIS . ISELASTICI. Gruter, 254, 4.

Caesars in the following sentences : " A man came forward
with a long beard and a haughty step, who was, among other
things, very much devoted to music. He often looked up to
the skies like one who meddled too much with forbidden
arts. When Silenus saw him, he asked : ' What do you
think of this sophist? is he looking for Antinous? Some
one should give him to understand that the youth is not
here, and tell him to give up his foolish tricks.' "[1] This
satirical opinion of Hadrian, coming from the mouth of a
clever man, who himself was emperor at a time when the
traditions of his predecessors still survived, is worthy of
attention. Julian describes him as a friend of the Muses, as
a sophist, a mystic and a lover of Antinous.

Antinous is certainly one of the greatest mysteries connected with Hadrian. The marble figure of this youth,
standing before us as Dionysus, casts a ghastly light upon
his history. It is a key to his biography. But it is of little
real assistance, even if like a torch it seems to illuminate
dark recesses in the soul of the emperor.

The nature of so uncommon a prince is a far more attractive study to the psychologist than the character of
such criminal lunatics on the throne of the Caesars as
Caligula, Nero, or Domitian. The misanthropic hermit
Tiberius alone affords equal interest, as a foil to the restless uneasy Hadrian.

The earliest biographers of the emperor are so much
embarrassed that they have only collected the most salient
contrasts in his character. Of pessimism and despair they
naturally remarked nothing in Hadrian ; that is only our
modern view. Is it a just one? Every line in the diary of
Marcus Aurelius shows that this imperial philosopher held
the world in melancholy contempt. But not in this fashion
did the richly-endowed nature of Hadrian display itself. He
ruled the empire like a noble Roman, with prudence and
strength. He enjoyed life with the joy of the ancients. He
travelled through the world, and found it worth the trouble.
He " restored " it, and embellished it with new beauty.

We certainly do not know what he thought of his whole

[1] Julian, *Caesares*, c. 9 : πολυπραγμονῶν τὰ ἀπόρρητα.—καὶ παυσάτω τοῦ
λήρου καὶ τῆς φλυρίας αὐτόν.

life at the end of it. He might, indeed, perhaps have agreed with the estimate of Marcus Aurelius : " All that belongs to the body is a stream, all that belongs to the soul a dream and a delusion ; life is a struggle and a wandering among strangers, and fame after death is forgetfulness."[1]

Hadrian was lavish on a great scale, more than most sovereigns before and after him. And he must therefore have often experienced the ingratitude of mankind. " How many burnings of Phaethon, how many deluges of Deucalion would not be required to punish the unfathomable wickedness of the world ! "[2]

As an older man, Hadrian assumes some of the characteristics of Timon of Athens. He hates and ruins his probably innocent friends together with his false friends, while he truly loves none. After the most painful struggle, he dies in the arms of Antoninus, taking farewell of his soul as it wings its flight into the unknown land with an ironical question, but a question without hatred, which breathes nothing but a pleasant recollection of this beautiful world.

Many things are reflected from Hadrian's mind, in the spirit of his time, and in them lies his value to the human race.

---

[1] Marc. Aurel. ii. 17 : ὁ δὲ βίος, πόλεμος καὶ ξένου ἐπιδημία· ἡ ὑστεροφημία δέ, λήθη.

[2] Πόσοι Φαέθοντες ἤ, Δευκαλίωνες ἱκανοὶ πρὸς, οὕτως ὑπεραντλον ὕβριν τοῦ βίου. Lucian, *Timon*, 4.

SECOND BOOK

THE STATE AND GENERAL CULTURE

CHAPTER I

The Roman Empire

THIS age, which has been called the happiest period of human history, produced so great an impression by its high state of culture and by the majesty of the Roman empire, that Greeks and Romans praised its splendour more eloquently than the philosophers of after days.[1] Even Pliny in his time, when he came to describe Italy, exclaimed with enthusiasm : " I speak of a country which is the mother and nourisher of all countries, which the gods have chosen to unite divided kingdoms, to improve manners, to knit together the tongues of many rude nations in one common language, to teach culture and sociability to men, in short to be a fatherland to all the peoples of the world."[2]

Aristides the Greek has extolled the magnificence of the empire no less enthusiastically than the Roman Pliny. His eulogy on Rome is a pompous flourish of courtly flattery, but it states facts and convictions, which themselves belong to the age. " The conquered," so said this celebrated orator of the time of Marcus Aurelius, " envy and do not hate their conqueror Rome. They have already forgotten that they were once independent, as they find themselves in the enjoyment of the blessings of peace, and share alike in all honours. The cities of the empire are resplendent with beauty and pleasure, and the whole world is adorned like a garden. Only the people who live outside the limits of the Roman dominion are to be pitied, if there are any such

---

[1] Compare Gibbon i., c. 2, at the beginning.
[2] *Hist. Nat.* iii. 6.

people.   The Romans have made the world a home for all.
The Greek like the barbarian, can roam freely everywhere
as if from fatherland to fatherland ; the passes of Cilicia, the
deserts of Arabia, the hordes of barbarians have now no
terrors for us; our safety lies in the fact that we are Romans.
The Romans have made the saying of Homer, that the
earth is common to all, an actual fact.   They have measured
the whole inhabited world, have bridged rivers, have carried
roads over mountains, have built cities in the desert, and
have ruled the world by law and custom."[1]

Half a century after Aristides, Tertullian the African
could speak of the Roman empire in the following terms:
" The world is equipped with everything, it becomes daily
more cultivated, it is richer in knowledge than in the past
ages.   Everything is accessible, everything is known, everything is full of activity.   Beautiful estates now cover what
once were frightful deserts, forests have been supplanted by
fields of corn, wild animals by flocks and herds.   Corn
sprouts in the sand of the desert, rocks are made productive,
marshes drained.   There are as many cities now as there
were formerly houses.   Bare islands and rocks no longer
inspire terror ; everywhere there is a dwelling, everywhere
a people, everywhere government, everywhere life."   The
human race, this father of the Church goes on to say, is so
numerous, that it already is a burden on the world.   Like
the Chinese, or like ourselves to-day, he is afraid of over-
population for which Nature he thinks can no longer provide,
and therefore he looks upon famine, pestilence, war, and
earthquakes as necessary means of relief.[2]

In the time of Hadrian the Roman empire extended from
the Atlantic Ocean to the Euphrates, from Scotland to
Mount Atlas and the cataracts of the Nile.   It contained
about ninety million people.   We cannot consider it remarkable either for its population or for its extent, for
the geographical dimensions of the Russian as well as of
the British empire exceed those of the Roman.   But the

[1] Aristides' *Encomium Romae* i., p. 348 *sq.* (Dindorf), with which compare the praise of Appian, *Praef.* c. 6.

[2] Pro remedo deputanda, tanquam tonsura inolescentis generis humani.
—Tertullian, *De Anima*, c. 30.

Roman empire stood out prominently among all ancient and modern states, as comprising in itself the noblest people of civilization, the most beautiful countries, and the most famous cities of the world, and was therefore the historic centre of ancient life.   The history of the peoples round the basin of the Mediterranean Sea was written in the creation of many forms of government, and the fact that these ancient countries were protected from the inroads of the barbarians enabled the Romans, in their insatiable desire for aggrandisement, to extend their borders.   In ever-widening circles they absorbed in their empire the Germans, the Britons, the Slavs and the Arabs.

The civilization of the empire was the sum total of the productions of antiquity in art as well as in science, both political and social.   These creations belonged essentially to the three great groups of the nations of the world.   The Semites indeed had disappeared politically with the downfall of their states in Asia and Africa, but a new religion had arisen out of Judaism, and this religion was beginning to spread through the empire.   On the other hand the Romans and the Hellenes were the predominant nations of the civilized world, the former as rulers and law-givers, the latter as men of art and culture.   The empire was divided, geographically, between the two nationalities, the East being Greek, the West Roman.   At the same time both languages were in general use throughout the world, and were understood by every cultivated man, whether in Rome or on the Thames, on the Nile or on the Euphrates.

The idea of the empire was based upon government, army, law, and culture, while it owed its political unity entirely to the central power of the emperor.   For in spite of uniformity of government, the peoples of the empire were separated from one another by creed and language, custom and history.   The Greeks of the East did not become Romanized like the Celts, the Dacians, and the Thracians of the West, who had merged themselves in the empire.   The division of East and West was so natural and so historical, that sooner or later the Roman empire was bound to fall into these two parts.   Even in the time of Hadrian, when Hellenism was the greatest intellectual force in the empire,

N

a reaction set in against it on the part of Latin learning. The epigram of Florus, the friend of the emperor, a poet from the completely Romanized Africa, is full of significance.[1]

While ancient Greece became a museum of antiquities, of whose treasures Pausanias, shortly after Hadrian, made a catalogue, a current of new intellectual life was constantly flowing from Hellenized Asia and Egypt towards Rome and the West. Art, literature, philosophy, new religions came thence. But the Roman instinct of government was still powerful enough not only to curb these influences, but generally to prevent any hostility between West and East from their contrary tendencies. This was one of the greatest facts in Roman history. For the empire was put together so mechanically that any part could be added or taken away without materially changing its character. It was a federal state of many nations; but it never possessed the characteristics of a modern monarchy like England and France. As an ancient organism the Roman empire, the great republic of the civilized world, rested on the peculiarity and independence of its self-governing states and communities which maintained their privilege of autonomy even after they had been converted from free countries into provinces and districts of Rome.

[1] *Anthol. lat.* ed., Mueller, i., n. 218: Cive romano per orbem nemo vivit rectius.

CHAPTER II

The Provinces of the Empire, their Government and their Relation to the Central Power. The Peaceful Development of their Civilization. Slavery

THE relations of the countries conquered by Rome to the central government were established by Augustus in 27 B.C., when he divided all the provinces of the empire into imperial and senatorial provinces.[1] In the last days of the republic seven of these were consular or military, and eight civil and praetorian. Those provinces which required no military force he handed over to the government of the senate. He himself kept all the others where stronger garrisons were needed, like the countries on the Rhine, the Danube, and the Euphrates. Under his successors the number of provinces was increased by conquest or by the division of larger territories, so that at the time of Hadrian's accession there were forty-five provinces, of which nine only belonged to the senate.[2]

The military force of thirty legions, which protected the empire, was stationed on its frontiers. In the whole of Italy there were no troops. Gaul had only one garrison of 1200 men at Lyons (*cohors* I. *Flavia urbana*); two legions, and afterwards one, protected Egypt. There was no soldier to be seen in any one of the five hundred cities of Asia.[3] The naval power of Rome was restricted to the fleets at Ravenna and Misenum, and to those on the Black and the North Sea,

[1] Dion Cassius, liii. 12. Suetonius, *Aug.* c. 17 ; Eckhel, iv. 236.
[2] Marquardt, *R. St.* i.², 489.
[3] Arnold, *Roman System of Provincial Administration*, p. 103.

on the Danube and the Euphrates, and at a few other stations. 350,000 men, Roman citizens and auxiliaries, sufficed to maintain tranquillity in this vast empire, while to-day Europe alone groans under the burden of more than two million soldiers in time of peace. The small strength of the army causes us perhaps more astonishment than anything else in the Roman empire, and it also explains the number of public works, the prosperity of the richly-adorned cities, and the flourishing condition of trade.

The emperor had therefore deprived the senate of military power, though it appeared as if he had magnanimously kept nothing for himself but burdens and dangers.[1] As a matter of fact he had both "the provinces of the senate and the people" in his power, as all proconsuls and praetors were under his proconsular authority which embraced the whole empire.[2]

The governors of the senatorial provinces were chosen annually by the senators from among the consuls and praetors. They generally bore the title of "Proconsul." In rank they took precedence of the imperial legates. They had ten or twelve lictors.[3] They were surrounded by a brilliant court, whose maintenance fell as a burden on the province. But they possessed no military power, not even the *Jus gladii*, though they could pass sentence of life and death on the provincials. The last vestiges of that tyranny which the proconsuls exercised in the provinces in the days of the republic, might occasionally come to light under the emperors, but could no longer have the same terrible consequences. Nothing, however, gave greater weight to the monarchy than the undeniable fact that the imperial provinces were the best governed and the least oppressed.

Their governors (*legati Augusti pro praetore, legati praetorii*) were chosen by the emperor himself, usually from consuls or ex-praetors, sometimes indeed from former aediles and quaestors. Subject to his approval they remained a

---

[1] Dion Cassius, liii. 12.   [2] Dion Cassius, liii. 15.

[3] Dion Cassius, liii. 13, 14. Eckhel, iv. 237. Asia and Africa were only governed by such proconsuls as had actually been consuls. On this account these countries were specially called proconsular, and their governors had twelve lictors.

shorter or longer time, but generally three years and more at their posts. Their rank was lower than that of the proconsuls ; they had only five lictors.[1] Their power was however greater, as their authority extended both over provincials and Roman citizens. They possessed the highest civil and military power in the province.[2] They gave judgment at their own residence, as well as in the courts. Legates of the legions and *Legati juridici*, whom the emperor appointed, stood at their side.[3] As they were under the control of the emperor, and were obliged to execute his commands, they could no longer rule as despots themselves. The salary, which rose to two hundred thousand sesterces for imperial, and to a million sesterces for senatorial governors, was intended to protect the people from exactions.

The exchequer was controlled by quaestors in the senatorial provinces, and by procurators in the imperial provinces. The emperor also sent procurators into the senatorial provinces, where they raised taxes which flowed into the fiscus,[4] independently of the proconsul. They had jurisdiction and increased power only according to circumstances ; but Judaea, Mauretania, Thrace, and other smaller countries were governed by procurators, who had also the complete administration of the country.

The financial ministers belonged either to the equestrian order, or they were freedmen of the emperor, and they did not always carry on so lucrative an office disinterestedly. Hadrian, who did not listen to any suggestions from his freedmen, punished guilty rulers with severity.[5]

The provincial taxes consisted of the poll-tax (*tributum capitis*), a tax on property, and a land tax (*vectigal*), from which every territory endowed with Italian rights was exempt.[6] The land-tax was paid chiefly in coin after

[1] Mommsen, *Bull. d. Inst.* 1852, p. 172.

[2] Savigny, *Röm. Gerichtsverf.* ii. 76 *sq.*, 81 *sq.*

[3] Marquardt, i.², 551 *sq.*, and the paragraphs on this subject in Arnold, *R. Prov. Administr.*

[4] Dion Cassius, liii. 15. Hoeck, *Röm. Gesch.* i. 2, 200.

[5] Spart. c. 16 : Et circumiens quidem provincias procuratores et praesides pro factis supplicio affecit.

[6] See the excellent description in Hoeck, i. 2, 204 *sq.*, and Savigny, *R. Steuerv. in Zeitschr. für gesch. Rechtswissensch.* vi.

Augustus had parcelled out the land.   Then came the taxes
that were farmed out, import and export duties, harbour
rates, road and bridge tolls.   The whole maintenance of the
state, the military expenses, which amounted even in the
time of Augustus to £4,500,000 sterling, the salaries of the
officers in the provinces, the corn-distributions, the maintenance of roads, the mail service, and the public buildings, were
raised from the provinces.   In this way more gold was taken
out of them than was returned to them, while the crowd of
Roman officials, the removal of their inhabitants to be
soldiers in foreign countries, the use of the Latin tongue in
judicial proceedings, all contributed to Romanize provinces
which had no culture of their own.

The income from the senatorial provinces was paid according to the arrangement of Augustus into the aerarium, the
public treasury ; the income from the imperial provinces into
the fiscus, which the *Procurator a rationibus* managed as
minister of finance.   Both treasuries existed for a long time
side by side.   As late as Marcus Aurelius, the right of the
senate to dispose of the aerarium was still acknowledged,
and even in the third century proconsuls raised tribute from
the senatorial provinces.[1]   But it was in the nature of the
principate that the emperor should occasionally interfere with
the financial matters of the senate, so that the importance of
the aerarium disappeared.   Hadrian established new officials,
the *Advocati fisci*, who represented in the provinces the rights
of the imperial treasury before the courts.[2]   In this way he
obviated the embezzlement and usurpation of land belonging
to the state.

There were countries which the emperor claimed for
himself, and which he governed by procurators.   Egypt
became the property of the house of Octavius after his
victory over Antony.[3]   The emperors sent viceroys there with
the modest title of *praefectus*, who ranked with the procurators of smaller provinces, like the Maritime and Cottian

---

[1] On these matters consult O. Hirschfeld, *Unters. über röm. Verwaltungsgesch.* i., p. 11 *sq.*

[2] Spart. c. 20 : fisci advocatum primus instituit.

[3] E. Kuhn, *Die städt. und bürgerl. Verfass. des röm. Reichs*, ii. 80.

Alps, Raetia and Noricum, provinces which were also imperial.[1]

The deep shadows which the Roman empire cast upon the nations which it absorbed were the loss of their political independence, which, as time elapsed, robbed them even of the power of self-preservation, and the bureaucratic machinery of despotism, which completely crushed national life while the welfare of the subjugated people remained entirely dependent upon the pleasure of the sovereign. The end, after a hundred years of happiness under the rule of Nerva's adopted family, was the increasing power of the satraps, and the impoverishment and decay of the national spirit. In the second century, however, the evil was not so apparent, and the loss of freedom by countries that had once been great, but were now exhausted, was certainly compensated by the advantage of sharing in the general prosperity and well-established order of the monarchy.

The movement of trade was more unrestricted than it has been ever since the fall of Rome. The same coinage had currency from the Pillars of Hercules to the Euphrates. The great system of high roads embraced the whole empire, and united all the provinces. The imperial post (*cursus vehicularius* or *publicus*) had already been established by Augustus. It was, indeed, only used in exceptional circumstances for private business, and was generally employed for state purposes and for the emperor's use.[2] The emperor often abused his power, so that the imperial post became an oppressive burden to Italy and the provinces. This may be compared with the burdensome *fodrum* of the Roman emperors in the Middle Ages, when they passed through Italy levying contributions on their journeys to Rome. Nerva first relieved Italy, and Septimius Severus the provinces as well, from the obligation of maintaining the imperial post. But we are also told of Hadrian that he threw

---

[1] Kuhn, ii. 83, 84. On Noricum, which was officially called a kingdom in the second century, see J. Jung, *Römer und Romanen in den Donauländern*, p. 25.

[2] Post diplomas, or free passes, were bestowed as favours, and were granted by Trajan and Hadrian to the sophist Polemon and his family. Philostr. (*Kayser*) ii., p. 44.

it upon the fiscus of every province in the empire. No emperor could have a greater inducement to make this service effective than Hadrian, the great traveller. He appointed a chief of the post in Rome, under the title of *praefectus vehiculorum*.[1]

Communication by water was also made easier. It was a sail of seven days from Ostia to Gibraltar, ten to Alexandria.[2] The trade of the world was never more flourishing. The city of Rome alone showed it ; for in the markets there, were gathered the productions of all the three continents of the world, and " all that seasons and climates, rivers and seas, the arts of Hellenes and barbarians produced was brought to Rome from every land and every sea."[3] The East sent its treasures, even those of the distant Indies, by Armenian merchants, to the Black Sea, to Dioscurias, and to the Phasis.[4] Goods from Babylonia, Persia, and India were all to be found in the markets of commercial cities like Ephesus, Smyrna, and Apamea. They came from the harbours of Arabia and the Red Sea, up the Nile to Alexandria. Myus Hormus sent fleets annually to India and Ceylon, which returned in January.[5]

The provinces had by this time renounced any individual power. Their national coherence was broken up, and they were artificially divided into communities and judicial dis-

---

[1] Spart. c. 7 : cursum fiscalem instituit, ne magistratus hoc onere gravarentur. E. Hudemann (*Gesch. des röm. Postwesens während der Kaiserzeit*, 1878, p. 22) rightly refers the *magistratus* to the municipal authorities (later Decuriones) in those places where postal stations were established. A list of *praefecti vehiculorum* will be found in Henzen, *Annal. d. Inst.*, 1857, p. 95. Upon imperial postal affairs see Mommsen, *R. St.* ii., 2, p. 956. O. Hirschfeld, i. 98 *sq.* H. Stephan, *Das Verkehrs- leben im Alterthum.*

[2] Pliny, *H.N.* xix. 1.

[3] Aristides, *Encom. Romae* (Dindorf), i. 326.

[4] Pliny, *H.N.* vi. 19. Strabo, xi. 506.

[5] For the Alexandrian, Indian, and Arabian commerce compare the *Periplus Maris Erythraei*, erroneously attributed to Arrian, but probably composed in the time of Nero. September was the month in which trade was most brisk in the Arabian Gulf. The harbours are : Myus Hormus, Adulis, Tapara, Malao, Mundi, Tabae, Opone, Muza, etc., as far as Taprobana.

tricts. Their old leagues were abolished ; for whenever
Rome made conquests, the senate lost no time in breaking
up such confederations.[1] The provinces, indeed, had the
right of forming unions of the cities for general purposes,
and of assembling deputies at a diet, which met yearly in
the capital under the presidency of the high-priest (*commune*,
concilium, or κοινόν in the East), and though these provincial
parliaments were allowed to make complaints about the
governors, and send envoys to the emperor, they were not
permitted to deliberate on the home affairs of the government. The object of their existence was to appoint the
times for public sacrifices and games.[2] For the central
point of provincial life was now the altar of the spirit of
Rome and Augustus, or the temple of his deified successors.
Tarraco was the first city to be permitted by Octavius to
build an altar to him, and other provinces imitated the
example of this servile flattery.[3] The provincial diets on
the whole, therefore, only served to confirm the obedience
of the provinces to the empire, which was surrounded with a
halo of divinity.

Roman rule was nevertheless a blessing to countries
which were no longer capable of freedom. It protected
them from civil wars, by which they had been lacerated, so
long as they were split up into small states, full of jealousy
and ambition. Plutarch said of Greece in his time : " Peace
and quiet prevail here. There are no military expeditions,
no more exiles and revolutions, neither despotisms nor other
evils of the Hellenes."[4] He might certainly have added that
there was no longer any creative political and intellectual

---

[1] As already under Mummius in Greece. Pausanias, *Achaica*, vii. 16, 6.

[2] Kuhn, *Städt. Verf.* i. 111 *sq.* Marquardt, *R. St.* 503 *sq.*, 510 *sq.*, and
in *Ephem. Epigr.* 1872, p. 200 *sq.* "die Zusammenstellung der Provinzial-
concile." Arnold, *Roman System of Prov. Adm.*, p. 202. The κοινά in
Asia, in Perrot, *Rev. Arch.* 1874, 11 *sq.*

[3] Huebner, *Hermes*, i., 1866, p. 111, on the emperor-worship in Tarraco.
This imperial worship, moreover, came from Asia ; under Augustus,
Ephesus, Nicaea, Pergamum, and Nicomedia were his privileged seats.
Krause, *Neokoros*, p. 12.

[4] Plutarch, *Moral.* ii. 460 (Wittenbach). Cur Pythia nunc non reddat
oracula.

life in his country. For the republics in Hellas, like the later republics in Italy, became great in the arts of peace, amid the din of war and the noise of revolutions. But this flourishing age of the small aristocracies and democracies had gone by. The history of the world took the place of local interests, and city and clan were superseded by humanity. Pliny could praise " the infinite glory of Roman peace," which made the most distant countries and their productions the common property of all.[1] Countries which, in the time of the republic, had been half laid waste, like Spain, Gaul and Africa, blossomed forth again under the blessings of peace. Asia and Syria experienced their last happy age. Whole districts in Asia were rescued from a nomad existence by the Romans, and the Saracens were the first to re-introduce the savage conditions of Bedawin life.[2]

The advantage of the peaceful development of the provinces, under a just government, is therefore not to be undervalued, and the fact remains which Aristides, and after him Gibbon, asserted, that the allegiance of the world to Rome was a willing allegiance. Only among the barbarians on the borders of the empire did the spirit of freedom which had been banished from the ancient states of civilization survive. On this account Tacitus looked sorrowfully upon the Germans. It must have been the endeavour even of the most civilized people whom the Romans subjugated by force of arms, to conform to the world-wide organization of the empire, and draw fresh vitality from it. They resigned themselves to their lot, the more readily as, in most cases, their national religion and constitution were respected by the wise maxims of the imperial government. They had renounced all opposition to the Roman dominion, or their struggle merely consisted in the endeavour to make themselves equal to the Romans in all political and civil rights. Even the provinces of the West already emulated Rome in their civilization, and in their profusion of native talent. They enriched Roman literature with brilliant names in every branch of knowledge, even in jurisprudence. Spain, Gaul, Africa, Illyricum gave in time great generals, and even

[1] Pliny, *Hist. Nat.* xxvii. 1 : immensa romanae pacis majestas.
[2] Renan, *Mission en Phénicie*, p. 837.

emperors, to Rome.   Rome civilized the West, and completed the work of Alexander the Great in the East.

By degrees the monarchy destroyed the legal barriers
between the subject countries and the imperial city.   Mae-
cenas had already advised Octavius to grant the same laws
and rights to the provinces, and to impose equal taxes on
all citizens.   Thus at the first dawn of the monarchy, the
equality of all nations was declared to be its object.   The
emperors bestowed Latin and Roman privileges, not only
upon cities but upon countries.   The *Jus Latinum* was conferred on the whole of Spain by Vespasian ; Hadrian gave
it to the province of Narbonensis, and he bestowed citizenship upon the whole of Upper Pannonia.[1]   If in this he
appeared only to follow the example of his predecessor, no
emperor before him did so much to facilitate the attainment
by the provincials in general of a legal standing in the
empire, by giving them equal rights with Rome.[2]   The title
" Multiplier of citizens" (*Ampliator Civium*), first found on
a medal of Antoninus, would certainly have applied to him.[3]
Admission to citizenship was indeed chiefly a financial venture, yet social conditions made it necessary, and the time
was at hand when Caracalla removed the last legal distinctions in the empire.   The great cosmopolitan principle
of Rome might truly have been called a sublime conclusion
to ancient history, if it had been really humane, and if it had
combined the rights of humanity with the rights of citizens.
But this was only hinted at theoretically by the Stoics, by
Seneca, Epictetus, and Marcus Aurelius.   The civil community and the whole economy of the state continued to
rest upon slavery, the most barbarous and the most fatal
institution of antiquity, and even the famous revival of trade
in the age of the Antonines, was essentially the work of
slaves.   The idea of free labour as the highest expression
of energy and strength and the source of all wealth in
national economy, had not yet been discovered by any

---

[1] Zumpt, *Comm. Ep.* i. 410 ; Mommsen, *C.I.L.* iii. 496, 498.

[2] Finlay, *History of Greece from its Conquest by the Romans*, p. 55.

[3] S.P.Q.R. AMPLIATORI CIVIUM ; Froehner, *Médaillons de l'Empire Romain*, p. 61.

statesman. Work generally was still the forced labour of slaves.

Slavery was the only basis for the independence of the ruling class. There was so great a force centred in the slaves that a suspension of their labour, if this could have occurred in the modern form of combination, would have made the existence of society impossible. The number of these unhappy creatures amounted to about a third of the population of the Roman empire. In a remarkable letter to the senate, Tiberius expresses his opinion on this vast number of slaves. He called them nations, and pointed to them and the latifundia as the ruin of the state.[1] He despaired of curing this terrible evil. Happily causes were at work which diminished slavery. Its main source had been wars of conquest, and when these ceased, slavery declined. It was daily becoming more unusual to see the inhabitants of cities sold *sub hasta* or *corona* as spoils of war on the high roads. But that it was still possible is shown by the fate of the Jews after the fall of Bether, under Hadrian. The more slavery diminished the better became the lot of the free husbandmen and labourers ; and the emperors endeavoured to improve their condition.[2]

Another cause of the diminution of slavery was the emancipation of the slaves. This had increased to such an extent since the civil war, that it was feared that the Roman citizens would be completely ruined by the admission of so many former slaves. For only a few among them could be men of character; long servitude must rather have destroyed their self-respect. Emancipation became finally a kind of luxury in Rome, for every great man boasted as much of the number of slaves whom he owned as of the freedmen who composed his court. Augustus had endeavoured to limit emancipation by the *Lex Aelia Sentia* and *Furia Caninia*, and

---

[1] Tacitus, *Ann.* iii., c. 53 : quid enim primum prohibere et priscum ad morem recidere aggrediar? villarumne infinita spatia? familiarum numerum et nationes?

[2] Jung, *Bevolkerungsverhältnisse des röm. Reichs, Weiner, Stud.*, 1879, p. 195. On the rise of free labour since the second century see Wallon, *Hist. de l'Esclavage*, iii., c. 3.

Tiberius by the *Lex Junia Norbana* had granted only a restricted Latin right to those slaves who were pronounced free without undergoing a formal ceremony.   But all classes of society were soon full of *libertini* ; they took possession of the court and the government, and as favourites and officers of the emperor's palace, they tyrannized over Rome and the empire.

CHAPTER III

Cities, Municipia, Colonies

APART from its division into political and ethnographical provinces, the empire presented a system of autonomous cities. The independence of the communities so long as it lasted, gave the Roman empire an imposing civic character, and contributed to the happiness of the age. Even after the fall of Rome the vestiges of municipal government afforded material for building up new states.

The Greek East, which, since its conquest by the Turks, displays merely the ruins of antiquity in its desolate regions and on its marshy coasts, was covered in the second century with cities and emporiums of commerce from the Black to the Red Sea. The same conditions prevailed in the north of Africa. Even under the Ptolemies, Egypt had not been so rich. In the West, Spain especially had many flourishing cities ; Ptolemy counted 428. But Italy, rich in cities, had never quite recovered from the civil wars. Her communities could no longer vie with those of Africa, Gaul, and Spain, and not until long after the fall of the Roman empire had Italy a brilliant period of city life, of which Rome had laid the foundation.[1]

The whole constitution of the empire rested upon the municipal system. To such an extent was the freedom of the community the political idea of antiquity, that the whole inner history of the empire is nothing but the development of this conception with which Rome first started. Every

---

[1] Milan was probably the largest city in Italy at this time, and more prosperous than Turin : Hadrian made it a colony. Zumpt, *Comm.*, *Ep.* i. 408. The Greek city of Naples was also flourishing.

degree of municipal freedom was represented in the empire according to the historical origin of the communities, and their legal relation to Rome itself—dependent and tribute-paying cities without any privileges, others with Latin and Italian rights, and finally free, autonomous communities. These differences weakened the feeling of national union among the countries which Rome had conquered. As in time of old, their patriotism became restricted within the walls of the city. Finally the municipal and colonial rights of Rome forced their way into the civic system of foreign countries. So it was easy for the emperors to allow the historical forms of the republican age to exist, and even to pass as protectors of their freedom.

While the vassal states—the ethnarchs, tetrarchs, and toparchs—were disappearing everywhere, the idea of free communities, united indeed with Rome, was still maintained.[1] They were relics of the ancient Greek polity, and even imperial Rome respected for several centuries its self-government by senate and people, its magistracy, its priesthood, its national festivals, its electoral assemblies and commercial laws. The toleration of the historical rights of free communities constitutes something really great, even though this conservative principle of Rome was dictated by necessity. For the conquered cities had to be spared and propitiated, and in allowing their own constitution to remain, endless trouble in governing them was spared to Rome.[2] As a matter of fact many free cities had never had equal powers of autonomy before. According to the law of Caesar they remained independent of the military and civil power of the provincial governor, and were free from garrisons and from having soldiers quartered upon them. They had the right to own property, and the privilege of coining, which the cities of the Greek Orient especially never lost. Only on emergency had they to furnish auxiliaries to the Roman legions. Cities with these high privileges were to be found chiefly in the countries of Greek civilization—*e.g.* Athens, Ephesus, Cyzicus, Sardis, Antioch, Laodicea, Byzan-

[1] Eckhel, iv. 262. Marquardt, *R. St.* i.², 71 *sq.* Kuhn, *Städt. Verf.* ii. 14 *sq.*

[2] Arnold, *Rom. System of Prov. Admin.*, p. 22.

tium, Troas, Samosata, or Amisus, Tarsus, Caesaraea, Tripoli and Tyre in Phoenicia, Seleucia and Massilia, Utica, Hadrumetum, and five others in Africa. Titles of honour, such as *Urbs sacra* and *Metropolis* were lavished upon them.[1] According to the favour or displeasure of the emperor, privileges were conferred or withdrawn as the examples of Rhodes, Cyzicus, Laodicea, and Antioch prove.

There was in general another side to the good fortune of the cities; for they preserved their autonomy only at the pleasure of the emperor. This is already shown by the title *Libertas*, which according to circumstances was a *relicta* or *concessa*, an *adempta* or *redempta* or *restituta*.[2] In consequence of the decay of civic energy and of financial difficulties, the free cities were obliged to admit imperial officials, correctors and curators, who regulated their money matters and their constitution, and ventured to encroach upon their autonomy.[3]

The Roman colonies too, were privileged communities. As settlements of the veterans, they originally formed strong stations for the Roman power in the conquered countries of the barbarians. These colonies were composed of the inhabitants themselves, ancient cities being rebuilt, or new cities founded by command of the emperor. Augustus established a number of colonies in different countries.[4] His successors did the same, and the colonies, in consequence, bore their names.[5] Hadrian founded several new cities, and bestowed

---

[1] For the metropolis, see Eckhel, iv. 273 *sq.* Marquardt, *R. St.* i. 343 *sq.*

[2] Augustus already had deprived cities of their freedom : urbium quasdam, foederatas—libertate privavit.—Suetonius, *Aug.* c. 47.

[3] Pliny, *Ep.* viii. 24. A *curator reipub. Comensis* (Orelli, 3898) appointed by Hadrian; even a curator appointed by Hadrian of the public works in Venusia 4006, of the baths in Beneventum, 3264; imperial *curatores calendarii publici* (officers of finance), in the municipalities (Henzen, *Annali. d. Inst.* 1851, 15); appointed by Hadrian in Canusium (Mommsen, *I.R.N.*, n. 1486). In the Greek cities the imperial officers of inspection were called διορθωτής and λογιστής. Marquardt, *R. St.* i.², 85. Kuhn, *Städt. Verf.* ii. 24.

[4] Eckhel, iv. 467 *sq.*

[5] Julia, Augusta, Claudia, Flavia, Trajana, Ulpia, Aelia, Hadriana, etc., to which often the designation Felix was added. Spanheim, *De Praest. et Usu Num.* ix. 766 *sq.*

the colonial right upon many ancient cities.[1]   This right, which was often given to communities which contained no colony, secured them self-government, with a senate and communal officials (*Duumviri* and *Aediles*).   The community might choose these magistrates, and pass resolutions.   But as in Rome, under Tiberius, all elections were made by the senate, so in the colonies they devolved upon the city senate (*Curia*).   The curiales chose the magistrates from among themselves.[2]   Seats in the senate were hereditary, and were filled up by election.   The colonies generally possessed Italian rights and citizenship ; they differed therefore from the municipalities, whose life as a community was less restricted.

Gellius has explained the difference between the colony and the municipium, by showing that the municipium had its own laws, and was not compelled to adopt the Roman law, against its wish.[3]   Hadrian once delivered a speech to the senate, in which he set forth clearly these distinctions ; [4] the occasion being that the municipia of Italica and Utica wished to participate in the colonial rights.   Tiberius, on the other hand, had complied with the wish of the city Praeneste to be converted into a municipium from a colonia, in order that it might keep its native rights.   On the whole, the condition of the colonies in the time of the emperors was privileged and desirable, because, as Gellius says, they were imitations of the greatness of Rome, and with less freedom, they had fewer obligations.   But the real object of the demand of these two municipia was the acquisition of the Italian right, which was granted to the colonies.[5]   By this right the colonists could be quiritary owners of land (*commercium*).   They also gained freedom from land-tax, and the right of self-government with muni-

[1] I have pointed this out in the respective provinces. See in general, Zumpt, *Comm. Ep.* i., c. 6.

[2] Savigny, *Gesch. des röm., Rechts im Mittelalter*, i., c. 2. In Africa so he remarks, the elections were not made as in other cities, by the decuriones alone, but by the whole people.

[3] Gellius, *Noct. Att.* xvi., c. 13.

[4] Gellius, *Ibid.*

[5] Puchta, *Institut.* i.[8], § 95, p. 243.

cipal magistrates.   The colonies, like the municipia, paid a
tax according to the Roman census, but the inhabitants of
the municipia differed from those of the colonies, in that
they were not Roman citizens.   By degrees these two kinds
of communities became more alike.[1]

The Latin right, too, the *jus Latii*, was bestowed, not only
upon magistrates, but upon whole provincial cities, which
thus occupied an intermediate position between peregrini and
Roman citizens.   Hadrian bestowed Latin rights upon many
cities.[2]

[1] On the general conditions of municipia and colonies.—Arnold
p. 216 *sq.*

[2] Spart. c. 21 : Latium multis civitatibus dedit.

CHAPTER IV

Italy and Rome

ITALY stood at first in the same dependent relation to Rome, as the provinces themselves stood to Italy. Only after the most bloody wars were the Italian cities admitted into the league of Roman citizens by the *Lex Julia* and *Plautia Papiria* (in 90 B.C. and 89 B.C.). Augustus had endeavoured to remedy the decay of prosperity and the depopulation of the country by establishing twenty-eight colonies, and by dividing all Italy into eleven regions. The fundamental character of Italy was the free constitution of the cities.[1] The people and the senate were the political elements in her municipalities and colonies. The highest office, which, like that of consul, lasted for a year, was filled by a *Duumvir* or *Quatuorvir*. He presided over the civil and criminal courts, but the condemned man might appeal to the comitia ; and later, after Hadrian had altered the laws of the Italian cities, to the imperial officials. The emperor himself sometimes filled the office of city magistrate.[2] Thus Hadrian became demarch in Naples, quinquennalis in Hadria, dictator, aedile and duumvir in the cities of Latium, and praetor in Etruria.[3]

By degrees the monarchy absorbed the independence of the Italian communities, which Caesar had guaranteed by the *Lex Julia municipalis*, the emperor usurping the power

---

[1] Savigny, *R. Gerichtsverf.* ii. 16 *sq.*

[2] The Popes did the same thing in the Middle Ages, by allowing themselves to be elected as *podestas* in the cities of the Church states.

[3] Spart. c. 19.

over them.　Hadrian, indeed, changed the entire position of
the Italian cities, as he put this privileged mother-country of
Rome on the same footing with the provinces, for he divided
Italy into four districts, and committed the administration of
justice, of which the city magistrates were deprived, to four
consulars.　An exception was made for the district around
Rome, which remained as before under the jurisdiction of
the praetor urbanus.[1]　Marcus Aurelius increased these four
districts of Hadrian, replacing the consuls by juridici of
praetorian rank.[2]　By this means the jurisdiction of the
cities was curtailed, and ·became eventually, as in the provinces, subordinate to the governors, without any material
change being made in the traditional municipal constitution.
After the time of Nerva, imperial curators controlled the
municipal treasuries.[3]

Rome too suffered a similar fate, for already under
Augustus her great political life ceased.　Monarchy had been
substituted for popular rights; for though in appearance
power was divided between the senate and the princeps, in
reality it was centralized in the hands of a single sovereign.
The perpetual outpouring of the energy of Rome into the
world had exhausted the civic life of the capital, and the
influx from the provinces had renewed and changed its
population.　It was Roman because it inhabited the city,
but, as representing so many nations, languages and religions,
it formed one complete picture of the empire.　The majesty
of the city was reflected in all the other cities of the empire,
and the dead forms of the republican past were still the
patterns of the law which Rome gave to the world.　When
the emperor bestowed civic rights upon the cities in the
empire, they were always allotted to one of the tribes of
Rome.[4]　The tribes, so wrote Ammianus Marcellinus in the

[1] Spart. c. 22.　Jul. Capitolinus, *Anton. Pius*, c. 2.　Appian, *Hist. Rom.*,
i. 38.

[2] Jul. Capitolinus, *M. Antonin. phil.*, c. 11.　Orelli, 1178, 3143.　Gruter,
1090, 13.

[3] Kuhn, ii. 29, 217.

[4] The emperors had new citizens and cities endowed with the civitas
enrolled in the tribes to which they themselves belonged, *e.g.* the Flavian
emperors in the Quirina, Trajan in the Papiria, Hadrian in the Sergia.—
Kubitschek, *De romanar. tribuum orig. et propagat*, p. 78.

third century, have long been idle, the centuries have gone to sleep, and the election contests have ceased, but throughout the world Rome is looked upon as mistress and sovereign, and the name of the Roman people is honoured.[1]

The city of Rome, as the seat of the emperor, was still the centre of all the governing forces of the empire, the repository and the market for all the creations of culture. The number of its inhabitants reached its highest figure under Hadrian and the Antonines, but it can only be approximately stated at one and a half million.[2] If we deduct the peregrini and the slaves who composed more than a third part of the population, there remain the three classes of Roman citizens—populace, equites and senators. As the two latter ranks held both the offices of state and the land, and as the means of industry for the citizens had been diminished by slave labour, a large part of the city population sank into the ignominious condition of a state-aided proletariate. Caesar had reduced the number who received corn to 150,000, but it rose again still higher.[3]

Like every other emperor, Hadrian gratified the Roman populace with doles of bread and with games. He was certainly not so lavish of public amusements as Caligula and Domitian, or as Trajan in the intoxication of victory, but he now and then gave 100 and even 1000 wild beasts to be hunted. At the games he threw the usual presents to the people. In honour of Trajan he ordered as indeed was customary, that balm and saffron should flow down the steps of the theatre. To Matidia and Plotina he gave magnificent funeral rites. He liked spectacles of all kinds, and gladia-

---

[1] Amm. Marcell. xiv. 477.

[2] Friedlaender (i. 51) admits that the population of Rome, according to present data, can only be hypothetically determined.—Pietro Castiglioni (*Della popolazione di Roma, Monograf. della citta di Roma*, 1878, ii. 251) assumes that under Claudius there were about 950,000 free men, and about 350,000 slaves.

[3] Under Augustus 210,000, under Septimius Severus 160,000 citizens and 40,000 praetorians. The most important concern therefore of the city was its provisioning by the corn-fleets from Africa, Egypt, Sicily, Sardinia, and Gaul. The *praefectus annonae* was one of the most influential officials in the empire.—O. Hirschfeld, *Die Getreide Verwaltung in der röm. Kaiserzeit. (Philol.* xxix.).

torial combats.   He never banished a hunter or an actor from Rome, and where was there an important city to be found in which he did not establish festival games?   No emperor founded or renewed so many in the course of his life.   The Olympian games which he permitted cities in Greece and Asia to celebrate are a proof of this.   As these games were connected with the worship of his own personal divinity, they are at the same time the strongest witness to Hadrian's boundless vanity.   Such Olympian games were never celebrated in Rome.

Hadrian treated the Roman people in the same way as Trajan, and of him Fronto said : " I consider it good policy that the prince did not neglect the theatre or the circus and arena, as he well knew that there are two things which the Romans applaud especially—the distribution of corn, and games.   The neglect of the important thing causes great harm, of the frivolous thing greater hatred, the crowd hungering more for games than for bread, because by the gift to the people (congiarium) those only who are authorized to receive the corn will be gratified, while by the games the whole population is pacified."[1]   This opinion brings to mind the words spoken by a pantomime actor to Augustus : " Know, Caesar, that it is a very great thing for you if the people are occupied with me and with Bathyllus."   It has been shown how Hadrian sought to win over the army by unusual gifts, and the nation in general by the great remission of debts. He improved the charitable institutions of Nerva and Trajan for boys and girls, by ordering that the boys should be provided for until they were eighteen, the girls until they were fourteen years of age.[2]

The liberality which makes such a display on the imperial coins was only too often the disguised handmaid of despotism, and was always an evidence of the unequal distribu-

---

[1] Fronto, *Prim. Hist.*, p. 249, ed., Niebuhr.

[2] Digest. xxxiv. 1, 14.   The date of this decree is uncertain. A *praefectus aliment.* connected with the repair of the roads for the first time under Hadrian. *C.I.L.* ii. 4510 *sq.* These praefects rank as public magistrates, probably first under Commodus.—Hirschfeld, *Unters. auf dem Gebiet der röm. Verwalt.* i. 114 *sq.* For these institutions, see Henzen, *Tab. aliment. Baeb*, in *Annal. d. Inst.*, 1845.

tion of earthly things. She would have been the first to be
banished from Plato's republic.   If these remedies, however,
which the best of the Roman emperors employed to
mitigate public misery could not cure it, they at all events
displayed a feeling of humanity growing with the growth of
knowledge, and were an evidence that the sovereign felt it
a duty to attempt to diminish the sufferings of mankind.

CHAPTER V

*The Equestrian Order.   The Senate and the Princeps.
The Imperial Cabinet*

THE two privileged classes in Rome were the knights and
the senators, and they too had lost their importance in the
state.

The Roman equites had originally been a part of the
army, subsequently the lower aristocracy of Rome, the
middle class between the highest aristocracy and the people.
After the law passed by C. Sempronius Gracchus they
formed an order of rank (*ordo equester*), including persons
capable of filling the office of a judge, capitalists and
farmers of the public revenue.   The equestrian order sank
so low under the empire that it was only coveted for
its outward marks of distinction, and for the opportunity
it afforded of acquiring wealth.   Even in Caesar's time the
knights were subject to the indignity of appearing on the
stage either voluntarily or for money.   The Roman knight
Liberius, who was compelled to recite a play that he had
composed, complained, in the prologue, of the insult that
had been offered to him.[1]

Augustus had in vain attempted to purify the equestrian
order from base elements.   He wished to make it a school
in which the sons of the better classes could be educated to
become officers and to fill curule and imperial posts.   And

---

[1] Macrobius, *Saturnal.* ii., c. 7 :

> Necessitas, cujus cursus transversi impetum
> Voluerunt multi effugere pauci potuerunt,
> Quo me detraxit paene externis sensibus ? . . .

on this very account the equestrian order was over-crowded.

Entrance was obtained surreptitiously by bribery and favour; the legal qualification of 400,000 sesterces (about £3300) was not maintained. The revival of the law did not avail to uphold the knightly dignity. For the emperors themselves bestowed it upon freedmen according to their caprice, so that the sons of gladiators and panders wore the golden ring which was degraded into a token merely of successful cunning.[1] Knights appeared continually as actors and gladiators. In the time of Nero they composed the imperial claque as followers of Augustus.

The better emperors always reverted to the principles of Augustus, and endeavoured to uphold Rome's high position, though the spirit of monarchy itself aimed at the destruction of all corporate bodies in order to replace them by the different ranks of officials. The equestrian citizens endowed with the horse of state were again to be a privileged corporate body, from which the higher class of officials was to be chosen. Alexander Severus never permitted freedmen to be raised to the equestrian order, as it was to be the school for senators.[2] It was Hadrian who did away with the influential position of the freedmen at court, and opened a new career to the equites by choosing most of his officers from among them. He made knights, procurators of the fiscus and of the imperial estates, of the mint, of the imperial post, of the mines, of the aqueducts, and of the corn market. It was chiefly the knights whom he chose to be his "friends" and "attendants" or secretaries, and they also composed his privy council.[3]

The senate, oppressed by the monarchy, had fallen so low that the ambassadors of Pyrrhus would no longer have recognized in it an assembly of kings, but of king's servants. The

---

[1] Friedlaender, ii. 250.

[2] Ael. Lampridius, *Alex. Sev.*, c. 19: seminarium senatorum equestrem locum esse.

[3] Spart. c. 22.   O. Hirschfeld, *Untersuch.* i. 30 *sq.*, 114 *sq.*, 169.   The prefecture of the annona was, from Augustus to Constantine, one of the highest equestrian offices, and the next step was the prefecture of Egypt. —O. Hirschfeld, *Die Getreide Verwaltung*, p. 46.

most important of the ruling and lawgiving corporations in Rome continued to exist only as a political idea, even though the greatness of the Roman people was founded upon it. For the senate had the right to choose the sovereign; it confirmed the emperors as often as the army raised them to the throne; it acquiesced in their adoption, and granted them the highest titles of honour. It could legally depose them, or it could refuse them consecration after their death. The emperor was therefore legally only the chief of the senate, the first among his peers.

When Octavius laid down his extraordinary powers in 27 B.C., and received the title of Augustus, he acknowledged the continuance of the rights of the senate with whom he legally shared his power. He himself was only to be the highest official of the sovereign people, not their irresponsible ruler.[1] The tendency afterwards was to deprive the old corporation of the empire of its constitutional character and to develop absolute power. Augustus purified the senate; he fixed its number at 600 members, who were endowed with the necessary wealth (1,200,000 sesterces, about £10,000). The dignity of the senate seemed consequently to be restored; but, as its law-giving power was controlled by the executive, it had lost its independence.[2] The Caesars succeeded in doing away with the dualism of sovereign and senate by an incessant struggle which lasted for two hundred years. Tiberius increased the independence of the senate in order, through it, to dominate the people. He deprived the people of the right of making laws and of electing magistrates, and gave this right to the senate. The senate was the tribunal for high treason, and the highest civil court of appeal. It confirmed all appointments, dignities and laws, in short every administrative act; that is to say, the emperor made his own will law through the apparent wishes of the senate. Tiberius thoroughly despised its slavish spirit, and Tacitus has shown what a miserable instrument of tyranny it became.

Caligula gave the right of election and legislation to the comitia, but restored it to the senate as the people did not

[1] Mommsen, *R. Staatsr.* ii.[2], 709 *sq.*
[2] Gibbon, c. 2.

know how to use their newly-acquired power. After the
murder of this lunatic, the wild idea occurred to the senators
of restoring the republic, but the guard set Claudius on the
throne. The third and most formidable power in the state,
the army, now came to the front, threatening to convert
Rome into a lawless military despotism. To hinder this, and
to maintain an even balance between the three powers, was
henceforth the most arduous task for the Roman government,
and it was almost accomplished by the extraordinary system
of law and administration which the monarchy adopted.
From Claudius, however, to the Flavian dynasty the praetorian guard was of more importance than the senate, which
had sunk into a mere council of 200 members.

Vespasian, who had risen from the plebeian class, stood
in need of the support of the senate to enhance his
authority. The monarchical party in the senate reduced the
republican party to silence, and the famous *Lex de Imperio*
decided in favour of the principate, making over to it again
all the power, which, during the republic, the people and the
senate, and afterwards Augustus, Tiberius, and Claudius,
had possessed. No one ever ventured to attempt to limit
the absolute power of the prince in the smallest degree
by establishing the right of the nation. The *Lex Regia* was
a declaration by the Roman people of their incapacity ever to
be free again. Nevertheless it increased the importance of
the senate by an act of authority, which the Flavians acknowledged. Many centuries afterwards the last of the Roman
tribunes, Cola di Rienzi, could derive from this state decree,
which he misunderstood, the inalienable rights of the Roman
people. Vespasian increased the number of the senate to
1000 members, admitting men from every province, and
in future no province, except Egypt, was refused admission.
Moreover, after the reign of Domitian, the emperors simply
appointed the senators.

The best of the emperors always maintained the honour
and importance of the senate, because they recognized that
its dissolution would deprive the monarchy of its only constitutional foundation. At their accession they made an
agreement with the senate, as the Popes used to do later on
with the college of cardinals. They looked upon it as a

particular corporation of the state, in which, theoretically, the sovereignty over the people was vested ; but this corporation became itself the instrument of their own sole power.

We may remember with what respect Hadrian treated the senate. He excused himself for having assumed the purple without its knowledge, begged for its ratification, and admitted that he was only the instrument to execute the senate's orders, promising to hold them always sacred. He did nothing important afterwards without it.[1] He restored its dignity by making the entrance into the curia more difficult. He was anxious about the income suitable to the senators' rank, and in order to maintain their position he revived the law that no senator should be engaged in trade, or should farm taxes.[2] He would not permit senators to be tried by the equestrian order ; they must be tried by their equals. He admitted the most distinguished senators into the circle of his friends, and often bestowed the consular dignity upon them. For the consulate had already been reduced to the duration of two months, so that annually twelve and more consuls were appointed of inferior rank to the two consuls who gave their name to the year.[3] The senate repaid the emperor's favour by complete submission. This union of both powers is commemorated by coins ; on one medal Rome stands between a senator and Hadrian, reaching out her hand to the emperor.[4] *Libertas publica* indeed makes a show with sceptre and Phrygian cap on a coin of Hadrian, like the theatrical figure which she has so often been in the world.[5]

Thus the separation which Augustus had effected between the jurisdiction of the princeps and the senate was maintained, for the senate still filled the proconsular offices in its

---

[1] Spart. c. 8.

[2] Dion Cassius, lxix. 16.

[3] Under Commodus there were as many as 25 consuls in one year.— Dion Cassius, lxxii. 12.

[4] Cohen, ii. 172. A famous medal of Hadrian commemorates the congratulations of the senate at new year. HADRIANUS AUG . S . P . Q . R.— AN . F . F . HADRIANO AUG . P . P. Froehner, *Les Médaillons de l'Empire Romain*, p. 42.

[5] Cohen, ii. 316.

provinces, diminished though they were in number, while the command of the legions was generally given in turn to men of senatorial rank.   But as a balance of power had not been created by an imperial constitution, the sovereign remained unfettered.   Rome was, according to her own idea, republican even under the emperors, and the ruler invested with power by the senate was only her chief magistrate, though at the same time an absolute despot, whose imperium was not founded on the law of heredity, nor upon any legal basis, and who was therefore only a lawful sovereign by usurpation.[1]   He had absorbed in his own person all the republican powers of the people, and these were not conveyed to Octavius by a *Lex Regia*, but he had acquired them gradually with the help of his friends in the senate.

The proconsular power for life was the basis of the imperium, for it gave Augustus and his successors the supreme military command and the highest judicial authority over the governors in the provinces, while the tribunate gave to the sovereign the rights appertaining to the people, and the consular power which he held or not, as he pleased, raised him above all other magistrates.   The old republican priesthood of the Pontifex Maximus made the emperor also the head of the state religion.

Imperialism, with its greed for power, continually urged the Roman state towards Byzantinism.   The emperor monopolised the whole administration.   He had also the right of coinage, for the senate was only permitted to issue copper coinage.   Imperial taxes, the post, the roads and streets, the aqueducts, the public buildings, the alimentary institutions, the grain distribution, the care of the city of Rome, the games,—everything |depended upon the emperor alone.   He defrayed the expenses from the public revenues that were set apart for him, to which also the senatorial provinces contributed.   The fiscus swallowed up the aerarium of the senate and the people.[2]

The emperor did not legally possess the right of electing

---

[1] Puchta, *Institutionen*, i., § 86 *sq.*

[2] For Asia, the largest province of the senate, there was a *fiscus asiaticus* which was managed by imperial procurators.—Hirschfeld, *Untersuch,* i. 12.

magistrates; but the consuls and the officials for his own provinces he appointed himself. His influence, however, determined the senate's choice, and even in the third century, when the struggle with the senate was decided in favour of absolute monarchy, the emperor appointed to all posts. The official system was the most powerful instrument of despotism, as it was the means of keeping the city of Rome in subjection to the sovereign. Imperial officials displaced those of the senate and the people, and thus the artificial system of the court and its ministers became merged in the government.

The most important order of magistrates which the emperors created was that of the prefects of the city and the praetorium. Augustus had revived the old republican office of the *Praefectus urbi*, a city magistracy, which represented the consuls in their absence, and from which Tiberius had created the imperial police office of Rome. The city prefect, under whom were the *Cohortes urbanae* and the *Praefectus vigilum*, had both civil and military power, and from the time of Nero he tried all crimes that were not political.[1]

The power of the commander of the praetorian body-guard, which always garrisoned the city, became more formidable after the time of Tiberius. Under Augustus, two officers of the equestrian order commanded these guards with purely military authority. Tiberius united these two commands, and this made the prefect of the praetorium the first officer after the emperor, but the guard, mistress of the empire. After Tiberius there were again two prefects, of whom one certainly must have been of higher rank. Attianus and Sulpicius Similis, then Q. Marcius Turbo and C. Septicius Clarus are known as prefects of Hadrian. The power of this magistracy, which had both civil and criminal jurisdiction in Italy until the time of Constantine, first assumed great proportions after Alexander Severus.[2] Hadrian himself gave the prefect of the praetorium a prominent place in the council of state.

The first idea of a cabinet council, or of a college of consuls and senators, of " friends and attendants " of the

[1] Geib, *Geschichte des röm. Criminal Processes*, p. 439.
[2] Geib, *Gesch. des röm. Crim. Proc.* p. 417.

sovereign, who were to help him in his administration of justice, originated with Augustus.[1]   Hadrian seems to have converted this council of private persons into a council of state, placing in it paid members, and thorough lawyers, like Julius Celsus, Salvius Julianus, Neratius Priscus, and others.[2]

The senate generally confirmed the appointment of the members of the council, who, by degrees supplanted the senate, not only in the administration of justice, but in the government itself.   For the council of state took the place of the senate, so that even in the time of Ulpian, the senatorial jurisdiction had become a mere tradition.[3]   After the end of the second century the *Praefectus praetorio* seems to have presided in the council, the colonel of the guard became a lawyer, and men like Ulpian, Papinian, and Paulus, could be considered thorough ministers of justice.[4]

Hadrian also reorganized the private cabinet of the emperor.   Since the time of Augustus, there had been three great offices of the palace on which devolved the administration of the empire ; the office of the treasurer (*a rationibus*), the secretarial office (*ab epistolis*), and the bureau for petitions (*a libellis*).   These three departments were managed in the first century by freedmen of the emperor, who on that account had such a powerful influence, that they really ruled the empire.

The power of the *Procurator a rationibus* extended over the whole empire, as all the income of the fiscus was managed by him, and all disbursements were made by him.   The board of secretaries had to look after the enormous mass of the imperial correspondence.   To them came the despatches and the reports upon the condition of things in the empire, and by them were issued the wishes of the emperor.   From their office, questions of the courts and the communities were

---

[1] On the customary *amici* and *comites* of the imperial court, see Friedlaender, i. 117 *sq.* and 190 *sq.*, the catalogue of Hadrian's friends.

[2] Spart. c. 18, c. 22.   Dion Cassius, lxix. 7.

[3] Geib, *Gesch. des röm. Crim. Proc.* 417, 419.

[4] Niebuhr, *Röm. Gesch.* Jena, 1845, v. 320.   On the council Mommsen, *R. St.* ii. 923 *sq.*; Hirschfeld, *Unters.* i. 201 ; Friedlaender, i. 1176 ; Geib, *Gesch. des. röm. Crim. Proc.*

answered, and commissions to officers in the army, and imperial privileges were made out. The two languages of the world required the separation of this department into two offices, one for Latin, and the other for Greek letters. Before Hadrian's time these were united in one, and it was by him that the offices were separated. It was natural that in this secretarial department, and particularly in the Greek division of it, distinguished literary men, rhetoricians and sophists should be associated in the government. Suetonius was Hadrian's first Latin secretary, Avidius Heliodorus from Syria his first Greek secretary. Heliodorus was a philosopher and a man of culture, who later fell into disfavour, but who was made prefect of Egypt under Antoninus.[1]

The post of head of the department for petitions and complaints from private persons (*a libellis*), was less influential, and this was filled in the time of Hadrian by the knight Titus Haterius Nepos. The emperor's answers were made in short remarks on the paper itself, and they served as a precedent for similar cases after Hadrian's time.[2]

The emperor Hadrian generally filled the highest offices of the court with knights. Even though, after his time, the office of finance (*a rationibus*) was occasionally filled by freedmen, he had made it into an equestrian procuratorship.[3] While before his time freedmen occupied the most important imperial offices of the state, he made an end of this favouritism, taking the personal character away from these offices, and converting them into magistracies. Hadrian was the first to draw an official class from the equestrian order, and to furnish the career of procurators and prefects with its different grades, which gave to the whole government a bureaucratic stamp.

His reforms indicate an epoch in the development of

[1] Waddington, *Mém. sur Ael. Aristide* in *Mém. de l'Inst. T.* xxvi. 1867, p. 217. The son of Heliodorus was Avidius Cassius, who rebelled against Marcus Aurelius. L. Julius Vestinus was also a secretary of Hadrian. *C.I.G.* 5900; Friedlaender, i. 99 *sq.*, *Anh.* iii. 165. A fourth not mentioned by name, on an inscription from Ephesus, probably also Celer., *ibid.*

[2] Hirschfeld, i. 207.

[3] Hirschfeld, i. 201.

absolute monarchy.   It was indeed Hadrian who laid the foundation for the state of Diocletian and Constantine. Aurelius Victor could therefore say of him that he gave the offices of the state and of the court that form which, on the whole, they retained until the fourth century.[1]

[1] The beginning of Byzantinism in the public service is shown in the idea of Alex. Severus of establishing an official uniform.   In animo habuit omnibus officiis genus vestium proprium dare et omnibus dignitatibus, ut a vestitu dinoscerentur.—Lampridius, *Al. Sever.*, c. 27.

CHAPTER VI

Roman Law. The Edictum Perpetuum. The Responsa. Roman Jurists. The Resolutions of the Senate and the Imperial Constitutions. The Reforming Spirit of Hadrian's Legislation

THE reign of Hadrian forms an epoch in legislation, not only by its scientific treatment of law, but by the philosophic maxims which it established on its basis. Hadrian, in the first place rendered great service by the *Edictum perpetuum.*

The annual edicts of those magistrates, who, like praetors, aediles, and governors of provinces, had the right of legislation (*jus edicendi*), were publicly proclaimed as their programme of justice when they entered upon office. They were, after the laws made by the people and the senate, the sources of the Roman law which prevails throughout the world. Caesar had already thought of collecting these edicts, but Hadrian first carried out his idea, probably in 131 A.D., with the help of the jurist Salvius Julianus, the great-grandfather of the emperor Didius Julianus.[1]

As no complete copies of this book of Julianus, but

---

[1] Only Jerome (*Chron.*) gives the date, 131 A.D. Eutropius, viii. 9, Spartianus and Dion Cassius are silent. The *Const. Tanta* in the *Cod. Justin.* Lib. i. Tit. xvii., § 18, expressly ascribes the composition of the *Edictum perpetuum* to Salvius Julianus and Hadrian, and says it was confirmed by a decree of the senate, of which the Greek constit. Δέδωκεν has nothing. The paragraphs of the edict are collected by G. Haenel, *Corpus legum ab Imp. R. ante Justinian. editar.*—Rudorff, *De juris-dictione edictum ; edicti perpetui, quae reliqua sunt*, 1869. Otto Lenel, *das Edict. perpetuum, ein Versuch der Wiederherstellung*, 1883. In general, Rudorff, *Röm. Rechtsgesch.* i. 268 *sq.*

merely sentences in legal writings, such as the Digests, have been preserved, its character remains doubtful. So much is certain, that Hadrian's reform of the edict did not create a completely new law-book. The most recent student of this subject does not look upon the *Edictum perpetuum* as a systematic whole, like our civil law, nor as a codification of a special part of Roman law, but believes that its contents were merely determined by historical events.[1]

The edict of Hadrian became a law of the empire by a resolution of the senate, and so served as a standard for law. The magistrates, indeed, continued to issue edicts, but they were bound to follow the Julian law-book, which was used in all jurisdictions.[2] In this way Hadrian advanced on the path of that uniform administration of justice which finally made Roman law the law of the world.

Jurisprudence, the only science of the Romans, had long been a power in the state. The decisions of men learned in the law (*responsa prudentum*) formed an important source of law. Gaius says: "The replies of jurists are the decisions and opinions of men who are qualified to make theses of law. If they are unanimous then their decision becomes law, but if not, the judge may take his own view of a case, and be guided by a rescript of the divine Hadrian."[3]

The importance of the jurists was maintained, although the emperors, following the precedent set by Augustus, endeavoured to limit their independence by bestowing the *Jus respondendi* upon them as a distinction. Hadrian fully admitted the authority of the jurists.[4]

His age is distinguished by a number of great lawyers. Juventius Celsus, who wrote thirty-nine books of Digests; Neratius Priscus, who wrote seven books membranarum and Salvius Julianus, whose main work comprised ninety books of Digests. Rather younger was Sextus Pomponius, who wrote a compendium of the history of jurisprudence

---

[1] Lenel, p. 9 *sq.* From the expression *componere* (*edictum composuit*) a scientific revision by Julian has been inferred.

[2] Brinz, *Zur röm. Rechtsgesch. in Krit. Vierteljahreschr. für Gesetzgebung.* xi. 471.

[3] Gaius, i. § 7.

[4] Puchta, *Inst.*, i.[8], p. 324.

down to the time of Hadrian. Javolenus Priscus and Pactumeius Clemens were men of note. The latter had been prefect of the city and Hadrian's legate in Athens, in Syria, in Cilicia, and consul suffectus in 138 A.D.[1] Contemporary with them, and active under the Antonines, are Aburnus Valens, Vindius Verus, Volusius Maecianus, Ulpius Marcellus, and the famous Gaius. These and other men bequeathed their scientific material and legal theories to the great jurists of the following century.[2]

The other main sources of law were the resolutions of the senate and the imperial constitutions. After the people's legislation had become effete, the republican right of making laws passed to the senate. Its consulta took the place of the leges. The emperor's will, however, decided the vote of the senate, as he either made the consuls acquainted in writing with his wishes, or he had a speech (*oratio principis*) read to them. After the time of Augustus the decrees of the senate bore distinguishing names, which were taken from their authors, or from the consuls, or from the emperors.[3]

The edicts and responsa, the rescripts, the decrees and mandates of the emperors, then became a new source of law under the definition *Constitutiones principum*.[4] They must have had the more weight as the emperor had the right of making laws for life, while the enactments of the magistrates, who held an annual tenure of office were in force only for a year, unless they were adopted by their successors.[5]

---

[1] Renier, *Inscr. de l'Algerie*, 1812.

[2] Capitolinus, *Anton. Pius*, c. 12 ; Dig. i. 2. The five great jurists—Gaius in the age of the Antonines, Aemilius Papinianus under Septimius Severus, Julius Paulus, Domitius Ulpianus and Herennius Modestus—were declared legal authorities by the Const. of Valentian III., A.D. 426. —*Cod. Theod.* Lib. i. Tit. 4.

[3] *Plancianum, Silanianum, Claudianum, Neronianum, ex auctoritate D. Hadriani*, or *auctore D. Hadriano*, for the designation *Hadrianum* is not found. The resolutions of the senate under Hadrian are collected by Burchardi, *Staats. und Rechtsgesch. der Römer*, § 106. Most of the civil laws passed by the senate occur in the time between Claudius and Septinius Severus. Puchta, *Inst.* i.[8], 295.

[4] Gaius, i., § 3.

[5] *Epistolae* and *Sententiae* of Hadrian are recorded by Dositheus at the beginning of the third century—*Corp. juris romani Antejustiniani*, by

The list of the decrees of the senate and of the constitutions of Hadrian's time, which have been preserved to us, show the advance of mankind with regard to personal and civil law. The influence of Stoic philosophy made itself felt on the stern Roman society. More powerful at the time than Christianity, which was only then in its infancy, it did much to mitigate the condition of women and slaves, and to curb the limits of paternal power. A milder feeling arose in cosmopolitan Rome, where the idea of what we call the rights of humanity began to stir in the mind of the lawgiver. Although no one ventured yet to propose the abolition of slavery, it was possible to suggest measures for its mitigation.

Time had gradually reformed the severe old laws, by which the master had power of life and death over his slaves, so that for the least offence he might scourge and crucify them. By the *Lex Petronia* (61 A.D.), the master was forbidden to condemn his slaves to fight with wild beasts, and they were permitted to repair to the statue of the emperor and to the asylum for refuge. But even Augustus had confirmed the law of the republic, which enacted that in the event of the murder of a master by his slave, all the murderer's fellow-slaves were to be put to death.[1] Hadrian was the first to forbid torture being applied to the slaves of a house whose master had been murdered. Those only whose proximity to the scene laid them open to suspicion were exposed to this terrible ordeal.[2] He forbade the arbitrary killing of a slave by his master,[3] and the sale both of male and female slaves to schools of gladiators and to procurers.[4]

Boecking, 1831 ; Haenel, *Corp. Leg.*, p. 85 *sq.* Dositheus, however, gives only one letter of Hadrian to Plotina, and the *Sententiae* are personal sayings of the emperor in the form of anecdotes.

[1] Tacitus, *Ann.* xiv. 42 *sq.* In the reign of Nero four hundred slaves were put to death on one occasion in this way.

[2] Dig. 29, 5, 1 ; 48, 18, 1.

[3] Spart. c. 18 : Servos a dominis occidi vetuit, eosque jussit damnari per judices, si digni essent. Geib however (*Gesch. des röm. Criminal Processes*, p. 459), has proved that this order remained only a 'pium desiderium,' and even Antoninus only forbade the unnecessary death of a slave.

[4] Spart. c. 18.

A matron who ill-used her slaves he punished with exile for five years.[1]　He limited the arbitrary power of the master, but he respected his rights so much that on one occasion he refused to the people the freedom of a charioteer, because he was not entitled to grant it.　When he saw one of his own slaves walking between two senators, he punished him for his presumption.

Hadrian also abolished the ergastula, those terrible prisons in which the proprietors of estates immured their fettered slaves, and where illegally enslaved freemen seem to have shared their fate.[2]　He protected, too, the freedom of those who had been illegally sentenced to the mines (*in opus metalli*). This frightful sentence involved the loss of freedom, and lasted for life.　But if, owing to some oversight of the judge the sentence was only for a certain period, Hadrian enacted that the condemned man should retain his position as a freeman.[3] Hadrian endeavoured to protect the rights acquired by emancipation, against the state and against private selfishness.　He refused manumission whenever its object was to deceive relations or creditors,[4] but he protected trustees who were freedmen from attempts to upset a will ; and he indeed decreed that a slave who had received his freedom as a legacy that was proved afterwards to be invalid, might redeem it by a sum of money.[5] According to the *Senatus consultum Claudianum*, an appendix to the *Lex Julia de adulteriis*, it was enacted regarding the connection of free women with slaves that, if it happened without the master's knowledge, they were to be considered slaves, but free, if the master had been apprised of the union. If the woman remained free, her child was a slave.　Hadrian altered this law, so that the child became free too.[6]　The foundation for these resolutions of the senate was the *Lex Aelia Sentia*, passed in the year 4 A.D., which enacted that

---

[1] Dig. i. 6, 2.

[2] Spart. c. 18 : Ergastula servorum et liberorum tulit.　Gaius, i. 53.

[3] Dig. 48, 19, 28.　The annulling of the *status libertatis* was only compatible with capital punishment, or with a lifelong punishment.

[4] Gaius, i. 47.　See also Dosithei, Lib. iii.　Boecking, § 10.

[5] Dig. 24, § 21.　*Cod. Justin. 2 de fideicomm. libertat.* (vii. 4), in Champagny, *Les Antonins*, ii. 43.

[6] Tacitus, *Annal.* xii. c. 53.　Gaius, i. 84.

an insolvent person and a master under twenty years of age could not give slaves their liberty. This law decided that the freedman who had become a Latin, if he had married a Roman woman, or a Latin colonist, and had a son one year old, might become a citizen. In the reign of Tiberius, the *Lex Junia Norbana* was added, which bestowed Latin rights upon slaves who had been freed by the private declaration of the master (*Latini Juniani*).[1]

Trajan had already enacted that any one who had acquired Roman citizenship as a gift from the emperor, without the consent of his master, might enjoy it for life, but after his death he was to be considered a Latin, on the ground that the law of testaments was connected with the *Jus Quiritium*, and so the masters were often without an heir. But the *Latinus Junianus* did not possess the right to make a will. He only who had legally acquired citizenship, or had obtained the consent of his patron, who had married and had a child, was in full possession of the rights of a citizen. Hadrian found this law of Trajan unfair, for it took away from freedmen at their death what they had possessed in life; he caused the senate, therefore, to decree that such freedmen should be treated as if they had acquired Roman citizenship by the *Lex Aelia Sentia*, or by the senatus consultum.[2]

The endeavour to increase the number of free citizens is everywhere apparent in Hadrian's legislation. He ordained that the children of a Latin and a Roman should be considered native Roman citizens.[3] The absolute power of the father over the life and liberty of his children, as established by the law of the Twelve Tables, was curtailed. This right emanated from the Roman citizenship, and Hadrian established by an edict that only a Roman citizen was to have this paternal power.[4] He made it difficult for the peregrini to obtain it. If they and their children had acquired Roman citizenship, the children could only be in the *Potestas patria*, if they were minors and absent, and if the

---

[1] Heineccius, *Antiq. R. Jurisprud.* i. 4 ; 5, 14 ; Ulpian, *Fragm.* xix. 4. xx. 8 ; xxv. 7.

[2] Gaius, iii., § 73.

[3] Gaius, i., § 30, 81, 84 ; Ulpian, *Fragm.* i., § 15.

[4] Gaius, i., § 55 ; Ulpian, *Fragm.* v., § 1 (*Instit.* Lib. i., Tit. ix.).

case had been thoroughly proved.[1]   It was also ordained that if anyone received citizenship ·when his wife was pregnant, the child, although a Roman citizen, was not to come under the *Potestas patria.*

The emperor was often implored by sons to free them from this power.   Trajan had once compelled a father to release his son who could no longer endure his cruel treatment; and Hadrian punished a father with banishment who had killed his son when hunting, on account of his too great intimacy with his step-mother.   But he punished him only as a highwayman, and from this case we learn that the murderous abuse of the paternal power in the time of Hadrian could not be punished as homicide.[2]

The histories of law record Hadrian's reforms with regard to wills and inheritances.   Like Trajan he was upright and liberal.   Both emperors disdained to usurp inheritances, and to follow the example of Caligula, Nero, and Domitian, who used simply to cancel wills in which they had not been mentioned.   Trajan had already abolished these abuses by an edict, and Hadrian never accepted legacies at the expense of the children.[3]   He gave the twelfth part of the paternal property to the children of those who had been sentenced to have their property confiscated, a humane arrangement which was in accordance with the principle of the emperor to discourage actions for high treason.[4]   His maxim was to augment the empire by men, not the fiscus by gold.[5]

The inferior condition of women was improved by fresh legislation.   The law that no Roman woman could make a will was in force as late as Hadrian, and this power Hadrian was the first to grant to women, by a decree of the senate.[6]   He also gave them the right to inherit from their deceased children, if they possessed the *Jus trium liberorum.*[7]   When a poor woman begged him to allow her to have something from the pension of her son, who

[1] Gaius, i., § 93, 94.   [2] Dig. 48, 9, 8.   [3] Spart. c. 18.
[4] Spart. c. 18.   [5] Dig. 48, 20, 7.
[6] Gaius, i., § 115 : Hadrian also gave the right of making a will to the veterans (*dimissis militia*), Gaius, ii. 12.
[7] Ulpian, *Fragm.* xxvi. 8 : According to the *Lex Julia* and *Papia Poppaea*, the law of the three children bestowed many privileges.

behaved undutifully to her, and the son declared that he did not acknowledge her as his mother, Hadrian answered: "Neither do I recognize you as a Roman citizen."[1]   The feeling of increased respect for women is also shown in the order of Hadrian, prohibiting the common bath to men and women, which had been customary since the time of Domitian.[2]

Dositheus, a grammarian in the time of Septimius Severus, collected a number of Hadrian's sentences, and this proves that the wise judgments of the emperor remained as anecdotes in the memory of men.   On the whole, it may be said that the legislation of Hadrian shows a moral advance in the feeling of human society.

The reforms which the emperor effected in the whole administration must have been so far-reaching that his reign may be called an epoch in the empire.   This we should see more clearly if we possessed less fragmentary records of the time.

[1] *Dosithei Magistri Interpret.*, Lib. iii., ed. Boecking, § 14.

[2] Spart. c. 18.   Dion Cassius, lxix. 8.   Elagabalus again permitted the *Balnea mixta*, so that Alexander Severus was again obliged to forbid it   Lampridius, *Alex. Sever.* c. 24.

CHAPTER VII

Science and the Learned Professions. Latin and Greek Literature. The Schools. Athens. Smyrna. Alexandria. Rome

THE imperial court from the time of Augustus had great influence upon letters in the empire. To be well-versed in the culture of the time, and as a patron to promote it, was an imperative duty for every Roman sovereign. No other monarchy in the world placed such a high value upon knowledge as did that of Rome, and no other imperial throne can show so long a line of cultured princes. But the atmosphere of a court hindered the steady development of learning. Censorship was practised even in the time of Augustus and Tiberius and the Flavian emperors banished philosophers from Rome as enemies of the monarchy. The despotism of the first century of the empire made literature barren until Nerva restored freedom of thought.

With Trajan, royal patronage again flourished, and the dependence of the learned professions upon the court was revived. Hadrian especially encouraged it. He himself, as a man of intellect, had mastered the whole province both of light and serious literature, as well as of art. Spartianus says of him : " He was intimately acquainted with Epictetus and Heliodorus among the philosophers, and without naming them individually, he surrounded himself with grammarians, rhetoricians, musicians, geometricians, painters and astrologers. Even scholars, who seemed useless in their own department, he was in the habit of dismissing with presents and honours."[1]

[1] Spart. c. 16.

This tendency lasted into the time of the Antonines.   Verus is an example of how princes were then brought up ; he was taught by the grammarian Scaurus, whose father had been the teacher of Hadrian, by the rhetoricians Apollonius, Celer, Caninius, Herodes Atticus, and by the philosophers Apollonius and Sextus.   In his Greek studies he had Telephus, Hephaestion, and Harpocrates for tutors.[1] Teachers and royal pupils were on intimate terms, an advantage to the schools.   This is shown by the correspondence of Fronto with the Antonines, and by the way in which Marcus Aurelius speaks of his numerous teachers.

Hadrian certainly often made the learned men of his court the butt of his humour, which alternated between urbanity and tyranny ; but he was throughout the patron of learning.   If pure learning no longer flourished it was not his fault.   His own taste was the product of the time, and intellectual currents cannot be stemmed by the most powerful sovereigns.   Literature, which never before had enjoyed so large a field as was at that time offered by the Roman empire, would have made great advances from the complete liberty of thought and teaching after the time of Nerva, if its creative power had not been already extinguished.   Rhetoric and grammar were in vogue in the second century, which produced neither classic poets nor great prose writers. Encyclopaedic knowledge was the characteristic of a time in which the Romans felt themselves masters of the world.   In the arts it brought a renaissance of style and form without ideas, and in literature it only shows a philological return to antiquity without any force of intellect.[2]   This tendency to archaism had long been perceptible, and had originated more probably from errors of taste, than as Niebuhr thinks, from the necessity of enriching the impoverished Latin language with words from the treasure-house of the oldest authors.[3]   Augustus had inveighed against philological anti-

---

[1] Capitolinus, *Verus Imp.*, c. 2.

[2] In relation to literature this is clearly shown by Martin Hertz, *Renaissance und Rococo in der röm. Lit.*, Berlin, 1865.   See also G. Bernhardy, *Grundr. der griech. Lit.*[5], p. 323 *sq.*

[3] Niebuhr (*Vortraege über röm. Gesch.*, iii. 231) thought too that the *Lingua rustica* arose at this time.   It is hardly fair to form an opinion

quarianism, for which he blamed Tiberius.[1]   The delight of
Hadrian and of the Antonines in obscure and archaic forms
of speech, appears chiefly to have been a rococo fashion of
the empire.   Spartianus says that Hadrian preferred Cato to
Virgil, and Coelius Antipater, a contemporary of the Gracchi,
to Sallust.   And he is said to have undervalued Plato, and
to have placed Antimachus, the precursor of the Alexandrian
art of poetry in the time of the Peloponnesian war, above
Homer.[2]

While the interest in Roman literature decayed, Greek
literature made a fresh start, and the Hellenes, not the Latins,
constituted the best talent of the age.   The brilliancy
of a fresh and increasing literature, full of the glittering
pomp of declamation, which originated in the schools of
the sophists at Smyrna, threw the Latin tongue into the
shade.[3]   But Latin had certainly conquered the West and
Africa, with astonishing rapidity, and, as the language
of law and government, it maintained in the East also the
prerogative of the ruling nation.[4]   It had to yield, however,
in literature, and even in aristocratic society, to the ascend-
ancy of Hellenism.   Greek, as the language of culture, stood
in the same relation to Latin as, in the time of Frederick the
Great, French stood to German ; and this relation between
the tongues was older than the empire.   Cato had already
blamed Albinus for writing a Roman history in Greek.
Lucullus, too, wrote the Marsic war in Greek, and Cicero the
history of his consulate.   Claudius composed histories of
Tyre and Carthage in Greek, and Titus wrote Greek
tragedies.   The sophist Aelianus, from Praeneste, a contemporary as it appears of Hadrian, wrote his works,

upon the language as a whole from barbarous Latin inscriptions.   Upon
the reaction against the modern literature of that time see Friedlaender,
iii. 335 *sq.*

[1] Suetonius, *Aug.* c. 86.

[2] Spart. c. 16; Dion Cassius, lxix. 4.

[3] Nicolai, *Griech. Literatur Geschichte*, ii. 425 *sq.*

[4] In the West there were more Latin than Greek schools.   In Philostratus
(*Vita. Soph.*, vol. ii. 9) Favorinus thinks it curious that he, a Gaul, should
speak Greek.   The Greek language, which had prevailed earlier in
Marseilles and Lyons, had been driven out.   Lucian had taught as a
rhetorician for a year in Gaul.

Stories of all Kinds and *Upon Animals* in Greek, and was considered a complete Philhellene.[1] The philosopher Favorinus, a Gaul, was also an enthusiastic student of Hellenic literature ; and Gellius preferred the Greek to the Latin language. Lucretius had already complained of the poverty of his mother tongue, an opinion which was confirmed by the younger Pliny in a letter to Arrius Antoninus, a perfect Philhellene and uncle to Antoninus Pius.[2] Hadrian himself preferred to write in Greek, and so did Marcus Aurelius and the orator Fronto. Suetonius and Apuleius wrote in both languages. The age of Hadrian, though it produced no striking genius among the Greeks, certainly diffused a refined Hellenic culture through the whole empire.

In all important cities, schools of one or of both the languages of civilization flourished. While Rome was the cosmopolitan centre of the arts and sciences, Smyrna, Alexandria, and Athens shone as the chief seats of Hellenism. After the time of Hadrian, Athens again became a much frequented university of philosophy and rhetoric. Its lecture rooms and libraries, which the emperor had greatly increased, attracted famous teachers and numerous students from all provinces.[3]

From Athens the sophists flocked into the Roman countries to acquire honours and wealth. In Athens the first public teacher was the celebrated Lollianus of Ephesus. The sophist Hadrian, who filled the professorial chair, first there and afterwards in Rome, received his living from Marcus Aurelius at the expense of the state, precedence on the occasion of festivals, exemption from taxes, the rank of a priest, and other honours.[4] Theodotus was the first teacher of the Athenian youth who received a salary from the emperor of 10,000 drachmas.[5]

Smyrna, the chief school of the Ionian sophists, shone

[1] Philostratus, *Vita Soph.*, vol. ii. 123.

[2] Pliny, *Ep.* iv. 3 and 18.

[3] Gellius, i. 2 : Ad capiendum ingenii cultum. On the library of Athens : Aristides, *Panathenaikos*, i. 306 (ed. Dindorf): βιβλίων ταμεῖα οἷα οὐχ᾽ ἑτέρωθι γῆς φανερῶς.

[4] Philostratus, *Vita Soph.*, vol. ii. 10.

[5] Philostratus, *Vita*, vol. ii. 73.

even more brilliantly than Athens.   The whole of Ionia, says Philostratus, in the life of Scopelianus, is a college of the most learned men, but Smyrna holds the first place among the cities, and gives the tone, like the zither, to other instruments.[1]   There Polemon taught and attracted innumerable pupils.   Other cities, too, such as Tarsus, Antioch, Berytus, and Carthage had famous schools, but their prosperity diminishes after the time of Hadrian.

Alexandria, the mother of Greek learning, outshone all other cities.   The youth of many countries assembled in her famous gymnasia, and in those libraries which Zenodotus, Callimachus, Eratosthenes, and Aristarchus had arranged.   Of these libraries the one in Alexandria which was connected with the Museum in Bruchium, the magnificent foundation of Ptolemy Philadelphus, had been destroyed by fire, at the time when Caesar annihilated the Egyptian fleet in the harbour.   Cleopatra had then replaced it by the library of Pergamum, which had been given to her by Antony. There was a second smaller library in the Serapeum.[2]

The Alexandrian school diffused a splendour over the civilized world which lasted longer than that shed by any university afterwards, whether of Paris, Bologna, or Padua. Long after the creative power of Greek genius was exhausted, encyclopaedic knowledge and Greek sophistry were to be found in the library and the Museum of Alexandria.   In this foundation of the first Lagidae, Ptolemy Philadelphus and Euergetes, all the methods of the philosophic as well as of the exact sciences were fostered for centuries.   The importance of the school of Alexandria lasted, though not uninterruptedly, as long as Alexandria itself.   There the treasures of classical literature were collected and arranged, the manuscripts improved, and the texts explained.   The Museum, indeed, whose splendid marble halls were close to the temple of the muses, within the circumference of the old royal citadel, was not merely an academy, but a place for the assembly of learned men,

---

[1] Philostratus, *Vita Soph.*, vol. ii. 29.

[2] Ptolemy Philadelphus seems to have founded both libraries. Fr. Ritschl, *Die Alexandrin. Bibliotheken unter den ersten Ptolomäern*, 1834, p. 14 *sq.*

many of whom received food and salary at the expense of the state. The high-priest of Egypt, who was at the head of this academical establishment was chosen by the kings before the Roman sovereignty, and was afterwards appointed by the emperors.[1] To the old Museum the learned Claudius added a new foundation—the Claudium ; but the professors degenerated into the hirelings of imperial vanity.

Hadrian confirmed the privileges of this honourable institution. As the greatest distinction of a learned man or a poet was to be a member of it, and as nomination depended upon the favour of the emperor, many abuses might easily prevail. But Hadrian was not the first emperor who gave the places in the Museum as sinecures to strangers not in residence, like the sophist Polemon of Smyrna, and Dionysius of Miletus.[2] He even made a mediocre poet, Pancrates, a member of the academy. He seems to have been a native ; but the national feeling of the Egyptians must have been deeply wounded when Hadrian appointed president of the Museum, and consequently high-priest of Egypt, a Roman named Julius Vestinus, who had been his secretary and director of the libraries in Rome.[3]

An historian of the Alexandrian school has erroneously ascribed the decay of the Museum to the too frequent abuse of Hadrian's favour in the appointment to its posts. The care, however, which the same emperor bestowed upon the schools in Rome and Athens, as well as in other cities, could scarcely diminish the importance of an institution that was already growing old.[4] For, even in the time of the Flavian

[1] Strabo, xvii. 794.

[2] Philostr., *Vit. Soph.*, vol. ii. 37. The expression for it is Ἀιγυπτία σίτησις or τράπεζα Αἰγυπτία.

[3] All his offices are enumerated in the inscription, *C.I.G.* iii. 5900 : Ἀρχιερεῖ Ἀλεξανδρείας καὶ Αἰγύπτου πάσης ... καὶ ἐπιστάτῃ μουσείου καὶ ἐπὶ τῶν ἐν Ῥώμῃ βιβλιοθήκων καὶ ἐπὶ παιδείας Ἀδριανοῦ. ... This is not cumulative but successive, and indeed in inverted order. See Friedlaender, i. 165. Matter. (i. 279) calls Vestinus the only president of the Museum whose name has been handed down to us.

[4] Matter, *Hist. de l'école d'Alexandrie*, 2nd ed., Paris, 1840, i. 265 *sq* The prize essays upon the Alexandrian Museum of Parthey and Klippel. 1838, may be compared, and the literature on the subject in Bernhardy, *Grundriss der griech. Lit.*, i. 539 *sq.*

emperors, the Museum must have fallen greatly into decay, for otherwise Dion Chrysostom could not have said that it was a school only in name.[1]   The learned society existed until the time of Caracalla, the terrible destroyer of Alexandria, who broke it up.   It was indeed restored, but could not regain its importance.   The famous library was destroyed, with the magnificent Serapeum, in 389 A.D. by the fanaticism of the Christians.

With regard to Rome, this city of the world was then the universal market for learned men, and the emporium of the already vast world of books.   The Roman libraries began to increase from the time of Lucullus, the founder of the first public library.   Henceforth Rome could vie in this respect with Athens and Alexandria.   Sulla brought the library of Apellicon, which he had stolen, from Athens to Rome. Augustus founded great libraries in the temple of Apollo Palatinus, and in the hall of Octavia.   Tiberius formed one in the capitol, Vespasian another in the temple of peace, and even Domitian enriched the libraries of Rome by copies which he had made in Alexandria.   Finally, Trajan founded the Ulpian library ; Hadrian formed a library at his villa at Tibur for his private use, and in Antium he possessed another ;[2] a third was connected with his famous academy, the Athenaeum.

Rome, in addition to every other advantage, could offer the richest treasures in books to learned men.   A golden age began for them under the Flavian emperors, with the single exception of the philosophers, whom Vespasian, and after him Domitian, indignant with the free thinking of the Cynics, had banished.   They returned in great numbers. Rhetoricians, philosophers and pedagogues flocked like a migration of nations into Rome, to seek their fortune.   The Athenian Demonax compared the philosopher Apollonius to an Argonaut going in search of the golden fleece,

---

[1] *Orat.* xxxii. *ad Alexandrinos*, p. 434 (ed. Dindorf).

[2] Philostratus, *Vit. Apollon.*, viii. 19.   Gellius, ix. 14, 3, xix. 5, 4, Graefenhan, *Gesch. der class. Philol.*, iv. 44, and Jahn, *Annal. Philol.*, ii. 360.   *C.I.G.* 5900, mentions L. Julius Vestinus as director of the library of Rome under Hadrian.   In Friedlaender, i. 165, an unnamed librarian of Hadrian, from a mutilated inscription at Ephesus ; also in Flemmer, p. 49.

when he sailed from Athens to Rome accompanied by his pupils.[1]

Vespasian laid the foundation for a Roman school, in which he established chairs for Greek and Latin rhetoricians, whose salary he paid from the fiscus.[2]   Hadrian enlarged this academy, and called it the *Athenaeum*.   He destined it, as the name leads us to conjecture, to the especial cultivation of Greek, though not to the exclusion of Roman literature.[3]   The chair of oratory was called a throne as in Athens.[4]   The Athenaeum contained such spacious meeting halls, that later on the senate could sometimes hold its sittings there.   Rhetoricians and philosophers discoursed in it, and poets contended for prizes.   This foundation of Hadrian was still existing in the time of Symmachus ; it can therefore be looked upon as the Roman university after the second century.[5]

The numerous schools of learning in the empire, which the emperor, the municipalities, and even private persons erected and promoted, show a high average of general culture, and a large class of learned men.   The ranks of this class became fuller, as after the regulations of Vespasian and Hadrian, rhetoricians, philosophers, philologists, and even physicians were exempt from the city burdens and offices.[6] How important the study of books had become may be per-

---

[1] Lucian, *Demonax*, c. 31 : Προσέρχεται ὁ ᾽Απολλώνιος καὶ οἱ ᾽Αργοναῦται αὐτοῦ.

[2] Suetonius, *Vesp.*, c. 18.

[3] Lampridius (*Alex. Sev.*, c. 35) says of this emperor: ad Athenaeum audiendorum et Graecorum et Latinorum rhetorum vel poetarum causa frequenter processit.

[4] Philostr. *Vit. Soph.*, ii. 93 : ὁ ἄνω θρόνος.   In the time of Marcus Aurelius the sophist Hadrian occupied it.

[5] Zumpt (*Bestand der philos. Schulen in Athen*, p. 44) believes that the Athenaeum was consecrated as a temple of Minerva.   Aurelius Victor, c. 14, calls it 'Ludus ingenuarum artium.'   Jul. Capitolinus, *Pertinax*, c. 11 ; Ael. Lampridius, *Alex. Sever.*, c. 35.   Kuhn, *Städt. Verfass.*, i. 95. Grasberger, *Erzieh. und Unterr. im class. Alterthum*, iii. 442.

[6] From gymnasiarchia and agoranomia, from the offices of priest, ambassador and judge, from military service and billeting, etc.   Kuhn, i. 104, according to Kriegel, *Antiqua Versio lat. fragmentor. e Modestini libro de excusationib.*, p. 44 ; also *Cod. Theod.*, xiii. 3.

ceived from Gellius, who composed his *Attic Nights* about
150 A.D.   He is a good example of the learning of his time,
and his work, precious from its antiquities and explanations,
is full of the greatest trivialities.   How he came by all the
material, he relates himself; he buys old books where he can
get hold of them, and makes extracts from them.[1]

Men of learning roamed about the streets like the mendi-
cant friars of the Middle Ages.   Reciters and orators were
to be heard in public places, and teachers sat in front of the
book-shops, where they offered, like mountebanks, to explain
this or that manuscript; for authority and antiquity were
everything in these degenerate days.   Passages from the
poets, or facts from ancient history, were explained with
elaborate phrases; an unusual word or an obscure term was
sought out, to make a display of the extent of historical and
philological knowledge.[2]   The ease with which such knowledge could be obtained stirred crowds of moderate intellects
anxious to make money by their learning.   But it was not
given to every one to be a Herodes Atticus or a Favorinus,
who could derive real advantage from the privileges of
literary men.   Not everyone could choose knowledge instead
of a trade or an art for his life's calling like Lucian, to whom,
in his youthful dream, the goddess appeared showing in a
dazzling light the wealth, the honour, the rank, and the fame
which awaited her followers in the world.[3]

[1] Gellius, ix. 4.
[2] The grammarian Domitius called such word-grubbing philosophers:
mortuaria glossaria, namque colligitis lexidia, res tetras et inanes, et
frivolas.—Gellius, xviii. 7 ; xiii. 30 ; xvi. 6 ; xviii. 4.
[3] Lucian, *Enhypnion*, c. 11.

CHAPTER VIII

Plutarch. Arrian. The Tactica. Philo of Byblus. Appian. Phlegon. Hadrian's Memoirs

AMONG the authors of the time one figure shines with the gentle light of humanity. This figure is Plutarch, the most versatile mind, and, with Favorinus, the most admired author of his epoch. Even to-day one of his writings is an ornament to literature.

Plutarch was born about 50 A.D., in that Chaeronea where, at the battle of Philippi, the freedom of Greece had found its grave. He studied in Athens under Ammonius, and then lived in easy circumstances in his native city. From there he travelled into Hellas and Egypt. He visited Rome too in the time of Vespasian. Here he gave lectures, and became friendly with the most prominent men, like C. Sosius Senecio, to whom he afterwards dedicated several of his *Parallel Lives*.[1] He acquired the Latin tongue, if only imperfectly.

Returning to Chaeronea, he remained there until his death, devoting his life to the muses as well as to the public service of his native place. No other personality in an age that was so full of contradictions, offers so beautiful an example of harmonious work and modest happiness. Plutarch, a philosopher of the ancient type, is the antithesis to Hadrian. The people of Chaeronea conferred upon him the office of priest. He was also priest of Apollo at Delphi, and Agonothetes at the Pythian games. Trajan bestowed upon

---

[1] R. Volkmann, *Leben und Schriften des Plutarch*, 1869, i. 36 *sq.* After 82 A.D. he came for the second time to Rome.

him consular honours, and in his old age, Hadrian is said to have made him procurator of Greece. Rome and Hellas, the two parts of the civilized world, honoured him. He died at Chaeronea about 120 A.D., aged seventy years.

The numerous writings of Plutarch, of which a large part has been lost, were circulated through the civilized world. Those that have been preserved are divided into two groups, the twenty-three biographies (βίοι παράλληλοι), and the moral writings (ἠθικά)—eighty-three writings in all.[1] They are not works of a genius which strikes out new paths in the world of thought, but they are the productions of reflection and experience based on a foundation of extraordinary learning. Rhetorical, grammatical, and antiquarian studies, together with ethics, form the leading characteristics of Plutarch's writings. To soften paganism by a gentler philosophy of life, which approached Christianity, is the great speciality of Plutarch, and he idealized both ancient religion and ancient history.[2]

In his essays he ably discusses the most diverse subjects, after the manner of the sophists. He inquires into scientific and even practical questions, and draws up rules of conduct, such as are contained in the manual of Epictetus and in the reflections of Marcus Aurelius. There are essays upon virtue and vice, upon equanimity, upon the love of parents, talkativeness, the love of money, upon envy and hatred, upon the education of children, upon the rules of conjugal life, the laws of health, fate, upon consulting oracles, upon the entertainment of the seven sages, the heroic deeds of women, the sayings of famous kings and generals, upon love stories, political doctrines, platonic researches as to the genius of Socrates, the origin of the mundane soul in Timaeus, the contradiction of the Stoics, writings against the Epicureans, physical investigations, upon the principle of cold, upon the envy of Herodotus, upon Isis and Osiris, etc. Plutarch followed no definite method of teaching, he was an Eclectic like Cicero.

---

[1] Volkmann, p. 99 *sq.* The catalogue, which is said to have been made by Plutarch's son Lamprias, contains 210 items.—*Plut. perditor. scriptor. fragmenta*, ed. Fr. Duebner, Paris, 1855.

[2] Thiersch, *Politik und Philosophie in ihrem Verhaeltniss zur Religion*, p. 15.

All these essays are of no value at the present time
except to the student of the history of culture, but the
collection of incomparable biographies of great Romans and
Greeks is still in the hands of educated people as a book of
universal interest.   Plutarch owes his immortality to it alone.
By it, he created a style in literature.   When he came from
Chaeronea to Rome, the capital of the empire made a profound impression upon him.   As he gazed at the monuments
of world-wide fame, he was overwhelmed by the thought of
the formidable power which could create so imposing a city.
Rome, on her part, recognized this deeply religious man as
an instrument of divine providence.   He freed himself there
from the prejudices of Greek vanity, which had made him
hitherto ascribe the greatness of the Romans, unlike that of
Alexander, to good fortune only, and not to their own
courage and sagacity.

The Greeks, moreover, since the time of Polybius had been
obliged to submit to the power of the Romans, by whom
their country had been subdued and ruined.   They lived
hereafter as descendants of the noblest race of humanity under
their rulers, to whom they had to pay allegiance even while
conscious of their own intellectual superiority.   This superiority was admitted by imperial Rome, who admired the ideals
of Greece and bowed humbly before them.   All the statesmen,
generals, and emperors of Rome acknowledged the aristocracy of the Hellenic intellect, from Flaminius, the Scipios,
and Cicero, to the Philhellenes, Hadrian and Marcus Aurelius.

It was a happy thought of Plutarch to give an historical
account of the parallel lives of the ancient civilized world,
and to reconcile them to one another.   In a list of biographies written in simple narrative he has contrasted the
national characters of Rome and Greece, and has created a
book of heroes from which earnest men in all ages have
drawn both instruction and inspiration.

Next to Plutarch, and of equal dignity, stands another
ancient Greek, Flavius Arrian, from Nicomedia in Bithynia,
one of the most striking personalities of his time.   He was
still living in the time of Marcus Aurelius, but his best work
belongs to the reign of Hadrian, for whom he wrote the
Periplus of the Black Sea.   He was one of those few Greeks

who filled high positions in the Roman state. He was a citizen of Rome and of Athens, then senator, consul between 121 A.D. and 124 A.D., and then governor of Cappadocia in the last years of Hadrian's reign. He was alike capable as statesman and general, as historian and philosopher.[1] Arrian might thus almost be looked upon as a new Xenophon.[2] He took this ancient Greek as a pattern for style and construction, and, like Xenophon, he wrote a book upon the chase.[3] His writings show that he was a practical man, without the glitter of sophistry, but without its grace.

In his youth he had been much engrossed by the philosophy of the Stoics, the best education for noble manhood. He was the most distinguished among the pupils of Epictetus. We only know the maxims of this sage through Arrian, for he collected them in the *Enchiridion*, and in the eight books of the discourses of Epictetus. Unfortunately his conversations of Epictetus, in twelve books, and his biography of him are lost.[4]

History owes important writings to Arrian, especially the work upon Alexander the Great, the hero of the Greek spirit, which he enriched by embodying the consciousness of Hellenic greatness. The Parthian wars of Trajan had revived the memory of Alexander. Arrian wrote seven books upon the expeditions of Alexander, and, as an eighth, the *Indica*. He made use of writings from the time of Alexander, so that his work is an important historical authority ; and he is the first of all the historians of Alexander who have come down to us.[5] His ten books upon the time of the Diadochi, and unfortunately his seventeen books also upon Trajan's Parthian war, are lost, and so are his eight books of Bithynian history from the earliest times to the last Nicomedes, who bequeathed his empire to the Romans.[6] Arrian's history of

---

[1] Arrian is still in office in 136-137 A.D.—Inscriptions from Sebastopolis in *Rev. Archéol. N.S.*, xxxiii., 1876, p. 199 ; in Duerr, *Anh.* 58.

[2] Photius, *Bibl.* 53.

[3] *Scripta minora*, ed. Hercher, 1854.

[4] Zeller, iii. 1, 661. Only four books of the dissertations (διατριβαί) have been preserved, and fragments in Stobaeus.

[5] Schoell, *Geschichte der griech. Liter.*, ii. 422.

[6] Photius says of it (*Bibl.*, 234) : τῇ πατρίδι δῶρον ἀναφέρων τὰ πάτρια.

Dion of Syracuse, and of Timoleon, and of the Alani have also disappeared.   To this last work was appended *The Expedition against the Alani* which has been preserved.   In his *Art of Tactics* he has described the different kinds of troops, their exercises, marches and commands for the use of civilians.

Military writings were suitable to the spirit of the age. Hadrian himself, though erroneously, has been credited with the authorship of a scientific military treatise under the title *Epitedeuma*; but his great passion for the army called forth works of this kind.[1]   The *Tactical Theory* of Aelian, who lived in Rome in the first half of the second century, scarcely belongs to them.[2]   But the famous work of Apollodorus upon siege tactics was expressly composed for Hadrian.[3]

The Greek authors who have treated of the history of the world, or of the history of Rome, and of separate countries, are numerous.   The loss of their works is vexatious enough. Suidas mentions Cephalion, who wrote a sketch of the history of the world from Ninus to Alexander, in the Ionic tongue; Jason of Argos, who wrote a work upon Greece; the Alexandrian Leander Nicanor, and Diogenes of Heraclea, who were both geographers.   Herennius Philo, a Phoenician from Byblus, wrote thirty books upon states and their great men.   He translated the *Sanchuniathon* into Greek in nine books, of which fragments are preserved in Eusebius, which however may be a forgery of this supposed Phoenician historical work by Philo.[4]   Crito, from the Macedonian Pieria, a

---

[1] R. Foerster, *Studien zu den griech. Taktikern* (*Hermes*, xii. 1877 p. 449 *sq.*), points out that the opinion that the writing of Hadrian was published by Urbicius and thus attributed to him is erroneous.   See Schoell, *Gesch. der griech. Lit.* ii. 75.

[2] H. Koechly und W. Ruestow, *Aelian's Theorie der Taktik*.   The view of Koechly that the τέχνη τακτική of Arrian belongs to Aelian, and that the work hitherto ascribed to the latter is a later edition of the same work, is disposed of by Foerster.

[3] Πολιορκητικά, *Veter. Mathemat.*, Paris, 1693.   *Poliorcétique des Grecs*, ed. Woescher, Paris, 1867, p. 137 *sq.*, with illustrations of the engines. In the preface to the work Apollodorus says that he was induced to write it by a production of Hadrian's.

[4] Euseb. *Praep.* i., c. 9.

travelling companion of Hadrian, wrote works on the history of Syracuse, of Macedonia, and of Persia, and upon the Dacian war of Trajan.

A happy accident has preserved a large part of the historical books of Appian the Alexandrian, who wrote his *Romaica* in the time of Antoninus Pius.   He treated the history of Rome until the time of Augustus, ethnographically, in twenty-four books, and he gave an account of the destinies of the separate countries until they became Roman provinces. We still possess the histories of the Punic, Syrian, Mithridatic, Spanish and Illyrian wars, and the five books of the Roman civil wars.   The dry, but useful work is confirmed by Polybius, and Appian shares the view with him as well as with Plutarch, that Rome's empire over the world was a divine dispensation.

Phlegon of Tralles, a freedman of Hadrian's, made himself famous by a chronological work.   It was a chronicle arranged according to the Olympiads, and it reached as far as Hadrian. Only fragments of it have been preserved.   Photius, who had read five books of the sixteen, said of it, that the style was neither popular nor Attic, the language without elegance, and the whole book tedious from a superabundance of detail. Eusebius however made use of this work.   Phlegon also wrote a description of Sicily, and of the topographical wonders of Rome, as well as of the Roman festivals.   All these historical and antiquarian writings are lost, with the exception of two unimportant works of this author, *Miraculous Stories*, and *Men of Great Longevity*, which have been preserved.

Phlegon stood so high in Hadrian's favour, that he entrusted him with the compilation of his memoirs, which he had written, following the example of Trajan.   According to the assertion of Spartianus, the memoirs were actually written by the emperor himself, who thirsted for immortality, but he published them under the name of Phlegon, doubtless in the Greek language.[1]   The memoirs of Hadrian, if we possessed them, would enrich literature with an imperial historian of rare intellect, and in spite of the unavoidable colouring of

[1] Spartianus (c. 16) certainly speaks of several freedmen who published the biography of the emperor under their own name, and then says : nam et Phlegontis libri Hadriani esse dicuntur.

many actions, would be the authentic source for the history of his life.   The memoirs of Hadrian would, too, have thrown an especial light on the general condition of Rome, and on the reigns of many of his predecessors.[1]   His life was written by many contemporaries, as well as by Philo of Byblus.

As these biographies are lost, our knowledge of one of the most remarkable epochs of imperial times can only be obtained from the scanty reports of two compilers who made use of the memoirs of Hadrian, namely, Spartianus, who lived in the time of Diocletian, and Dion Cassius, who lived in the early years of the third century, whose information is only conveyed to us in the epitome of Xiphilinus.   Irreparable, too, is the loss of the Roman historical work of Marius Maximus, who continued the biographies of the emperors by Suetonius, and who wrote at the end of the second and the beginning of the third century.   The life of Hadrian, which he treated, was made use of by Spartianus, and also by Aurelius Victor.[2]

[1] Dion Cassius, lxvi. 17, in one place quotes the scandalous stories which accuse Titus of the poisoning of Vespasian, and refers expressly to the opinion of Hadrian.   Can we suppose that he read this in the autobiography?

[2] On the biographers of Hadrian: H. Jaenecke, *De vitae Hadrianae Scriptoribus*, 1875.—J. J. Mueller, *Der Geschichtschreiber L. Marius Maximus*, 1870.—J. Plew, *Marius Maximus als Quelle der Scriptores H. Aug.* 1878: also by the same author, *Quellenuntersuchungen zur Geschichte des K. Hadrian*, Strassburg, 1890.—Aem. Pierino, *De Fontib. Vitar. Hadriani et Septimii Severi Impp. ab Aelio Spartiano conscriptar*, 1880.— J. Duerr, *Die Reisen des Kaisers Hadrian*, 1881, p. 73 *sq.*

CHAPTER IX

Florus. Suetonius. Geography. Philology

THEY were, then, essentially Greeks who wrote the history of the world and of Rome, after this task had been executed by Latins until the second century. The Latins henceforth gave way to the Greeks. They could, indeed, point to Tacitus, who survived the reign of Hadrian, but with him ended the great national list of Roman historians. The succeeding authors show the decay of historical literature, which no longer bears any trace of a lofty conception of events.

Two Latin historians belong to this time, Julius Florus and Suetonius. Florus made an abridgment of Livy's *History of Rome*, which has been preserved, and which was highly thought of in the Middle Ages.[1]

C. Suetonius Tranquillus, a Roman of culture and ability, but without any great originality, was more important. The son of a knight and a favourite of the younger Pliny, who corresponded with him, he was born in 77 A.D.[2] In the schools of rhetoric at Rome, Hadrian as a youth must have known this companion of his maturer years. When he became emperor he made him his secretary, but Suetonius lost his post because he had approached the empress too familiarly. The later circumstances of his life are

---

[1] *J. Flori. Epitom. de T. Livio bellor. omnium annor.* dxx, *Libri duo*, ed. O. Jahn, 1852, then Halm, 1854. Florus is called sometimes Julius sometimes L. Annaeus. Whether he was identical with the poet P. Annius Florus is uncertain.

[2] Pliny, *Ep.* i. 18 ; iii. 8 ; v. 10, in which he asks him to publish his works,—appellantur quotidie et flagitantur.

unknown.　Most of his grammatical, critical, and historical writings, wherein he seems to have taken Varro as a pattern, have been lost.　He wrote on the games of the Greeks and Romans, upon the customs of the Romans, a life of Cicero, and a list of famous men.[1]

Suetonius owes his fame to the biographies of the first twelve emperors, which he wrote in 120 A.D., and dedicated to his friend Septicius Clarus, before he himself had fallen into disgrace with the emperor.　The happy idea of describing biographically the development of the empire of the first century contributed as much as the poverty of the literature upon the imperial period to give great importance to this work.　It is written slightly and simply in a pleasant, easy style, but his treatment of character is wanting in artistic unity and in depth of conception.　The biographies swarm with anecdotes, chiefly of a scandalous character, in which the influence may be perceived of the court of an emperor, who was accustomed to treat the world and its great men with irony and caprice. But the wealth of material and the trustworthiness of the information derived from the archives of many families, make the work of Suetonius always an important historical authority.　This history of the emperors is a monument of Latin literature, wherein the national instinct, as in Tacitus, of writing Roman history from an imperial stand-point, is displayed.　Hadrian may probably have suggested the work to Suetonius.

The science of geography must have received fresh life from the travels of the emperor; but the only work of travel of Hadrian's time is the report of Arrian upon the circumnavigation of the Black Sea.[2]　The study of geography, a product of Greek learning, was warmly encouraged in Rome, after the time of Caesar, by the government.　The gigantic works of Strabo and Pliny mark an epoch in the study of geography in both literatures of the world.　Under the

---

[1] Suidas, 934 *sq.*　J. Regent, *De C. Suetonii vita et scriptis*, 1851.　*Suet. Tranquilli praeter Caesarum libros reliquiae*, ed. A. Reiffenscheid, 1860. Gellius, ix. 7, p. 472.　Teuffel (*Röm. Literaturgesch.*) quotes a *Historia ludicra* by him.

[2] Bunbury, *Hist. of Ancient Geography*, ii. 510.

Antonines, geography came to the front when the great catalogue of roads was made by the genius of Claudius Ptolemaeus for the use of mathematical geography as well as for astronomy and chronology. The observation of the heavens by the ancients was reduced by this Alexandrian to a system which prevailed until the time of Copernicus. The same thing happened with the science of medicine, for the Greek, Claudius Galen collected the experience of antiquity, and dominated the scientific opinion of thirteen centuries. This great man was born at Pergamum in Hadrian's reign, in 131 A.D.

Special activity was displayed in the time of Hadrian in grammatical and philological studies. Many Latins, and more Greeks, are distinguished in this field of literature as atticists, lexicographers, and etymologists. In the same way the Alexandrians Orion, Apollonius Dyscolus, the famous predecessor of Aelius Herodianus, Hephaestion, Nicanor of Cyrene, Aelius Melissus, Heliodorus, Aelius Dionysius from Halicarnassus, and Telephus of Pergamum may be mentioned.[1] Among the Latin philologists are Valerius Pollio, Quintus Terentius Scaurus the commentator on Plautus and Virgil, Flavius Casper, Velleius Celer, Domitius, Caius Apollinaris Sulpicius, Julius Vestinus, and others. These studies were the foundation of the eloquence which, with art and science, formed the whole culture of the Roman and Greek world.

---

[1] Upon the grammarians : Nicolai, *Griech. Literaturgeschichte,* ii. 316 *sq.* Gräfenhan, *Gesch. der class. Philol.,* Band iv.

CHAPTER X

The Schools of Roman Oratory. Roman Orators. Cornelius Fronto

DURING the republic, when the life of the state was on the Forum and in the Curia, and when its fate was being determined by the struggle of great parties, the Roman people developed the most brilliant political oratory. In Rome the art of speaking formed part of the education of the citizen. Men of war and of the camp were at the same time finished orators such as Metellus, Licinius Crassus, Antony, Pompey, Caesar, and Brutus. As late as the civil wars oratory preserved its practical character; then the dialectic of the Greeks, which penetrated into the world, transformed literature and rhetoric. The art of oratory was now fashioned after Greek models. Cicero was its first exponent.

The stream of political passions became stagnant in the monarchy, which deprived speech of freedom, and even of the dignity of resistance. What were now the *Causae centumvirales*, the private cases in comparison with those historical state trials of the republic? "I do not know," said Messala, "if those old writings have come into your hands, which repose in the libraries of our predecessors; they show that Pompey and Crassus became great not simply by force of arms but by their eloquence, that the Lentuli and Metelli, the Luculli and Curiones, and other great men, have devoted much attention to these studies, and that no one of that time attained to power without the gift of oratory. The brilliancy and the importance of the subjects by which eloquence is enhanced are also to be considered. For it makes a great difference whether the subject of the speech is a theft, or a point of law, or an interdict, or whether it concerns the canvassing of the comitia, the oppression of the allies, and the murder of citizens." [1]

The Romans of the empire lamented the loss of their proudest national possession, for Rome had no longer anything, as in the days of Cicero, to oppose to the arrogance of Greece. "All the intellects," said Seneca, "which shed light upon our studies were born at that time. Afterwards the art of oratory decayed, either from the corruption of the times, or because ambition aimed afterwards at lower things, such as office and money. The minds of the idle youth are enervated; no one any longer passes wakeful nights in toil over an honourable occupation. The dishonourable study of song and dance makes the mind effeminate, and the anxiety to be distinguished in unclean vices is stamped on the young men." [2]

The spirited dialogue of Tacitus upon rhetoricians attributes the decay of eloquence since the foundation of the monarchy to a false system of training in oratory. Formerly young men learnt the art of oratory publicly in courts and assemblies, and according to the custom of the republic they earned their spurs in the impeachments of great men. The brilliant speeches of Crassus when nineteen against Caius Carbo, of Caesar when twenty-one against Dolabella, of Asinius Pollio when twenty-two against Caius Cato, are notable instances. But now young men attend the theatre of so-called rhetoricians, who teach them to ruin their intellect by senseless exercises and contemptible tricks.

Petronius in the *Satyricon* has described this rhetorical education with masterly touches. In his opinion the young men are only made stupid by the host of idle things and sentences they are taught, so that when they come to the Forum they feel themselves transplanted to another world. [3]

---

[1] *De oratore dialogus*, c. 37.

[2] Seneca, *Controv*. i. prooem.

[3] This passage is elucidated by the introduction (proemium) to the 4th book of Seneca's *Controversies*, where we are told that an orator, Latro Porcius, was on one occasion so disconcerted in the Forum that he asked the judges to let him go to a basilica.

They hear nothing practical in the schools, only of pirates loaded with chains, of tyrants who command sons to cut off their father's heads, and of decrees against the plague which order that three or more young women should be sacrificed. Finally, every speech and action is steeped in honey, and encrusted with opium and sesame. "Recently," says Petronius, "this windy garrulity came from Asia to Athens, and breathed upon the spirits of our youths with a pestilential breath. Who afterwards could rise to the eminence of Thucydides, who to the fame of Hyperides? A vigorous poem could never be written, but everything was after the same pattern, and was not likely to last. It was the same with the art of painting, which decayed after the Egyptians ventured to invent a traditional style for so great an art." [1]

Not only form and matter, but the two kinds of scholastic oratory, the persuasive (*suasoriae*), and the controversial (*controversiae*), had been imported into Rome from Greece.[2] Exercises such as the following were given: Alexander takes advice whether he should march into Babylon, as the augur prophesied evil if he did; the Athenians consult whether they should remove the Persian trophies, as Xerxes threatens to return if this is not done; Agamemnon deliberates whether he should sacrifice Iphigenia, as Calchas foretells that unless this is done the Greeks cannot depart. Then there were controversies which resembled those sophistic quibbles that served to while away the time in learned society and at the banquets of the rich. They were schools for advocates and pettifoggers, as well as for the man of polished good breeding.

The education of the incipient orator until he reached perfection, seems as pedantic as these gymnastics of the intellect were senseless. Quintilian has spoken plainly about it in his discourses on oratory. There are precepts borrowed from the dramatic art about the use of the emotions by which the judges were to be moved, about declamation and modulation of the voice, about gestures and pantomime, and the artistic use of the limbs. The eyes should now be

[1] Petronius, *Satyricon*, c. 2.
[2] On the schools of oratory: Friedlaender, iii. 343 *sq.* Grasberger, *Erziehung und Unterricht im class. Alterthum*, iii. 353-390.

fixed, now dim, now moving, here sparkling with delight, there blinking, and so to say leering (*venerii*). For only a simpleton will keep the eyes quite open or quite shut. Then follow rules upon the rhetorical use of the lips, chin, throat, neck, and shoulders, and minute directions about the play of the hands. For instance, does it not make a splendid effect when the hands are wrung at that declamation of Gracchus: "Whither shall I most miserable flee? Whither shall I turn? To the Capitol? Ah! it trickles with my brother's blood. To my own house? Perchance, to see my unhappy mother sorrowing, and falling into a swoon?"

It would be a mistake, however, on account of this scholastic pedantry, to undervalue the importance of oratory in the world at that time. It trained the best intellects, and aroused the interest of society in literature and art. Even in its decay it was an ornament to life, and so much of a necessity to the nature of the southern people, that among the Italians of a later age, rhetoric revived with the renaissance of ancient literature. In the empire it took the place of the drama and the press. All the Caesars went through its schools, not only because it adorned despotism with fine phrases, but because it was generally indispensable to a liberal education.

Vespasian appointed the first public teachers of oratory in both languages in Rome, and the provinces afterwards bestirred themselves to attract celebrated rhetoricians. But no emperor promoted the art of oratory as much as Hadrian, who had himself an excellent knowledge of rhetoric.[1] In his time several Roman orators flourished, such as Calpurnius Flaccus, Antonius Julianus, the master of Gellius, Castricius and Celer.[2]

But the most famous orator of all was Cornelius Fronto, an Italian, born however at Cirta, in Numidia, at the beginning of the second century. He studied in Alexandria, and shone as a forensic speaker in Rome in the time of Hadrian, who made him a senator. Fronto says on one occasion in a letter to Marcus Aurelius, that he had often praised his

---

[1] Philostratus (*Lollian*, vol. ii., p. 42) means this when he says of him : ἐπιτηδειότατος τῶν πάλαι βασιλέων γενόμενος ἀρετὰς αὐξῆσαι.

[2] Speeches of Calpurnius Flaccus delivered in school are in existence. Teuffel, 351.

grandfather by adoption in the senate, that he had honoured him greatly, but did not love him, as love implies confidence and familiarity.[1] Dion calls him the first advocate in Rome.[2] He became so rich by his industry, that he bought the gardens of his patron, and built baths.   After he had been consul for two months in 143 A.D., he refused the trouble-some honour of proconsul of Asia.   He found himself in the same relation as Seneca to the future emperor.   But if to Seneca it proved a curse that Nero had been his pupil, it became a blessing and a source of lasting fame to Fronto that he had been the teacher of the noblest of all rulers, Marcus Aurelius. This emperor repaid the care of his master with a touching affection, and Fronto had nothing to complain of in his illustrious pupil, except that he deserted rhetoric for philosophy.   Their correspondence is the monument of an interesting friendship.   It shows us the character of Fronto, who, though self-satisfied and subject to many weaknesses which were fostered by his calling as an orator, and by his position as tutor to a prince, was, notwithstanding, possessed of many honourable traits of genuine humanity.[3] From many letters and discourses, as, for instance, from the *Alsiensian Holidays*, in which he exhorts his pupil to a keener enjoyment of life, we may perceive that Fronto at the bottom was no dry pedant.   Toward Lucius Verus, who was his second pupil, he does not always appear sincere; he flattered Verus, but Marcus Aurelius considered himself fortunate in having learnt from his master to be truthful.[4]

About 160 A.D. Fronto was at the zenith of his fame; he died about 175 A.D.[5]

[1] Fronto, *ad. M. Caesar*, ii. 4 : Divom Hadrianum avom tuum laudavi in senatu saepenumero studio impenso et propenso quoque.

[2] Dion, lxix. 18 : ὁ τὰ πρῶτα τῶν τότε Ῥωμαίων ἐν δίκαις φερόμενος.   Orator nobilissimus, as Eutropius, viii. 12, calls him.

[3] See his letter, 'De nepote amisso,' wherein he ventured to attribute to himself the 'integer vitae scelerisque purus.'

[4] 'Quod verum dicere ex te disco.'—In *Fronto*, iii. 12, iii. 18, Aurelius writes that he is grateful to him, 'quom cotidie non desinis in viam me veram inducere, et oculos mihi aperire.' His praise in the *Meditations*, i. 11.

[5] Bernhardy, *Grundriss der röm. Liter.* 5 Auflage, p. 839 ; Teuffel, 355. On Fronto's *cursus honorum* before his consulate: Renier, *Inscr. Rom. de l Algérie*, 2717.

As an author he must be considered the pedantic advocate of antiquarianism in Latin literature. If Quintilian took Cicero as a model, Fronto kept to the style of Cato, Ennius, Plautus, and Sallust. He would have nothing to do with the art of Greek orators, but he imitated the style of the oldest Romans. For this he was admired by Gellius. It was the age of philological enthusiasm for antiquated forms of speech, which made both style and language absurdly distorted, obscure, and unmusical, and only proved the inevitable decay of literature. The writings of Fronto, among which there are fragments of a treatise against the Christians and of his history of the Parthian war, were first discovered, though in a very imperfect condition, by Angelo Mai in the Ambrosian Library and in the Vatican.[1] They were at first welcomed with enthusiasm, as unexpected remains of antiquity, and were even over-estimated.[2] Then they were under-valued and neglected.[3] Fronto's material is often very trivial as merely a subject for rhetorical exercises. Among them is to be found a praise of indolence, of smoke, and of dust. But one must be a Swift to be able to talk intellectually about a broomstick. Fronto's correspondence with the Antonines is most important as an historical document descriptive of the culture of the age. Yet it displays

[1] Editions by Angelo Mai, Milan, 1815 ; Berlin, 1816 (by Niebuhr) ; Rome, by A. Mai, 1823, 1846. Minucius Felix refers to his attack upon the Christians, *Octavius*, c. 30.

[2] The discovery of Fronto by Angelo Mai was greeted with special warmth by Giacomo Leopardi. After the discovery of the books of Cicero's *De Republica*, the poet addressed to Mai the famous ode *Italo ardito*. See on the discovery of Fronto the jubilee pamphlet of Ateneo di Bergamo: *Nel primo Centenario di Angelo Mai, Memorie e Documenti*, by Benedetto Prina, 1882.

[3] Fronto is one of the best examples of the abuse of the art of oratory and of the degradation of language. For Fronto see Roth, *Bemerkungen über die Schriften des M. Cornel. Fronto*, 1817. Bernhardy, p. 840, calls him a witness to the impoverished literature of the second century. Martin Herz has drawn an unfavourable picture of him in *Renaissance and Rococo in der röm. Literatur*. Macrobius, *Saturnalia*, v. i : quatuor sunt, inquit Eusebius, genera dicendi : copiosum, in quo Cicero dominatur : breve, in quo Sallustius regnat, siccum quod Frontoni adscribitur ; pingue et floridum, in quo Plinius secundus. . . .

but a mediocre intellect, the product of an age devoid both of thought and action. Fronto wrote, too, some letters in Greek and an *Eroticus*.

Roman oratory did not produce any classic literature after the time of Cicero. Quintilian himself in his work, *De institutione oratoria*, only set up a standard text-book for the acquisition of the art of rhetoric. While in Rome rhetoric was always directed to practical and forensic oratory, Greek rhetoric was a free art of polite letters and of literature.

CHAPTER XI

Greek Sophistry. Favorinus. Dionysius of Miletus.
Polemon. Herodes Atticus and other Sophists

THE sophistry of the second century was a wonderful display of the activity of the Greek intellect. It lasted, with
many fluctuations, until the time of Justinian, and Neoplatonism, a product of the Renaissance of Platonic philosophy
in its relation to Christianity, continued to exist by its side,
and expired with it.

While the Roman national intellect after the golden age
of its poets and prose writers was becoming exhausted, the
Hellenes filled a gap in the literature of the world, for the
ever-oscillating scale between the Greek and Latin genius in
the empire inclined again to them. Sympathy for Hellas
had greatly increased at the imperial court since the time of
Claudius and Nero. Even a Domitian was fond of the Greek
character. He organized the contests at the Capitol after the
pattern of the Olympian games, presiding over them himself in Greek garb, his head adorned with a golden wreath.
In the reign of Nerva, Dion Chrysostom, grandfather of
the historian Dion Cassius, heralded the revival of Greek
oratory; but its victory was decided by the Philhellene
Hadrian. Sophistry owed a new life to him, and a second
era of Greek eloquence arose from the study of ancient
literature. Although tainted with the spirit of an age poor
in great subjects and ideas, oratory yet attained such elegance
and mastery of form and expression that the world at the
time was charmed. Though these declamations upon mythological subjects and historical events of the Greek past seem

trivial to us now, the literature of the sophists is always a reflection of the cosmopolitan culture of the Roman empire. It seemed, indeed, so important to that age that it found a historian in Philostratus.

As the Greek school of sophists was the pattern for Latin rhetoric, what is said of one applies to both. The times of Pisistratus, Solon, and Pericles, of Philip, and Demosthenes, Homer, and the poets, and, above all, the Attic orators, afforded the material. The main point was to cultivate the art of dramatic expression, and the greatest accomplishment, to be able to improvise readily at the moment. For this they not only studied the ancients but nature as well. Herodes Atticus had learnt the art, so says Philostratus, of touching the heart, not only from the tragic poets but from life. Marcus of Byzantium compared the versatility of sophistry to the play of colours in the rainbow, and Philostratus could not better describe its difficulty than by the remark he made upon the fifty-six years of its life after the death of Polemon. At this time he said, age would begin in other sciences, but the sophist is still a youth, for the older he grows the more he improves.

We cannot find fault with the sophists if they glorified eloquence as the finest flower of the human intellect, for they lived upon its fruit ; but a large part of the cultivated world also considered it the essence of all intellectual perfection. When even a Roman orator carried away his audience, we may imagine the enthusiasm which a Greek excited among Greeks, as often as he caused the music of a language to be heard which was still the language of the world, and paramount even in Rome. The Greeks, we may suppose, alone knew and enjoyed the virtuoso's feeling for eloquence as a fine art. Their delicate ear could alone appreciate the melody of metre like the sound of a lyre and a flute. Polemon was in the habit of laughing after delivering long sentences, in order to show how little he was fatigued. It was all artificial, but it passed for art.

Sophistry was so greatly admired by the world that its acquisition was preferred to the highest dignities. The name of sophist, and the pleasure of being allowed to declaim, was bought at a great price. Philostratus speaks of a rich young man who allowed himself to be praised as a reciter by his parasites, remitting even the interest to his debtors if they attended his lectures. Polemon, too, had borrowed money from him, but disdained to listen to him often. The young orator accordingly threatened him with an action for debt. Polemon determined to gratify his vanity, but, unable to endure his prattle, he exclaimed, "Varus, you had better bring your action." The sophists had their own claqueurs; Aristides especially asked Marcus Aurelius, who wished to hear him, that his friends might be allowed to applaud.[1]

The rhetoricians travelled about like players, and gave performances. If they were famous the cities celebrated their arrival with festivals. They often bestowed civic rights upon them, erected statues to them, gave them a voice in their most important affairs, and made use of them as ambassadors to the emperor. In this way Marcus the rhetorician, obtained the favour of Hadrian as ambassador from the Byzantines. Cities like Smyrna and Pergamum certainly owed fresh splendour to the sophists. The desire for fame, and the vanity of these sophists found sufficient food in the theatrical character, and the poor achievements of the Hellenic world of the time, which was in the habit of raising monuments to mediocrity, and to all that was dazzling, bewildering, and ostentatious. Patriotism, however, explains the power of the rhetoricians, particularly among the Hellenes. For they recalled to the Greeks the fame of their name, the deeds of their ancestors, and the treasures of their literature, which they pretended survived in their own productions. Even if the influence which Philostratus says that Apollonius had upon Vespasian is exaggerated, it is still a fact that the Roman emperors recognized sophistry as a power.[2] They paid homage to it as it represented the intellectual life of the Hellenes, and with it they were obliged to come to terms, if they wished to be in the forefront of their epoch. They were also very anxious to be recognized by the Hellenism of the East as the successors of Alexander, and with Olympian trumpets the sophists freely sounded its praise. Even a Pliny did not extol the universal

[1] Philostratus, *Vita Soph. Aristides*, vol. ii. 88.
[2] Philostratus, *Vita Apollon.* v., c. 31.

greatness of Rome with such enthusiasm as the Greek orators of the age of the Antonines.[1]

The chief seats of sophistry were Smyrna and Athens, Ephesus and Pergamum, then Antioch, Berytus, and other Phoenician cities.   From Prusa, in Bithynia, came the leader of this new school of oratory, Dion Chrysostom, who was born in the middle of the first century, and was still famous in the time of Trajan.   In the age of the Antonines, sophistry reached its height.   The number of these rhetoricians is legion.   Hadrian himself is to be counted among them.   His speeches and discourses were collected and read, and Photius has bestowed moderate praise upon them; but none of them exist.[2]

It is strange that one of the most famous Greek sophists of this time was a Gaul.   This was Favorinus, from Arelate. At least Philostratus placed him in this class, although he was really a Platonic philosopher, and was always described as such by his pupil Gellius.[3]   Favorinus was a man of great experience and calm judgment, if Gellius is not carried away by affection in describing him.[4]   Philostratus maintained that he was an hermaphrodite, without beard and with the voice of a eunuch, and yet so fond of women that he was accused before a consul, of adultery.   His Greek education must have made him particularly sympathetic to the emperor Hadrian.   Spartianus mentions him especially among the learned men of Hadrian's court.   That he was a trained courtier may be seen from the following anecdote: One day Hadrian set him right on a scientific question, and Favorinus at once gave way.   When friends blamed him, he answered: "Let me always believe that he is

[1] On the sophists in general: Lud. Cresollius, *Theatr. veter. rhetor.* i., c. 8 ; A. Westermann, *Gesch. der griech. Beredsamkeit*, p. 198 *sq.* Passages in question in Friedlaender.

[2] Photius, 100 : Μελέται διαφόραι—εἰς τὸ μέτριον ἀνηγμέναι καὶ οὐκ ἀηδεῖς.   Of his sermons and orations, Charisius, *Art. Gramm.* ii. 129, 240.

[3] Gellius, i. 3; x. 13 ; xvii. 12.

[4] Gellius, iv. 1 : Sic Favorinus sermones in genus commune a rebus parvis et frigidis abducebat ad ea, quae esset magis utile audire ac discere, non allata extrinsecus, non per ostentationem, sed indidem nata acceptaque—xvi. 1.

the wisest man in the world who commands thirty legions."

It is surely nothing more than a fable that the fame of Favorinus aroused the jealousy of the emperor, so that he endeavoured to supplant him by promoting his adversaries. But he seems to have really fallen into Hadrian's disfavour without however being ruined. He could point to three things as the greatest marvels in his life : though a Gaul, he was a Hellene, though a eunuch, he was accused of adultery, and though he had the emperor for an enemy, he yet remained alive.[1] The Athenians are said to have thrown down the bronze statue which they had erected to him, in the belief that Hadrian was his implacable enemy, and even then he knew how to console himself. In spite of the harmony of his studies with those of the emperor, he did not share his predilection for antiquarian literature, nor his mystical disposition. This is proved by the discourse which he delivered in Rome against astrologers.[2] It may have offended the emperor, who would besides have been annoyed by the arrogance of Favorinus. However ridiculous the vanity of such sophists may have appeared, it must, nevertheless, be admitted that they, like the Cynics, knew how to maintain the dignity of intellect, even before the imperial throne.

Favorinus was not friendly with Polemon. Ephesus took the part of Favorinus, Smyrna that of Polemon. Literary quarrels were as rife then as in the scholastic Middle Ages, and in the time of Poggio and Valla, when the literary activity of antiquity was imitated. Philostratus concluded from this quarrel that Favorinus was a sophist, as jealousy only occurs in members of the same profession. Favorinus got on better with his pupil Herodes Atticus, to whom he left his books, his house in Rome, and his black Indian slaves. He was also friendly with Plutarch, who dedicated his treatise on the principle of cold to him, and he valued the celebrated Dion Chrysostom as his especial teacher.

Favorinus, one of the versatile men of his time, had great

---

[1] Philostratus, *Favorinus* at the beginning : Γαλάτης ὢν ἑλληνίζειν, εὐνοῦχος ὢν μοιχείας κρίνεσθαι, βασιλεῖ διαφέρεσθαι καὶ ζῆν.

[2] Gellius, xiv. i.

fertility in production, and in that respect he was like Plutarch. But only a few fragments of his writings have been preserved. Ten books of pyrrhonian tropes were considered his best work. Gellius praises his elegant Greek, whose charm was not to be attained in a Latin discourse; and Philostratus, his fascinating utterance, his speaking eye, and the melody of his words, "for even those who did not understand Greek listened to him with pleasure; he enthralled them by the sound of the language which appeared like a song to them."[1]

Dionysius of Miletus, a pupil of the Assyrian Isaeus, shone also among the rhetoricians. Hadrian gave him a post in the Museum at Alexandria, made him a knight, and even governor of a province.[2] The assertion therefore that the emperor wished to ruin this sophist too, out of envy seems incredible. Dionysius, full of self-reliance, said once to Heliodorus, Hadrian's private secretary: "The emperor can make you rich, but he cannot make you a sophist."[3] He travelled about in many cities, and had a school for oratory in Lesbos. He died at Ephesus, where he was buried on the finest site of the city, a monument being raised in his honour. As he was older than Polemon, the talent of the young rhetorician made him uneasy. He once heard him in Sardis, where Polemon had come from Smyrna to plead in an action, but he was wary enough not to jeopardize his own fame by accepting the challenge which Polemon offered him. Dionysius is said to have been distinguished for his unaffected style in the delivery of his lectures. He imparted his rare memory as a mnemonic art to his pupils, from which those who were envious of him maintained that he accomplished such results by the aid of Chaldean magic. Philostratus remarks about this: "There are no artificial aids to memory, nor ever will be. Memory indeed teaches the arts, but is not itself to be taught by any art, as it is a gift of nature, and a part of the immortal soul."[4] Memory is the queen of all things, according to Sophocles.

[1] Philostr. vol. ii. 11.
[2] So at least Philostratus maintains, ii. 37 : σατράπην μὲν αὐτὸν ἀπέφηνεν οὐκ ἀφανῶν ἐθνῶν.
[3] Dion Cassius, lxix. 3.   [4] Philostratus, vol. ii., p. 36.

Other famous sophists of that time were Alexander of Troas, Scopelianus, Sabinus, Asclepius of Byblus, Lollianus of Ephesus, and Marcus of Byzantium. Lollian was the glory of Athens, where he first filled the chair of oratory. Philostratus calls him an upright and well-disposed man. He became rich by his teaching of the theory and practice of oratory. The senate at Athens erected a statue in his honour.[1]

All the sophists of this age were outshone by Polemon and Herodes Atticus. They were not only the recognized masters of their art, but they lived like princes in the possession of great riches, and were honoured by their age as demi-gods.

Polemon, of a consular family in Carian Laodicea, was the head of the Ionian school, and the pride of Smyrna. As he attracted thousands of pupils, he acquired such importance that he ruled the city. He made peace among factions, controlled the government, endeavoured to restrain luxury, and to restore the feeling of independence to the citizens by not bringing their disputes before the proconsul, but by having them settled at home. Such civic activity was the finest side in the life of the famous sophists. They could be justices of the peace, patrons, and advocates for their cities before the emperors. Polemon understood so well how to win the favour of Hadrian for Smyrna, that on one occasion the emperor gave the city ten million sesterces, with which the citizens built warehouses, a temple, and the most splendid gymnasium in the whole of Asia.[2] It was no wonder that the sophist was rewarded with great honours. Among other dignities, Smyrna bestowed upon him and his posterity the right of presiding at the Olympian games, and the command of the sacred ship of Dionysus.

Trajan, Hadrian, and the Antonines honoured Polemon in every way. He often came as ambassador from Smyrna to Rome. Hadrian appointed him to make the speech at the dedication of the Olympieum in Athens. What finer occasion than this for making a speech could a sophist desire! Unfortunately this splendid oration has been lost. Philos-

[1] Inscription in Spon, *Itin.* ii., p. 336.
[2] Philostratus, ii. 43.

tratus says that he spoke wonderfully. Polemon lived in
great style. On his journeys he took with him costly furniture, horses, slaves and dogs, and he sat like a Mark
Antony on a richly adorned carriage. It must have been a
brilliant and luxurious world at that time, if a single sophist
could appear in such state. Philostratus says the same
thing of the Tyrian Hadrian, and of Herodes Atticus.
Polemon he says, rose to such greatness, that he conversed
with cities as their sovereign, and with princes and gods as
their equal. When once the proconsul of Asia, who was
afterwards the emperor Antoninus Pius, took up his quarters
in the house of the absent sophist without ceremony, Polemon,
returning home at night, turned out the uninvited guest, and
the Roman proconsul submitted. So even in those days
talent asserted itself in the presence of the ruler. Polemon's
quarrelsome temper has been mentioned before. He did not
attack all sophists who were of equal reputation, at all events,
neither Scopelianus nor Herodes Atticus. The latter was
his genuine admirer ; when the people once called out that
he was the second Demosthenes, he made answer : " I am
the second Phrygian" (Polemon). It is to this great reverence
that Philostratus ascribes the fact of Herodes leaving Smyrna
secretly in the night, in order not to be forced into a contest
with him.

Polemon was a great extempore speaker. His delivery is
described as glowing, powerful, and as full of sound as a
trumpet. He was called the Olympian trumpet. His
thoughts appeared to his hearers as lofty as those of Demosthenes, and as inspired as the utterances from the tripod. The
pomp and verbosity of the Ionian school seem not to have
been foreign to his style. Philostratus indeed was obliged to
defend him against those who accused him of flowery speaking
and over-nicety. At one time Marcus Aurelius writes to
Fronto, "I have been hearing Polemon declaim for three days.
If you ask me what I think of him, I must say that he seems
to me like a very active and earnest farmer, who on his large
estate only grows corn and vines, whereby he obtains the
finest and most luscious fruit. But on this land there are no
fig-trees from Pompeii, no vegetables from Aricia, no roses
from Tarentum, no pleasant groves, or thick woods, or shady

plane-trees. Everything is calculated more for use than pleasure, more to be praised than to be loved. But I must not be hasty and presumptuous in a rash judgment, which I give upon a man of such fame."[1]   We are obliged to accept this critical opinion as authoritative, as we possess nothing of Polemon except two funeral orations upon the heroes Cynegirus and Antimachus, who fell at Marathon.[2]   He died in the reign of Marcus Aurelius, about 153 A.D., at the age of fifty-six years, from voluntary starvation, as an incurable illness made him despair of carrying on the practice of his beloved art.

Still more attractive and more instructive is the figure of Herodes Atticus, the famous benefactor of the city of Athens, which received as much glory from this one man as from its great benefactor on the throne of the Caesars. This fortunate man united, in a rare combination, the riches of Croesus with as many gifts of the Attic muses as his time could appreciate.

He was born at the beginning of the second century in the famous Marathon,[3] and claimed to be descended from the Aeacidae. Polemon, Favorinus, Scopelianus, and the Athenian sophist Secundus, were his teachers, and Taurus the Tyrian introduced him to the philosophy of Plato. Herodes soon seemed to eclipse all his contemporaries. His memory too has lasted longer than theirs; but this superiority he owes less to his ability, than to the liberal use he made of his fortune. His father Atticus, had found a treasure in one of his houses near the theatre at Athens, which the generous Nerva allowed him to keep. This good luck, and the fortune of his mother, made Herodes more than rich. But he under-

---

[1] Fronto, *Epistolar.* ii. 8, p. 40 : cum de tantae gloriae viro existimo?

[2] Ἐπιτάφιοι λόγοι—*Laudationes duae funebres*, ed. Orelli, 1819 ; *Declamationes quae extant duae*, rec. Hink, Lips. 1873.

[3] His birth seems to have taken place either in 95 A.D. or 101 A.D., according to Philostratus, *Vit. Herod.* c. 14, where his first meeting with Hadrian in Pannonia is mentioned, and this Olearius (*in Vita Herodis*) believes to have happened in 119 A.D. Franz (*C.I.G.* iii., p. 922*b*, 925) assumes this as correct. Herodes would then have been twenty-five years old, while Heyse assumes eighteen years. Keil, in Pauly's *Real. Lexicon Artik. Herodes Att.*, takes 101 A.D. for the year of his birth. But none of these calculations are certain.

stood how to spend his money in the most magnificent way.

He was a young man when he appeared before Hadrian in Pannonia, but he did not succeed in the speech which he delivered. He approached the emperor for the first time in Athens in the winter of 125-126 A.D., and after that he began to be famous. Hadrian then made him overseer of the free cities of Asia, in which office he displayed great liberality. He loved fame above everything, for he scarcely undertook his buildings simply from motives of benevolence or from enthusiasm for art. His most ardent wish was to cut through the Isthmus of Corinth. The necessity of uniting both the seas of Greece by a navigable canal had long been felt, and Nero, during his stay in Corinth, had not only drawn a plan for it, but had begun the work.[1] The traces of the cutting by Nero are still to be seen in the narrowest part of the isthmus, where the ancient Diolkos used to stand, and the engineers of the present day have followed these traces. It was Nero's own capricious inconstancy, and his sudden return to Rome, which induced him to abandon the enterprise.[2] The science or the superstition of the time is therefore not to be blamed. None of the emperors after Nero thought of it again. But Herodes was the first to whom the idea occurred, and it does no little honour to the noble mind of the sophist. The account of Philostratus is doubly interesting to-day, when after the lapse of centuries, the canal has been completed. As Herodes was journeying one day to Corinth with the Athenian Ctesidemus he said, on reaching the isthmus, "I have been trying for a long time to leave a monument to posterity, which shall convince mankind that I have really lived, but I despair of ever attaining such fame." His companion remarked that the fame of his discourses, and of his architectural works, would never be equalled by anyone, but Herodes answered : "My works are perishable, and time will

[1] Suetonius, *Nero*, c. 19 : Dion Cassius, lxiii. 16.

[2] Lucian, *Nero*, c. 4. Egyptian geometers asserted that the water-level of the two seas was not alike, and that therefore, after the cutting of the isthmus, the island of Aegina would always be in danger of being flooded. This opinion, however, was only a pretence, for it was in fact the rebellion of Vindex which called Nero away from Greece.

destroy them ; my discourses too will be found fault with, first by one and then by another, but the cutting through the isthmus would be an immortal and almost superhuman work ; yet it seems to me that to pierce through the isthmus is the work more of Poseidon than of a mortal."[1]

This opinion of Herodes shows that the technical difficulties of the undertaking were still considered very great. Pausanias relates that the Pythia had advised the people of Cnidus to pierce through their isthmus, and remarks : "It is difficult for men to offer violence to the gods."[2] Herodes Atticus would have been just the right man, in spite of Poseidon, to undertake cutting through the Isthmus of Corinth ; only, as Philostratus asserts, he had not the courage to beg permission from the emperor to do it, as he was afraid of being blamed as presumptuous, if he undertook a work which the talent of Nero had not been able to carry out.[3] The relinquishment of this project for the canal will scarcely have troubled Herodes less than the fact that not he, but Polemon, delivered the Olympian inaugural address. In Athens, however, he filled the office for life of high-priest of the emperor-worship.[4] He was also Archon Eponymus.[5] There must have been a spark of divinity in the private individual who scattered millions like Hadrian, who erected buildings and delivered lectures like Pericles in Athens, who adorned many other cities with magnificent works, and who was honoured by them, not merely for his wealth but for his talent. But the son of this demi-god did not know his letters ; his father had twenty-four boys brought up with him, to each of whom a letter of the alphabet was given as a name, but it was of no avail. To display his sorrow at the

---

[1] Ἡ δὲ τοῦ Ἰσθμοῦ τομὴ ἔργον ἀθάνατον καὶ ἀπιστούμενον τῇ φύσει, δοκεῖ γάρ μοι τὸ ῥῆξαι τὸν Ἰσθμὸν Ποσειδῶνος δεῖσθαι ἢ ἀνδρός.—Philostr. ii. 60.

[2] Οὕτω χαλεπὸν ἀνθρώπῳ τὰ θεῖα βιάσασθαι.—Pausanias, *Corinth.* ii. 1, 5.

[3] Οὐκ ἐθάρρει δὲ αὐτὸ αἰτεῖν ἐκ βασιλέως, ὡς μὴ διαβληθείη διανοίας δοκῶν ἅπτεσθαι, ῇ μηδὲ Νέρων ἤρκεσεν.—Philostratus, *ut supra*.

[4] *C.I.A.* iii., n. 478, 664, 665, 735, 1132.

[5] *C.I.A.* iii., n. 735, 736, and 69*a*. Vidal-Lablache (*Hérode Atticus*, p. 34) assumes for this the year 135 A.D., but Dittenberger, "Die attische Pana-thenaiden-era" (*Comment.* Mommsen, p. 252), the year 127-128 A.D. He probably became archon after his return from the office of *corrector* of the free cities of Asia (Keil).

death of his wife, the rich Roman lady, Appia Annia Regilla,
Herodes had his house painted black, and darkened with
black Lesbian marble, for which, as well as for many other
theatrical representations of his grief, he drew upon himself
the mockery of Lucian.[1]   If this was fantastic folly, the
flattery of the Athenians in striking out of their calendar the
dáy on which Panathenais, one of the daughters of Herodes,
died, was still more absurd.   These Greeks carried the worship
of genius so far that they actually imitated the voice, the
walk, and the dress of a sophist who was dead, as in the
case of Hadrian of Tyre.[2]

Herodes is said not to have lived on good terms with the
wife whom he mourned so ostentatiously, and his enemies
even accused him of having employed a slave to murder her.
Philostratus dismisses this accusation with the other, that
Herodes, when he was overseer of the free cities in Asia,
actually quarrelled with the proconsul there, Antoninus who
was afterwards emperor; but it may be gathered from similar
anecdotes how great the pride, the quarrelsomeness and bad
temper of the man must have been.   The sophists of that
age very nearly succeeded in becoming tyrants in the cities.
In other times a citizen with such command of the money
market as Herodes, would have made himself master in the
republic of Athens, and would have founded a dynasty, as in
later ages the banker Cosmo de Medici succeeded in doing
in Florence.   The crowd of his slaves, servants, officers and
clients would have composed an army, and his freedmen
outraged the Athenian people, in whom the democratic spirit
still survived, by their insolent behaviour.   The Athenians
could at last no longer endure the imperious conduct of
their benefactor.   A party was formed against him, as in
earlier times one had been formed against Pisistratus.   The
party was led by the two Quintilians, who were the governors
of Greece.   The brothers Condianus and Maximus Quintilius, Ilians by birth, were celebrated for their intellect, their
wealth, and their love for one another; for with perfect
unanimity they filled together the highest offices.   Marcus
Aurelius treated them with the greatest respect.   (Commodus
afterwards had them put to death.)   The Athenians now

[1] Lucian, *Demonax*, 24, 25, 23.   [2] Philostratus, ii. 10.

begged these brothers to appear for them against Herodes before Marcus Aurelius, and they brought an action against him in 168 A.D. for his high-handed conduct in the affairs of the city, and for the excesses of his slaves. Herodes and his adversaries, among whom was the sophist Theodotus, placed themselves before the judgment-seat at Sirmium. The dispute really caused the downfall of the sophists from their position in Athens, but it did not end so much to the disadvantage of the accused that the emperor withdrew his favour from him.[1] Embittered, and at variance with Athens, the aged Herodes withdrew to his villas at Cephisia and Marathon, and here he died about 177 A.D. The Ephebi of Athens carried away his corpse by force, and buried it with great honour in the Panathenaean stadium, which he himself had magnificently adorned. His pupil, Hadrian of Tyre, pronounced his funeral oration. The Athenians inscribed on his monument: " Here lies Herodes of Marathon, son of Atticus, honoured by the whole world, and builder of this place."[2]

The writings of Herodes are lost. His *Ephemerides* is said to have been a clever work. Philostratus remarks that he imitated Critias in his manner of speaking, that it was less convincing than insinuating, and that it flowed as smoothly as a stream of silver on which sparkled grains of gold.

[1] Philostratus has given a detailed account of this. See also Hertzberg, ii. 399 *sq.*
[2] Philostratus, ii. 73.

CHAPTER XII

Polite Literature. Hadrian as Poet. Florus. Latin Poets. Greek Poets. Pancrates. Mesomedes. The Musician Dionysius of Halicarnassus. Greek Epigrams of Hadrian. Phlegon. Artemidorus and his Dream Books. The Romance of the Golden Ass

THE last wave of the worn-out poetic spirit of the Romans endured only until the time of Hadrian. The national poetry of Rome became extinct with Statius, Martial, and Juvenal. Juvenal, whose last fortunes are obscure, wrote satires in the time of Hadrian. The prince upon whom the muses set all their hopes, mentioned in the introduction to the seventh satire, is a reference to this emperor.[1] To poets and poetasters, he gave what they longed for, gold with both hands, but he could not endow them with the gifts of the muses. Greek as well as Latin literature no longer found expression in the higher ranks of poetry.

As a dilettante, Hadrian sought to express himself in verse like nearly every emperor, or prominent man in Rome.[2] He wrote love-songs and hymns to Plotina.[3] The Latin anthology ascribes some epigrams to him, of which none would do particular honour to a poet. Among them is an

---

[1] In *Sat.* xv. 27 (L. Aemilius) Juncus is mentioned as consul (suff. 127 A.D.). Friedlaender, iii. 461.

[2] Spart. c. 14: Et de suis dilectis multa versibus conposuit; amatoria carmina scripsit. Dion. lxix. 3: Καὶ πεζὰ καὶ ἐν ἔπεσι ποιήματα παντοδαπὰ καταλέλοιπεν.

[3] The hymns are mentioned by Dion Cassius, lxix. 10.

epitaph on Soranus, who boldly swam across the Danube with the Batavian cavalry, and an epitaph as well on the imperial charger Borysthenes. But it is doubtful whether these verses, and the dry epigram on the Amazons, are really his.[1] The well-known verses which he exchanged with P. Annius Florus are genuine. He seems to have asked the poet to accompany him on his journey to the north, and Florus declined the honour in the following trochaic trimeters :

> " I would rather not be Caesar,
>   Have to haunt Batavian marshes,
>   Lurk about among the Britons,
>   Feel the Scythian frosts assail me."

Hadrian replied :

> " I would rather not be Florus,
>   Have to haunt the Roman taverns,
>   Lurk about among the cookshops,
>   Feel the bossy bowl assail me." [2]

Spartianus considered these trifles which would have passed as impromptus at a banquet, worthy of record, and it is wonderful that they have lived. Florus was an intellectual man, as is shown by the fragment of his Latin work, the introduction to the dialogue on the school theme whether Virgil was an orator or a poet. In this he related some of his own experiences.[3] He was an African by birth. He came

[1] Lucian Mueller (*Claudii Rutilii Namatiani, De Reditu suo*, Lib. ii., 1870, p. 26) has greatly reduced the number of genuine Hadrian epigrams. Hadrian's epigrams in the *Anthol. lat. ed.* Meyer, n. 206-211.

> [2] " *Ego nolo Caesar esse,*
>   *Ambulare per* [Batavos,
>   *Latitare per*] *Britannos,*
>   *Scythicas pati pruinas.*"

> " *Ego nolo Florus esse,*
>   *Ambulare per tabernas,*
>   *Latitare per popinas,*
>   *Culices pati rotundos* " (?)

Spart. c. 6. The English version is that of Mr. Hodgkin. (Tr.)

[3] Found at first by Oehler in Brussels, edited by Ritschl, *Rhein. Mus.* 1842, i. 302 *sq.* The literature on the subject in Teuffel, 341.

to Rome as a boy, and appeared as a poet. But Domitian refused him the wreath of honour which he had won at the contest on the Capitol, as he did not wish to give such a prize to Africa. The injured poet hereupon left Rome, and wandered through the wide world, until he settled in Tarraco; here he kept a school of rhetoric. The scene of the dialogue is laid in the groves of the temple. The interlocutor is surprised that Florus remains in the provinces and does not revisit Rome, where his verses are recited, and where his famous Dacian triumph is applauded on the Forum. We do not know whether this poem had the real triumph of Trajan for its subject, or the shameful transactions of Domitian with Decebalus, which the senate rewarded with triumphal honours. Florus was again in Rome in Hadrian's reign, and became friendly with him. But he would not accompany the restless emperor, as he had grown tired of wandering about the world.

This precious fragment throws a gleam of light on the poet's life, which was so full of romantic adventures. His biography would have been a reflection of the literature of the time, and of Hadrian's court of the muses;[1] but we know nothing more about him. The epigrams of Florus in the Latin Anthology show that he could lay claim to the fame of a talented poet, even though his *Pegasus* did not rise far above the regions of mediocrity.[2]

The Latin poets who were famous in the time of Hadrian were Orion from Alexandria, a Greek, indeed, but who composed a Latin panegyric upon the emperor, Voconius, Julius

[1] A contribution to this in F. Eyssenhardt, "Hadrian und Florus," in *Samml. wissenschaftl. Vortraege*, xvii., 1882.

[2] *Anthol. lat.* ed. Meyer, n. 212-221. On the spitefulness of women.—On Apollo and Bacchus.—On Roses (the best). The epigram, n. 220, is full of the poet's pride:

> " Consules fiunt quodannis et novi proconsules,
>   Solus aut rex aut poeta non quodannis nascitur."

The epigrams have been collected by Lucian Mueller, *Claud. Rutil Namat.*, p. 26 *sq*. The question, whether *The Night-Festival of Venus* is by Florus, is disputed.—C. H. O. Mueller, *De P. Anno Floro poeta et carmine quod Pervigilium Veneris inscriptum est*, 1855. The literature on Florus in Teuffel.

Paulus, and Anianus Faliscus, an Etrurian writer of idylls.[1] Rome swarmed at this time with versifiers. Pliny the younger once wrote: "This year has produced a great cluster of poets; scarcely a day has passed in the whole month of April, on which one of them was not to be heard." And then he complained about the indifference of the public.[2]

The Greek poets seem to have been more numerous and more gifted than the Latin poets. Evodus from Rhodus, Erycius from Thessaly, Pancrates the Alexandrian, who celebrated Antinous, and was repaid by a post in the Museum, and particularly Mesomedes of Crete, all enjoyed some reputation. Mesomedes was a freedman of Hadrian, and, as court singer to the harp, he was as high in his favour as once Menecrates had been in that of Nero. He too, extolled Antinous. It is lamentable that we do not possess any of these Antinoids. The subject was romantic enough, and even in our own day has been made use of for a romance. They would have made clear to us how the fate of the youth, whose appearance we know only through the plastic art, was mirrored in the works of the poets, and what moral they extracted from this melodrama. Numerous poems must have been dedicated by the courtiers of the emperor to his deified boy. The rhetorician Numenius of Troas also wrote a consolatory discourse upon Antinous.[3] Hadrian rewarded the Antinoid of Mesomedes with a pension which Antoninus withdrew from the poet from motives of economy; but Caracalla erected a monument to him, which proves that the talents of this harp-player had made an impression on the time.[4] Two epigrams and a hymn to the Nemesis of Mesomedes have been preserved, with which Synesius was acquainted in the fifth century. As a virtuoso in singing and playing the harp he often

---

[1] Teuffel, 353, 3.　Lucian Mueller, *ibid*, p. 34 *sq.*

[2] Pliny, *Ep.* i. 13.

[3] Παραμυθικὸς εἰς ᾽Αντίνοον Suidas s.v. Numenios.

[4] Dion Cassius, lxxvii. 13: τῷ τε Μεσομήδει τῷ τοὺς κιθαρῳδικοὺς νόμους συγγράψαντι, from which it follows that Mesomedes had compiled the rules of his art. The *Chron. Euseb.* for 146 A.D. specifies him as κιθαρῳδικῶν νόμων μουσικὸς ποιητής.

triumphed in musical contests, and thus won Hadrian's heart.[1]

The emperor, too, was a dilettante in music. On that account he paid honour to a famous musician, Aelius Dionysius of Halicarnassus, the composer of a theory and history of music, giving him the name of his own gens Aelius. It is uncertain whether the hymn to Calliope is to be ascribed to him or to another musician of the same name. The hymns to this muse, to Helius and the one mentioned above of Mesomedes, are the only songs which have come down to us, with ancient Greek notes.[2] An historian of music has called them valuable antiquities which cannot serve as a standard of Greek music in its time of prosperity, and he compares these poems, elegantly composed of traditional phrases, with the bas-reliefs of the same epoch, which are designed with conventional figures.[3]

Hadrian was so conversant with both languages that he attempted to write Greek as well as Latin verses.[4] We possess five of his epigrams, among them the dedicatory inscription of the Dacian booty, which Trajan had offered to Zeus Casius. In an epigram dedicated to Eros, Hadrian begged the son of the sweet-speaking Cypris, who lived in Heliconian Thespiae, by the flower garden of Narcissus, graciously to accept the offering of a bear which he had killed when on horseback, in return for a breath of the favour of Aphrodite Urania. The elegance of these verses is only derived from the richness of the Greek language.[5]

Spartianus tells us that the emperor composed a very obscure work under the title *Libri Catachannae.* This

---

[1] Suidas, *Mesomedes* : ἐν τοῖς μάλιστα φίλος.

[2] See Bellermann, *Die Hymnen des Dionysios und Mesomedes*, 1840.

[3] Ambros, *Gesch. der Musik*, i. 451.

[4] Dion Cassius, lxix. 3, calls him φύσει δε φιλόλογος ἐν ἑκατέρᾳ τῇ γλώσσῃ.

[5] Kaibel, *Ep. gr.*, n. 811. Among the Greek epigrams the longest is that to Jupiter Casius. *Anth.* vi. 332. Other epigrams, vii. 674; ix. 137, 387 (also ascribed to Germanicus), ix. 17; ix. 402 (doubtful). A Greek epitaph on Hector in Cramer, *Anec. gr. Oxon.* iii. 354 ; *Scholia ad Tzetzis Chiliad.* ii. 78. A Greek epigram, probably by Hadrian, on the poet Parthenius, in Kaibel, n. 1089. Tillemont's error (*Adrien*, p. 443), that the emperor had composed an Alexandreis is due to the confusion of the names Adrianus and Arrianus.

seems to have been a wonderful satire in imitation of
Antimachus.[1]   It has been said of Hadrian that he wished
to supplant Homer by this composer of the antiquated epic
Thebais, and the tendency of his taste in this direction was
ascribed to the envy which made him grudge their deserts,
not only to the living but to the dead.[2]   In his time the
Alexandrian Chaennus, son of Hephaestion, wrote an *Anti-
Homer* in twenty-four cantos, and this is a proof of the
perverse view taken by the schools of the grammarians of
that time.

The poetry of Hadrian's time presents but scanty
material to the historian of literature ; but there is one
species of composition which he can examine as a sign of
the dark side of the century, namely, the stories of daemons
which merge into the fabulous and satirical romance of the
time.   Phlegon wrote *Miraculous Stories* in which he tells
the most irrational anecdotes of ghosts, among them being
the story which was the origin of Goethe's *Bride of Corinth.*
All these fables contain neither the interest of a gruesome
imagination, nor the value of a hidden moral.   They are
crudely and unskilfully invented.[3]   The demand for such
things was very great at the time, for the decay of religion
stimulated superstition, and, from the emperor down to the
slave, every one was interested in magic, demonology, and
astrology.   The endeavour to treat dreams scientifically, as
a source of revelation, was a proof of this mystical tendency.
Every one believed in the power of dreams, like Galen, who
accepted them as medical signs ; like Pausanias, who made
up his mind through a dream not to write upon the Eleu-
sinium, and like Lucian, who was prompted by a dream to
become a sophist instead of a sculptor.

Hermippus of Berytus, a pupil of Herennius Philo, had

---

[1] The word has been used of grafted trees which produced different
kinds of fruits (Forcellini, *Lex.* s.v. Catachanna).   The best explanation of
καταχήνη, as a satirical composition, is given by Th. Bergk, *De Antimachi
et Hadriani Catachenis, Zeitschrift für Alterthumswissensch* (ed. Zimmer-
mann), 1835, p. 300.

[2] Dion Cassius, lxix. 4 : μὴ μόνον τοῖς ζῶσιν ἀλλὰ καὶ τοῖς τελευτήσασι φθονεῖν.

[3] *Phlegontis Tralliani opuscula gr. et lat.* ed. Franz. *Fragmenta* ed. C.
Müller, 1849, in *Fragm. Histor. Graecor.*, vol. iii.

already written a history of dreams in the time of Trajan and Hadrian. His successor was Artemidorus Daldianus of Ephesus, the chief seat of all daemoniac superstition. In the preface to his *Oneirocritica*, or *Dream Interpretations* he boasts of having given a true and generally useful work to the world, in which the whole Greek literature upon dreams was collected.[1] In fact, he almost passed his life travelling through countries and islands to procure materials for his work.

Artemidorus first established the difference between *oneiros* and *enhypnion*. One prophesies the future, the other the present; one continues to act upon the soul in its waking hours, the work of the other terminates with sleep. The dreams of the first kind are speculative, indicating the subject of the dream, as if one dreamt of a shipwreck which afterwards really took place, or allegorical. According to his theory, oneiros is a figurative movement of the soul, something which exists outside consciousness and by which the soul delivers an oracle to mankind, giving it either no time or only a certain time to look into the future. The allegorical dream foretells events by the most sympathetic image. For instance, the head denotes the father, the foot the slave, etc., etc. If a man is poor and dreams he is born, it signifies fortune to him, for a child must be maintained and must have a guardian; if he is rich, however, it is a sign that he will lose control over his property, for a child is not *sui juris*. The interpretation is often not devoid of ingenuity. It is founded chiefly on the relation in which the dreamer may be supposed to be to the vision. A large head denotes wealth, places of honour, triumphal wreaths, if the dreamer does not already possess them; in which case it denotes cares and anxieties. Long and well-kept hair promise happiness; unkempt hair, misfortune and sorrow. Wool instead of hair means illness; a shaven head, mischief. If a man dreams that he hears ants creeping in his ear, it means health and many listeners to the sophist, but to anyone else it means death, as the ants live in the earth. If an unmarried woman dreams that she has a beard, she may reckon upon having a husband. If an accused man dreams that he is

[1] Artemidorus, *Oneirocritica*, ed. Reiff, 1805, ed. Hercher, 1864.

beheaded, he need no longer fear the executioner, for a head cannot be cut off twice.

In this way Artemidorus goes through the list of visions proceeding from dreams of physical activity to dreams of mental activity and to the whole world of apparitions.

While in Phlegon's writings the anecdotes of ghosts serve only for amusement, the attempt was made by Artemidorus to treat the dream psychologically. The Greek Lucian and the Latin Apuleius afterwards attacked the belief in apparitions and demonology, though quite unsuccessfully, by their satires. Lucius Patrensis is said to have been the real author of the romance of the Golden Ass. Lucian continued it, and Apuleius, who was born at Madaura in Africa about the middle of Hadrian's reign, was the last editor of this obscene, but valuable picture of the manners of the time of the Antonines. Literature owes to him the preservation of the story of Cupid and Psyche, one of the sweetest poems of antiquity, which is set as a pearl in this filthy romance. This platonic allegory of the soul rising to celestial happiness through the purgatory of sorrow, seems like the farewell of dying paganism, which forebodes its change into Christianity. Marble groups of Cupid and Psyche, or their images represented on sarcophagi, cannot be authenticated before the second century.[1]

We are not sufficiently enlightened as to the structure of the Greek romance of this epoch. Iamblichus of Syria seems to belong to this period, of whose Babylonian histories (the love story of Rhodanes and Sinonis) Photius made extracts. The circumstances of this and other Roman writers are obscure, and unquestionably a whole literature of this class has been lost, whose birthplace must have been Ephesus.[2] The military expeditions of Trajan had opened up the East

---

[1] Gaston-Boissier, *La religion Romaine d'Auguste aux Antonins*, ii. 120. Upon the legend of Cupid and Psyche and other traces of folk-lore in antiquity, Friedlaender, i., p. 468 *sq.* A highly cultivated Roman lady, Donna Ersilia Caetani Lovatelli, has enriched the literature on this subject by a beautiful treatise—*Amore e Psiche*, Rome, 1883.

[2] The date, too, of the *Ephesiaca*, or love story of Anthia and Abrocomas, by Xenophon of Ephesus cannot be determined. Erwin Rohde, *Der griech. Roman und seine Vorlaeufer*, p. 360 *sq.*

afresh to the realm of fancy, and Hadrian encouraged relations with these distant countries. The literary circles of
Greece, Asia, and Egypt were brought by him into nearer
connection with each other and with the West. It was a
restless age. Side by side with the travels of Hadrian arose
the imaginary travels of romance. These romances must
have been very much the fashion, as Lucian ridiculed them
in his *True Stories*. At the beginning of the third century,
these journeys of adventure were worked into a famous
romance of a social and religious tendency by Philostratus,
in which Apollonius of Tyana wanders through the world
like a heathen Christ. Paganism defended itself in vain
against the degeneration of the power of the old religion
into wild romance which was brought about by the irony of
the Atheists, as well as by the fantastic ideas of the Neopy-
thagoreans and the Platonists.

CHAPTER XIII

Philosophy. The Stoa. Epictetus and the Enchiridion. Stoicism and Cynicism. Demonax of Athens

THE philosophical schools of Athens however still continued to exist even in this age. In Rome, Greece and Asia they could show many celebrated names, like Rusticus and Severus, the teachers of Marcus Aurelius, Taurus, Favorinus, Secundus, Theon, Timocrates, Alcinous and others. Platonists, Peripatetics, Pythagoreans and Stoics maintained the traditions of the ancient systems of thought, and if philosophy could derive advantage from freedom of thought, this was certainly offered to her in the fullest measure by the Roman empire. Freedom of thought and teaching was absolute in the empire. Oenomaus of Gadara could deny the gods in the time of Hadrian, without being condemned to drink the cup of hemlock. The Flavian emperors indeed, even Vespasian, had driven the philosophers out of Rome, but that was on account of their political principles. Philosophy, however, had become unfruitful, the age was worn out and impoverished in ideas. Christianity could traverse these shallows of thought without effort. It encountered no Plato and no Aristotle, but their formulas only which no longer satisfied the mind. Philosophy and the old religion were equally effete.

The few thinkers of that time escape our view, as we do not possess their writings; but Lucian has taken care that the beggarly philosophic proletariate is visible to us in its thousands. In *Hermotimus* he exposes the folly of the syllogisms as well as of the beliefs and opinions of the average philosopher, and shows us how happiness consists only in practical actions. In *The Sale of the Philosophers*, and in the *Fisherman*, he drowned all these follies in the floods of his wit. His mockery, however, was only aimed at these caricatures, for he was not so superficial as to despise the heroes of thought.

Among the schools of philosophy of the time of the empire there was still one of historical importance, that of the Stoics. Neoplatonism, indeed, is a production of the time, and was combined with Christianity in the Gnosis, but it was not until the third century that it was formed into an effective system by Plotinus. After Quintus Sextius founded the school of the Stoics in Rome, Stoicism remained the profession of faith of the noblest minds among the Romans. It formed the really aristocratic character which knew how to die with greatness of soul. Under the empire the Stoa had its martyrs as well as Christianity. Musonius Rufus and Seneca were its brilliant representatives in the first century. In the second century it came into power, ending its glorious age with Marcus Aurelius on the imperial throne.

Rome, with her crime and her slavery, but also with her cosmopolitanism, was the natural field for Stoic morality, while in the East, the schools of Zeno and Chrysippus had long fallen into decay.[1] Even Epictetus, the head of the new Stoicism, a Greek from Hierapolis in Phrygia, was brought up as a slave of the freedman Epaphroditus under Nero in Rome, where he was a pupil of Musonius Rufus and of Euphrates. Expelled with all the other philosophers by Domitian, he lived and taught at Nicopolis in Epirus. The year of his death is unknown; but he died either in the last years of Trajan or in the earliest years of Hadrian. For the assertion of Spartianus that Hadrian was acquainted with Epictetus is certainly doubtful, but cannot be refuted.[2] After the days of Nerva the Stoa had become a public

[1] See Gellius, i., c. 2, where Herodes Atticus silences a young man who wishes to be a Stoic and airs his syllogisms, by a few words from Epictetus. Arrian, *Dissert.* ii., c. 29.

[2] Spart. *Vita Hadr.*, c. 16. See Zeller, *Die Phil. der Griechen*, iii. 1, p. 660. The life of Epictetus in the edition of Arrian (1683). Macrobius, *Saturn.* I. ix., quotes the epigram of Epictetus, δοῦλος Ἐπίκτητος.

power, and could not therefore escape the notice of Hadrian. But his sophistical nature forbade him to become wedded to any one mode of thought. He respected Epictetus, without being a Stoic. The noble image of this teacher of virtue, who could say of himself that though born a slave and a cripple, and though poor as Iros, he was still a favourite of the immortals, has been preserved to posterity by Arrian ; for what Plato and Xenophon were to Socrates, this statesman of Hadrian was to Epictetus.

The *Enchiridion* is the Stoics' gospel of the second century, the guide for all the practical conduct of life. For morality is the kernel of the Stoic school, which recognizes the doctrine of ethics as its highest theme, and therefore renounces speculation. This book of morals has so much in common with the teaching of the Gospels that it has been ascribed to a Christian author.[1] But this harmony is also so strongly marked in the writings of Seneca, that it has been supposed that he was a secret Christian. It is also noticeable in Marcus Aurelius, and in truth the morality, which could elicit even from the Stoics the command to love their enemies, is so sublime, their submission to the will of God so complete, that this moral current in the mind of the heathen world seems to prove the historical necessity for Christianity.[2] And still more it provokes the question, whether from Stoicism alone a universal religion like Christianity, perhaps in the form of a philanthropic brotherhood, would not have grown up, without miracles and dogmas and without a priesthood, even if Jesus of Nazareth had not appeared. For the rest, the Stoics placed little value upon Christianity, and this fact proves that their ideas were independent of those of the new religion. They were astonished at the readiness with which martyrs suffered death, but they did not admire it. They

γενόμην, καὶ σώματ' πηρὸς, καὶ πενίην 'Ιρος, καὶ φίλος ἀθάνατος. There is an Altercatio Hadrieni Aug. et Epicteti Phil., a game comprised of questions and answers, not devoid of wit, which has come down from the Middle Ages like the Disputatio Pippini cum Albino Scholastico.

[1] Stoici nostro dogmati in plerisque concordant.—Hieron. *in Esaiam*, c. 11.

[2] The Stoics, however, did not agree with the Christians in the belief of the immortality of the soul. The soul was to them something corporeal though of the finest matter.

looked· upon it as a fanatic obstinacy, or as a custom which had become epidemic, but not as the act of philosophic conviction, which made heroes of Cremutius Cordus, Thrasea and Helvidius Priscus.[1]

At the beginning of the *Enchiridion* we are told that man has only his actions in his power. These are free; but everything outside the human soul, like fortunate circumstances, etc., is not free, and over them he has no control. We should not therefore complain of the want or loss of such things, we should only ask for what is ours, that is, for the things over which we have control; all others we should despise. Stoicism may be comprised in the words: endure and renounce! The chief thing is to be able to distinguish rightly between what is possible for us and what is not possible. Everything depends upon the way in which we look at things. The objectiveness which forces itself upon our desire is a fantasy, that is, a vision accepted by the idea, and our business is to find out what is real in this fantasy. A man must not then allow himself to be drawn away by his desires to the fantasy. As then the conceived idea, or the pure subjective thought is the principle and criterion for the truth of everything, so by it is all truth preserved, and the world of the Stoics becomes merely a formal and abstract world. It is not things themselves which move us, but the conceptions which we form of them.[2] Epictetus expressed this practically when he says that all injuries do not come from the offender, but from our view of them. The transition to Scepticism or Pyrrhonism is thus easily made.

The Ego is the one concrete thing as opposed to the abstract. The Stoic took refuge within himself to preserve his freedom. This freedom however is imaginary, because the other side, namely, the real world, is wanting. Man is composed of body, soul and mind. To the body belong the senses, to the soul the desires, and to the mind the opinions. The Aesthesis is the animal. It receives an impression, but the Hormesis is animal as well as human, and

---

[1] Epictetus (*Dissert.* iv. 7) and Marcus Aurelius (xi. 3) cast a glance of disapproval upon such martyrs. Otherwise they take no notice of the Christians.

[2] *Enchiridion*, c. 10.

is peculiar both to a Phalaris and a Nero. The true wise man is he who lives conformably to the inner daemon, not allowing himself to be dazzled by a number of illusions, but submitting himself to fate.[1] For as understanding is common even to those who are godless and practise shameful things in secret, there must be something special for the good, which others do not possess. This consists in equanimity, resignation, and the withdrawal of the inner mind from all that may disturb it.

From this logic, in which the subjective thought is made the starting-point, is built up the fabric of practical moral philosophy. The chief idea has been already given, that the wise man should not let himself be carried away by things, but should find out what they are, and live according to pure reason. Accordingly as things exist only in appearance, imagination, or thought, they produce the Stoic fortitude, but at the same time enjoin an active prosecution of the aims of life. First see what kind of affair it is with which you have to do, and then see if your nature has strength for it.[2] By this means arrogance, ambition, and love of power are avoided, and it follows that every one quietly fulfils the task which nature has appointed for him.[3] Zeno and Chrysippus defined virtue as life according to nature, or self-preservation according to reason. The Stoic takes the world as it is, and his idea of justice consists in the discharge of duties. This principle forms the transition to fatalism.

According to Plutarch, fate is the world-soul, and is a circle, because everything which happens in heaven and earth moves in a circle. But it is universal, and stands in the same relation to the individual, as the universal power of the civil law stands to the citizens. Without referring to them individually and particularly, they are in subjection to it. Plutarch has justly recognized, that the individual is the individual only through the universal. He distinguishes between things directly and indirectly predestined. The former are included in fate, the latter are the definite consequences of the former. In the same way, many

[1] Marcus Aurelius, iii. 9.   [2] *Enchiridion*, c. 26.
[3] *Enchiridion*, c. 13 ; *Dissertat.* i. 2.

things contained in the law like adultery and murder are not lawful, but other things which follow definitely from the law, are lawful. Therefore, he says, everything is comprised in fate, but individual things cannot with justice be ascribed to it, and hence everything happens according to its own nature. In nature the possible precedes the event. The possible is either something which really happens, and then it is necessary, like the rising and setting of the stars, or something which might be prevented from happening, and then it is chance. Luck is a combination of causes; it happens, it is true, in conjunction with our actions, but independently of our will; as, for instance, if a man digs up a plant, and finds gold. Chance is a wider conception than luck, which only refers to mankind. Plutarch goes on to say that, the first and the highest providence is the intelligence of the only God, His beneficent will towards everything divine, and of divine order. The second is that of the divinities of the second grade, who settle the affairs of mortals. The third is that of the genii who move round the earth and direct the acts of men. Now fate is dependent upon the first providence, that is God, who made everything good and beautiful, who allotted souls to man, and gave to each his own star. In Plutarch fate coincides with the world, or the productive power of nature. The tendency to monotheism is evident, but it is not developed, as the mythological polytheism is maintained, intervening between the highest God and the soul of man, like a Platonic doctrine of daemons. Justin, who does every justice to the Stoics, proves the paradox which is contained in the fact that they deny freedom, and yet lay down moral laws.[1]

In the Stoic renunciation of the world there is a similarity to ascetic Christianity. In the writings of Seneca, Epictetus, and Marcus Aurelius, sentiments entirely Christian are to be found, such as, that man should consider himself as a part of the Divinity, indeed, even as a son of God, and that on that account he should preserve his moral dignity as an inhabitant of the earth, and should love his fellowmen, even slaves, as they are all descended from God. Neoplatonism is allied

---

[1] Just. Mart. *Apol.*, p. 45 ; also Tatian, *Cont. Graec.*, p. 146 C, D.

to this tendency, its view being that life will be completed by being raised to the contemplation of God.

As a branch of the Stoa, the Cynics formed a community of some size in the Roman empire. Underneath the rough exterior of the sect there were qualities which commanded respect. In its dogma Cynicism is opposed to the polytheism of the heathens, and particularly to the belief in the gods. In the philosopher Oenomaus it seems to have reached its height as Nihilism. The theory of life of the Cynics is the moral opposition to despotism through the consciousness of the inner freedom of the soul. Even before the Christians ventured openly to contend against the tyranny of the Pagan state, the late followers of Diogenes and Antisthenes did so with the assurance of heroes of virtue. Their manly pride before the throne of the sovereign often degenerated into beggarly impudence, and on that account Vespasian banished all the philosophers from Rome, with the exception of the highly cultivated Musonius Rufus.

Though Lucian himself did not admire Cynicism, he held up a patriarch of this school as a pattern of virtue. This was Demonax of Cyprus, who in the time of Hadrian and the Antonines enjoyed the greatest respect at Athens. He lived like a new Diogenes, without posing as an eccentricity. His nature, says Lucian, was full of Attic graces; he was never heard to use a common expression or a severe faultfinding word. He attacked faults but not those who committed them. The work of his life was to make peace. He looked upon every one as related to him, because he was a man.[1] He never sacrificed to the gods, and he disdained to be admitted into the mysteries. Accused on that account of godlessness, he entered the assembly of the people, and said: "Athenians, I stand here garlanded before you; now put me to death, for in your first sacrifice you have had no signs of good omen."[2] The people were so fond of him, that all houses stood open to him; and anyone thought himself fortunate if Demonax appeared to spend the night. Many of his sayings, with which he rebuked the vanity of men, particularly of the great, were passed from mouth to mouth. When he

---

[1] οὐκ ἔστιν ὅντινα οὐκ οἰκεῖον ἐνόμεζεν, ἄνθρωπόν γε ὄντα.

[2] *Demonax*, c. 11 : allusion to Socrates.

felt that his end was approaching, he repeated to his friends the speech of the herald at the end of the combat.[1] He then took no more food.   When Demonax had ended his long life of nearly a hundred years in this way, the Athenians buried him like a hero at the public expense, showing that they placed as high a value upon philosophical greatness of character, as upon the most brilliant oratory of the sophists.

On the whole, Stoicism had a softening effect upon the legislation of the Romans, especially upon that of Hadrian, enlarging the philosophic spirit of justice towards every one, while at the same time, long before the effect of Christianity became apparent, it served as a consolation to innocent sufferers.[2]   Midway in the reign of terror of the Caesars the republican mind could take refuge in Stoicism, and then could incorporate in Marcus Aurelius the ideal of a prince.   In his *Meditations* this emperor acknowledged that he had formed his character after the model of the heroes of liberty, Cato and Brutus, Thrasea and Helvidius.   He owed this sympathy for them to the instruction of Claudius Severus, who had taught him that the best state was that in which the citizens were treated according to the principles of equality, and where the liberty of the subject was the most important point.[3]

Finally, Stoic philosophy, quite independently of Christianity and from its conception of the unity of the world, set up as the highest aim of civilization, the idea of humanity and of the rights of men.   If there were nothing more remaining of it than the idea of cosmopolitanism and of the brotherhood of man, this would be enough to give it a very high place among the systems of philosophy.[4]

[1]
Λήγει μὲν ἀγὼν τῶν καλλίστων
ἄθλων ταμίας, καιρὸς δὲ καλεῖ
μηκέτι μέλλειν.

[2] Herder, *Ideen zur Geschichte der Menschheit*, iii. 14, 5.

[3] *In se ipsum*, i. 14.

[4] Marcus Aurelius, iii., calls man πολίτην πόλεως τῆς ἀνωτάτης ἧς αἱ λοιπαὶ πόλεις ὥσπερ οἰκίαι εἰσίν and iv. 4, the world πόλις, and in c. 23 even πόλις Διός. In the same way Musonius, entirely in the sense in which Augustine conceives the civitas Dei, speaks of the πολίτης τῆς τοῦ Διὸς πόλεως. Zeller, iii. 1, 279.

CHAPTER XIV

Peregrinus Proteus

IN *Peregrinus Proteus* Lucian has caricatured Cynicism. It is the philosophic charlatan whom he ridicules. The history of this adventurer throws a light upon the moral conditions of the age of Hadrian. The Cynic Peregrinus Proteus was born at Parium in Mysia at the beginning of the second century. From a restless love of travelling, which seems to have been an attribute of the men of the time, as well as from a thirst for knowledge, he journeyed through many lands, like Hadrian. He penetrated into philosophic and religious secrets. In Palestine he learnt the mysteries of the Christians, and joined their community. Lucian looked upon his going over to this sect merely as an act of insanity. The "wonderful wisdom" of the Christians only appeared ridiculous to him.[1] As a man of education and ability Peregrinus enjoyed their respect, filling indeed one of the chief offices of the community, and suffering persecution.[2] He was captured and imprisoned for participating in the Christian mysteries, whereupon he experienced the brotherly love of the Christians in such great measure that he acquired a good income under "this title" (namely, that of martyr). "For these people," says Lucian, "display incredible activity in cases which concern their community; they spare neither trouble nor expense." What Lucian thought of Christianity is shown by what he says later

---

[1] *Perigrin.* c. 11.

[2] He calls the Christian offices which Proteus held, according to heathen notions, προφήτης, θιασάρχος and ξυναγωγεύς; then he became προστάτης.

of its professors: " These poor devils imagine that they are immortal, and that they will live for ever; therefore they despise death, and many indeed even seek it.   In addition, their first Lawgiver inculcated the belief that they were all brothers, and they went so far as to deny the gods of the Greeks, to pray to that crucified Sophist, and to live according to His precepts.[1]   All other goods they despise, possessing them in common, without having any convincing proof for these opinions.   If any cunning scoundrel comes to them, it is easy for him soon to become rich, and to laugh at the simpletons."   Lucian relates that the Christian communities in Asia sent delegates to mitigate the fate of prisoners.

Peregrinus was, however, thrust out of the community, as he was found guilty of eating forbidden meat.   He then continued his adventurous life as a Cynic in Egypt and Italy, where he appeared as a freethinker and a demagogue, and acquired great fame.   Banished from Rome by the prefect of the city, he then wandered to Elis.   Here he gave vent to his slanderous disposition.   " First he wanted to persuade the Greeks to take up arms against Rome, then he blamed a man distinguished for his culture and worth (namely, Herodes Atticus) because, among other services to Greece, he had made an aqueduct to Olympia, in order that the spectator at the games might not faint from thirst.   He reproached him for this good action as if he had thereby rendered the Greeks effeminate."

Yet in Peregrinus an impulse towards something higher can be discerned, which, however, took a false and fanciful direction.   The Cynic finally committed suicide with theatrical ostentation, from weariness of a life which could not give him satisfaction of any kind.   The Stoics defended suicide, and considered it an honour rather than a disgrace.   It is said of the philosopher Euphrates, whom Pliny admired, that he died voluntarily after Hadrian had granted him the poisoned cup.[2]

According to Eusebius, Peregrinus Proteus burnt himself

---

[1] ἐπειδὰν—τὸν δὲ ἀνεσκολοπισμένον ἐκεῖνον σοφιστὴν αὐτῶν προσκυνῶσιν, c. 13.

[2] Dion Cassius, lxix. 8.   Hadrian condemned suicide as a crime only in the case of the Roman soldier because he considered it a case of desertion.—Grasberger, *Erziehung und Unterr. im class. Alterthum.* iii. 75.

in 168 A.D. This tragical farce, as Lucian calls it, took place at Olympia, whither it is quite probable that the Cynic had gone in order to make a sensation. He and his friends had sent out an invitation as if to a play. A discourse was given upon death by fire, in the gymnasium, and Peregrinus himself delivered what was practically his own funeral oration before an assembly. Lucian only heard part of it, as, for fear of being crushed to death, he avoided the crowd. " I heard him say, however, that he wished to place a golden crown upon a golden life, for he who has lived like Hercules must die like Hercules, and return into the aether. He wished also to be a benefactor to the world, and to show how death may be despised. For this reason every one must be his own Philoctetes. Here the weakest and the simplest among the crowd burst into tears and exclaimed, ' Live for the Greeks!' Others, who had stronger nerves, called out, ' Do what you have determined to do.' This seemed considerably to disconcert the old man, for he may have expected that the mob would have restrained him from dying by fire, and have compelled him to live on against his wishes. He trembled so much that he was not able to speak any more."

After the games were over and many strangers had left, the great spectacle was really acted at Olympia. It was midnight, and the moon shone as a witness to the mighty deed. Peregrinus came with the leading Cynics, accompanied by Theagenes of Patrae. Each Cynic carried a torch. The pile, composed of pine chips and dry brushwood, was laid in a hole twenty stadia from the Hippodrome. Proteus laid aside his wallet, his Cynic's coat and club of Hercules, and appeared in a dirty white linen under garment. He then took incense, threw it into the flames, and exclaimed, turning his face to the south, " Spirits of my parents, receive me kindly." With these words he sprang into the fire and disappeared, as the flames, blazing up all round, closed over him. The Cynics stood round the pile gazing with silent grief, but without shedding tears. Peregrinus probably wished, by the circumstances of his death, to bequeath wonderful legends to posterity, and this object would have been defeated if he had burnt himself at the games before assembled Greece. The exaggerated statement of Lucian is, however, throughout hostile to the man, and barely in accordance with the truth. Gellius heard the teaching of this same Peregrinus at Athens, and acknowledged him to be an honest man, and Ammianus mentioned him as a famous philosopher.[1] Yet his voluntary death must have made a great impression on the minds of men; for the Christian apologist Athenagoras, a younger contemporary of Proteus, informs us that his statue was erected at Parium, and that oracular power was ascribed to it.[2]

[1] Jacob Bernays, *Lucian und die Kyniker*, p. 60 *sq.*

[2] Hujus etiam statua oracula dicitur edere.—Athenagoras, *Legat. pro Christianis*, c. 26.

CHAPTER XV

Alexander of Abonotichus

THE honesty of Lucian with reference to Peregrinus may be doubted, but the brilliant colours with which he has painted the character of the religious charlatan in *Alexander of Abonotichus* are, on the whole, to be accepted as correct. Nothing so clearly shows the degeneration of the ancient religion into priestcraft and absurdity as the history of this Cagliostro of the second century. Lucian, the Voltaire of the time, had the good fortune to come into personal contact with this adventurer. He was a close spectator of his audacious conduct and of his actions in this farce of religious delusion, and he has shown us to what a height the stream of superstition can rise when priestcraft is encouraged by the credulity of the foolish mob.

Alexander, a Greek from Abonotichus in Paphlagonia, was the hero of this religious comedy, a man of majestic appearance, of great cunning and powerful intellect. He had prosecuted his studies in the wide field of human folly, with one of those necromancers who carry on their dark, but profitable, business under the guise of the science of medicine. After the death of his master, Alexander joined himself to a man of letters from Byzantium. Accident put it into the head of these two comrades, who were travelling over the world, to appear in great style, as workers of miracles if not as founders of a religion, and to grow rich by a wholesale manufacture of oracles. They came to Chalcedon with a serpent, which they had bought at Pella in Macedonia, and had trained for their purpose. There they buried two bronze tables in the temple of Apollo, on which was written that the god Aesculapius would come with his father Apollo, to Pontus, and would take his seat at Abonotichus. The discovery of these tables caused the expected sensation, and paved the way for Alexander's reception in his favoured native city, for on the rumour of the approaching appearance of Aesculapius the council of Abonotichus decided to build a temple for the god. The charlatan reversed the proverb, that a prophet has no honour in his own country, for he knew his locality. After playing his game first in superstitious Macedonia, he could, as Lucian asserts, find no more suitable spot for carrying out his plan than a city of the Paphlagonians, " where the simple people are accustomed to stare at every soothsayer who asks a riddle, if he comes accompanied by a player on the flute and the cymbal, as if he were a messenger from heaven." [1]

While his comrade remained behind in Macedonia, where he soon after died, Alexander made his entry into his native city. He appeared in a purple garment and white cloak, with long flowing curls, having a crooked sword in his hand, such as Perseus was represented wearing, for he asserted that he was descended from this hero. He announced his divine ancestry in the following verses :

> " This man you see is offspring of Perseus, and the darling of Apollo,
> Alexander of divine descent from the blood of Podalirion."

The conjurer first prepared his countrymen for the great event by cunning tricks, acting as if he were possessed. The temple was being built at Abonotichus ; in a ditch under the foundation Alexander concealed an egg, in which he had enclosed a small serpent. Some days after he appeared, strangely attired and as if mad with excitement, in the market-place. He leapt upon an altar and announced the near approach of Aesculapius, while the people remained on their knees praying. Chaldaean and Hebrew phrases gave the needful magical colour to his prophecies. He then rushed to the ditch, sang a hymn to Aesculapius and Apollo, and called for the gracious appearance of the god at Abonotichus. He brought the egg out in a cup and broke it, the Paphlagonians raising a cry of delight when the god appeared in their city in the shape of a young serpent. Abonotichus

---

[1] *Alexander*, c. 9.

was immediately filled with swarms of the curious and the wonder-loving, who assembled from far and wide. The spectacle was as like as one egg is to another, to the scenes that were publicly enacted in our own time at a spot in a great country which suddenly sprang into notoriety, but with this difference that at Abonotichus in Paphlagonia Aesculapius appeared, while in France it was the Virgin Mary.

In a few days the prophet was to be seen in a small house, seated upon a divan. Around him was coiled the serpent, grown already to great size, the serpent of course which he had brought with him from Pella and had trained. It displayed a human head, moved its mouth, and stretched out a black tongue. The obscurity of the room, the crowd and the feverish excitement of the people accomplished the desired effect.

In the meantime processions by degrees streamed into Abonotichus from Bithynia, Galatia and Thrace. Artists portrayed the new god in bronze and silver, in marble and clay, and sold the figures in great quantities, as the figures of saints are sold to-day in places of pilgrimage. Alexander gave the name Glycon to this god:

"Glycon am I, a grandson of Zeus,
    And a light to humanity."

Need we be surprised that this magician really succeeded in establishing a temple and worship for his divinity? He had the women on his side, for he was a very handsome man. Lucian, indeed, only narrates facts, when he says that many women boasted of having had children by Alexander, and that this was indeed confirmed by their fortunate husbands.[1] A regular oracle was established in the temple of Aesculapius. Questions were brought to the prophet for his oracle on a sealed tablet, which he then opened so cleverly that none could perceive it.[2] He answered them in verse, for correct form had to be given to the deception. We can imagine

---

[1] *Alexander*, c. 42.

[2] Lucian mentions the artifice which was then employed to open writings without being detected. The seal was either detached by a hot needle, without destroying it, or an impression was taken of it. They were therefore in the second century not so far behind our present secret police.

that like a father confessor, Alexander had sufficient opportunity to get the people into his power who came to him
for advice, and to make many who were inclined to show
dangerous political tendencies dependent upon his silence.
He was also cunning enough to make friends with other
frequented oracles, especially with the priesthood of Apollo
at Clarus and Didyma, and Amphilochus, so that he often
referred to their prophetic source, and said, instead of giving
an answer, "Go to Clarus and hear what there my father
foretells."

Lucian gives many proofs of the crafty cunning of the
impostor in working the oracles. But his success made him
in the end so audacious that he became careless, and was
deceived by ingenious people who saw through his game.
"I asked him," so says Lucian, "on a slip of paper whether
Alexander had a bald head, and as I had sealed the leaf so
that it could not easily be opened without suspicion, he
wrote upon it a dark oracle which ran, 'Sabardalachis Malach
Attis was another.'[1] Another time I asked him on two
different slips when the poet Homer was born. As my servant had told him that the question was about a remedy
for pains in the hip, on one slip he wrote these words,
'Anoint yourself with Cytmis and with the dew of Latona.'
On the other, which the servant had told him was an inquiry
whether I should journey to Italy by sea or land, he wrote
the following reply, which had nothing to do with Homer,
'Dread the journey by sea, the way by land is more to your
advantage.'"

Such mistakes did not prevent the prophecies of Alexander becoming famous far and wide. Even Severian, the
governor of Cappadocia, when he took the field against the
Parthian king Vologeses II., sent to demand an oracle,
which however turned out badly for him. This happened
at the beginning of the reign of Marcus Aurelius. The
prophet sent his agents into all the countries of the
empire to advertise his fame. He won a footing even in
Italy, where he found believers and adherents among

[1] As Abonotichus could not contain the number of inquirers, Alexander
despatched many by similar night oracles, that is to say, he laid the slip
under his pillow, and the god revealed himself in a dream.

the highest aristocracy in Rome and at the emperor's court. He attached Rutilianus, one of the most prominent Romans, to him, by giving him his own daughter, of whom he said Selene was the mother, in marriage, upon the express command of the god Aesculapius. Rutilianus is said to have even persuaded the emperor to allow two lions to be thrown into the Danube, because Alexander considered this sacrifice was needful to secure the Romans their victory over the Marcomanni. The sacrifice was of no avail, for the imperial army suffered a terrible defeat. The lying prophet made use with great skill of the excitement in the minds of people in the empire, which was caused by this war and by the plague, which in 167 A.D. laid waste many countries. His travelling emissaries spread everywhere the dread of pestilence and earthquakes, and offered the amulets of Alexander as a protection against them. While the plague lasted, Lucian assures us, that nearly over every house-door a foolish line was to be seen, which Alexander had sent into every country, which ran : " Phoebus, with flowing locks, drives away the clouds of sickness." [1]

There seems to have been a whole joint-stock company of impostors whom the prophet employed in the manufacture of his oracles. All these helpers, temple servants, registrars, oracle makers, secretaries, and interpreters of the questions which were addressed to him in different languages, received a good income. In order to attract the crowd he established a mystical festival of three days, with torchlight processions, and all imaginable priestly pomp. Dramatic pantomimes were performed, representing the delivery of Latona, the birth of Aesculapius, and of the god Glycon.[2]

This audacious comedy was maintained for thirty years, without its chief actor being put in prison. Sensible people indeed began to see through it, but power failed them to overthrow the juggler, as he had struck his roots too firmly in the nation. He was particularly afraid of the enlightened Epicureans and the Christians, and incited the populace to stone them wherever they showed themselves. Lucian, too, would have repented his temerity if he had not been saved by an accident. The story he tells is almost fabulous.

---

[1] *Alexander*, c. 36.   [2] *Alexander*, c. 38.

When the prophet heard of his arrival, he asked him to come and see him. Lucian came with a few soldiers, whom the governor of Cappadocia had given him as an escort on his way to the sea. Embittered for a long time by the fact that the sophist had ventured to dissuade Rutilianus from his marriage, Alexander wished to destroy him; but he appeared friendly to him, and in a private interview he succeeded in opening Lucian's eyes to his own advantage.

Lucian here confesses, probably with the intention of making a good story, his weakness as a man of the world. He made use of the hint, and went openly away from his enemy, apparently as a friend. Alexander lent him a boat for his voyage to Amastris, but he gave orders secretly to the pilot to throw him into the sea. The sailors, however, put him on shore at Aegiali, whence some people from the Bosporus sailing by, brought him to Amastris. What may be true of this story Lucian alone knows. He says further that he had endeavoured in vain to bring the impostor to justice. " It was Avitus, the governor of Bithynia and Pontus, who frustrated my attempt, entreating me to abandon it, for Alexander would never be punished, even if he were unmasked, on account of his connection with Rutilianus. So I was obliged to keep quiet, for it would have been madness to bring complaints before a judge so disposed."

Alexander remained unmolested. His deception became a power, indeed a recognized religion. He even obtained the emperor's permission to change the name of the city Abonotichus to Ionopolis, which still survives in the modern Ynebolu.[1] The lying prophet died in possession of his divine honours. His comrades disputed among themselves for the succession to the dignity of prophet, which, however, Rutilianus would not grant to any of them. The oracle of Glycon, however, existed for a long time after the death of the magician, and he himself was honoured by statues, medals and inscriptions, as well as by a ceremonial worship.[2] In

---

[1] Mionnet, *Suppl.* iv., p. 550: Abonotichos quod et Ionopolis, nunc Aineh-Boli vel Inebolu.

[2] Athenagoras (*Legatio pro Christianis*, c. 26) says that statues of Alexander and Proteus were standing at Parium, where was also the tomb of Alexander: Alexandri adhuc in foro sepulcrum et simulacrum est . . .

Ionopolis the service of Glycon still existed in the middle of the third century.[1]

Alexandri autem statuae sacrificia publicis sumptibus et dies festi, tanquam exaudienti Deo peraguntur.   Dacian inscription upon the god Glycon: *C.I.L.* iii., n. 1021, 1022.   Coins of Abonotichus or Ionopolis, of Marcus Aurelius, and L. Verus represent the serpent with the human head (Ιωνοπολείτων Γλύκων).   Eckhel, ii., p. 383, 384.   Mionnet, *Suppl.* iv., p. 550, n. 3, 5 ; n. 4.   Coin with two serpents (l'un d'eux faisant des sifflements à l'oreille de l'autre).   An inscription from Blatsche in Macedonia in honour of Draco, and of Dracaena and Alexander, *Ephem. Epigraphica, C.I.L. Suppl.* ii. 331, n. 493.

[1] Renan, *Marc Aurèle*, p. 51.   Coins of Nicomedia, with the dragon and the human head, as late as 240 A.D., *ibid.*

CHAPTER XVI

Oracles. Plutarch their Apologist. Hadrian's Mysticism. The Deification of Antinous

THERE was a renaissance of oracles in this wonder-loving century. In the first century they had fallen into decay from the spread of intelligence, but the mysticism of the East, which permeated the ancient worship of the gods, tended to revive them. The same Nero who had questioned the oracle at Delphi, undermined its authority by plundering the temple of Apollo, and carrying off the treasures. The Pythia was dumb. She had long deserved the contempt of mankind by her lies and venality, as Cicero had already remarked.[1] She had shamelessly flattered the matricide Nero by venturing to compare him with Orestes and Alcmaeon.[2] Trajan, however, seems to have restored the Delphic oracle, and Hadrian consulted it about Homer's birthplace.[3] Although Plutarch speaks of their decay, none of the famous oracles were absolutely dumb. But the probable cause of their diminished attraction lay in the fact that the public preferred to turn to new manifestations which suddenly came into fashion, such as the oracle of Glycon at Abonotichus. The old oracles still existed, particularly those of Apollo in Delos

---

[1] Cicero, *De divin.* ii. 57.

[2] Lucian, *Nero*, c. 10. In spite of this, Nero wished to have the opening of the abyss of the Pythian oracle blocked, so that Apollo might be silent for ever.

[3] Bouché-Leclercq, *Divination dans l'antiquité*, iii., p. 200. There are no imperial coins from Delphi, except of Hadrian (one referring to Antinous), of Antoninus Pius, and Faustina. Bormann, *Bull. d. Inst.*, 1869, p. 45.

and Argos, in Xanthus, and Clarus near Colophon, that of Trophonius in Lebadea, of the Branchidae at Didymae near Miletus, of the sun-god of Heliopolis, and that at Hierapolis in Syria.[1]   But they were all more or less worn out.

Plutarch admitted this with sorrow in his discourse on the decay of the oracles, and he took pains to bring back the powers of prophecy into repute.[2]   These powers were, in his opinion, not answerable for this decay, for they had appointed daemons as oracle priests, and daemons were not gods, but rather beings of a nature at once mortal and immortal, and as they had at the same time a bodily existence, they could change to good or bad, and could even vanish.   For this he refers to Plato, Empedocles, Xenocrates and Chrisippus.   To make the matter quite clear he relates the history of the downfall of Pan.   In the time of Tiberius, some sailors heard, on one of the Grecian coasts, the name called out of their pilot Thamus, and a voice which said, "When you come to the height of Palodes then make it known that the great Pan is dead."   Thamus did this, whereupon a great sighing was heard.   Tiberius inquired into this occurrence and confirmed it.   Daemons can therefore perish. We smile, too, over the trouble which Plutarch has taken in the *Daemon of Socrates*, to explain prophecy by the genius, whose voice was particularly audible to a philosopher of so pure a mind.   He emphatically takes this genius to be an oracle-giving daemon.

The Epicureans made light of this new belief in oracles and daemons.   Oenomaus, of whose writings Eusebius made an abridgment, laughed at the oracles as deceptions of conjurers.[3]   But the criticism of the school of Epicurus, and the wit of Lucian, were of no avail, for the credulous common people took no notice of them ; while apologists for the oracles were to be found among the first intellects of the time,

---

[1] Doellinger, *Heidenthum und Judenthum*, p. 649 *sq.* Friedlaender, iii. 527 *sq.*   Marquardt, *R. Staatsv.* iii. 95.   The history of the most eminent oracles in Bouché-Leclercq.

[2] *De Defectu Oraculorum.* In. c. 5 he complains that in Boeotia, which formerly was full of oracles, the one at Lebadea alone exists.   See also *Cur Pythia nunc non reddat Oracula.*

[3] Eusebius, *Praep. Evang.*, v. and vi. : φωρὰ γοήτων.

as the example of Plutarch has shown. Soothsayers and star-gazers from Egypt and Chaldaea swarmed in the Roman empire, and carried on a profitable business. People crowded in procession with offerings to their altars, to their images of saints and talismans, and to their mystical secret closets, where departed spirits were seen, and dead men were heard to prophesy. Lucian and Favorinus attempted in vain to ridicule the idea that our resolutions and actions can be determined by the position of the stars.[1]

If such an intellectual man as Hadrian was addicted to the secrets of astrology, and practised the arts of Eastern necromancy, his example must have lent as much weight to these delusions as the Papal Bulls gave to the belief in magic and witchcraft. Before he ascended the throne, omens of his imperial dignity reached him from the Sibylline books and the poems of Virgil, from the oracle of Jupiter Nicephorus, and from the Castalian fountain near Antioch, which he then had walled up as dangerous.[2] As a skilled astrologer, he inquired into his own future, and it was said of him, that he calculated the events and actions of every day beforehand.[3] Pliny the younger believed in omens and signs of wonder as well as Suetonius, whose history of the Caesars is full of accounts of the strangest prodigies. It may be seen on what a fertile soil the Christian love of the marvellous fell in the Roman world.

The mystical disposition of Hadrian is indicated by a Sibylline poet, who addresses Rome thus :

" But as soon as fifteen imperious kings have ruled over you,
　Enslaving the people from morning until evening,
　Then will come a prince grey-haired who is named after the sea,
　Who travels over the world with profane footsteps, bringing presents
　And treasures in silver and gold, many more than the enemy has.
　All these things he amasses, and then sails homewards with the booty.
　He knows all mysteries too, magical and hidden,

[1] Favorinus on Astrology, in Gellius, xiv. 1.

[2] Ammianus Marcellinus, xxii. 12, 8 ; Sozomen, *H. Eccl.* v. 19.

[3] The remarkable passage in Spartianus, c. 16 : mathesin sic scire sibi visus est ut sero kalendis Januariis scripserit, quid ei toto anno posset evenire, ita ut eo anno quo perit usque ad illam horam qua est mortuus scripserit, quid acturus esset.

Points out a boy as a god, and destroys what is sacred,
Unbolting the doors of the ancient mystic illusion."[1]

It is here asserted of Hadrian, that he penetrated into
all mysteries, and this agrees with what Tertullian and Julian
have said of him.[2] Although it is not known that he was
initiated into any but the Eleusinian mysteries, it is not
to be doubted that on his travels he became acquainted with
many of the mysteries of Greece, Syria and Egypt. For
his spirit of inquiry was certainly as great as that of Septimius
Severus, of whom Dion said, that he left nothing human or
divine unexplored.[3] There are traits in Hadrian as a child of
his time, which make him appear related to a Peregrinus and
an Alexander. He too, degenerates into the religious conjurer; he invents a new god, and an oracle which wins
acceptance like the Paphlagonian god of Glycon. Did this
imperial caprice arise from the consciousness of the divinity
which was ascribed to him, as to all the Caesars, by the
servile flattery of mankind? His attempt too, to become
the founder of a religion may also have been ironical. Did
Hadrian despise the folly of mankind, and on that account
make fools of them? Was he only an artist when he created
the god Antinous, the embodiment of beauty? Was he at
the bottom an atheist like Lucian and the Epicureans? No
one can say; the religion of this enigmatical man remains a
mystery to us. Nor was he a follower of any one philosophic
system. Spartianus says of him, that he was ardently devoted
to the worship of the Roman gods, despising strange gods, by
which Syrian and Egyptian divinities are to be understood.[4]

[1] *Sibyll.* viii. 50 *sq.* (ed. Alexandre, Paris, 1869):

Καὶ μαγικῶν ἀδύτων μυστήρια πάντα μεθέξει
Παῖδα θεὸν δείκνυσιν ἅπαντα σεβάσματα λύσει
Κἀξ ἀρχῆς τὰ πλάνης μυστήρια πᾶσιν ἀνοίξει.

See also v. 46 ; xii. 163-175.

[2] The expression of Tertullian about Hadrian, 'quamquam curiositatum
omnium explorator,' refers also to religious mysteries, as it occurs in connection with Christianity.—*Apologet. adv. gentes*, c. 5.

[3] μῆτε ἀνθρώπινον μῆτε θεῖον ἀδιερεύνητον καταλιπεῖν, Dion Cassius, lxxv. 13.

[4] Spart. c. 22: Sacra Romano diligentissime curavit, peregrina con-
tempsit. Tiberius forbade aegyptios judaicosque ritus, Suetonius, *Tiber.*
c. 36.

As head of the state, he showed the religion of the state the reverence that was her due. In Rome he restored old temples and built new ones. On the coins of Hadrian are to be seen the three divinities of the Capitol. One medal represents Jupiter as protector of the emperor himself; the god stands as a colossal figure, holding the thunderbolt in his right hand, which is stretched over Hadrian, while he shields him with his cloak. The emperor's attitude is that of a suppliant; he is depicted as a small figure, recalling the humility of Christian kings or of the Popes, who in imitation of the heathen method of representation before the time of Christ, are portrayed on mosaics as dwarfs.[1]

Pausanias, indeed, called Hadrian one of the most god-fearing emperors, with reference most likely to his temple building.[2] He built temples enough, but this he may have done as an artist; and, moreover, he dedicated them to no god, but left them without a name.[3] There is no doubt that he willingly agreed to his own elevation as Olympian Zeus.

If temples were erected to the majesty of Hadrian, they would surely also be erected to the companion whom he raised to equal divinity with himself? By the apotheosis of Antinous, Hadrian stamped his imperial seal upon the superstition of the century. But this act made much less impression upon the contemporary world than it has made upon posterity. Apotheosis was the greatest honour in antiquity which could be given to mortals, associating them with the gods as heroes, and honouring their memory with festival games. The deification of mortals passed from

[1] Froehner, *Les Médaillons de l'Empire Romain*, Paris, 1878, p. 28 : HADRIAN . AUG . COS . III . P . P.—JOVI CONSERVATORI. A large bronze of Trajan with the legend CONSERVATORI PATRIS PATRIAE has the same motive, and Froehner ascribes it to the Flavians. There are similar medals, on which Jupiter Custos protects the emperors Marcus Aurelius and L. Verus.—Medals of Hadrian, HADR . AUG . P . P.—JOVI OPT . MAXIMO S.P.Q.R., p. 29. Other medals of Hadrian referring to the gods of the Capitol, p. 26 *sq.*

[2] Ἁδριανοῦ τῆς τε ἐς τὸ θεῖον τιμῆς ἐπὶ πλεῖστον ἐλθόντος, v. 14. In the Middle Ages, too, all kings who built churches and cloisters were considered god-fearing, and William of Sicily was for that reason called the "Good."

[3] Lampridius, *Alex. Severus*, c. 43.

U

Paganism into the Christian Church in the form of beatification and canonization. Altars were dedicated to the saints as heroes of the faith. The Italians of the Renaissance recognized the connection between the two apotheoses, the heathen and the Christian, quite correctly when they spoke of the saints as *Divi*. But, on the whole, Paganism was more sparing than the Christian Church of its apotheoses. The ancient calendar of heroes pales before the myriads of Christian saints, and the sixty folio volumes of the *Acta Sanctorum*. The Spartans cannot be blamed for deifying their Lycurgus, nor the people of Smyrna for offering sacrifices to Homer, nor the Athenians, who placed among the immortals the heroes who fell at Marathon. But the Greeks, unfortunately, took the contemptible flattery of Asia Minor for an example, and deified power. In the time of the Diadochi they honoured the followers of Alexander even in their lifetime as gods, and then they raised to the skies the Roman generals, Flaminius and Sulla. This worship of men would cause less sensation in Egypt where the Lagidae had inherited the divine honours of the Pharaohs. Augustus was glorified in hieroglyphic inscriptions as a child of the Sun.[1]

The Romans, indeed, adopted the idea of apotheosis from the Greeks, and Caesar first received consecration as Divus Julius. A comet which appeared in the sky was declared to be his soul.[2] Emperor-worship then became the real religion of the state, and the provinces of Europe were obliged to conform to it. Tacitus has told us how the cities of Asia vied with each other through their ambassadors, in begging the favour from Tiberius of being allowed to build a temple to him.[3] There was scarcely a city of importance in Greece which had not solicited the honour of the Neocoria, that is, the distinction of the temple-worship of the emperors of Rome.[4] Every emperor was already a god in his lifetime.

---

[1] Doellinger, *Heidenthum und Judenthum*, p. 14.

[2] Suetonius, *Caes.* c. 88. A temple was erected to him on the Forum by Augustus, the real founder of emperor-worship, on which in general see Preller, *Röm. Mythologie*.

[3] Tacitus, *Ann.* iv. 55.

[4] Hermann, *Gottesdienstliche Alterthümer der Griechen*, § 12.

In a work of art Augustus is represented as Jupiter, with his foot on the globe, close to Livia, who stands by him in the guise of Venus. A famous bas-relief at San Vitale in Ravenna represents him in the same fashion.[1] If the Olympieum in Athens had been completed in his time, he would have been worshipped there as Zeus, before Hadrian.

The apotheosis of Antinous loses, therefore, its distinction as soon as it is brought into connection with the ideas of the time, but it retains its moral enormity when we consider what this deified youth was in his lifetime. Every one knew his history as well as the citizens of Abonotichos knew the origin of their prophet Alexander. The profane caprice of Hadrian would scarcely be excused in the judgment of thoughtful contemporaries by the idea that the sacrificial death of the youth entitled him to the fame of a hero.[2] Dion expressly says that the emperor became a laughing-stock, when he asserted that he had seen the star of Antinous.[3] But it is a melancholy reflection that the gods were not only laughed at by the critical spirit of the atheist, but that the belief in them arose merely from the servility and fear of men.

In Antinoe, Hadrian set up an oracle to his favourite, with soothsayers and all the other needful theatrical apparatus.[4] He proceeded much in the same way as the lying prophet Alexander, and like him he stooped to write oracles in verse.[5] As there was already an Ethiopian god of oracles in this

---

[1] A. Conze, *Die Familie des Augustus, ein Relief in S. Vitale zu Ravenna*, 1867. A bronze statue from Herculaneum also represents Augustus as Jupiter.

[2] Such is the interpretation of Hausrath, *Neutestamentliche Zeitgesch.* ii. 480. I certainly think that Antinous' sacrificial death recalls the death of Osiris and Adonis.

[3] Διὰ ταῦτα μὲν οὖν ἐσκώπτετο.—Dion, lxix. 11.

[4] The προφῆται or oracle priests of Antinous in Antinoe are referred to by Hegesippus in Eusebius, *H. E.* iv., c. 8.

[5] Spart. c. 14 : et Graeci quidem volente Hadriano eum consecraverunt oracula per eum dari adserentes, quae Hadrianus ipse composuisse iactatur. It is hard to say where Hadrian could impart oracles to inquirers, as the temple of Antinous in Besa can only have been finished after his departure from Egypt.

place, the ancient Besa, the emperor blended him with Antinous in one person.   The Egyptians could still worship Besa in him, while he was Antinous to the Greeks.[1]

If the ruler of the world became the prophet of the new divinity, he was sure to find recognition for his creature so long as he lived.   But nothing shows more clearly the strong necessity for worship among mankind at that time, than the fact that this oracle of Antinous was still in existence in the third century.   Origen believed that in Antinoe, magicians and daemons carried on their mysterious existence.[2]

Antinoe was a Greek city, and it was the Greeks generally who acknowledged the Hadrianic god, and spread his worship abroad.[3]   It might flatter their national vanity that the honour of Olympia had been bestowed upon one of their countrymen.   In their eyes Antinous might signify Hellas, and the emperor could not carry his Philhellenic sympathies further than by raising a Greek to be a god.   To the importance of a regular form of worship, however, Antinous did not attain, although Greece and Asia vied with each other in honouring him by altars and images.   His chief seat in Hellas was Mantinea.   For the emperor made use of a far-fetched genealogy, in which the Nicopolitans in Bithynia were said to have been colonists of Mantinea, in order to build a temple there to his Adonis.[4]   He founded a yearly festival of dedication, and instituted games to be held every five years.[5] Pausanias saw many statues of Antinous in Mantinea, and beautiful pictures in the gymnasium there, representing him as Dionysus.

In Athens too he was honoured with games.   His statue was found in the ruins of the theatre.   A marble chair was placed as a seat of honour for the priest of Antinous among

---

[1] Bouché-Leclercq, iii. 394.

[2] Origen, *in Cels.* 3. 36.   Tertullian, *Apol.* c. 13.   Clement Alex. *Protrept.* 43.

[3] The passage in Spart. c. 14, also points this out.

[4] Pausanias, viii. 9, 7.   Medal in Fabretti, 462.

[5] Eusebius, *H. E.* iv., c. 8, mentions Hegesippus, at whose time the ἀγών, Ἀντινόειος was still celebrated.   This ecclesiastical writer lived in the middle of the second century.

the spectators.[1] In Eleusis he passed as Iacchus, and here too festival games were held in his honour.[2]

Many other Hellenic cities have glorified him on their coins as Dionysus or Iacchus, as hero and divinity. These coins are from Tarsus, Adramyttium, Adrianotherae, Amisus, from Ancyra, Mantinea, Bithynium, from Corinth, and Delphi, from Hierapolis, Cyzicus, Nicomedia, Nicopolis, from Sardis, Tyana, Smyrna, and Alexandria.[3] On a Corinthian coin Antinous is holding the winged Pegasus by the bridle ; the horse is supposed to be Borysthenes, Hadrian's charger.[4] One of the finest busts of Antinous is on a medal from Nicopolis or Bithynium, his native city.[5]

Sometimes he is represented with Harpocrates, his companion in the society of the gods, sometimes with Apollo or Hermes. A griffin, a goat or a bull, a panther and a thyrsus, the moon and the stars, indicate one or another god whose incarnation he is. For Antinous was never considered a new god, but only a new manifestation of one of the existing deities. This was also often the case with the deified emperors. For the most part he appears in the guise of Dionysus, because this seemed most in accordance with his youthful beauty. His handsome appearance contributed largely to the fact that the worship of Antinous did not come to an end with Hadrian, for art has, in its portrayal of man, adopted him as a type of youth.

But the worship of Antinous was confined to the East. In the Latin West he made no impression upon the imagination of men, and here little attention was paid to the Greek youth. But it is striking that Marcus Aurelius, in his *Meditations*, when he mentions by name Hadrian's most con-

[1] Ἰερέως Ἀντινόου, *Ephem. Archeol.*, 1862, p. 162, n. 158. Rhusopulos *ibid.*, p. 215, upon that statue ; p. 202, upon the Ἀντινόεια ἐν ἄστει. Mention of a ἱερεὺς Ἀντινόου ἐφήβου, from which Semiteles assumes that Antinous was honoured in Athens as Ephebus.

[2] Ἀντινόεια ἐν Ἐλευσῖνι distinguished from those of Athens : ἐν ἄστει Lenormant, *l'Antinoüs d'Eleusis, Rev. Arch.*, 1874, p. 217.

[3] Eckhel, vi. 528 *sq.* ; Cohen, ii. 267.

[4] Maffei, *Gemme antiche*, ii. 193.

[5] ΑΝΤΙΝΟΟΝ ΘΕΟΝ Η ΠΑΤΡΙC, R) ΒΕΙΘΥΝΙΕΩΝ ΑΔΡΙΑΝΩΝ, Mionnet, *Suppl.* iv., pl. 1. Those from Smyrna, flatteries of Polemon, in Cohen, ii. 268, and at the same place coins with Antinous and Hadrian.

fidential friends such as Celer, and the otherwise unknown Chabrias and Diotimus, never alludes to Antinous.[1] This silence must have been intentional.   As a Stoic, Marcus Aurelius would despise the farce of Antinous.   We do not know if Hadrian took any particular trouble to naturalize his divinity in Rome.   He was never acknowledged there publicly, as it would have required a decree of the senate; and he had no temple in Rome.   There are no Roman coins of Antinous, but a few inscriptions prove the existence of his worship there and in Italy, and for this the emperor was probably indebted to the Greeks.   Servile souls, however, would not be wanting among Romans and Latins.   As Justin Martyr said many a one will have sacrificed to the new god from eye-service and from fear, and will have put up his image in their houses.   An inscription found on the field of Mars, from the temple of Isis, mentions Antinous as equal with the divinities of Egypt; so he must have had an altar in the Egyptian temple at Rome.[2]   It is uncertain whether this inscription belongs to the time of Hadrian; but we shall not be far wrong in thinking that the death of his favourite in the Nile first made the emperor himself a follower of the worship of Isis.   Spartianus indeed commends him for despising strange gods, and it is not clear that Hadrian publicly participated in Rome in the mysteries of Isis, as did Domitian, and afterwards Commodus and Caracalla.   The villa at Tivoli, however, bears witness to his connection with the gods of Egypt, even if only from the standpoint of art.   From this villa come the colossal marble figure in the Vatican which represents Antinous as Osiris, and the Harpocrates of the Capitol, his divine companion, who is depicted as the genius of silence, his finger on his lip.

From the Tiburtinum a Latin inscription may have been carried to Tivoli, where it was found, comparing Antinous with Belenus.[3]   But a Latin inscription from Lanuvium, the

---

[1] Marcus Aurelius, viii., 25, 37.   Do Chabrias and Diotimus, he asks, still sit at the grave of Hadrian?   It would be ridiculous.

[2] Ἀντινόῳ συνθρόνῳ τῶν ἐν Αἰγύπτῳ θεῶν Μ. Οὔλπιος Ἀπολλώνιος Προφήτης. C.I.G. iii., n. 6007.

[3] Antinoo et Beleno par aetas formaque par est cur non Antinous sit Belenus. Q. Siculus.—Orelli, 823. Belenus was a Celtic god and idealized

present Civita Lavigna, proves that there was a temple in
the neighbourhood of Rome in 132 A.D., only three years
after the death of the deified youth, with a priesthood belonging to Diana and Antinous, a combination of divinities which
is very singular.[1]   Another inscription speaks of a priesthood
of Antinous in Naples, and it is probable enough that one
should have been found in a Greek city.[2]   But in Ostia too
there seems to have been a temple of Hadrian's god, for the
statue that was found in the Lateran Museum represented
him as Vertumnus.[3]   Whether it was a statue in a temple,
or whether it adorned some public garden, or belonged to a
private owner, we do not know.   As the colony of Ostia
had received many benefits from the emperor, it might have
wished to show its gratitude by acknowledging his god.

It cannot be supposed that Lucian, who laughed at all
gods, legitimate as well as barbaric, spared Antinous.   But
with the prudence of a man of the world, he would not scoff
at deified emperors, or at the deified creature of an emperor;
only in one single passage in his *Assembly of the gods* he
may have thought of Antinous, when he mentions Ganymede.[4]
He did not venture to let him appear in Olympus, and this
recognition was also refused him by the emperor Julian.   For
in his satire upon the Caesars he makes Silenus say, on the
appearance of Hadrian in Olympus, that it was useless to look

as Apollo, Fabretti, 325;   Preller, *Röm. Mythol.* i³., 270.   The inscription seems ironical; either it means the Celtic god or that Belenus was
a beautiful youth belonging to Siculus, who seemed to him to deserve
the divine honours of Antinous.

[1] Henzen, 6086: in templo Antinoi . . . cultorum Dianae et Antinoi.
The birthdays of Diana, as also of Antinous (*V. Cal. Dec.*) were celebrated,
but this date cannot be accepted as the birthday of Antinous; consult on
this inscription the remarks of Mommsen, *De collegiis et sodaliciis Romanorum*, p. 114.

[2] Orelli, 2252.   The municipium of Bovillae, near Rome, erected this
inscription to a Roman knight, Myron, probably a Greek, who, under
another title, was also designated as *Fretriacus Neapoli Antinoiton et
Eunostidon, i.e.* a member or president of a phratry *cultorum Antinoi et
Eunosti.*

[3] Benndorf und Schoene, *Die antiken Bildwerke des lateran. Museum*,
n. 74.

[4] *Assembly of the gods*, c. 8.

for Antinous among the gods, for he was not there. Like
Marcus Aurelius, Julian too despised this Antinous farce.[1]
Hadrian's Ganymede as, according to Prudentius, Antinous
was called, was reason enough for the Christians to brand
the heathen religion with boundless immorality. The Apologists might indeed be grateful to the emperor; they all speak
of Antinous.[2] They have not used too strong colours,
when they speak of the unchastity of the Asiatic priests, and
even of human sacrifices. Hadrian is said to have abolished
these in the worship of Mithras, but Commodus again allowed
them. And after all was the death of Antinous anything
more than a mystical human sacrifice?[3]

---

[1] Julian, *Caesares*, c. 9.

[2] Justin. Mart. *Apol.*, ii. 72 : τοῦ Ἀντινοόυ τοῦ νῦν γεγενημένου, ὅν καὶ πάντες
ὡς θεὸν διὰ φόβου σέβειν ὥρμηντο. ἐπιστάμενοι τίς τε ἦν καὶ πόθεν ὑπῆρχε. Athenagoras, *Apol.* 34. Tatian, *contra Graecos*, p. 149. Prudentius, *contra
Symmach*, i. 271.

[3] About human sacrifices, Justin. Mart. *Apol.* i., p. 50. Tatian, *contra
Graec.*, p. 165. Lactantius, *Divin. inst.* i., c. 21. Tertullian, *Apol.*, c. 9.
Compare what Lampridius, c. 8, says of Elagabalus : caedit et humanas
hostias lectis ad hoc pueris nobilibus et decoris.

CHAPTER XVII

Attempts to restore Paganism.   Plutarch and Lucian

GREAT efforts were made, especially by the philosophers of the Platonic and Pythagorean schools, to prevent the decay of the ancient religion by reforming its morals.   With Celsus, about whom little is known, except that he belonged to the age of Hadrian, Paganism began its struggle against the ever-growing power of Christianity in the days of Marcus Aurelius.[1]   In the third century, the Athenian sophist Flavius Philostratus, the friend of the empress Julia Domna, wrote his famous romance *Apollonius of Tyana* as a reply to Christianity.

Though Philostratus was the first to make the historical figure of this early Pythagorean philosopher (who did not escape Lucian's satire),[2] the Antichrist of Paganism, yet long before his time there had been similar accounts and biographies of Apollonius, written by Damis, by Maximus of Aegae, and by Moeragenes.   Hadrian himself kept in his library at Antium a collection of Apollonius' letters, probably only because he admired him as the greatest of magicians.[3]

While Epicureans and Cynics in their atheism renounced the ancient mythology, while Sceptics and Stoics were indifferent whether the gods existed or not, the Platonic

---

[1] His writing Ἀληθὴς λόγος is preserved in the extracts in Origen, *contra Celsum*; Kellner, *Hellenthum und Christenthum*, p. 25 *sq.*   Most likely this was the Celsus to whom Lucian dedicated the history of the lying prophet Alexander.

[2] *Alexander*, c. 5.

[3] Philostratus, *Vita Apollon.* viii. 19.

theology arose, and made desperate efforts to save the old dogmas. These attempts could only originate in Greece, where religion had not degenerated into the ridiculous excesses of Eastern worship, but formed an historical element in the nation, and they were supported both by philosophy and art. A highly-educated man like Plutarch took the most childish delight in the ancient Olympus. An enemy of materialism, he was the champion of the new Platonic doctrine. He wrote dissertations against the views of Epicurus and the Stoics, in which he made violent attacks upon the godlessness of the age, whose morals he undertook to improve by the doctrine of Plato. With the courage of a priest inspired by the fear of God, he inveighed against the vices of the time, the luxury and sensuality, the love for youths, the gladiatorial fights, the oppression of slaves. If there was anyone who could show in a world where the old faith was decaying, that philosophy and veneration for the gods produce happiness, it must have been Plutarch, who was in himself the most contented and most fortunate man of the antiquity that was soon to perish.

His industry and thoroughness, his acquaintance with the old philosophers and poets, his fervent zeal and his noble morality are highly to be praised, but his logic is utterly weak. The ground of the ancient religion which he wishes to defend, gives way under him, for these Olympian deities are only petrifactions; they may adorn an art museum, but philosophy can never again restore them to moral and intellectual power. Plutarch takes refuge, as Plotinus and Porphyry after him, in the misty realm of daemonology. The daemons are obliged to appear as intermediate beings, taking upon themselves the follies and crimes of the gods, in order that the gods may be saved as abstract beings from moral ruin. He shelters himself too behind allegory, and the moral meaning of mythology,[1] and becomes a complete mystic. Though he combats the vulgar supersti-

---

[1] *De audiendis poetis*, an interesting work in which Plutarch shows young men how to treat the myths of the poets, namely, morally and artistically, so that what the poets say is not to be considered absolutely true, but is to be interpreted according to the situation and idiosyncrasies of the characters.

tion of the people, he still clings to the delusion of auguries and necromancy.

The writings of Plutarch can scarcely have been convincing to a philosopher of the time, but they appealed all the more to the sentimental as moral books of devotion.   In his discourse upon the *Daisidaemonia*, is contained the principle of his ethics, that men should love, not fear the gods.   According to his view, ignorance arises from two sources, godlessness and superstition.   The godless man disbelieves in the gods, in order that he may not be obliged to fear them ; the superstitious man believes in them, but he looks upon them as beings who inspire horror and dread.   The gods, however, are not to be hated, but are to be treated with confidence, hope, and affection.   Plutarch developed these views still further in his work against the Epicureans, where he wishes to prove that man cannot live happily by following the atheistic doctrines of Epicurus.   It is better to cling to the belief in the gods, to honour and even to fear them, than to abandon all hope, and in " evil times " all recourse to the heavenly powers.   A sojourn in the temple, banquets and plays give more pleasure, when they are celebrated in connection with sacrifices, mysteries and dances.   For the thought of God delivers man from fear, and fills him with excessive joy.   But he who has renounced Providence can have no part in this joy.   Bravely, too, does Plutarch defend the belief in immortality and in reunion after death.   His youthful contemporary, the Greek rhetorician Aelius Aristides from Hadriani in Mysia, a pupil of Polemon attempted, like Plutarch, with real piety and enthusiasm to restore the ancient belief in the gods.[1]

In opposition to such visionary attempts of the Pythagoreans and Platonists to prop up sinking Olympus by daemonology, and by a system of ethics which approached Christianity, Lucian appeared as their most formidable foe. The sophist of Samosata seems insignificant beside the priestly figure of Plutarch, but he carried weapons which were formidable enough.   The multitude are more susceptible to the ridiculous than to the sublime.   We can estimate the

[1] See his orations on gods, and the work of Baumgart, *Aelius Aristides als Repräsentant der sophist. Rhetorik*, 1874.

effect produced at the time by the pitiless but popular satires of this pamphleteer, by the fact that his writings even to-day make the most striking impression, although many contemporary references can no longer be understood. Lucian despised Christianity; this new mystery of "the crucified magician" appeared to him, as to the emperor Hadrian, and to every one in the higher circles of society, something so absurd, that he only contemptuously mentioned it in a few places in his writings.[1]   Nevertheless, his atheism became one of the strongest allies of Christianity, and his wit made a breach in the ancient faith which no philosophy or doctrine of ideas of the Neoplatonists could ever heal.

Lucian gave the death-blow to ancient mythology by his dialogues of the gods.   His polemics are directed, like those of the Christian apologists, against anthropomorphic fables. The weaknesses of the gods are turned into ridicule.   Zeus is a chatterer, a boaster, a Don Juan; Mercury, a thief; Bacchus, a drunkard; Apollo, a deceitful soothsayer.   The myths of Homer, the *Metamorphoses* of Ovid, the tragedians are all despised on account of their preposterous and fabulous tales.   These remarks apply to the native, and consequently ancient gods of Greece.   Lucian proceeds to review the whole fantastical Olympus of his time, which swarms with strangers. It is a theocracy or combination of gods which produced in the last centuries of Paganism a chaotic religion.   The gods migrating into Rome from foreign provinces find themselves in the Pantheon of the empire, and become citizens of Rome. What is said of Rome may be said of the empire.   Religion is broken up into a thousand sects.   These gods, genii, and daemons are innumerable; the more foreign and mysterious they are, the more they look like Egyptian and Chaldean deities, the more they are sought after.   The gods of Greece,— Zeus, into whose place the emperor stepped, Apollo, whose oracle at Delphi had lost its charm,—were willingly exchanged and united with the powers of the mystic service of nature,

---

[1] Strictly speaking, only in *Alexander* and *Peregrinus;* for other passages, as in *Philospeudes,* c. 16, in the *Vera Historia,* and in the *Fight of Endymion with Phaethon,* can only be considered as containing strained allusions to the Christians. Kellner, *Hellenismus und Christentum,* p. 89 *sq.*

with Isis and Osiris, with Serapis and Anubis, with Attys and Adonis, with Mithras, Astarte and the Nature goddess Rhea. This great goddess herself has a hundred names (which are to be found in the eleventh book of Apuleius): she is the goddess of Pessinus, the Paphian Venus, Minerva, Ceres, Diana, Proserpina, Isis, and Cybele in Hierapolis, whose worship Lucian has described in his *Syrian Goddess*.[1]

In the *Assembly of the gods* he makes Momus complain of the novices who have sneaked into Olympus, and who have sat down with the ancient gods to an equal portion of nectar and ambrosia. Above all, Jupiter is particularly anxious to save Ganymede, and he would take it very ill if Momus tried to injure his favourite by attacks upon his ignoble descent. But Attys and Corybas and Sabazius and the turbaned Mithras, who cannot speak one iota of Greek, much more all these Scythians and Getae, who have been made into gods by their own people, how do they come into Olympus? Or Anubis, the dog's face swathed in linen, the bull of Memphis, the ibis, the apes? All this Egyptian nonsense Jupiter himself thinks disgraceful, but admits that there is some hidden meaning in it. Lucian laughs at the mysteries, naïvely making Momus ask: "Do we require mysteries to know that gods are gods, and that heads of dogs are heads of dogs?" The piece closes with a decree commanding the gods to appear before a commission, and show their pedigree.

In the dramatic farce too of *Jupiter Tragoedus*, the chaotic mixture of all national religions is turned into ridicule with biting sarcasm. With inimitable wit Lucian makes the gods take their place according to their value in metal. On the urgent summons of the herald Mercury they come running in, gods of gold, of silver, of ivory, of bronze

---

[1] How great was the mixture of religious ideas after the fusion of the Syrian worship of gods with that of the Greeks is apparent in the temple of the Syrian goddess in Hierapolis. It is a pantheon or museum of statues, where are to be found Rhea-Juno, Jupiter, Baal-Apollo, Atlas, Mercury, Lucina, Semiramis, Sardanapalus, the Trojan heroes, Stratonice, Combabus, and in the portico there are colossal pillars, on one of which twice a year a man remains seated sleepless for seven days, as a pillar saint.—Lucian, *Dea Syria*.

and of marble.   The barbarian gods, Bendis, Attys, Mithras, Anubis take the front seats because they are made of
gold.   This gives rise to most comical scenes.   Lucian
derides the gods for their ridiculous anthropomorphism.   The
question turns on a quarrel between two argumentative philosophers, the Epicurean Damis and the Stoic Timocles, which
Jupiter says he overheard as they were walking towards the
Poecile at Athens.   Damis denied the existence of the gods,
which Timocles maintained.   The latter is nearly being defeated, when Jupiter separates the parties by the approach of
night.   On the following day the dispute is to be resumed.
Jupiter has summoned a meeting of the gods to devise means
by which the victory may be assured to the weak-headed
Timocles, as the honour and the existence of the heavenly
powers are at stake.   He makes a speech to the citizen-gods,
with expressions from the first Olynthian oration of Demosthenes, in which he soon breaks down.   The gods, according
to their different characters, give the most ridiculous advice.
Meanwhile, Hermagoras, the statue of Hermes Agoraeus,
comes running up from the Athenian market-place, and
announces the beginning of the philosopher's dispute.   The
heavens are opened, the gods look down.   " As we cannot
do more," says Jupiter, "we will at least pray with all our
might for Timocles."   The absurdity of this idea is most
ingenious.

     The argument proceeds.   Timocles merely produces weak
arguments for his belief, while the Epicurean dismisses the
idea of a Divine Providence, as well as of individual deities,
with biting wit; a Providence which permits evil, gods which
are arbitrary creations of the people, sometimes human beings,
sometimes the elements, onions, crocodiles, cats, apes, earthen
pots and dishes.   Timocles then makes as little way with
the theological argument of the *consensus gentium* as with the
other proofs which he brings forward ; but he finally saves
himself by the following masterly syllogism : " If there are
altars there must be gods, and as there are altars, therefore
there are gods."   This is merely an appeal to the custom of the
people and to authority.   The people would be furious if they
were deprived of their formulas, their images of the gods, their
robes of purple, and their theatrical costumes.   In conclusion,

Jupiter says: "For all that, Mercury, it was a fine thing which king Darius said of Zopyrus; and I confess too, that I would rather have one champion like Damis, than ten thousand Babylons."

The continuation of *Jupiter Tragoedus* is given by Lucian in *Jupiter Convinced*. A Cynic begs permission from Zeus to ask him a few questions. He only wants to know if it is true as said by Homer and Hesiod, that no one can escape from the goddess of destiny, and from the fates. Jupiter says this is so, and also admits that fate rules over the gods; he is therefore obliged to concede that they are only idle machines. With this avowal Olympus itself is destroyed, and prediction by oracle is represented as an absurdity; for what does it avail for mortals to seek to know the future, if they cannot escape the decree of destiny? In the same way the judgment after death of good and bad will be annulled, for if destiny rules over everything, moral freedom and responsibility for our actions are no longer possible.

Everything which Plutarch discussed with such care, oracles, mysteries, providence and fate, collapses before these syllogisms of the Cynics and the Epicureans. Lucian is indefatigable, when it is a question of destroying ancient dogma. He despises the oracles of Trophonius and Amphilochus, which were still important in his day, and he especially despises the most legitimate of all, the Delphic oracle. In *Jupiter Tragoedus* he makes Momus ask Apollo, if, as Apollo is so great a soothsayer, he will tell the gods which of the two philosophers will carry off the victory. Apollo first makes the paltry excuse that he has not got his oracle apparatus at hand, the tripod, the frankincense, and the Castalian fountain, and then he allows a very foolish prophecy to be extracted from him.

The doctrines of the immortality of the soul, and of the life in Elysium and Tartarus, are no less the objects of Lucian's irony. To these belong his dialogues of the dead, reminding us often in their scenes of Dante's *Inferno*. No one escapes his scourge, neither Socrates nor Empedocles (half-roasted on Etna), nor Pythagoras, who in the joyless Hades no longer despises the forbidden bean, as doctrines change in the Stygian world. Achilles, Alexander, Hannibal, what are they in the lower world? What has become of Alexander, worshipped after death as the god Ammon and the Indian Bacchus? He who now shares the fate of other shadows in a world where there are no distinctions, and where the worms which feed on kings are all-powerful, is used as an example by the scoffing, though worldly-wise Lucian to illustrate the absurdity of imperial apotheoses. Lucian agrees with the philosophy of Marcus Aurelius and of Hamlet that all is vanity, that heroic deeds, costly possessions, and the best attempts to attain the ideals of life are but an empty show. Here he meets the Stoics on their own ground, unintentionally, and falls like Voltaire into a contempt for life and for mankind.

Plutarch is therefore right in the caution which he gives (in his work on the Epicureans), against this pessimism which arises from godlessness. But Lucian is not to be taken too literally, for he soon becomes an Epicurean again, praising the present moment as the only certainty in life, and valuing above all contentment, moderation and modest self-esteem. The ideal is non-existent for him. Absolute science, philosophy, religion, are only objects of satire, the rest is merely the enjoyment of the moment; beyond that there is nothing.

In this way Lucian, the critic of the Greek and Roman world, arrived at Nihilism, like the encyclopaedists of the eighteenth century, setting up instead of the gods, the goddess of the common human understanding, or of reason on the throne. The words of Fronto, the royal tutor, who possessed no spark of Lucian's wit, ring out wonderfully, and are almost like the words of a prophet of the French Revolution, when he says on one occasion, that many temples have been built to fortune, but that to reason there has been neither a statue nor an altar erected.[1]

Meanwhile the perpetual needs of the soul, which could no longer find satisfaction in the insipid worship of the gods, sought among the mysteries for a deity who had not yet been profaned. It was no longer Greece but the East, the birthplace of religions for the whole world, whence these rites came. The mind of Europe was turned towards the

---

[1] *Ep*. iii. Quis ignorat—templa fana delubraque publica fortunae dicata, rationi nec simulacrum nec aram consecratum.

East.   From thence the Asiatic religions penetrated into the West, finding each one their adherents, as they proclaimed more or less the power of repentance, and the immortality of the soul.   This attracted numerous followers to the worship of Mithras especially in the third century.   The political, as well as the intellectual centre of gravity of the empire, seemed to incline gradually to the East.   Trajan had already sought it there, and it was in the East that Hadrian travelled most frequently, and with the greatest pleasure.   The theatre of the world's history was transferred to the East under the two Severi, under Elagabalus, the priest of the sun, and under the thirty Tyrants.   The newly-established empire of the Sassanidae was the centre of future events, until Constantine took his seat at Byzantium and made Christianity, the most powerful and the most profound of all the mysteries of the East, the religion of the world.

CHAPTER XVIII

The Spread of Christianity. The Christian Religion a "Religio Illicita." Hadrian's Toleration of the Christians. Rescript of Hadrian to the Proconsul Fundanus. The Christian Apologists

THE Christian religion was not a hundred years old when Hadrian ascended the throne, and it already had adherents in every province of the empire. It came from Palestine, and penetrated by way of Damascus over the commercial highways of the Phoenicians into Asia Minor, by Troas into Greece, and by Cyprus towards the West. In every emporium of the Mediterranean Christianity had taken its place among the heathen.[1]

The destruction of nationalities by the Roman empire, the weakness of the heathen state church in consequence of the decay of the ancient religions owing to the mixed kind of worship, philosophic atheism and scepticism on one side, the morality of the Stoics on the other, credulity in miracles, and the craving for salvation by means of fresh mysteries, the depravity of manners, despotism, and the slavery of the lower classes,—all these things had combined to prepare the ground throughout the Roman empire for the doctrine of the apostle. The first general language of the Church was everywhere the Greek language.[2] It was only through the Roman empire

---

[1] Movers, *Phoenizien*, iii. 1, p. 1 *sq.*

[2] Even the Roman liturgy was Greek ; and as late as the third century Greek epitaphs of the Popes are found in the catacombs (De Rossi, *Roma Sotter.* ii.). In the second century the Roman bishops were chiefly Greeks (Evaristus, Telesphorus, Hyginus, Anicetus, Soter, Eleutherius).

that Christianity became a world-religion. In the time of Hadrian a network of well-organized communities was spread over the whole empire, from the Euphrates as far as Gaul, Spain, Britain and Roman Africa.

It has been remarked that this emperor rendered a service to Christianity by transforming Jerusalem into a Roman colony, and by thus compelling the Christian community of Palestine to renounce for ever the national limits of Judaism. From that time the original metropolis of the Christian Church could never again be its ruling centre, which from historical necessity Rome became. Although the bishopric there had at first no greater authority than that of Antioch and Alexandria, or even than the churches in Ephesus and Smyrna, in Corinth and Carthage, there were many circumstances which combined to support the claim of the bishops of Rome to the supremacy, namely, the majesty of the imperial city, the legend of the foundation of the Roman church by Peter, and finally, its extraordinary wealth.[1] No great personality laid the foundations of the empire of these Roman priests.[2] Their history, as late as the second century, is almost legendary, and it was not until three hundred years after Hadrian, when the victory of Christianity was assured, that a prominent figure appeared among the bishops of Rome.

The struggle with sects which began in the first hour of its foundation, and the other heroic struggle, under repeated persecutions, with the Roman state, gave the Christian Church a particularly dogmatic stability and strength of faith.

Even in the second century the Christians were looked upon by the Roman government as fanatical adherents of a mystery which was considered foolish and contemptible. But their sect was no longer confounded with Judaism. It was understood to be a peculiar society of Christiani or Galilaei, and as, unlike the synagogue of the Jews, it could make no claim to public toleration, it fell under the ban of Trajan's law, which forbade illegal societies. The Christians were persecuted in the days of Nero and Domitian. But after

[1] Renan, *Marc Aurèle et la fin du monde antique*, p. 23 : le trésor commun du christianisme était en quelque sorte à Rome.

[2] Karl Hase, *Kirchengesch.*, p. 62.

Domitian until the time of Decius, there was, in the opinion
of Lactantius, no further persecution of the Christians.

But if there were such persecutions under Trajan and
Hadrian they were not general, nor were they ordered by
imperial edicts.   They were merely local, caused in the cities
by popular tumults, by private hatred, and by the eager
officialism of the Roman governors.   While Eusebius and
Jerome, Augustine and Orosius speak of a persecution of the
Christians by Hadrian, Lactantius and Tertullian know
nothing of it, and even Melito of Sardis, whose apology to
the emperor Antoninus Pius has been preserved by Eusebius,
merely mentions the persecutions under Nero and Domitian,
and recalls as a contrast to them Hadrian's gracious rescript
to the proconsul Fundanus.[1]

In the Jewish war of Barcocheba, the Christians had suffered
much from the vengeance of the infuriated Romans, and their
devotional places in Jerusalem had been built over, destroyed
and desecrated by the colonists of Aelia Capitolina.   From
this fact Sulpicius Severus drew the erroneous conclusion,
that Hadrian was an enemy to the Christians, although in
the end he forbade as wicked this so-called fourth Christian
persecution.[2]   Legend, but not authentic history, recognizes a
few martyrs of Hadrian's time.   As such, are pointed out
the Roman bishop Alexander, whose crypt has been found
near the seventh milestone on the Via Nomentana, and the
holy Symphorosa and her seven sons to whom the famous
church of the seven brothers on the Via Tiburtina was
dedicated.[3]

[1] Eusebius, *H. Eccl.* iv. 26 : Tertullian, *Apologet. adv. gentes*, c. 5, only
knows of the persecution of Nero, and mentions Hadrian expressly as one
of the emperors who enacted no laws against them.

[2] *Sulp. Severus*, ed. Halm, ii. 31.   Dodwell, *Dissert. Cyprian*, xi., § 22.

[3] Eusebius knows no single martyr of Hadrian's time.   The death of
Alexander is placed by him before the emperor's accession, in 132 A.D.
by the Lib. Pontificalis.   The death of Symphorosa and her sons is only
laid in the time of Hadrian by a martyrology ascribed to Julius Africanus.—
Hausrath, *Neutestamentl. Zeitgesch.*, p. 529.   Irenaeus, iii. 3, is the only
writer who speaks of the martyr Telesphorus.   The catalogue of martyrs
under Hadrian in Champagny, *Les Antonins*, iii., p. 46, 94, is destitute
of all foundation.   The legendary number of 4000 martyrs under Hadrian
is rejected by De Rossi, *Roma Soterr.* ii., c. 27.

Like all Romans of distinction, Hadrian viewed the Christians with contempt, as is shown by his letter to Servianus from Egypt.   He looked upon them as fanatics of a Syrian mystery, which horrified the cultivated heathen, as its central point was the ignominious crucified Christ.   Tacitus, and even Suetonius, Hadrian's secretary, described them as refractory and gloomy heretics who were cursed with the *odium generis humani.*[1]   This was the fixed opinion in court circles, in spite of the converts which the gospel had already made, even in the imperial palace in the time of Nero and the Flavian emperors.   Among the mysteries of the East which excited the curiosity of Hadrian, the teaching of the apostles would scarcely have found a place.   His mind, however, was so free and open that he never showed himself an enemy to Christianity; he was more tolerant than the Stoic Marcus Aurelius, who considered it his duty to apply the severity of the imperial law to the professors of the new religion.[2]   The opposition of the Christians to the worship of the imperial gods, and their heterogeneous society had only hitherto called forth the sentence of the prefect, without provoking the learning of the heathen to a contest.   None of the literary men who surrounded Trajan and Hadrian cast a critical glance upon the meaning of the dogmas of the Galilaeans.

Under the Antonines, however, they began to be an object of interest to heathen sophists, and with the increasing power of the Christian religion came apologies for paganism. The list begins with the philosopher Celsus, about 150 A.D., and goes on to Philostratus, Porphyry, Iamblichus, to the emperor Julian and the sophist Libanius, to Eunapius and Zosimus, and the Neoplatonist Proclus until towards the end of the fifth century.[3]

So far was Hadrian from being a persecutor of the Christians that, in fact, he was looked upon as their patron. For Dion maintains that he paid them honour, and Anto-

---

[1] Suetonius, *Nero*, 16 : Genus hominum superstitionis novae et maleficae; *Domitian*, c. 15 : Comptentissima inertia.

[2] This is shown by the martyrs of Lyons, Renan, *Marc Aurèle*, c. 19.

[3] See Kellner, *Hellenismus und Christentum*.

ninus Pius was of the same opinion.[1] In Eusebius the much
discussed rescript is to be found, which Hadrian addressed to
the proconsul of Asia, Caius Minucius Fundanus, on the
strength of the representations made by his predecessor,
Quintus Licinius Granianus, about the riotous proceedings
in the courts over the trial of Christians.[2] According to
Roman law the followers of Christianity were sentenced if
they avowed their Christian name, but if they disowned it
they were set free. The judge punished the name and not
the crime (*flagitia cohaerentia nomini*).

, This loss of civil rights by the Christians was established
as a principle by Trajan, who gave orders in his letter to
Pliny, that the Christians should not be sought out, but
should be punished, if they were found, and convicted. By
this epoch-making order the Christian profession of faith was
declared to be a forbidden religion (*religio illicita*).[3] It remained the standard in conformity with which successive
emperors acted. It was of the greatest importance to the
Christians to escape from this position. Their apologists
used legal means to have the name separated from the deed,
and if they had succeeded, their creed would have become a
recognized religion.[4]

There has been a wish to see some favour of this kind in
Hadrian's rescript, in which he instructed the proconsul of
Asia not to condemn persons accused of Christianity on the
mere clamour of the people and of tale-bearing sycophants,
but to investigate the accusation carefully, to pronounce
judgment if there were proof of criminal actions in keeping
with the accusation, but to punish severely slanderous complaints.

The famous rescript of "the great and illustrious emperor
Hadrian" was added by Justin Martyr to his first apology,
which he presented to the emperor Antoninus and his
adopted sons, Marcus Aurelius and Lucius Verus, in 138 or

---

[1] Dion Cassius, lxx. 3, says of Antoninus : καὶ τῇ τοῦ Ἀδριανοῦ τιμῇ ἦν ἐκεῖνος
ἐτίμα χριστιανούς, προστιθείς; but this may be an addition by Xiphilinus.

[2] *H. Eccl.* iv. 9.

[3] F. Chr. Baur, *Das Christenthum und die christl. Kirche*, 1860, p. 438 ;
Neander, *Gesch. der. christl. Relig.* i.[2] 171.

[4] Tertullian, *Apolog.* c. 2.

139 A.D. Eusebius translated the Latin text into Greek.[1] Its genuineness has been disputed; but the proconsuls of Asia who are referred to are not to be doubted from the records. Licinius Granianus governed this province in 123 or 124 A.D., and his successor was C. Minucius Fundanus, the friend of Pliny and Plutarch.[2]

In the decree sent to Fundanus a device of the Christians has been perceived to secure for Christianity the status of a recognized religion by an imperial edict of toleration. It has been shown that this rescript of Hadrian was never taken as a guiding principle by the judges, that under Hadrian's successors the persecutions of the Christians still went on, and that the maxims of Trajan were employed in all lawsuits, while the apologists continued to complain and to demand for their co-religionists equal civil rights.[3] These doubts are supported by a rescript composed in favour of the Christians, and ascribed to the emperor Antoninus Pius, which is more than questionable.[4]

To such doubts it has been replied that Justin could not possibly venture to appear before Hadrian's successor with a forgery, especially as Bishop Melito of Sardis referred to Hadrian's rescript, in the apology which he addressed to Marcus Aurelius.[5] But both bishops might have accepted in good faith a forgery that was circulated amongst the Christians. The opinion that no Christian forger would have been satisfied with asking so little in favour of his

---

[1] *Apolog.* i., c. 68, vol. i; *Opp. Justini*, ed. Otto, Jena, 1876. Runus has preserved the Latin text; the Greek is from Euseb. *H.E.* iv., c. 9.

[2] Waddington, *Fastes des prov. Asiatiques*, p. 197, 199. The name of the first is Q. Licinius Silvanus Granianus Quadronius (*C.I.L.* iii., 4609, Borghesi, viii. 96 *sq.*).

[3] Baur, *Das Christenth. und die christl. Kirche*, 1860, p. 492 *sq.*, doubts the genuineness; see also Th. Klein, *Bedenken gegen die Echtheit des Hadr. Christen-Rescripts* (*Theol. Jahrbuch*, 1856, 387 *sq.*); the literature on both sides in Otto, *Justini M. Opp.* i., p. 191, note.

[4] Antonini Ep. ad. Commune Asiae (πρὸς τὸν κοινὸν τῆς ᾿Ασίας),—Appendix to Justin (Otto, 3, i. 244), and in Euseb. iv. 13. This edict was not added by Justin himself to his apology to Antoninus, for if he had been acquainted with it he would have made use of it instead of the rescript of Hadrian which said so little.

[5] Eusebius, iv., c. 26.

co-religionists, is more to the point.　For the contents of the rescript refer merely to a more just and equitable dealing with the Christians.　It was contrary to Hadrian's humane character to order that any encouragement should be given to the activity of avaricious informers.[1]　On the whole, however, his decree is so indecisive that it gives neither a rule for legal procedure, nor for what constitutes "illegal" acts of the Christians.[2]　If the Christians had understood the rescript to be really an edict of toleration, they would unquestionably have laid the greatest stress upon it.　But Justin did not do this; he tells the emperor plainly that he bases his demand for equality in civil rights for the Christians less on Hadrian's letter than on the consciousness of justice itself.

The rescript to Fundanus, as Melito assures us, was only one of many of the same kind which Hadrian addressed to the governors of provinces as instructions for their guidance. His successors did not in any way consider it a statute of the constitution, but it lost its power, and the Christian community remained as before, a Hetaeria, standing outside the constitutional law.[3]

Eusebius is certainly mistaken in representing Hadrian's letter as a consequence of the apologies for Christianity which were presented to the emperor by Quadratus, a pupil of the apostles and afterwards bishop of Athens, and by Aristides the philosopher.　This may have occurred during the emperor's first residence in Athens in 125 or 126 A.D;[4] but these early Christian apologies with which Eusebius was acquainted are lost, so that the most ancient apology we possess is that of Justin to Marcus Aurelius.[5]

---

[1] ἵνα μὴ τοῖς συκοφάνταις χορηγία κακουργίας παρασχεθῇ.—See Neander, i. 173.

[2] τι παρὰ τοὺς νόμους πράττοντας.　By this I do not understand merely ordinary crime, but crime affecting religious matters, denial of the gods, contempt for the genius of the emperor, etc.

[3] P. Aubé, *L'Apologétique chrétienne au IIe Siècle*, Paris, 1861, p. 50 *sq.*, has pointed this out clearly.　The genuineness of the edicts of Hadrian, as of the Antonines, is maintained by Carl Wieseler, *Die Christen Verfolgungen der Caesaren*, 1878, p. 18 *sq.*, but he does not consider that they prove that the Christians enjoyed religious liberty.

[4] Cavedoni, *Nuovi cenni cronologici intorno alla data precisa delle principali apologie* (p. 3), quite arbitrarily places these apologies in 123 A.D.

[5] Carl Werner, *Gesch. der apolog. und polem. literatur der christl.*

It is difficult to fathom the motive which induced these two Athenians in their own native city, where nothing had been heard of the persecutions of the Christians, to intercede for them with Hadrian. We cannot, however, help treating this remarkable fact as historical. Some event in the communities of Greece, perhaps some local persecution or oppression, may have induced them to take the step; and the emperor, who admitted so many learned men and sophists to his presence, would scarcely refuse to receive these two Athenians, one of whom wore the garb of a philosopher. He probably laughed at them as a new kind of Greek charlatan, who worked wonders and raised the dead in the name of Christ, while the community at Athens might hope for some good result from the love of justice and humanity, as well as from the intelligence of the emperor. But it would be going too far to think that the Christians of Greece had noticed the "dissatisfied truth-seeking" mind of Hadrian, or had any reason to suppose that his view of the world was similar to theirs, and that therefore the way was open to an attempt at his conversion.[1]

Not until the century of Eusebius was this humane and intellectual emperor counted a secret Christian or friend of the gospel. Lampridius relates that Alexander Severus wished to admit Christ among the gods, and that this was also in Hadrian's mind, as he erected temples in every city without statues, which on that account were simply called temples of Hadrian. But the emperor was diverted from this plan, because, when the oracle was consulted, an answer was returned that if this were done, all men would become Christians, and all other worship in the temples would cease.[2]

In the Sibylline books too, is to be found a favourable opinion of Hadrian by a Christian poet, who says of him: "A

Theologie i., 86; Gaston-Boissier, *La religion Romaine d'Auguste aux Antonins*, i., p. 5. The Mechitarists in Venice published in 1878 *S. Aristidis, philosophi atheniensis, Sermones duo*, of which one is supposed to be the apology to Hadrian; its genuineness, however, is doubted by Renan, *l'Église chrétienne*, praef. vi.

[1] This is the opinion of Hausrath, p. 534.

[2] Lampridius, *Alex. Sev.*, c. 43. Of such temples of Hadrian, those in Tiberias and Alexandria became Christian churches in the fourth century : Renan, *l'Église chrétienne*, p. 43.

king with a brow of silver, who bears the name of a sea, will build temples and altars in every city, will travel through the world on foot, and will understand all magic mysteries. So long as he, the prince of men, the sweet singer, the lawyer, the just judge reigns, will peace prevail. But he himself will fall, snatched away by his own destiny."[1]

The apologists know nothing of any secret leaning of Hadrian to Christianity; but they endeavour with great skill to establish the relation of their own faith to paganism. They became converts to Christianity from the school of the sophists and of Plato, so that they still wore partially the garb of a philosopher. Justin Martyr from Flavia Neapolis or Shechem in Samaria, proved the immortality of the soul by the representations of necromancers and magicians, of poets and philosophers of antiquity. He called the Sibylline books, the songs of Homer, the comedies of Menander, the tragedians, Plato and the sophists to witness to the truths of the Christian religion; and in the same way, Athenagoras attempted to prove the unity of God from Euripides and Philolaus, from Lysis and Plato, from Aristotle and the Stoics.[2] Justin looked upon the Platonic doctrine of the Logos as an incomplete manifestation of God to the heathen, and he connected it with the Christian theory of life.[3] It is nothing new he says that Christ as the Logos, born the Son of God, was crucified, and dead, and ascended into heaven. One need only think of Hermes as the Logos, the interpreter and teacher of Dionysius and Asclepius, and of Perseus the son of Danaë; and why should the emperors be placed among the gods? Everyone thinks it a fine thing to be like the gods. The connection of Christianity with the religions of the world lay therefore in the historical feeling of the early Church, and the golden saying of Justin proceeded from this view, "all those who have lived according to reason ($\lambda\acute{o}\gamma o\varsigma$) are Christians, even though they were considered atheists, like Socrates and Heraclitus, and other great Greeks, and like Abraham, Ananias, and Azarias among the barbarians."[4]

[1] *Sibyll.*, xii. 163-175, ed. C. Alexandre, Paris, 1869, and v. 46, where Hadrian is called πανάριστος ἀνὴρ καὶ πάντα νόησει.

[2] Athenagoras, *Leg.*, p. 5 *sq.*

[3] Justin, *Apol.* ii., p. 66 *sq.*

[4] *Apol.* ii., p. 83.

A breath from the ancient temples, and from the philosophic schools of the heathen, penetrated not only into the forms of Christian worship, but into its spiritual existence. Faith in oracles and prophecies was so firmly rooted in the minds of men that even Christians could not free themselves from it.   This explains the origin and the universal use of so many prophetical writings and apocalypses, like those of Abraham, Thomas, and Peter, and like the prophecies of Hydaspes and of the Sibylline books, to which Justin and the other apologists referred.

From the union of Greek and Oriental ideas with Christianity sprang Gnosticism, a mystical theory of life founded on dualism, which had one foot planted in the paganism of Plato, and the other in the revelation of the Christian doctrine. Gnosticism was really developed in the time of Trajan and Hadrian, to which epoch the schools of Saturninus in Antioch, of Basilides, Valentinus, and Harpocrates in Alexandria belong.

CHAPTER XIX

*Art among the Romans. Hadrian's Relation to Art.
Activity of Art in the Empire. Greek Artists
in Rome. Character of the Art of Hadrian's Age*

THE age of Hadrian has left a deeper impression in the
world by its marvellous fertility in the productions of art
than by anything else. Authors and inscriptions, ruins and
numerous beautiful works in the museums of Europe bear
witness to this fact. The joyous, if no longer creative, art of
the time appears like a last renaissance of antiquity, and
offers throughout a parallel to the new birth of Greek literature. It was cosmopolitan, for since the time of Alexander
the Great, Greek art had not possessed a home. Its works
were the property of the world. Its schools, indeed, were
still carried on in the Greek cities under Roman rule, but
Rome itself had become the nucleus of artistic activity. The
empire, the inheritor of the ancient world of art, was lord of
its treasures, and bestowed copies of them upon every nation.

The art as well as the literature of Greece was a necessity
for the luxurious in the Roman empire. The emperors spoke
and wrote in Greek, and endeavoured to become connoisseurs
of the beautiful. In the first century, indeed, of the empire
the feeling of Rome for art was still so barbarous, that the
beautiful works of Greek sculpture and painting were carried
off to Rome in large quantities. Caligula and Nero went on
with the plundering which Marcellus had begun in Sicily,
and Fabius Maximus in Tarentum, and which afterwards,
Flaminius, Fulvius Nobilior, Metellus, and Cornelius Scipio,
Paulus Aemilius and Mummius carried on all over the lands

of Hellas. This was changed under the Flavian emperors, and from their time to the days of Constantine, Greece was robbed of no work of art.[1]

The Caesars had shown the splendour of the empire in Rome itself by the magnificence of its buildings and art treasures. The city had reached the height of its beauty in the Forum of Trajan, and this great emperor had given a fresh impetus to all the arts. He may be compared with Pope Julius II. in giving great encouragement to works of art, but he was devoid of any great feeling for art itself. To him she was the handmaid of the empire, which was glorified by her greatness and by his triumphs ; his most magnificent building served to enclose his own tomb. Hadrian's attitude towards art was that of Leo de Medici in the time of the Renaissance. From an intellectual superiority he loved art passionately, looking upon it as the essence of Hellenic and Roman culture. His inclination for art is more strongly expressed than his pleasure in literature, and it was more easily gratified by the resources of the empire. An artist himself, revelling in all intellectual tastes, he sought his highest enjoyment as a ruler, in buildings and in art. In Antinous, Hadrian deified beauty, giving him as the type of his ideal to the artists of his time. He only ventured to deify Antinous because he was beautiful, and the artists were among the foremost of his contemporaries who made converts for the new god.

The Renaissance of the antique is one of the most marked features in Hadrian's mind, and his chief attraction lay therefore in Athens. When he completed the Olympian temple there, and again made the city of Pericles the chief city of Greece, it seemed as if he hoped to awaken the genius of Greece on the banks of the Ilissus. And here he deceived himself. The difference between his age and that of the later Italian Renaissance is the difference between youth and age. The Italian Renaissance was preceded by a

[1] The only emperors who plundered Hellas were Caligula and Nero, Leake, *Topogr. Athens*, Introd., p. xlv. On these plunderings see Petersen, *General Introd. to the Study of Archaeol.* 1829 ; Sickler, *Gesch. der Wegnahme vorzügl. Kunstwerke*, 1803 ; Voelkel, *Ueber die Wegfuhrung der Kunstwerke*, 1798.

long barbaric age which it eventually conquered. Its art
steadily improved from Nicola Pisano to Michael Angelo,
from Cimabue to Rafael, and was displayed later by a
galaxy of brilliant intellects, whose creative power is one of
the most astonishing phenomena in the history of civilization.
Not in sculpture as in antiquity, but in painting, did the
modern Renaissance find its most fertile domain ; it culmin-
ated in the celestial and glorified beauty of woman in the
ideal of the Madonna, while the last pagan Renaissance closed
with the repetition of the ancient ideal of manly beauty in
the Dionysus-Antinous.

Hadrian visited and favoured every city which contained
schools of Greek art, but he could not call Phidias and
Polignotus back to life to animate the forms of antiquity
with new ideals. Though it is a mistake to compare his age
with the best times of Greece, it is nevertheless true that
art then flourished for the last time. Its reign was short,
for under Hadrian's successors the philosophy of the Stoics
became predominant, and to them beauty was a matter of
indifference. Winckelmann was of opinion that Hadrian
could no longer befriend art, as the spirit of liberty had disappeared from the world, and the fountain of glorious and
sublime thoughts was dried up.[1] This cosmopolitan age could
only become illustrious by making every classic idea serve
an intellectual purpose. It imagined that it was being
illuminated by the sun of Greece, but this borrowed light
was merely an after-glow. To undervalue it on this account
would be a mistake, as our own art of sculpture to-day
resembles that of Hadrian, and can scarcely be more simple
in the conception of its highest ideals. If Hadrian failed
in his attempts to revive the arts, the fault lay in the times,
not in himself. In this he was like the emperor Julian,
who attempted the restoration of the ancient religion ; but
Hadrian was more fortunate. It may be said that he retarded
the decay of art by at least half a century, and that as an
enthusiast for art he rendered this service to the ancient
world. The emperor Julian did not acknowledge his services
to antiquity when he drew his portrait in the *Caesars*.

In the time of Hadrian the fancy of the artist had long

---

[1] *Geschichte der Kunst*, xii. 309, c. 1, § 22.

exhausted the supply of beautiful forms, but the antique still remained, and religion still connected man and his ideal wants with the whole range of ancient sculpture. Artists who in the second century created an Apollo and a Zeus, a Diana and a Venus, might still believe in the power of these deities, and thus approach more nearly to the mythological truth of Nature than the artist of Christian times, who gives to his academical composition the name of any ancient divinity indifferently. Their greatest misfortune was that they were condemned to imitation, as the value of their creations was measured by the still numerous masterpieces of the golden age of Greece. Their own age seems to have paid little attention to them. We know the names of many even mediocre learned men, poets, and sophists of the age of Hadrian, but only a few names of artists survive. Pliny complained of the decay of the arts in his time,[1] and Pausanias never mentions the masters of his age. In his work *The Dream*, in which the arts of the sculptor and the sophist struggle to possess him, Lucian tells us that the artists enjoyed no respect.[2] They were no longer original, their art consisted merely in reproduction.

The Museums of Rome, and perhaps the Torlonia Museum in particular, give a clear idea of the wholesale imitation of the antique, and their rich contents form an epitome of the group of Roman designs which were devoted to the sculptural decoration of villas. On the whole, however, the art of Hadrian's age bears the stamp of the consciousness of supremacy of the Roman empire, while its all-embracing activity dazzles our imagination, merely as the expression of its ordinary demand for beauty. Our capitals, which equal or exceed the population of imperial Rome, are not as much adorned with public works of art, as any thriving municipality in the time of Hadrian. The pride of our galleries are the fragments from antiquity, especially from the imperial period; art and the love of art having so completely disappeared from the minds of the people generally, that it is only by the few, who are both highly cultivated and rich, that they are indulged in, to an extent which would

---

[1] Pliny, *H.N.* xxxv. 2, 2. Painting an expiring art, xxxv. 11.

[2] *Enhypnion*, c. 9.

have excited the smile of a Hadrian or a Herodes Atticus.

The motives for spirited inventions were certainly wanting in that ageing world; it was over-ripe, but still keen for enjoyment, and a genuine desire for luxury and beauty took the place of originality and skill. Never was this more universal. We are surprised at the artistic decoration of Pompeii, which was only a small country town; we must imagine the work of painter and sculptor there, carried out through the empire, in order to conceive the aspect of its cities in the times of Hadrian and the Antonines. This wealth of beautiful works presupposes a prosperity that is hardly credible, and legions of artists in large and small societies.

On the whole, the best artists under the empire were Greeks. After the fall of Greece, sculptors and painters, who were often slaves and freedmen, found their way to Rome and to the West. They inspired their barbaric conqueror with the taste for beautiful things, and worked for him. From the booty taken from Macedonia, Quintus Metellus erected temples to Jupiter and Juno, wherein he placed the works of Praxiteles, Polycletes, Dionysius and Philiscus which he had carried off. At the same time these temples were richly ornamented by the Greeks Sauras and Batrachus, while Pasiteles carved the statue of Jupiter in ivory. This master founded a Greek school of art in Rome in the time of Pompey; he was the master of Stephanus, the sculptor of the statue of the Ephebus in the Villa Albani. Stephanus also carved the Menelaus, and the beautiful group of the Electra and Orestes in the Villa Ludovisi are supposed to be original.[1] Zenodorus, the sculptor of the colossus of Nero, was no less famous in his time. The migration of the masters of Greek art to Rome must have lasted a long time, for before Constantine and his successors had gathered together the art treasures of the expiring Greek world on the Bosporus, Rome was the universal museum of art. These artists could never have wearied of contemplating the creations of Greece, of which more were to be found in Rome than in

---

[1] Friedrichs, *Bausteine*, n. 715.

Athens.[1]   The widest field lay open for their activity, a field
which has never been offered to the arts before or since.
The projects of the emperors were worthy of their position
as rulers of the world, and the claims of luxury were insatiable.   Architects, sculptors and painters, lived in a golden
age; they had plenty to do in the realm of art, from the
magnificent building of a temple down to a pleasant country
house, and from the ideal figure of a god to the furniture
of a dwelling.   Greeks had been employed in the service of
the magnificent Trajan, and the best among them became
the teachers of the dilettante Hadrian.   How many artists
must have found their way from Greece to Rome in his
reign![2]   A few names of Greek masters of his time have been
preserved; Aristeas and Papias from Aphrodisias designed
the two centaurs on the Capitol, and Zeno, from the same
city in Caria, was probably their contemporary.   He inscribed
his name on a Hermes in the Braccio Nuovo, and on the
so-called senator in the Villa Ludovisi.[3]   It is strange that
the figure of Antinous cannot be ascribed to any one of
these masters.

The artists did not furnish merely the capital of the empire
with beautiful works, but they adorned the provinces as well,
particularly in the West.   Rome may be considered the great
market where statues of the gods, portraits of distinguished
men, and objects of the greatest luxury were produced as in
a manufactory.   Material was brought in ships from the
distant marble quarries of the empire to Ostia, and was then
conveyed to Rome.   The remains of these imperial marble

[1] On the material for the study of art in Rome: O. Jahn, *Aus der
Alterthums Wissensch., die alte Kunst und die Mode*, p. 239.

[2] Studios of artists in imperial times have been found, especially on the
Campus Martius and about Navona.   Pellegrini, *Bull d. Inst.*, 1859,
p. 69; Bruzza, *Inscr. dei marmi grezzi Annali d. Inst.*, 1870, p. 137;
Benndorf and Schoene, *Lateran. Museum*, p. 350.

[3] Overbeck, *Gesch. d. griech. Plastik*, ii[3]., 398, 454; Brunn, *Gesch.
der Künstler*, i. 573; G. Hirschfeld, *Tituli statuarior. sculptorumq.*,
Berlin, 1871, ascribes n. 172, two statues in the Villa Albani with the
name of Philumenos to Hadrian's time.   The names of other Greek
artists are Erato, Menophantus, a Phidias and Ammonius, of the year
159 A.D., n. 169, 170, 171.

store-houses give an idea of the extent of the trade and art of sculpture in Rome.

On the whole, the period of art in Hadrian's time shows, with increased production, a refinement of technique and a brilliancy of invention, which are its characteristics. The school became academical and conventional; it attained the greatest elegance, but the sparkle of genius was lost in a cold polish. At the same time the barrier of national and provincial distinctions was broken down; for the same style was represented in the most diverse circles of culture by a systematic uniformity, so that a work of art found in Britain looks like one of the same period found in Rome or in Ephesus.[1] Taste in Rome set the fashion for the provinces. People in Germany and in Gaul were anxious to possess works which were admired in the capital. Fresco painting as a decoration for the interior of houses also came into vogue throughout the empire.[2]

[1] Gerhard, *Roms antike Bildwerke; Röm. Stadtbeschr*, i. 280; Friedlaender, iii. 249.

[2] Helbig, *Untersuch. über die campan. Wandmalerei*, p. 137.

CHAPTER XX

The Progress and Production of Art. Furniture.
Gems. Medals. Precious Stones. Paintings.
Portraits in Marble. Historical Relievo

THE magnificence of the imperial designs was natural in an
age when the love of the beautiful was universal. Hadrian
spent fabulous sums on his undertakings, and his example
was followed, from motives of patriotism, by many cities
and citizens. The emperor like Leo X. in another age,
was eventually blamed for his building craze. Marcus
Aurelius praised his father by adoption, Antoninus, for having been free from the mania.[1] But the art of building drew
in its train all the other fine arts, for the temple of architecture enclosed them all.

In those days secular architecture predominated over
sacred architecture. To the gods indeed, especially to those
who had come into fashion from Asia, new temples were
later still erected. Even in the third century Aurelian
reared magnificent temples to the sun-god, and Constantine
also built temples for the gods; but, generally speaking,
the want was already supplied in Hadrian's time, for the
great shrines of Greek and Roman worship were numerous
and perfect, and, like our cathedrals of to-day, they could
not be equalled. The restoration of ancient temples was
more frequent than the building of new temples. On the
other hand, emperors and nobles erected innumerable palaces
and villas, and cities built their theatres and baths, their
gymnasia and libraries. All these places became museums

[1] *In se ipsum*, i. 13.

of art. The galleries of Europe have been provided with sculpture from one single villa of Hadrian's.

All branches of art and industry which contributed to the luxury of the age flourished greatly. The furniture of that time still bears the stamp of classic beauty. The massive marble candelabra in the Vatican, the most beautiful of the kind in antiquity, the large and richly adorned vases and cups of marble, like the vase of *rosso antico* with swans at the four corners, and the Egyptian vase of black granite in the Capitol, all came from Hadrian's villa. Amid the ruins of the temple of Venus and Rome were found the colossal faces of Medusa in the Braccio Nuovo, which show on what a grand scale the ancients represented the gloomy dæmoniacal powers.

The coins and medals of Hadrian's time (the large imperial bronze medallions begin, according to Winckelmann, with this emperor) are of exquisite taste, and are distinguished —especially the Egyptian medals—by a surprising wealth of imagination in their use of symbols. The medals are small works of art which delight the eye and enchant the imagination.[1] Their subjects are, it is true, either derived from ancient ideas, or are actually copied from Greek patterns, like the splendid medallion which represents the winged Victory dashing through the air in a chariot drawn by two horses.[2] Other beautiful specimens of Hadrian's time show the figures of deities in the Greek style : Jupiter enthroned, with Victory on his right hand, Diana Lucifera, Apollo playing on his lyre before the Muses, Asclepius, Vesta, Hermes with the ram, Cybele in a chariot drawn by four lions. Many are completely Roman, like the medallions which represent Hadrian, standing erect between five military banners, which he seems to salute with his hand. Others display the Roman she-wolf or Moneta Augusti, the figure of a beautiful woman with scales and a cornucopia, or of Felix Roma who is seated upon a pile of weapons near a

[1] W. Froehner (*Les Médaillons de l'Empire Romain*) has collected the best of Hadrian's coins in the section "Hadrian." He calls the medals of the age of the Antonines, an anthology after the great poets.

[2] Froehner (p. 34) quite arbitrarily refers this precious medallion to the Jewish war.

trophy, while in the background a winged Victory raises a shield.[1] Another medal represents the senate and the people in the guise of an old man with a sceptre and a genius, while between them stands a burning altar.[2]

Connoisseurs maintain that the stones cut in the time of Augustus, the work of Dioscorides, are more beautiful than those of Hadrian's time, as the art of carving gems began to decay after the time of Claudius.[3] But the wonderful gem of Claudius and of his family hardly shows any falling off.[4] Hadrian himself eagerly collected carved stones and precious cups. The imperial treasury grew so rich in this respect that Marcus Aurelius defrayed the cost of the war against the Marcomanni out of it, after the public sale of these collections had lasted for two months on the Forum of Trajan.[5] Beautiful cameos with the bust of Hadrian and of Antinous have been preserved.[6] The emerald, on which the heads of Hadrian and Sabina are cut, is considered especially fine. The mine where this stone was mainly found was at Djebel Zaborah in Egypt.[7]

The mines of this country and of Numidia furnished the coloured marble and rare stones with which the houses of the rich were adorned. Greece had never known such luxury in marble. We search vainly to-day in Athens for traces of it, while in Rome an inexhaustible supply of coloured marbles from imperial times supports a flourishing trade. The excessive use of marble certainly shows the degeneracy of taste, but the fashion began before Hadrian's time, though the luxury in coloured marbles may then have been at its

---

[1] This medallion, too—HADRIANUS AUG . COS . III . P . P—FELIX ROMA . (Cohen, ii., p. 167, n. 714)—is referred by Froehner to the same victory over the Jews.

[2] IMP . CAESAR TRAIANUS HADRIANUS AUG.—SENATUS POPULUSQUE ROMANUS VOTA SUSCEPTA.—Cohen, ii., p. 222, n. 1406.

[3] King, *Antique Gems and Rings*, i. 190.

[4] Eckhel, *Pierres gravées*, pl. 7.

[5] Julius Capitolinus, *M. Aurel.*, c. 17.

[6] Eckhel, *Pierres gravées*, pl. 8, in sardonyx, though, I think, the likeness of the portrait doubtful; pl. 8, Antinous in sardonyx, with a mask of Silenus on his head. Mariette, *Traité des pierres grav.*, pl. 64, Hadrian on a white agate, Sabina on a cornelian.

[7] Friedlaender, iii. 72 ; according to King, p. 297, 8.

height.[1] For most of the pieces of sculpture of rare or
colossal stone come from the buildings of Hadrian.[2] Porphyry was then used in architecture, but it was not employed
for sculpture, although statues of this material had already
been brought by Vitrasius Pollio to the emperor Claudius
from Egypt. Pliny who tells us this, says they found
neither approval nor imitators, and porphyry was not used
for statues until after the decay of art in the third century.[3]
But they were carved out of *rosso antico*[4] With small
regard for taste, busts were carved even from alabaster,
like those of Hadrian and Sabina in the Capitol. A bust
of the emperor is in existence, of which the face is carved in
alabaster, but it may be of later date. Large engraved scarabei
in coloured marble are to be found, which prove the revival of
this Egyptian art in Hadrian's time. It is quite probable
that the fancy for valuable marbles actually helped to
destroy the taste for bronze statues. While Pompeii and
Herculaneum have furnished rich treasures in bronze, nothing
remarkable of this kind has been found in Hadrian's villa.[5]
The museums of Rome, which contain the fragmentary remains of works of art from the time of the empire, are
generally poor in fine bronze.

The art of the painter, like the decorative art of the
worker in marble, was very active throughout the empire.
Hadrian doubtless adorned his villa at Tibur with many
mural paintings, representing the scenery of the cities and
countries which he had admired on his travels; and the
landscape of the Nile, which was particularly dear to the
Romans, would not be wanting. As the emperor had also
the vale of Tempe symbolically depicted in his villa, it seems
that he had a strong appreciation of beautiful scenery. But
no investigation has brought to light remains of important
paintings from the villa at Tibur; only a few fine mosaics
have been preserved. In the Vatican is the large portrait-

---

[1] Friedlaender, iii. 66, is of this opinion.
[2] Gerhard, *Roms ant. Bildwerke; Röm. Stadtbeschr.*, i. 297.
[3] Pliny, *H. N.*, 36, 11, 3; Letronne, *Inscr. de l'Egypte*, i. 142.
[4] According to Friedrichs, *Bausteine*, n. 760, no statue of this material
can be proved to have been made before the time of Hadrian.
[5] Gerhard, *Roms ant. Bildwerke*, p. 297.

mosaic of Dionysus and Apollo, with many rural scenes; and in the Capitol is the famous mosaic of the doves, the Roman copy of a work of Sosus of Pergamum.

We can form no correct opinion whether during the imperial times the decorative art of the sculptor and the painter merely repeated ancient designs, or produced original work as well. There was only one domain in art in which the Romans were independent of the Greeks, and that was in portraiture and in historical scenes in relievo. The fashion of portraits among the Romans had its origin in their family affection and love of history, and in no other nation of the world has the art of portraiture played so great a part. Under the empire, the busts too of famous Greeks were made in quantities for the adornment of palaces and gardens.

The portraiture of the Romans was maintained at this high level until the time of the Severi. The bust of Commodus Hercules which was discovered a few years ago, and which is now in the new Museum of the Capitol, illustrates the same technical school of Hadrian's time. Portraits and busts of this emperor and his wife are numerous in all the museums of Europe, for there has scarcely been another prince in honour of whom cities, corporations and private individuals erected so many statues. The most famous busts of him are in the Capitol, in the Vatican, in Naples, and in the Louvre. The most faithful likeness appears to be the excellent bust of Hadrian on the staircase of the palace of the conservators; but the marble is unfortunately disfigured by a blemish on the chin. Of the numerous statues of the emperor at Athens, none worthy of note are in existence.[1]

Like other emperors, Hadrian was represented in the form of a deity. In a statue on the Capitol, he is represented as Mars offering sacrifice.[2]

The imperial statue acknowledged to be that of Hadrian,

[1] In the collection at Athens there are few busts of Hadrian to be found; a doubtful bust in the National Museum from the theatre of Dionysus, and an authentic bust; in Varvacion a doubtful head of the youthful Hadrian, which was found at the same time as the colossal head of Lucius Verus in the theatre of Dionysus. Milchhoefer, *Die Museen Athens*, 1881.

[2] See Cohen, ii., p. 185, n. 951, the medal MARTI.

in the Museum of the old Seraglio at Constantinople, is worthy of notice; the emperor is clad in a coat of mail, and is in such a warlike attitude, that his foot is set upon a prostrate prisoner.[1]

Altogether, the production of portraits at this time was astonishingly great. A mass of inscriptions, too numerous to peruse, but which are valuable as historical records, belong to the pedestals of these honorary statues. The emperor himself erected many statues for his favourites. He almost covered the world with images of Antinous and of Aelius Verus; but to many other persons less dear to him, dead as well as living, he dedicated statues.[2] He even erected an equestrian figure in the temple of Bellona to the barbarian king Pharasmanes. Dion observes that he honoured Turbo and Similis with public statues.[3] Unfortunately these and the likenesses of other friends and statesmen of Hadrian are lost, or can no longer be distinguished, as they are without a name. Whose is that intellectual head in the Braccio Nuovo, not far from the statue of Demosthenes, which arrests our attention? A young Roman of fashion, with well trimmed beard and locks flowing over his brow; this head is an example of the distinguished world of Hadrian's time, and of the brilliant treatment of a portrait.

The historical relievo of the Romans has also its own peculiar characteristics. It suited the Latin taste for individuality. Great national events, wars and battles, expeditions and triumphs, could in this way be historically portrayed. The Romans, indeed, had no Phidias, who might have adorned the frieze of a temple for them with the ideal figures of a state festival; but this art of relievo was applied to the triumphal arches and to the honorary statues, which are peculiar to their historic worship. The remains of this art in Rome are unfortunately very fragmentary, and only illustrate the short period of fifty years of its prime.[4] As Domitian's numerous triumphal arches

[1] Sorlin-Dorigny, *Hadrien, Statue trouvée en Crète, Gazette Archéol.*, 1880, vi., 52, pl. 6.

[2] Dion, lxix. 7 : ὅθεν καὶ εἰκόνας πολλοῖς—ἐς τὴν ἀγορὰν ἔστησεν.

[3] Dion, lxix. 18.

[4] Ad. Philippi, *Ueber die röm. Triumfal. Reliefe (Abhandl. der phil.*

have perished, we only possess fragments of the ancient sculptures from the arch of Claudius in the Villa Borghese, the ideal reliefs on the arch of Titus, the realistic reliefs on the triumphal arch and on the column of Trajan, where Roman art probably reached its zenith in the portrayal of historical events by groups of figures. Then we have remains, which are of much less artistic value, of sculptures on the arch of Marcus Aurelius and in the bas-reliefs of his column; and, finally, the figures on the arches of Severus and Constantine, which clearly indicate the decay of art.

Hadrian was no warrior prince; he had no victories to commemorate. If he was represented as Mars this flattery was only meant to show the attention he paid to the army. We know of only one equestrian statue of Hadrian, and this stood before the temple of Zeus in the Roman colony of Jerusalem. Perhaps, too, Hadrian was represented on horseback on the triumphal arch at Antinoe. He did not offer himself as an historical subject to the plastic art. But probably the two coffers of marble decorated with bas-reliefs, which were excavated from the Forum at Rome in the year 1872, refer to him. They display inside the colossal figures of the three sacrificial animals (*Suovetaurilia*), and outside, solemn acts of state; here the burning of the bonds, there a scene before the emperor, which seems to refer to the institution for poor children. The style resembles that of the time of Trajan or Hadrian. Nothing prevents our seeing in the first scene a monument to the great remission of debt, while the other may easily represent the extension of Trajan's *Alimenta Italiae* by his successor. This charitable establishment was often symbolized on medals and in marble, as on Trajan's triumphal arches in Rome and in Beneventum, and on a bas-relief in the Villa Albani which refers to the benefactions of Antoninus to poor girls (*Puellae Faustinianae*).[1]

hist. Classe der kön sächs. Ges. der Wissensch. Bd. vi. iii. 1872). According to him the flourishing state of this art lasted from Titus to Trajan, from 81 A.D. to 117 A.D.

[1] Henzen, *Bull. d. Inst.* 1872, p. 273 *sq.*, was the first to explain these reliefs from the Forum, and to ascribe them to Trajan. See the literature upon it in Orazio Marucchi, *Descrizione del Foro Rom.* 1883, p. 87. Henzen is now (April, 1883) inclined to ascribe the reliefs to Hadrian.

CHAPTER XXI

Ideal Sculpture. Its Cosmopolitan Character. Imitation of Ancient Masterpieces. Review of the Works of Art found in Hadrian's Villa. The Statues of Antinous

IN the domain of ideal sculpture the art of this age displays a thoroughly cosmopolitan character. It reproduces with equal taste the types of the epochs of Greece as well as of Egypt. It portrays all the ancient treasure of fables, together with the grecianized legends of Syria and the mysterious secrets of the Nile. And if these symbols are localized in Athens and Smyrna, in Ephesus, Alexandria and Carthage, in Rome they are cosmopolitan. There is a world-sculpture as there is a world-literature. The man of this period stands on a pinnacle of culture from which he surveys the creations of past ages. The mixture of divinities involves also a mixture of styles, but when the gods descended from their temple-niches to adorn palaces, their strange forms were conventionally polished and their barbaric names translated into Latin.

We can at once recognize the images of Egyptian gods of Hadrian's time in the Vatican museum by the smoothness of their modernized forms, which no longer agree with their ancient worship. It was then the custom to look upon many of the gods with antiquarian interest, just as we gaze to-day at the carvings of the people of Thibet and Mexico. There were amateurs who looked at a Pallas from an archaic temple, an Ephesian Diana, or a Vesta such as is in the possession of the Torlonia Museum, with

more pleasure than at the ideal forms of the Juno of
Polycletus and the Athene of Phidias.   Authorities on the
art of the period have advanced the theory that the
favourite subjects at the time were representations from
the group of myths connected with Bacchus; and they have
based their theory on the numerous reliefs of Dionysian
dances, and of Cupids on sarcophagi and vases, and on
many works of Hadrian's time, like the Fauns in the
Vatican, the Satyr with the vine in the Capitol, and the
two Centaurs of black marble.   But this may be entirely
accidental, while the Dionysus figure of Antinous gives the
exact idea of the youth himself.   The works which come
from the villa at Tibur are copies of an ancient style.   The
celebrated Barberini Faun in Munich belonged to the
mausoleum of Hadrian.   It is no matter of surprise that
more works of sculpture were excavated from this one
villa of the emperor than from Pompeii,[1] but it is amazing
that even his tomb should have been as richly furnished.
So late as the time of Belisarius, the Greeks who were
besieged there, protected themselves against the assault
of the Goths with fragments of marble statues.   From
the ruins of the tomb the colossal bust of Hadrian in the
Sala Rotonda of the Vatican was brought to light.[2]   The
fan of white and black granite in the cabinet of the Laocoon comes also from the mausoleum.   The temple of
Venus and Rome was certainly another museum of works
of art, from which came the famous mask of Medusa.

No emperor had more favourable opportunities than
Hadrian for procuring antique works of art from Greek
cities.   We may assume that he bought many on the spot,
and that others were given to him as presents, as he took
nothing by force.   Instead of carrying off an obelisk from
Heliopolis to his villa he had one set up there which had
been sculptured in Rome.   Instead of surrounding himself
with stolen masterpieces he was satisfied with copies of
them.

[1] R. Foerster, *Die bildende Kunst unter Hadrian (Die Grenzboten)*,
1875, i. 105.
[2] See on the Barberini Faun, Luetzow, *Münchener Antiken*, p. 51.
Friedrichs (*Bausteine*, n. 656) believes it to be a Greek original.

The number of ancient and modern works of art which Hadrian placed in the rooms of his villa must have been so great that it probably did not fall short of the contents of the Vatican Museum. If we could see this artistic Pantheon as it stood, we should obtain a clear conception, not only of the range of contemporary art, but of the society of amateurs of whom the emperor himself was the most brilliant representative. And the mere collection of works found in this villa is sufficient to prove that Hadrian had there formed a museum of works of art of every age and style. A hundred styles and forms are visible there from the vase of marble adorned with bas-reliefs, and the great candelabras, to the torso of the weeping Niobe (in the Vatican), a copy of the Iris of Phidias from the Parthenon, and the statues of the gods Zeus and Hera, of Apollo and of Aphrodite. There are statues of the muses, busts and statues of poets and philosophers, the graceful heads of Tragedy and Comedy, the head of Aristophanes, the bas-relief of the forsaken Ariadne, Harpocrates and a row of Egyptian deities. Antinous, too, is to be found there with vestals, fauns, satyrs, centaurs, the Attic fragment of the birth of Erichthonius, the Artemis of Ephesus, the so-called Flora (in the Capitol), Nemesis, Psyche, the Amazons, the Jason or Hermes (in Munich), Meleager, Adonis and the sleeping Edymion (in Stockholm), the Discobolos of Myron (in the Vatican), the Antinous (in the Capitol), Ajax with the body of Achilles (the fragments in the Vatican), and many others.

If the locality where some antiquities have been discovered makes it at least probable that they belong to the time of Hadrian, there are many others which may be of the same period, though it cannot be proved. We may ascribe the famous statue of the Nile in the Vatican to this epoch. In the Torlonia Museum a figure of the Nile in black marble, with cornucopia, palm branch, and sphinx, recalls the type of Hadrian's Egyptian coins. Works like the bas-relief of Daedalus and Icarus in *rosso antico* in the Villa Albani, the bas-relief of Medea in the Torlonia Museum, the Amazons by Polycletus in the Capitol and the Vatican, the Cupids with their bows drawn, the discus throwers, the figures of Mars, the copies of Apollo Sauroctonos, the figures of Venus by Praxiteles, the sleeping satyrs, many Niobe groups by Scopas,—might as easily come from the time of Hadrian as from the earlier days from which the copies of the Laocoon and the Apollo Belvedere were derived. We certainly find it difficult to distinguish between the art of the time of the Roman emperors and the art of Alexandrian times, and we cannot even fix the age in which to place the Laocoon.[1]

As the art of the two first centuries of the empire bears no traces of originality, but is merely the repetition of ancient ideals, it portrays no distinct characteristics of the age. It only displays the highly accomplished technique of a school inspired by the most cultivated taste. Form had attained such elegance that thought was lost in insipidity, as we may see in the theatrical heads of women in the Sala Rotonda, in the Centaurs, and in the bas-reliefs of Antinous. The academic smoothness of form almost reminds us of Canova and Thorwaldsen; but if these masters of the latest renaissance succeeded, by returning to antique models, in freeing sculpture from quaint disfigurements, no such thing was possible in the time of Hadrian. For this period was rather the final development of the antique itself; its close was necessarily marked by the transition from the real to the apparent. It was the same with Greek sophistry, which would have ended in empty bombast if, like the schools of sophists in Smyrna, Athens and Constantinople, it had survived the triumph of Christianity and had lasted through the rise of the barbarians until the sixth century.

The art of Hadrian's time sought to reach its highest ideal in the type of Antinous. The insane desire of the emperor to create a new divinity was rendered possible only by the rare beauty of his favourite. All who took part in this comedy no doubt laughed at it: the Greeks at the freak of the emperor, and the emperor himself at the world of flatterers; but Hadrian looked with more satisfaction at the influence which the form of his deified favourite began to exercise upon art, than at the increase of superstition, which was promoted by the worship of Antinous. The images

---

[1] Friedrichs, *Bausteine*, p. 426.

and statues which he carved himself cannot sustain the criticism of artists, but his Bithynian god was recognized by them as an ideal form. The figure of Antinous may, indeed, be looked upon as Hadrian's own production in art, for he doubtless gave the direction for it to the sculptor. He appears in numberless statues, bas-reliefs and gems, as a genius and hero, or as a particular divinity.[1]

Although the representations of Antinous are all ideal, there is an historical portrait for their foundation. He has a personality. In every case we see a face bowed down, full of melancholy beauty, with deep-set eyes, slightly arched eyebrows, and with abundant curls falling over the forehead. The thick lips, the broad chest, and the effeminate figure suggest sensuality; but this is redeemed by traits of melancholy. It is the beautiful expression of a nature which combines the Greek and the Asiatic, only slightly idealized. Knowing as we do the fate of Antinous, we read it in this sorrowful figure, for the artists knew of the death of sacrifice to which Antinous dedicated himself. The mysterious sadness in the features of Antinous would attract the observer, even if he could not give the name to the statue. And yet these beautiful features are smooth and devoid of expression; a young man stands before us who has experienced nothing, and who tells us nothing.

When the statues of Antinous were discovered at Tibur, they created the same excitement in the world of art of the eighteenth century as the most famous antiques had created at the beginning of the sixteenth. Their value was overestimated. Winckelmann praised the Antinous of the Villa Casali enthusiastically, and especially the bas-relief of the Villa Albani.[1] The colossal head of Antinous by Mondragone, which was found at Frascati, and has been in the Louvre since 1808, was pronounced by him to be the finest thing which has come down to us from antiquity after the Apollo of the Vatican and the Laocoon. It certainly surpasses in beauty the colossal bust which was found at Tibur, and which now stands in the Sala Rotonda of the Vatican, and

---

[1] According to Dion Cassius (lxix. 11), Hadrian dedicated statues to Antinous throughout the world (ἀνδριάντας), and especially statues to be worshipped (αγάλματα).

the other bust which was taken from Tibur to the Villa
Albani.[1]   But the great art critic would have expressed himself still more enthusiastically if he had seen the colossus of
Antinous, which was found at Palestrina in the year 1793, and
which was given by Pius VI. to duke Braschi.   A few years
ago Pius IX. had it removed from the Lateran Museum to the
Sala Rotonda.   It is unquestionably the most brilliant statue
of the Dionysus-Antinous.   The wreath of ivy is twined
amid his flowing locks, and on his head he carries a pine-
apple ; the ample upper garment which was originally ornamented with gold and ivory, is fastened on the left shoulder,
allowing the right arm, the breast and part of the body to
be seen.   In his left hand the young god holds on high a
thyrsus.   The decorative principle of painting is strongly
expressed in this Bacchic statue, and admirers of severe
beauty of form will prefer it to the Antinous Hero in
the Museum at Naples, and to the more famous statue in
the Capitol.   The latter, a nude youth, his head bowed to
the right in a dreamy attitude, looks like a Narcissus or a
Hermes.   The statue is one of the most perfect figures of
the revival of art in Hadrian's time, as the so-called Antinous in the Belvedere was proved by Winckelmann to be
a Hermes from the best Greek epoch.

The celebrated marble group too of Ildefonso, which was
formerly called Sleep and Death, or Orestes and Pylades,
has been taken since the time of Visconti to be a representation of Antinous and of his sacrificial death.   In it we are
supposed to see the garlanded youth who gives himself to the
angel of death on behalf of the emperor; the angel kindles the
flame on the altar, and gently leads the victim to Proserpine.[2]

---

[1] The opinion of Winckelmann that the relief figure was placed on a
chariot as a consecration statue is contested by Levezow, *Ueber den
Antinous, dargestellt in den Kunstdenkmälern des Alterthums*, Berlin,
1808. Levezow, however, speaks only of eighteen busts and ten statues.
Overbeck, ii., p. 444.

[2] Huebner, *Antike Bildwerke in Madrid*, p. 73 *sq.*—Friedrichs, *Bausteine*,
n. 754. Doubts expressed by Welker, *Alte Denkmäler*, i. 375 *sq.* Friedrichs (*Bausteine*, n. 833) is certainly mistaken in thinking that he recognizes Antinous in a Trajan relief on the arch of Constantine (Bellori
according to veteres arcus Aug. triumphales, table 32), in the suite of
the emperor Trajan.

That the statues which have been hitherto called after Antinous are to be reckoned among the best of Hadrian's time
is certain, as they come chiefly from the imperial palaces.
But they and other statues or busts only represent a fragment of the plastic works which glorified Hadrian's favourite.[1]
Dion expressly says that the emperor dedicated statues and
images to him all through the inhabited world ; and there are
many badly executed busts of Antinous, which prove that
the figure was used commonly for ordinary decorations. His
statues in Egypt and in the Greek cities must have been
numerous.   A naked figure of a youth has been found in
the theatre of Dionysus at Athens, which is taken to be
Antinous ; it has been placed in the National Museum there
with another of Egyptian style which was found at Marathon,
and which probably belonged to a villa of Herodes Atticus.[2]
In the year 1860 Lenormant found a statue of Antinous
made from Thasian marble at Eleusis.[3] He was honoured
there as a new Dionysus. It is generally the youthful divinities of Olympus, Hermes, Apollo and Dionysus, in whose
image the deified youth was represented.   There is therefore nothing original in the type beyond the outlines
of his portrait.   On this account later criticism passes
almost too contemptuous a sentence on the extravagant
admiration of Winckelmann, which, however, Levezow did
not share.   Even the celebrated bust by Mondragone is
condemned by the superior art critic.[4]

The statue of Antinous, however, is a true ideal of
youthful beauty, which art created from the life of the
time.   Other works of sculpture which are ascribed to
Hadrian's epoch can only be looked upon as portraits of
doubtful accuracy, but the statues of Antinous are the only
authentic evidence of what the plastic art could do in the

---

[1] The Torlonia Museum, too, possesses several busts of Antinous in the
character of Dionysus; one of them, No. 403 in the catalogue, comes from
the Villa Hadriana. K. O. Müller, *Handbuch der Archäol. der Kunst*,
3 ed. § 203, has collected the statues and medals of Antinous.

[2] Milchhoefer, *Die Museen Athens*, p. 6, 23.—Rhusopulos in *Arch.
Ephem.*, Athens, 1862, p. 215.

[3] Lenormant, *L'Antinous d'Eleusis, Rev. Arch.*, 1874, p. 217 *sq.*

[4] Overbeck, ii. 445.

time of Hadrian.   If after the discovery of genuine masterpieces from the best days of Greek art, such as the sculptures of the Parthenon and the Hermes of Olympia, the
work in the statues of Antinous must be reckoned inferior,
it nevertheless proves that the age in which they were
created was still in possession not only of a complete
mastery of technique, but also of a keen appreciation of
form.   Certainly the type of Antinous must be considered
one of the last products of the art of antiquity, even if it
is a tame conclusion to the Greek ideal.

CHAPTER XXII

Architecture. Munificent Civic Spirit of the Cities. Hadrian's Love of Building. Antinoe. Roads to Berenice. Other Buildings in Egypt. The Temple at Cyzicus

HADRIAN'S greatest passion was building. With the Roman empire for his sphere, he probably surpassed every other ruler in the number of his buildings. The title of " Founder of the World" might have been ascribed to him with even more justice than to his predecessor Trajan.[1] But the passion was not confined to the emperor alone ; provinces and cities were infected by the same mania. During this peaceful epoch the taste for the fine arts became highly developed in the cities, and the patriotism of the citizens sought to augment the fame of the past by fresh monuments. The cities of Greek Asia, which were the richest of that time, particularly distinguished themselves by their devoted love for their country. The same munificent patriotism flourished in Italy, Gaul and Spain ; the communities vied with one another in the erection of private and public buildings, like the Greek republics in their best days, or like the Italian cities in the Middle Ages.

Rich citizens endowed their native cities with fine buildings, or they presented them with the means for that purpose. Only after the times of Nerva and Trajan had cities acquired the right of accepting legacies through the medium of a trustee, and this important right was confirmed to them unconditionally by a decree of the Senate in the

[1] Eutropius, viii. 4, speaks of Trajan as orbem terrarum aedificans.

time of Hadrian.[1]   From this flowed a fresh source of revenue, as it became a point of honour to bequeath money for patriotic purposes.   Inscriptions and other evidence, even before the time of Hadrian, give numerous proofs not only of the wealth, but of a patriotism that we can scarcely imagine in every province of the empire.   A consul in Trajan's time gave to the city of Tarquinii more than three million sesterces for buildings, and his son increased this sum.   A citizen gave to his native city, Laodicea, 2000 talents for the same purpose.   In Naples two brothers, Stertinius, spent their fortune in adorning the city, and in Massilia the physician Crinus built the city walls at his own expense.   A priestess at Calama in Numidia gave 400,000 sesterces to build a theatre, and Numidia Quadratilla built an amphitheatre and a temple at Casinum. Private persons built the large colonnades in the wonderful city of Palmyra, and Greek sophists in Smyrna, Pergamum, Cotyaeum, Antioch, Ephesus, and other cities, built porticos, baths and theatres.[2]   One sophist alone, Herodes Atticus, could emulate even Hadrian in adorning Athens and many other cities with splendid works.[3]

Where great undertakings were concerned the provinces were obliged to provide the means.   In the time of Trajan eleven cities of Lusitania bore the cost of the great bridge over the Tagus at Alcantara.   The provinces sometimes complained of these oppressive taxes for public buildings, and they could not be undertaken without the emperor's permission.[4]   Hadrian had made Herodes Atticus overseer of the cities of Asia, and had allowed him to build an aqueduct at Troas at an estimate of three million denarii ; the bold sophist spent seven millions upon it, and the province complained that its whole power of taxation was exhausted.[5]   But the liberality of the emperor was always

---

[1] Ulpian, *Fragm.* 34, 28.

[2] In Ephesus I saw traces of the hall discovered by Wood, which was built by the sophist Damianus from the ruins of the temple of Diana.

[3] For this activity in building by private persons, see Duruy, v. 138 *sq.* Friedlaender, iii., in the section Architecture.

[4] *Dig. L.* 10, 3.

[5] Marquardt, *Röm. Staatsverwaltung*, ii. 296.

ready to help in such cases, and we are told by an inscription that Hadrian bore the largest share of the cost in making the road from Beneventum to Aeclanum.[1] He gave an aqueduct to Dyrrhachium, which Alexander Severus afterwards restored.[2] For the gymnasium at Smyrna he gave such a large sum that the work was at once accomplished with the help of other contributions.[3] Companies with large capital were formed, which offered important buildings to rival contractors.

It was due to Hadrian's influence that all the provinces of the empire vied with one another in the erection of architectural monuments. If we possessed a complete catalogue of the buildings which arose from his private liberality the number would appear fabulous to us. For in all parts of the world where he travelled he left temples, gymnasia, aqueducts and roads as monuments of his journeys.[4] He was always accompanied by architects and engineers and by an army of masons, who were classed in military order.[5]

In the first place, there were cities which he partially or completely rebuilt. Many were called after him—*Aelia, Aeliopolis, Hadriana,* or *Hadrianopolis.* These were situated in Thrace, in Bithynia and Lycia, in Macedonia, in Illyria, in Cyrenaica, in Egypt, in Pontus, Syria, Paphlagonia and Caria.[6] Spartianus says that as he did not like to give names to his works he called many cities *Hadrianopolis,* like Carthage and a part of Athens. The names for these cities were only transitory, but the name Aelia clung to Jerusalem for centuries.

The motives at times were extraordinary which caused Hadrian to build different cities. In Mysia he founded Hadrianotherae, in order to commemorate his love of

[1] Of 1,716,000 sesterces the inhabitants of the immediate vicinity contributed only 569,000.—Mommsen, *I.R.N.* 628 *sq.*

[2] *C.I.L.* iii. 709, in Duerr, *Suppl.*, n. 85.

[3] χιλιὰς μυριάδας. *C.I.G.* 3148.

[4] Ejus itinerum monumenta videas per plurimas Asiae atque Europae urbes,—Fronto, *Princip. Hist.*, p. 244.

[5] Aurelius Victor, *Epitome* 14.

[6] Tile-inscriptions indicate an unknown city of Hadrian, Manpsus, *Ephem. Epigraph.* on *C.I.L.* iv. 332.

hunting, in the place where he had killed a boar.[1] We
have a coin of Antinous from this city bearing for arms
a boar's head.[2]

In honour of Antinous he built Antinoopolis or Antinoe
in the Heptanomis, on the site of the small city of the god
Besa on the eastern bank of the Nile. Ptolemy mentions
it as the metropolis of a particular Nomus Antinoitis, which
must have been made by Hadrian. Opposite to it lay
Hermupolis.[3] Antinoe as an essentially Hellenic city was
built not in the Egyptian, but in the Greek style.[4] It
had the regular form of a long quadrangle through which
ran the main street. At the north end, ruins of the
mausoleum of Antinous are to be seen, while on the south
the remains still exist of a magnificent temple with a fine
Corinthian portico. Colonnades line the streets, of which
three run across the city. On the harbour by the Nile a
triumphal arch with three gateways was erected on Corinthian pillars, with equestrian statues at each side. The cost
of the pillars in Antinoopolis must have been astonishing.
Where the principal streets met, honorary statues were
erected, one of which was dedicated later to Alexander
Severus and his mother, according to the inscription on
the pedestal. Ruins of baths, of a circus and gymnasium
lie outside the city, which must have presented a bright
and cheerful appearance.

Hadrian especially distinguished Antinoe by giving her a
Greek form of government. In Antinoe alone among the
Greek cities of Egypt was there a senate. And to create
a future for her by commercial intercourse he had a road
made to Berenice, provided with fountains, watch-towers,
and stations. As the road described by Pliny went from
Coptus to Berenice, Hadrian's new road seems to have
been made to the nearest port, probably to Myus Hormus,

---

[1] Spart. c. 20. Dion, lxix. 10.

[2] Eckhel, vi. 530.

[3] Ptolemy, 107 ; Mannert, x. 1. 395. In the city of Abydus there
was an oracle of Besa ;—Ammian. Marcell. xix. 12, p. 539.

[4] Letronne, *Inscr. de l'Egypte*, i. 171 ; Hirt, *Gesch. d. Baukunst der
Alten*, ii. 383.

and then to have been carried on to Berenice along the Red Sea.[1]

Hadrian did much to beautify Alexandria, which was already rich in works of art. Alexandrian coins display a temple with the figures of Serapis and of the emperor, and with the word Adrianon. In Alexandria too, it appears there was a Hadrianeum, which was turned later into a gymnasium, and then into a Christian church.[2] Imperial likenesses of Hadrian have been found in the remains of temples at Denderah, Esneh, and Medinet Habu, from which we may conclude that he erected buildings there in the usual Egyptian style, as the Ptolemies did before him.[3] At the celebrated porphyry quarries near Jebel Dokhan, and amid the ruins of a fortified city and an unfinished temple, Greek inscriptions of Hadrian's time have been found.[4]

As the emperor erected his buildings chiefly on his journeys, the course of these has only to be followed to discover his memorials. With the exception of Rome, he seems to have done less for the Western than for the Eastern provinces of the empire, the reason for this probably being that the East with its splendid and famous cities offered him greater inducement to leave monuments of his reign behind him.

He built a great number of temples in Asia, many of them for no special purpose; and on this account they were called in later days simply temples of Hadrian.[5] These temples without a divinity may well have been destined by the vain emperor for his own worship.

The temple at Cyzicus, which was so magnificent that it was numbered among the seven wonders of the world, belonged to this class. Marcus Aurelius probably finished it and dedicated it to his predecessor Hadrian, in 167 A.D. Its columns, monoliths 12 feet in thickness and 150 feet

---

[1] At Sheikh Abad, the ancient Antinoe, Mariette discovered an inscription of Hadrian of 25th of February, 137 A.D., which refers to this road. E. Miller, *Rev. Archéol. N. S.*, xxi., 1870, 314.

[2] Greppo, p. 222; according to Epiphanius, *Haeres.* xix. 2, op. i. 728.

[3] Champollion, *Lettres écrites d'Egypte*, p. 92; in Greppo, p. 221.

[4] Letronne, *Inscr. d'Egypte*, I, 418.

[5] Spart. c. 13.

in height, shone from the summit above the Propontis like a Pharos.   Aristides praised the temple in his inaugural address, speaking of it as the most beautiful which had ever been seen.   Its remains are still in existence.[1]

Hadrian enriched many cities in Greece and Asia with theatres, baths, gymnasia and aqueducts.   He rebuilt Jerusalem, he restored Stratonicea, Nicaea and Nicomedia.[2]   He gave a million on one day to the city of Smyrna ; with this she built a corn market and a gymnasium, which surpassed all others of Asia in beauty, and erected a temple to Hadrian himself on the promontory.   In Ephesus he built a temple to the genius of Rome which was also his own genius, an aqueduct in Alexandria Troas, and a harbour at Trebizond.

[1] Aristides, i. 382, does not say by whom it was built.   Cedrenus, p. 437, Malalas, p. 279, and the *Chron. paschale*, 254, ascribe it to Hadrian. Malalas maintains that he had his statue placed on the roof with an inscription, and adds ὑπερ ἐστὶν ἕως τῆς νῦν.   The Hadrianic coins of Cyzicus do not bear the design of the temple, but it was found on one of Antoninus Pius, Mionnet, ii. 450.   On this temple and its ruins, Perrot et Guillaume, *Le temple d'Adrien à Cyzique* and *Explorat. archéol. de Galatie*, etc.   See also Marquardt, *Cyzicus und sein Gebiet.*, p. 131.

[2] Stratonicea was rebuilt and called Adrianopolis by Hadrian.   Stephen Byz., on this city.

CHAPTER XXIII

*Buildings of Hadrian in Athens and in other Cities
of Greece. Buildings of Herodes Atticus*

FOR no other country did Hadrian manifest his preference
with such magnificence as for Greece, and especially for
Athens. There is no stronger testimony to the universal
affection in which this city was held, than the list of foreign
rulers who honoured and adorned her like a divinity with
great piety, after the loss of her freedom. Antigonus and
Demetrius, Ptolemy Philadelphus, Attalus and Eumenes of
Pergamum, Antiochus Epiphanes, Caesar, Augustus and
Agrippa, even Herod the King of the Jews, all loaded the
city of Solon and Pericles with benefits, and adorned it
with magnificent buildings.[1] Even in the time of Trajan
the posterity of Antiochus IV., the last king of Commagene,
continued the list of the princely patrons of Athens. Their
family tomb, the so-called monument of Philopappus, still
stands in partial preservation on the summit of the Museum hill.

The last splendour of Athens is connected with the
names of Hadrian and the Antonines. Hadrian erected so
many buildings in Athens that it almost looked as if he
would have liked to live there, and he probably would
have made this city his residence if his duties to Rome
had permitted. He renovated and embellished the city.
He built a temple to Zeus Panhellenius and to Hera, and
then a Pantheon after the pattern of the one in Rome.
Pausanias admired in this magnificent structure the one
hundred and twenty pillars of Phrygian marble, of which
the walls of the halls were also built. Later on he built
a fine gymnasium, with one hundred columns of Lybian

---

[1] Enumerated in Wachsmuth, *Die Stadt Athen*, i. 602 *sq.*

stone, and a library.   From the description of Pausanias this library must have been a specially fine architectural work, richly adorned with statues and pictures, and having a roof of gold.[1]

An inscription in the Pantheon contained the list of all the buildings of Hadrian in the cities of Greece and elsewhere,[2] and the loss of this inscription is therefore greatly to be deplored.   A Corinthian stoa of grey marble is to be seen now in the neighbourhood of the bazaar, and is taken to be the remains of Hadrian's gymnasium.   The temples we have mentioned probably formed a quarter of their own, but their exact position cannot be determined.[3] In the Panhellenion it is most probably Hadrian who is represented in the image of Zeus with Sabina as Juno.

Hadrian could scarcely add anything to the Acropolis, whose temples and innumerable sacred gifts covered the surface of the rocky plateau ; but it is believed that he reconstructed the great staircase of white marble which led to the Propylaea.[4]   A rebuilding of the theatre of Dionysus is also ascribed to him, partly from the fact that the place for the spectators was divided into thirteen parts, corresponding to the thirteen tribes of Hadrian's time, partly from inscriptions, and partly from the circumstance that in the theatre a statue of Antinous has been found.[5]

Hadrian's most important building in Athens was the temple of the Olympian Zeus.   Pisistratus had begun to build this famous sanctuary, but after the expulsion of his house it remained unfinished, until Antiochus Epiphanes gave a commission to the Roman architect Cossutius, to finish the temple which had fallen into oblivion.   But it still remained incomplete.   Livy however could say that it was one of the temples in the world whose design was worthy of the

---

[1] Aristides, i. 18, 9 ; *Panath.* i. 306 (*Dindorf*), calls the library βιβλίων ταμεῖα, οἷα οὐχ ἑτέρωθι γῆς φανερῶς καὶ μάλα τῶν ᾿Αθηνῶν κόσμος οἰκεῖος.   Bibliotheca miri operis—Euseb. *Chron.* ed. Schöne, ii. 167.

[2] Pausanias, i. 55.

[3] Bursian, *Geogr. von Griechenland*, i. 291 *sq.*

[4] Beulé, *Les Monnaies d'Athenes*, p. 394, and *l'Acropole d'Athenes*, p. 129, draws this conclusion from coins.

[4] Rhusopulos, *Archeól. Ephem.*, Athens, 1862, p. 287.   Wachsmuth, *Stadt Athen*, i. 692.

greatness of the god.[1]   The completion of the Olympieum
was interrupted for a long time.   It shared the fate of
many a cathedral of the Middle Ages, for the intention of
friendly princes and allies to finish the temple at the public
expense and to dedicate it to Augustus, was not carried
out.[2]   Hadrian found the temple of Cossutius to be a
building with ten Corinthian pillars at each end and
twenty at each side in double rows.[3]   Spartianus, Dion
Cassius and Philostratus all affirm that Hadrian really
completed the temple ; and Philostratus says that the
Olympieum was at last finished, after a period of five
hundred and sixty years (which is rather too short a
reckoning from Pisistratus to Hadrian), that Hadrian dedicated this great and laborious work of centuries, and that
the sophist Polemon delivered the opening address.[4]

According to Pausanias, the Olympieum was four stadia
in extent.   The temple was 173 feet in breadth, and 359
feet in length, and had a peristyle of 132 columns of
Phrygian marble, whose diameter at the base was $6\frac{1}{2}$ feet,
and whose height was about 60 feet.   In the temple Hadrian
placed a colossal statue of Zeus, made of gold and ivory, for
which the Olympian masterpiece of Phidias had probably
served as a model.[5]   Pausanias also saw there two statues of
Hadrian in marble from Thasos, two more in Egyptian
marble, and bronzes erected to Hadrian by the colonies which
stood before the columns.   In fact the peribolus was filled
with statues of the emperor, while the city of Athens had
placed a colossus in his honour in the Opisthodomus.   So
many tiresome repetitions of the same figure in the same
place was only a deplorable evidence of the servility of the
Greeks to the all-powerful emperor, their political god.   The
theatres, halls and streets of Athens were filled with statues
of the one Hadrian, for private individuals, priests, tribes and
communities vied with one another in paying homage to

[1] Livy, xli. 20.

[2] Suetonius, c. 60.

[3] Vitruvius, 3, 2, 7.   Hirt, *Gesch. der Baukunst*, ii. 151.   The temple in
Athens was the only one of the kind *Hypaethros Decastylos*.

[4] Philostratus (*Kayser*), vol. ii., p. 44.

[5] Representation on an Athenian coin in Beulé, p. 396.

their "benefactor."[1]   Pausanias saw him placed in the Stoa Basileios close to Conon and Timotheus, as Zeus Eleutherius.[2]   In the citadel, the council of the Areopagus, the council of the five hundred, and the demos had erected a statue in his honour in gratitude for all "benefits."[3]

As a serpent of Erechtheus was preserved in the temple of Athene Polias, the emperor wished in the same way to place his own genius in the Olympieum, and he caused an Indian serpent to be set up there—an absurd comedy which was not far removed from the Glycon serpent of Alexander.   In his immeasurable vanity he was not afraid to look upon himself as an associate of Zeus, for the Olympieum was dedicated to him.   But neither his ambition, nor the profane flattery of the Athenians went so far as to call the temple merely the Hadrianeum.   The same priest performed the service for both the Olympians, the god of heaven, and his imperial ape.

Of the splendour of the temple there is nothing left but the foundations and fifteen columns that are still standing. These colossal pillars produce the effect even to-day of something quite foreign in Athens; they seem rather to belong to Baalbek and Palmyra, than to this city of the muses, where, notwithstanding the severe Doric style, every building was characterized by fine proportion and taste.   Perhaps there were some citizens even in the Athens of that time who preferred the ancient Parthenon to this gigantic temple. At the same moment when the sophist Polemon was delivering the inaugural address at the Olympieum there was probably a handful of despised Christians praying in the house of their bishop on that Areopagus where St. Paul had preached the gospel seventy years before.   A few centuries

---

[1] A list of them in *C.I.A.* n. 487 *sq.*

[2] Pausanias, i. 3, 2.

[3] *C.I.A.* n. 465.   The names of the sculptors of the Hadrian statues in the Olympieum have been lost except two, Xenophanes, son of Chares, who executed the statues in marble from Thasos, and Aulus Pantuleius son of Caius, who carved the Milesian statues, *C.I.A.* n. 476, n. 480, and Hirschfeld, *Tituli statuarior.* n. 159, 160.   Xenophanes is called in the inscription τεχνείτης, Pantuleius ἀνδριαντοποιός, and distinguished as Ἐφέσιος ὁ καὶ Μειλήσιος (ἐποίει).

later the Christians of Athens built a chapel to the apostle
John in the deserted temple of Zeus, and the remains of
Hadrian's magnificent building were in this way probably
saved from complete destruction.[1]

The Olympieum was the centre of Hadrian's new city of
Athens, which stretched from the eastern slope of the
Acropolis to the Ilissus, and to it was probably assigned the
thirteenth tribe Hadrianis.　The emperor did not hesitate to
call this new quarter Hadrianopolis.[2]　On the marble arch
of triumph which led to it and to the precincts of the temple,
may still be read on both sides, towards Athens, as well as
towards the Olympieum, the following lines : " This is Athens
the ancient city of Theseus ; this is the city of Hadrian and
not of Theseus."[3]　In each niche of the second storey of the
entrance gate the statues of Theseus and Hadrian were
doubtless placed.[4]　The arch is almost in complete preservation, and no unprejudiced observer would say that
this insignificant work was in proper proportion with the
magnificence of the Olympian temple.　For the rest, the
city of Hadrian was not surrounded with walls, but the
eastern wall was pulled down when the new quarter was
added.[5]　An aqueduct supplied the city and its gardens with
water which came from Cephisia and was stored at Lyca-
bettus, in a tower adorned with Ionian pillars.　The emperor
Antoninus Pius completed this aqueduct in 140 A.D.[6]

Hadrian adorned many other Greek cities with public
buildings which Pausanias mentions in his description of
different provinces.　In Corinth he built baths and an aqueduct which carried the water from the lake of Stymphalus
into the city ; he restored the temple of Apollo at Megara,

---

[1] The chapel was called σταῖς κολόνναις or εἰς τὰς κολόννας from the columns
of the temple, by which it was supported.　A. Mommsen, *Athenae
christianae : ecclesiae propre Ilissum sitae.*

[2] Spart. c. 20 : Novae Athenae, so called in the inscription of the
aqueduct ; νέαι Ἀθῆναι Ἀδριαναί in Stephen Byz. sub v. *Olympieion*,
Wachsmuth, i. 688.

[3] ΑΙ Δ ΕΙΣ ΑΔΡΙΑΝΟΥ ΚΟΥΧΙ ΘΗΣΕΩC ΠΟΛΙC.
　　ΑΙ Δ ΕΙΣ ΑΘΗΝΑΙ ΘΗΣΕΩC Η ΠΡΙΝ ΠΟΛΙC.

[4] Forbiger, *Hellas und Rom.* iii. 210.

[5] E. Burnouf, *La ville et l'acropole d'Athènes aux diverses époques*, p. 9.

[6] *C.I.L.* iii. n. 549.

and he widened the rocky road of Sciron, the narrow and dangerous road over the Isthmus to the Peloponnesus, by making gigantic foundations, so that carriages could pass each other. In the Phocian Abae he built a temple to Apollo, a stoa at Hyampolis, and in the temple of Juno at Argos he placed a peacock of gold adorned with precious stones. He did a great deal for Mantinea on account of Antinous. He restored its ancient name to this city, which had been called Antigoneia in honour of the Macedonian king Antigonus, the father of Perseus. He restored the temple of Poseidon Hippios there, by encasing the original of wood in a new building. He built a splendid temple to Antinous in Mantinea which he filled with statues and pictures of his favourite. He dedicated a monument to Epaminondas with an inscription which he wrote himself. When he was initiated into the mysteries at Eleusis, he no doubt adorned the city with buildings, and the idea for the magnificent Propylaea of the temple of Demeter probably arose there.

It is characteristic of this period with its love for art, that even a Greek private individual like Herodes Atticus, could emulate Hadrian. Pausanias draws attention to the benefits which this rich sophist conferred upon Athens and upon other cities. It says little for him that he dedicated four gilded horses with ivory hoofs and two gold and ivory Tritons in the temple of the Isthmian Poseidon and two statues of Demeter and Proserpine in the gymnasium at Olympia. He built at Athens in memory of his wife a splendid Odeum, whose remains, in the Roman style, are still in existence. He caused the Panathenian stadium over the Ilissus to be paved with Pentelican marble. The stadium was still a wonder in the time of Pausanias, and had hardly its equal in size, for Hadrian once had a thousand animals hunted there. Herodes also built a stadium of marble at Delphi, a theatre in Corinth, baths at Thermopylae, an aqueduct at Olympia, another at Canisium in Italy, and a splendid villa, Triopium, near Rome, on the Via Appia, where to-day is the vale of Cafarelli. It is no wonder that all the Attic tribes dedicated statues to this generous man.

CHAPTER XXIV

Hadrian's Buildings in Italy. His Villa at Tivoli

APART from Rome and his villa at Tibur, Hadrian seems to have shown less regard for Italy than for the Hellenic countries. This perhaps was because he spent the greater part of his reign in travelling, or because the Italian cities had no charm for him. But our information is scanty, and Hadrianic inscriptions in Italy are remarkably scarce; though in this country, too, he was extolled as restorer.

He seems to have favoured especially two colonies, Auximum (Osimo) and Mediolanum; the latter assumed the name of Aelia.[1] Inscriptions in honour of Hadrian are to be found at Teano, Sorrento, Puteoli, and in an unknown place Forlanum.[2] The colony of Ostia boasted that he had supported and honoured her with all care and liberality.[3] He probably built the theatre whose remains are considered to belong to the time of Hadrian.[4] Inscriptions record the restoration of roads, of the Cassia from Chiusi to Florence, of the *Via Augusta* by the Trebia and of the road to Suessa.[5] He built a harbour at Lupiae, the ancient Sybaris and the modern Lecce.[6] At Gruttae on the Adriatic Sea he restored the temple of the *Dea Cupra* or the Etruscan Juno.[7] According to Spartianus, he drained the

---

[1] COL . AEL . FEL . MEDIOLANENSIS, Zumpt. *Comm. Ep.* i. 108.

[2] Mommsen, *I.N.R.* 2112, 3990. Greppo, p. 59.

[3] *C.I.L.* vi. n. 972, 133 A.D.

[4] *Notizie degli scavi, Accad. d. Lincei*, 1880, p. 469.

[5] Greppo, p. 57 *sq.* In Falerii he seems to have constructed a new road through the Forum ; Orelli, 3314.

[6] Pausanias, *Eliac.* vii. 19.

[7] Gruter, 1016, 2.

Fucine lake. This had been a plan of Caesar's, but neither he nor Claudius accomplished it, and Hadrian's undertaking could only have been a revival of the Claudian enterprise.

But the villa at Tivoli stands out above everything that Hadrian created, and unlike anything else in the world, forms his most splendid monument. It cast into the shade Nero's golden house. The ruins of this Sans Souci of an imperial enthusiast for art, cover even now an area of about ten miles, and present the appearance of a labyrinth of decaying royal splendour. Hadrian began to build his villa early in his reign, and went on with it until his death.[1]

It may be doubted whether the site he selected was happily chosen. The villas of the Romans at Tusculum and Frascati, and by the falls of the Anio at Tibur, were all more open and more pleasantly situated than this villa of Hadrian ; but he required a large space. It stood on a gentle elevation well below Tibur, where the view on the one side was limited by high mountains, but on the other side extended to Rome and its majestic Campagna, as far as the sea. The landscape was watered by two streams, and close by, the Anio afforded an abundant supply of water. From the Lucanian bridge near which it is conjectured was the main entrance to the villa, were to be seen for miles the wonderful pleasure-grounds stretching over hill and dale. The villa was as large as a city, and contained everything that makes a city beautiful and gay; the ordinary and commonplace alone were not to be found there. Gardens, fountains, groves, colonnades, shady corridors and cool domes, baths and lakes, basilicas, libraries, theatres, circuses, and temples of the gods shining with precious marble and filled with works of art, were all gathered together round this imperial palace.

The large household, the stewards with their bands of

---

[1] A column of *giallo antico* found there bears the date of Hadrian's second consulship (118 A.D.). Bruzza, *Iscr. dei marmi grezzi*, p. 187 n. 221. Stamps on bricks from the walls run from 123-137 A.D. Nibby, *Contorni di Roma*, iii. 651. According to Aurelius Victor, c. 14, he was still building palaces there after he had made over the government to Aelius Verus.

slaves, the bodyguards, the swarms of artists, singers and players, the courtesans and ladies of distinction, the priests of the temple, the men of science and poets, the friends and guests of Hadrian ; these all composed the inhabitants of the villa, and this crowd of courtiers, idlers, and slaves had no other object but to cheer one single man who was weary of the world, to dispel his ennui by feasts of Dionysus, and to delude him into thinking that each day was an Olympian festival. Hadrian here beguiled the time in the recollections of his Odysseus-like travels, for this villa built according to his own designs, was the copy and the reflection of the most beautiful things which he had admired in the world. The names of buildings in Athens were given to special parts of the villa. The Lyceum, the Academy, the Prytaneum, the Poecile, even the vale of Tempe with the Peneus flowing through it, and indeed Elysium and Tartarus were all there.[1]

One part was consecrated to the wonders of the Nile, and was called Canopus after the enchanting pleasure-grounds of the Alexandrians. Here stood a copy of the famous temple of Serapis, which stood on a canal, and was approached by boat. The inauguration of a worship of his Antinous, which Hadrian did not attempt in Rome, he achieved at his villa. The most beautiful statues of Antinous come from a temple in the villa. An obelisk only twenty-seven feet in height, did honour in a hieroglyphic inscription to the " Osirian Antinous, the speaker of truth, the embodied son of beauty." He was depicted upon it as offering a sacrifice to the god Ammon Ra. If the empress Sabina survived the erection of the obelisk, she must have reddened with anger at the inscription, which declared that the emperor had erected this pious monument in conjunction with his wife, the great queen and sovereign of Egypt, to whom Antinous was dear.[2] It may be supposed that the worship

[1] Spart. *Vita*, at the end.

[2] Ungarellius, *Interpret. obeliscor. urbis Romae*, 1842, p. 172. Lepsius, *Röm. Stadtb.* iii. 2, 604. The obelisk stands on the Pincian in Rome, where the Pope had it placed in the year 1822. Elagabalus is said to have taken it from the villa at Tivoli and to have set it up in the amphitheatre Castrense, and there it was found among the rubbish.

of Antinous increased the influence of Egypt upon Roman art. It had long been the fashion to decorate houses and villas with scenes from the Nile, and with pictures of the animals and customs of Egypt. The wall-paintings of Pompeii and many mosaics, like the famous mosaic of Palestrina, and the mosaic in the Kircher Museum are sufficient to prove this.[1] But Hadrian had transplanted Egypt itself to his villa. Sphinxes and statues of gods carved out of black marble and red granite surrounded the god Antinous, who was represented as Osiris in shining white marble. The temples built in Egyptian style were covered with hieroglyphics.

At a sign from the emperor these groves, valleys, and halls would become alive with the mythology of Olympus; processions of priests would make pilgrimages to Canopus, Tartarus and Elysium would become peopled with shades from Homer, swarms of bacchantes might wander through the vale of Tempe, choruses of Euripides might be heard in the Greek theatre, and in a sham fight the fleets would repeat the battle of Xerxes. But was all this anything more than a miserable pretence in comparison with the fulness and majesty of the real world through which Hadrian had travelled? The emperor would after all have surrendered all these splendid stage scenes for one drop from the rushing stream of real life, for one moment on board his gala boat on the Nile, or on the Acropolis at Athens, in Ilium, Smyrna and Damascus, amid the acclamations of his devoted people. Epictetus would have laughed to see the emperor amusing himself with a collection of the wonders of the world, and would have called it sentimentality; and perhaps Hadrian's famous villa is an evidence of the degradation of the taste of the time.

Its extent was too great to be a Tusculum of the Muses; nor was it adapted to serve as a romantic hermitage, or as a place for repose. A Roman emperor of this period could not be content unless he was in the midst of splendour on a

---

[1] The first was found in the year 1638 in Palestrina, the other on the Aventine, 1858. See *Gazette Archéol.* vi. 1880, p. 170 *sq.* "Mosaique du Musée Kircher," and *Catalogo del Museo Kircheriano*, i. 265 *sq.* These mosaics must be considered as copies of Alexandrian carpets.

great scale. Hadrian might have written over the portal of his villa, *magna domus parva quies*. If the villa at Tivoli shows the strength of the impression made by the Greek world on the imperial traveller, its incredible extravagance can only be explained by his mania for building. Country seats are the least famous buildings of princes, for they serve only their own fleeting pleasure, but a ruler like Hadrian, who had provided the cities of his empire with so many public works, may be more easily forgiven than a Louis XIV., if for once he thought of himself.

We do not know how often he stayed at the villa ; it was his favourite resort in his later years, and it was there that he dictated his memoirs to Phlegon. He possessed other beautiful country-houses at Praeneste and Antium.[1] He died at Baiae, not in his villa at Tivoli. After his time the villa was more and more rarely inhabited by the emperors, until it suffered the fate of all country seats. Constantine was doubtless the first to plunder it, in order to carry off its marbles and works of art to Byzantium. At the time of the Gothic wars it existed only as a desolate world of wonders ; the warriors of Belisarius were the first to encamp in it, and then those of Totila. Its ruins in the Middle Ages were called Ancient Tivoli. Its columns and blocks of marble had been stolen, its statues burnt to powder. But many things remained hidden amid the protecting rubbish, over which olives and vines had been planted. The recollection that this charming wilderness of ruins had once been a pleasure resort of Hadrian, lasted a long time. Many years before excavations were begun there, the intellectual Pope Pius II. visted these ruins, and described them in melancholy words, which we may quote.

"About three miles outside Tivoli the Emperor Hadrian built a splendid villa for himself, as large as a city. Lofty and spacious arches of temples are still to be seen, half ruined courts and rooms, and remains of prodigious halls, and of fish ponds and fountains, which were supplied with water by the Anio, to cool the heat of summer. Time has disfigured everything. The walls are now covered with ivy instead of paintings and gold embroidered tapestry. Brambles and

[1] Philostratus, *Vita Apollon.* 8, 20.

thorns grow in the seats of the men clad in togas of purple, and serpents make their home in the bed chamber of the empress. So perishes everything earthly in the stream of time."[1]

Antiquities were first looked for in the villa at Tivoli in the time of Alexander VI., when statues of the Muses and of Mnemosyne were found.[2] In the sixteenth century Piero Ligorio first made a plan of the villa, then it was described by Re, and after 1735 those excavations were undertaken which have brought so much sculpture to light. Piranesi made his great plan of the villa.[3] In the year 1871, the Italian government took possession of it, and the excavations were carried on, but they had no great result,[4] for everything of importance had been discovered in the eighteenth century. The villa had been so completely ransacked at that time, that there was scarcely anything left of its enormous supply of marbles. Here and there floors of mosaic are to be seen; the best preserved consist of small white stones with designs in black. The extent of mosaic flooring alone has been estimated at 5000 square miles, while the astonishing variety of decorations on the pillars, pilasters, niches, and walls is a brilliant testimony to the development of art at that time.[5]

The grounds of the villa now consist of a mass of ruins, large and small. Remains of temples, which, according to fancy, are called after Apollo, Bacchus, Serapis, Pluto, etc., of basilicas, baths, and theatres are scattered within the spacious enclosure.

The use of some of the buildings is still apparent, the long rows called *cento camerelle* indicating the quarter of the

[1] Pii II. *Comment.* v. 138.

[2] Nibby, *Contorni di Roma*, iii. 656.

[3] *Re delle antichità Tiburtine*, Rom 1611. *Pianta della Villa Tiburtina di Adriano*, by P. Ligorio and Fr. Contini in the last edition of 1751. Plan by Piranesi in 1786. Upon the excavations in the eighteenth century, Fea, Winckelmann's translation, ii. 379 *sq.*

[4] Floors of mosaic were found, and a beautiful perfect statue which seems to represent a Bacchus. Tadolini the sculptor, who has just (spring of 1883) restored and shown it to me, values it more highly than the Antinous of the Capitol.

[5] *Notizie degli Scavi (Accad. d. Lincei)*, 1883, p. 17.

imperial guards, which could contain 3000 men; the high walls of a magnificent porticus are taken to be the Poecile.[1] The Canopus looks now like a green valley, where at the end are ruins from the temple of Serapis, and the vale of Tempe can be distinguished as a deep depression, bordered by the mountains of Tivoli.[2]   The scenery of the so-called Greek theatre was still so well preserved, that in the time of Winckelmann, when the Dionysus theatre in Athens was still in ruins, it gave the best idea of an ancient theatre.[3]

The original use of many of the other buildings and ruins is obscure, and the attempt is vain to form a whole from these fragments of the fairyland, whose central point must have been the palace of the emperor.

[1] The Poecile, the so-called *Aula dei sette sapienti*, the centre of the so-called *Teatro Marittimo*, and many halls, corridors, courts, nymphaei, were brought to light in 1873.   *Notizie degli Scavi*, 1880, p. 479.

[2] Poecile, Tempe, and Canopus, are the three places which can be decided almost with certainty; see L. Meyer, *Tibur eine röm. Studie*, Berlin, 1883.

[3] Winckelmann, vi. 291.

CHAPTER XXV

*The City of Rome in Hadrian's Time. Buildings of
the Emperor in Rome. Completion of the Forum
of Trajan. The Temple of Venus and Rome.
Hadrian's Tomb.*

WHEN Hadrian became emperor, he found the city of Rome
not only complete in its essential characteristics, but almost
extending to the limits which Aurelian afterwards fixed by
the walls which he built.[1] The Flavian emperors had
restored the Capitol in all its splendour; the imperial
palace on the Palatine had been magnificently rebuilt by
Domitian; the Forum Romanum had preserved its monumental character, and during the time between Augustus
and Trajan, the great system of imperial fora had been
completed. On the ruins of Nero's golden house Vespasian
and Titus had built the Coliseum, and baths which reached
to the Esquiline, where they joined those of Trajan on the
Carinae. The Circus Maximus had been rebuilt by Domitian, and completed by Trajan; the stadium of Domitian,
the present Navona, shone in fresh beauty, and adjoined the
Pantheon and the baths of Agrippa and Nero. The number
of aqueducts was increased by Trajan.

Nobles and citizens had emulated the emperors in their

---

[1] This remark at least applies to the time of Marcus Aurelius and of
Commodus, who, about 175 A.D. established a boundary line for Rome,
by *lapides*, and this line corresponded to the later walls of Aurelian.
De Rossi, *Piante Icnografiche di Roma*, c. vii,—Limiti di finanza
stabiliti da Marco Aurelio e da Commodo.

love of building; palaces, villas, and gardens covered the hills and valleys of Rome. All the arts had contributed to adorn the wonderful city, and Roman architecture in its union with the style of Greece, and in its magnificence and grandeur, had already reached its zenith in the buildings of the Flavian emperors, and of Trajan. In the time of the Antonines, an intelligent observer like the Greek Aristides could say that the whole world had produced nothing like Rome.

The knowledge that he could not surpass the work of his predecessor Trajan in Rome, must have moderated Hadrian's passion for building; and though it is incorrect to say that he was not fond of Rome, his long periods of absence must have estranged him from the capital. The time, moreover, had arrived when Rome ceased to be the only object for the ambition of the emperors. This is the explanation of the fact that Hadrian, who surpassed all other emperors in his passion for building, did not embellish the capital of the empire with a great number of fine monuments. There are very few Roman local inscriptions in existence which refer to the buildings of Hadrian.[1]

Nevertheless, the monuments which he executed in Rome are magnificent; and if to these we add the building of the immense villa at Tivoli, it cannot be said that Hadrian was less active in promoting art in Rome than Trajan. He drew the plans himself for many buildings, which no emperor before or after him could do. We are bewildered when we try to imagine the masses of marble which must at this .ime have been discharged on the banks of the Tiber. No emperor made use of so much valuable stone from Paros, from Scirus, from Luna, Phrygian marble from the quarries of Sinnada (*pavonazetto*), Numidian marble (*giallo antico*),

[1] *C.I.L.* vi. 1, n. 1240. Restoration of the *ripae Tiberis* and of the *cloacae*, 121 A.D.; n. 976. Restoration of the Auguratorium (Palatine?), 136 A.D.; n. 1233. Restoration of the Cippi of the Pomerium, 121 A.D. As Hadrian had made no conquests, he could not, like Claudius, Vespasian and Trajan, enlarge the Pomerium; n. 973. Building of the *pons Aelius*, 133 A.D.; n. 975. Inscription in honour of the overseer of the region in the Capitol, 136 A.D.; this shows Hadrian's great activity for Rome. No. 981: a mutilated inscription of an unknown restoration.

porphyry and granite from the Thebais, and Carystian marble from Mount Ocha.   Carystian marble (*cipollino*) was very much used in the time of Hadrian.   The greatest number of marked blocks found in the emporium were of this kind of marble.   Even the names of the imperial overseers of this quarry, the slaves Cerealis and Hymenaeus, have been preserved.[1]

Like every other emperor, Hadrian restored the monuments of Rome ; among them many temples not mentioned by Spartianus ; the Septa, the Basilica of Neptune, the Forum of Augustus, the Pantheon, which had been injured by lightning in the time of Trajan, and the adjoining baths of Agrippa.   He probably also embellished the interior of the Pantheon.[2]

Hadrian began his new buildings by completing the Forum of Trajan ; here he first consecrated the Templum Divi Trajani, which the senate had erected to this emperor.   It was the only temple upon which Hadrian placed his own name ; then he continued the west side of the Forum, and finished it with a triumphal arch.   On the same side behind the column of Trajan, there arose a magnificent temple with columns of granite built by the senate to the emperor Hadrian.[3]   The system of imperial fora thus extended to the

[1] Bruzza, *Inscr. dei marmi grezzi* (*Annal. d. Inst.* 1870), p. 137 *sq.*   A column of Numidian marble found in the villa at Tibur, bears the date of Hadrian's consulate (118 A.D.) ; a block of *cipollino* in the emporium with the date of the consulate of Augurinus (132 A.D.) ; the two columns of the Marmorata bear the date of the consulate of Aelius Caesar and Balbinus (137 A.D.).

[2] Spart. c. 19. In the baths of Agrippa near the statue of Minerva, only brick-stamps of Hadrian of the year 123 A.D. have been found.   There are stamps which prove a restoration of the Pantheon by Hadrian between 123 A.D. and 127 A.D., which was the time of the restoration of the Septa and the Basilica of Neptune. *Notizie degli scavi* (*Accad. dei Lincei*), 1881, p. 280-283. Stamps of Hadrian's time were found in the Palatine stadium (*Notizie*, 1877, p. 201), and in the newly excavated square of houses in the Forum. For some inscriptions from the Forum Hadriani, see Jordan, *Sylloge Inscr. Fori Rom. Eph. Ep.* iii.

[3] Coins of Hadrian (Eckhel, vi. 509 *sq.*) representing a temple with ten columns (S.P.Q.R. EX. S.C.) refer to this ; *Röm. Stadtb.* iii. 2, p. 107.   It is the site of the Palace Imperiali, where the inscription of the great remission of debt was copied by Anonymus of Einsiedeln.

edge of the Campus Martius, and on this account Hadrian restored the Septa and the Basilica of Neptune, which were adjacent.[1] The Antonines went on with these buildings, and a new forum was erected round the column of Marcus Aurelius.

According to Spartianus, Hadrian also built the temple to the *Bona Dea*;[2] but the biographer has overlooked the Greek gymnasium or Athenaeum, whose site is unknown.

Hadrian's most magnificent building in Rome was the double temple of Venus and Rome in the *Via sacra*. It was his own design. The imperial dilettante wished to immortalize himself by a monumental work without parallel, and this temple was in fact the largest and the most magnificent temple in the city. The architect is unknown. It was not Apollodorus, though his fall indeed, has been connected by a legend with this building. This Syrian from Damascus was the greatest genius among the architects of the second century. We do not know the whole extent of his works, but the fact that in addition to an Odeum and a gymnasium for Trajan, he built the magnificent forum and the bridge over the Danube, is enough to make his name remembered. Whether Apollodorus was ever employed by Hadrian is doubtful. Dion relates that the emperor laid before him his ground-plan for the temple of Venus and Rome, and that the architect pointed out many mistakes; in particular, he criticised the size of the statues of both gods, saying they would lift the roof if they rose from their seats—a stupid remark, which would also have applied to the colossus of Zeus by Phidias, in Olympia. By the command of Hadrian, Apollodorus is said to have been first banished, and then put to death.[3] There is nothing, however, to confirm this legend; on the contrary, Hadrian not only asked the great architect to edit the *Poliorcetica*,

[1] According to Nardini, ed. Nibby, iii. 119, the temple (basilica?) of Neptune appears to have been close to the Septa of Agrippa; the porticus Neptuni was built by him. Hadrian, moreover, had a theatre pulled down on the Campus Martius, which Trajan had built. Spart. c. 9.

[2] It was a temple of the Bona Dea upon the Aventine, which Hadrian probably restored. Nardini, iii. 279.

[3] Dion Cassius, lxix. 4.

but also commissioned him to make a colossus of Luna as a companion to that of the Sun.[1]   It is certainly possible that Apollodorus suffered from the emperor's caprice, and was no longer employed upon important buildings.   His brilliant career came to a conclusion with Trajan, and his end is unknown.   It is supposed that it is his likeness that decorates the triumphal arch of Constantine, where it was placed when the architect robbed one of Trajan's arches of its reliefs.   It represents a man in Greek dress, who hands a drawing to the emperor Trajan.[2]

According to Hadrian's plan, the magnificent building of Venus and Rome consisted of two large temples united under one roof; for the semi-circular apses at the end of each cella joined one another at the back.[3]   A vaulted roof covered the whole space ; inside, the walls were adorned with coloured marble, outside, with white marble from Paros.   The front of the temple of Rome faced the Coliseum, the front of the temple of Venus the Forum, and each was approached by a flight of marble steps; for the magnificent building stood upon a walled-in terrace which is still in existence.   Ten Corinthian pillars stood before each front, and twenty along the sides.   A Pronaos stretched towards the Forum, and the whole building was enclosed by a granite colonnade.[4]   The pediments were ornamented with carvings ; statues adorned the niches of the cellae, and pictures no doubt represented the mythical foundation of Rome.   In the two tribunes were placed the colossal figure of Venus Victrix, and of the genius of Rome, both seated, and in a warlike attitude.   Venus held

---

[1] Spart. c. 19 : Aliud tale (simularum) Apollodoro architecto auctore facere molitus est.   Nothing is known of this colossus.   Neither Spartianus nor Eutropius nor Aurelius Victor say anything of the death of Apollodorus.   Duruy, iv. 395, has well pointed out the absurdity of the tale.

[2] Niebuhr, *Vorträge über Röm. Gesch.* iii. 221.

[3] Prudentius, *in Symmachum*, i. 219.

> Delubrum Romae (colitur nam sanguine et ipsa
> More Deae, nomenque loci ceu numen habetur)
> Atque urbis, Venerisque pari se culmine tollunt,
> Templa, simul geminis adolentur tura deabus.

[4] A *Pseudodipteros decastylos*, Adler, p. 181 ; Hirt, ii. 371.   Niebuhr in the *Röm. Stadtb.* iii. 1. 299 *sq.*, with appendices by Bunsen.

in her right hand a Victory, in her left a lance; Rome, the globe and lance.[1] A roof of gilded bronze-tiles covered both temples. The edifice was remarkable for its combination of Greek and Roman forms; for it united the rectangular plan of the temple with the building of the arch in the most striking manner.[2] Hadrian caused the marble colossus of Nero, a work of Zenodorus, to be placed at the commencement of the *Via sacra*, between this temple and the amphitheatre, where the pedestal is still preserved. This difficult undertaking was accomplished by the engineer Decrianus with the help of twenty-four elephants. Spartianus remarks that the gigantic statue was dedicated to the sun after it had been deprived of the face of Nero. In all probability it was Vespasian who caused this to be done when the colossus was being prepared, after the burning of Nero's house.

Hadrian had dedicated the temple to the genius of the city as well as to the ancestress of Caesar's house, a true Roman idea; it had reference also to the festivals on the anniversary of the city of Rome which had been newly instituted by him, and which received in his time and probably from him, the name *aeterna*. The temple afterwards was generally called *templum urbis*.[3] It surpassed the Jupiter of

[1] Eckhel, vi. 510. Roma was afterwards also represented in this way, the statue in the villa Medici. See Reifferscheid in *Ann. d. Inst.* 1863, p. 363 *sq.* Coins of Hadrian VENERI GENETRICI. Venus, Victoria at her right, her left hand resting on a shield on which the flight of Aeneas is represented. Cohen, ii. p. 226, n. 1444, 1446. A similar one in *Bull. Comunale*, 1877, p. 78. The COS, iiii. is a mistake.

[2] Lübke, *Gesch. d. Architectur*, i. 200.

[3] Athenaeus, viii. 361. Eckhel, vi. p. 510 refers two coins of Hadrian with VENERIS.FELICIS and URBS.ROMA.AETERNA to this building, although the latter coin represents a temple with six columns. From two coins of Antoninus Pius, ROMAE.AETERNAE and VENERI.FELICI, Niebuhr, p. 301 has inferred that Antoninus Pius finished the temple. The coin of Antoninus ROMAE.AETERNAE in Cohen, ii. p. 340, n. 698, represents the front of a temple with ten columns, and reliefs on the pediments. The legend ROMA.AETERNA first appears in the time of Hadrian. Cohen, ii. pp. 214, 215, n. 1299 to 1303. Rome seated on armour holding in her right hand the heads of the sun and the moon, in her left a lance. The buildings of Hadrian are not immortalized by coins like those of Trajan. According to the chronicle of Cassiodorus (ed. Mommsen), the Temple of Venus and Rome was built in 136 A.D., or rather consecrated, and

the Capitol and Vespasian's temple of Peace, and it was not
even dwarfed by the Flavian amphitheatre and the villa.

At the same time that this magnificent building and the
villa at Tibur arose, Hadrian remembered that he was mortal,
and caused his tomb to be built.   The site selected was the
garden of the Domitia, near the triumphal way, which led to
the city over the triumphal bridge.   He wished to give a
new appearance to this quarter of the Vatican.   He founded
a circus there, which he destined for the festival games in
honour of his divinity.   The Goths under Vitiges entrenched
themselves in this circus, and its remains were visible until
far into the Middle Ages, behind the Mausoleum.[1]   Hadrian
could not, like Trajan, find his last resting-place under a
splendid column erected in his honour in the centre of the
city of Rome, decked with glories of war and conquests,
but he was determined to build himself a tomb more
beautiful than that of Augustus (where there was no more
room left), more worthy of admiration than the mausoleum of
Halicarnassus, and not surpassed in durability even by the
Pyramids of the Pharaohs.   And in truth the vain emperor
created a monument, whose ruins, with the additions which
it received in the Middle Ages, form still one of the most
striking architectural features of Rome, though the Vatican
be near for comparison.   Hadrian devoted many years to
this building, which he no doubt planned himself.[2]

The mausoleum rising several storeys high, adorned with
statues and shining with the splendour of marble, must have
been a magnificent sight.   But no correct description of it has

this view is also taken by Fea, *Varietà di Notizie*, p. 143.   Nissen, *Das
Templum*, p. 202, disputes the passage in Athenaeus, viii. 361, which
determines the date of the foundation to be on the festival of Palilia
(21st of April), and places it on the festival of Floralia (28th of April to
3rd of May).   The foundation on the festival of the Palilia is, however,
the more probable.   See Preller, ii. 356.

[1] Procopius, *De bell. Goth*, ii. 2, 1, speaks of the circus, but does not
mention its name.   In the Middle Ages it was called theatrum Neronis ;
it is shown on a plan of the city of the thirteenth century, and on other
plans.   De Rossi, *Piante icnograf. di Roma*, p. 85.   The remains of the
circus, close to the Castle of S. Angelo, were still seen by Blondus and
Fulvius ; Nardini, iii. 363.

[2] That it was being built already in 123 A.D., is proved by brick stamps
bearing the consular year.

come down to us, and the picture that has been attempted of it from the meagre account of Procopius of Labacco, Piranesi, Hirt, Canina, and others, is partly imaginary.[1] The gigantic building consisted of a square basement of travertine blocks, fifteen palms in height, still in good preservation, though half covered over with earth. At each corner of this basement, four horses of gilt bronze are said to have stood upon the foundation, which was faced with blocks of marble, and surrounded by a Corinthian colonnade. The tomb of Caecilia Metella with its frieze of bulls' heads and with the architrave under which the inscriptions of the dead were placed, must clearly have been used by Hadrian as a pattern. In this hall, as well as on the platform of the tower, which was approached by a flight of steps, works of sculpture were placed, statues of horses and men, as Procopius says, of the most admirable workmanship, and there the statue of Hadrian, a work of enormous size, is also said to have stood on a quadriga.[2]

From the portal of the mausoleum, which was closed by a bronze door (the famous *porta aenea* of the Middle Ages), a vaulted winding passage, similar to the passage in the pyramids of Egypt, led up to the imperial sepulchre, which occupied the centre of the large round tower. The sepulchre was quadrangular, built of massive blocks of stone, which once were faced with valuable marble. There were four large niches to receive sarcophagi, and cinerary urns could be placed on shelves close by. A porphyry sarcophagus in the middle of the chamber contained the remains of the emperor.

Over the large round building there seems to have been a second smaller one in the shape of a temple with pillared halls, and a winding passage in it led to another sepulchre.[3] We do not know how the dome of this temple was finished ; the opinion that it was crowned by the large bronze pine-

[1] In mediaeval plans of the city the mausoleum is represented as a tower of two storeys rising from a quadrangular substructure. This is the way in which Filarete, who was the first artist to handle the subject, has depicted it on the bronze doors of St. Peter's.

[2] Procopius, *De bell. Goth.* i. 22; Panvinius, *urbs Roma*, p. 114; Winckelmann, xii. c. 1, 290.

[3] Bunsen, *ibid.* p. 418.

cone which now stands in the court of the Belvedere is not well founded.[1] The original entrance to the tomb is now walled up. It faced the Aelian bridge over the Tiber, which the emperor built not far from the triumphal bridge, and probably then destroyed. The new bridge resting upon seven arches of travertine, and richly adorned with statues, was already built in 134 A.D. But Hadrian did not live to see the completion of the mausoleum. It is even uncertain whether he buried his wife Sabina and his adopted son Aelius Caesar there; perhaps this was only done by his successor Antoninus Pius, who removed the ashes of the emperor from Puteoli, and deposited them in the mausoleum. An inscription says that Antoninus consecrated the tomb of his parents by adoption, Hadrian and Sabina, in 139 A.D.[2]

The magnificent mausoleum was the conclusion of the life and actions of the emperor Hadrian. After the fall of the empire it served as dungeon, citadel, and fortress of Rome during the gloomy centuries of the Papacy, and its melancholy history can be read in the chronicles of the Eternal City in the Middle Ages.

[1] Lacour-Gayet (*Mélanges d'Arch. et d'Hist., Ecole française de Rome*, 1881, p. 312 *sq.*), proves that the *pigna* does not come from the mausoleum, and supports the view of authorities on the Middle Ages, who maintain that it crowned the dome of the Pantheon. This certainly cannot be proved.

[2] See the first of the titles of the mausoleum, n. 984-995; *C.I.L.* vi. 1.

BIBLIOGRAPHY

Adler, Friedrich. Erläuterungen zum Stadtplan von Ephesus. (*Königliche Akademie der Wissenschaften. Abhandlungen.*) 8°. Berlin. 1873.

Ahrens, Franz Heinrich Ludolf. De Athenarum statu politico et literario inde ab Achaica foederis interitu usque ad Antoninorum tempora. 4°. Gottinguae. 1829.

Alexandrian Chronicle. Chronicon Paschale. Ad exemplar Vaticanum recensuit L. Dindorfius. (*Corpus scriptorum Historiae Byzantinae.*) *Gr.* and *Lat.* 8°. Bonnae. 1828.

Ambros, August Wilhelm. Geschichte der Musik. 4 voll. 8°. Breslau. 1862-78.

Antoninus Augustus. Vetera Romanorum itineraria ; sive A. A. itinerarium cum integris … notis ; itinerarium Hierosolymitanum … curante P. Wesselingio. 4°. Amstelaedami. 1735.

Apollodorus Damascenus. Poliorcetica excerpta ex libris A. Veterum mathematicorum A … opera. *Gr.* and *Lat.* Fol. Parisiis. 1693.

Appian Alexandrinus. Historia Romana, ed. Ludovicus Mendelssohn. 2 voll. Sm. 8°. Lipsiae. 1879-81.

Aristides, Aelius. Aelius Aristides ex recensione G. Dindorfii. 3 voll. 8°. Lipsiae. 1829.

—— S. Aristidis, philosophi atheniensis ; Sermones duo. Venice. 1878.

Arnd, Carl. Der Pfahlgraben nach den neuesten Forschungen und Entdeckungen. 8°. Frankfurt a. M. 1861.

Arnold, William Thomas. The Roman system of Provincial Administration to the accession of Constantine the Great. 8°. London. 1879.

Arrian, Flavius. Τεχνη Τακτικη, Ἔκταξις κατ᾽ Ἀλανων, Περιπλους Ποντου Εὐξεινου, Περιπλους της Ἐφυθρας Θαλασσης—Ἐπικτητου Εγχειριδιον, του ἀυτου Ἀποφθεγματα καὶ Αποσπασματα. … Ex recensione et museo N. Plancardi. *Gr.* et *Lat.* 8°. Amstelodami. 1683.

—— Arriani Nicomediensis scripta minora. Recognovit R. Hercher. *Gr.* 8°. Lipsiae. 1854.

Artemidorus. Oneirocritica ex duobus codicibus MSS. … item indices adjecit J. G. Reiff. *Gr.* 2 voll. 8°. Lipsiae. 1805.

—— Oneirocriticon, libri V. ex recensione R. Hercheri. *Gr.* 8°. Lipsiae. 1864.

Aschbach, J. Die Consulate der Römischen Kaiser von Caligula bis Hadrian. (*Kaiserliche Akademie der Wissenschaften.*) 8°. Wien. 1861.

—— Ueber Trajans steinerne Donaubrücke. (*Kaiserlich-Königliche Centralcommission zur Erforschung und Erhaltung der Baudenkmale.*) 4°. Wien. 1858.

Athenaeus. A. Deipnosophistarum libri quindecim ex optimis codicibus ... emendavit ac supplevit ... commodisque indicibus instruxit J. Schweighäuser. *Gr.* and *Lat.* 14 voll. 8°. Argentorati. 1801-1807.

Athenagoras. Legatio pro Christianis : C. Gesnero interprete. (J. P. Migne, *Patrologia Graeca*, tom. 6.) 4°. Parisiis. 1857.

Aubé, Barthélemy. Essai de Critique Religieuse. De l'Apologétique Chrétienne au IIe siècle. Saint Justin Philosophe et Martyr. 8°. Paris. 1861.

Augustan History. Historiae Augustae scriptores sex .. ad postremas I. Casauboni ... editionis excusi. 12°. Lugduni Batavorum. 1621.

Aurelius Victor, Sextus. Origio gentis Romanae.—De viris illustribus urbis Romae. Historia abbreviata de Caesaribus.—Epitome de vita et moribus Imperatorum. (B. C. Haurisius, *Scriptores Historiae Romanae Latini Veteres*, tom. 2.) Fol. Heidelburgiae. 1743-48.

Basnage de Beauval, Jacques. Histoire des Juifs depuis Jésus Christ jusqu' à present. 9 tom., 15 parts. 12°. La Haye. 1716.

Baumgart, Hermann. Aelius Aristides als Repräsentant der sophistischen Rhetorik des zweiten Jahrhunderts der Kaiserzeit. 8°. Leipzig. 1874.

Baur, Ferdinand Christian von. Das Christenthum und die christliche Kirche der drei ersten Jahrhunderte. 8°. Tübingen. 1860.

Bellermann, Johann Friedrich. Die Hymnen des Dionysius und Mesomedes. Text und Melodien nach Handschriften und den alten Ausgaben bearbeitet von Dr. F. B. 4°. Berlin. 1840.

Bellori, Giovanni Pietro. Veteres arcus Augustorum triumphis insignes ex reliquis quae Romae adhuc supersunt, etc. Fol. Romae. 1690.

Benndorf, Otto. Beiträge zur Kenntniss des attischen Theaters. (*Zeitschrift für die oesterreichischen Gymnasien.*) 8°. Wien. 1875.

—— Vorläufiger Bericht über zwei oesterreichisch-archäologische Expeditionen nach Klein-Asien von O. B. 8° Wien. 1883.

Benndorf, Otto, und Schöne, Richard. Die antiken Bildwerke des Lateranensischen Museums beschrieben von O. B. und R. S. mit ... photo-lithographischen Tafeln. 8°. Leipzig. 1867.

Bernays, Jacob. Lucian und die Kyniker. ... Mit einer Uebersetzung der Schrift Lucians über das Lebensende des Peregrinus. 8°. Berlin. 1879.

Bernhardy, Gottfried. Grundriss der griechischen Literatur : mit einem vergleichenden Ueberblick der Römischen. 8°. Halle. 1876.

Beulé, Charles Ernst. Les Monnaies d'Athens. 4°. Paris. 1858.

—— L'Acropole d'Athenes. 8°. Paris. 1853-54.

Boecking, Eduard. Corpus juris Romani Antejustiniani consilio E. Boeckingii, etc. Praefatus est E. B. 4°. Bonnae. 1841.

Boissier, Gaston. La Religion Romaine d'Auguste aux Antonins. 2 tom. 8°. Paris. 1874.

Borghesi, Bartolommeo. Ouvres complètes publiées par les ordres et aux frais de S. M. L'Empereur Napoléen III. 4°. Paris. 1862.

Bormann, Eugenius. De Syriae Provinciae Romanae partibus capita nonnulla. 8°. Berolini. 1865.

Bouché-Leclercq, A. Histoire de la divination dans l'antiquité. 8°. Paris. 1879.

Brinz, Alois von. Zur römischen Rechtsgeschichte. (*Kritische Vierteljahrschrift für Gesetzgebung und Rechtswissenschaft.*) 8°. München. 1859.

Bruce, John Collingwood. The Roman wall: a historical, topographical, and descriptive account of the barrier of the Lower Isthmus extending from the Tyne to the Solway. (*The Geology of the district traversed by the Roman wall. With geological map and sections by G. Tate, etc.*) Third edition. 4°. London. 1867.

Brunn, Heinrich. Geschichte der griechischen Künstler. 2 voll. 8°. Braunschweig. 1853, 1859.

Bunbury, Edward Herbert. A history of ancient geography among the Greeks and Romans from the earliest ages to the fall of the Roman empire. 2 voll. 8°. London. 1879.

Burchardi, Georg Christian. Geschichte und Institutionen des Römischen Rechts. 8°. Kiel. 1834.

Burnouf, Emile. La ville et l'Acropole d'Athenes aux diverses époques. 8°. Paris. 1877.

Bursian, Conrad. Geographie von Griechenland. 2 voll. 8°. Leipzig. 1862-71.

Buxtorfius, Joannes, the Elder. J. Buxtorfi. P. Lexicon Chaldaicum, Talmudicum et Rabbinicum ... opus XXX. annorum nunc demum, post Patris obitum, ex ipsius autographo ... in lucem editum a. J. Buxtorfio filio. Fol. Basileae. 1639.

Caignart de Saulcy, Louis Félicien Joseph. Recherches sur la numismatique Judaïque. 4°. Paris. 1854.
—— Les derniers jours de Jérusalem. 8°. Paris. 1866.
—— Numismatique de la Terre Sainte: Description des monnaies autonomes et impériales de la Palestine et de l'Arabie Pétrée, ornée de 25 planches, etc. 4°. Paris. 1874.

Callimachus. Callimachi hymni, epigrammata et fragmenta ex recensione T. J. G. F. Graevii cum ejusdem animadversionibus. Accedunt ... R. Bentleii commentarius et adnotationes, etc. *Gr.* and *Lat.* 2 voll. 8° Ultrajecti. 1697.

Cassel, Selig, afterwards **Paulus.** (Ersch und Gruber *Allgemeine Encyclopedie der Wissenschaften.*) 4°. Leipzig. 1818.

Cassiodorus, Magnus Aurelius. Opera omnia. (J. P. Migne, *Patrologia Latina,* tom. 69-70). 4°. Parisiis. 1865.

Castiglioni, Pietro. Della popolazione di Roma, dalle origini ai nostri tempi. 4°. Roma. 1878.

Cavedoni, Celestino. Biblische Numismatik … aus dem Italienischen übersetzt und mit Zusätzen versehen von A. von Werlhof. 8°. Hannover. 1855-56.

Cedrenus, Georgius. Georgius Cedrenus, Joannis Scylitzae ope ab J. Bekkero suppletus et emendatus. (*Corpus Scriptorum Historiae Byzantinae,* pars 24.) *Gr.* and *Lat.* 8°. Bonnae. 1828, etc.

Centerwall, Julius. Spartiani vita Hadriani commentario illustrata. Disputatio prior. (*Upsala Universitets Arsskrift.*) 8°. Upsala. 1870.

Champollion, Jean François. Lettres écrites d'Egypte et de Nubie en 1828 et 1829. Collection complète accompagnée de trois Mémoirs inédits. 8°. Paris. 1833.

Charisius, Flavius Sosipater. (H. Keil, *Grammatici Latini,* vol. 1.) 8°. Lipsiae. 1857.

Clarke, Edward Daniel. The tomb of Alexander, a dissertation on the sarcophagus brought from Alexandria and now in the British Museum. 4°. Cambridge. 1805.

Clarke, Hyde. Ephesus ; being a lecture delivered at the Smyrna Literary and Scientific Institution. 8°. Smyrna. 1863.

Clemens, Titus Flavius Alexandrinus. Κλημεντος του 'Αλεξανδρεως τα ευρισκομενα παντα. C. Alexandrini opera quae extant omnia juxta edit. Oxon. an. 1715 ; accedunt N. Le Nourry Commentaria. 2 tom. *Gr.* and *Lat.* (J. P. Migne, *Patrologia Graeca,* tom. 8, 9.) 4°. Parisiis. 1891, 1890.

Cohen, Henry. Description historique des monnaies frappées sous l'Empire Romain communément appelées medailles impériales. 7 tom. Deuxième edition. 8°. Paris. 1880-1890.

Cons, Henri. La Province Romaine de Dalmatie. 8°. Paris. 1882.

Conze, Alexander Christoph Leopold. Archäologische Untersuchungen auf Samothrake ausgeführt. … (Bd. I.) Von A. C., A. Hauser, G. Niemann. (Bd. II.) Von A. C., A. Hauser, O. Benndorf. Mit Tafeln und … 36 Holzschnitten. 2 voll. Fol. Wien. 1875-1880.

Corsini, Edoardo. Fasti Attici in quibus Archontum … aetas atque praecipue Atticae Historiae capita … deposita describentur, novisque observationibus illustrantur. 4 tom. 4°. Florentiae. 1744-1756.

Cramer, John Antony. Anecdota graeca e codd. manuscriptis Bibliothecarum Oxoniensium descripsit J. A. C. 4 voll. 8°. Oxonii. 1835-1837.

Cresollius, Ludovicus. Theatrum veterum rhetorum … expositum libris quinque. 8°. Parisiis. 1620.

2 B

Curtius, Ernst. Peloponnesos, eine historisch-geographische Beschreibung der Halbinsel. 2 voll. 8°. Gotha. 1851.

—— Beiträge zur Geschichte und Topographie Kleinasiens. (*Philosophisch-historische Abhandlungen der Königl. Akademie der Wissenschaften.*) 8°. Berlin. 1873.

—— Inschriften aus Kleinasien. (*Hermes, VII.*) 8°. Berlin. 1873.

Derenbourg, Joseph. Essai sur l'Histoire et la Geographie de la Palestine d'après les Thalmuds et les autres sources rabbiniques. 8°. Paris. 1867.

Deyling, C. E. Dissertatio de Aeliae Capitolinae historia et origine. (D. S. Deylingi, *Observationum sacrarum...pars prima*, pt. 5.) 4°. Lipsiae. 1735, etc.

Dierauer, J. Beiträge zu einer kritischen Geschichte Trajans. (Max Buedinger, *Untersuchungen zur Röm. Kaisergeschichte.* Vol. 1.) 2 voll. 8°. Leipzig. 1868.

Dion Cassius. των Διωνος του Κασσιου ...'Ρωμαικων ιστοριων τα σωζομενα. Dionis Casii historiarum Romanarum quae supersunt ... emendavit ... notas adjecit. F. G. Sturz. *Gr.* and *Lat.* 9 voll. 8°. Lipsiae. 1824-1836.

Dion Chrysostom. Διωνος του Χρυσοστομου Λογοι. Dionis Chrysostomi Orationes. Recognovit et praefatus est L. Dindorfius. *Gr.* 2 voll. 8°. Lipsiae. 1859.

Dittenberger, Wilhelm. Die attische Panathenaiden Aera. (*Commentationes philologicae in honorem T. Mommseni. Scripserunt amici*, etc.) 4°. Berolini. 1877.

—— Hadrian's erste Anwesenheit in Athen. (*Hermes, VII.*) 8°. Berlin. 1873.

—— Die Attischen Phylen. (*Hermes, IX.*) 8°. Berlin. 1875.

Dodwell, Henry. Dissertationes Cyprianicae. 8°. Oxoniae. 1684.

—— Dissertationes in Irenaeum. 8°. Oxoniae. 1689.

Doellinger, Johann Joseph Ignaz von. Heidenthum und Judenthum. Vorhall zur Geschichte des Christenthums. 8°. Regensburg. 1857.

Dositheus. Quae ex Dosithei magistri interpretamentorum libro tertio ad jus pertinent D. Adriani sententiae et epistolae et tractatus forensis maxime de manumissionibus. *Gr.* et *Lat.* ... emendavit commentariisque instruxit E. Böcking. (*Corpus Juris Romani Antejustiniani.*) 4°. Bonnae. 1841.

Duerr, Julius. Die Reisen des Kaisers Hadrian. (*Abhandlungen des archäologisch-epigraphischen Seminars der Univ. Wien.*) 8°. Wien. 1881.

Duruy, Victor. History of Rome and the Roman People, ed. by J. P. Mahaffy. 4°. London. 1886.

Eckhel, Joseph Hilarius von. Doctrina nummorum veterum conscripta a J. E. 8°. Vindobonae. 1792-8.

—— Choix des pierres gravées du Cabinet Impérial des Antiques, représentées en XL. planches, décrites et expliquées par E. Fol. Vienne. 1788.

Eisenmenger, Johann Andreas. Entdecktes Judenthum. ... In zwei Theilen. 4°. Königsberg. 1711.

Epictetus. *See* Arrian, Flavius.

Epiphanius, Saint, Bishop of Constantia in Cyprus. Epiphani Episcopi Constantiae opera. 8°. Lipsiae. 1859-1863.

Eusebius, Pamphili, Bishop of Caesarea in Palestine. Omnia opera. (J. P. Migne, *Patrologia Graeca*, tom. 19-24.) 4°. Parisiis.
—— Chronicon. Eusebi chronicorum libri duo.... Edidit A. Schöne. 2 voll. 4°. Berolini. 1875-1876.

Eutropius, Flavius. Eutropii breviarium historiae Romanae. Editionem primam curavit D. C. G. Baumgarten-Crusius, alteram H. R. Dietsch. 8°. Lipsiae. 1849.

Ewald, Georg Heinrich August von. Geschichte des Volkes Israel bis Christus. 7 voll. 8°. Göttingen. 1864.

Eyssenhardt, F. Hadrian and Florus. (R. Virchow and F. von Holtzendorff-Vietmansdorf, *Sammlung gemeinverständlicher wissenschaftlicher Vorträge*, Ser. XVII.) 8°. Berlin. 1882.

Fabretti, Ariodante. Racolta numismatica del R. Museo di Antichità di Torino. Monete Consolari. 8°. Roma. 1876.

Fabricius, B., *pseud.* **Heinrich Theodor Dietrich.** Der Periplus des Erythräischen Meeres ... mit ... Anmerkungen ... von B. F. 8°. Leipzig. 1883.

Falkener, Edward. Ephesus and the temple of Diana. 4°. London. 1862.

Fea, Carlo. Miscellanea filologica, critica e antiquaria (che contiene specialmente notizie di scavi di antechitor ordinati da E. Fea). 2 tom. 8° Roma. 1790-1836.
—— Varieta di notizie economiche fisiche antequaria sopra castel Gandolfo Albano Ariccia Nemi, loro Laghi ed Emissarii, sopra scavi recenti di antichità in Roma, e nei contorni, fabriche scoperte, sculture e iscrizioni trovatevi, ec., ec. 8°. Roma. 1820.

Finlay, George. A history of Greece from its conquest by the Romans to the present time, B.C. 146-A.D. 1864. A new edition, revised ... by the author and edited by ... H. F. Tozer. 7 voll. 8° Oxford. 1877.

Flemmer, Hans Morten. De itineribus et rebus gestis Hadriani Imperatoris secundum numorum et inscriptionum testimonia commentatio. 8°. Hauniae. 1836.

Florus, Lucius Annaeus. J. Flori Epitomae de Tito Livio bellorum omnium annorum D.C.C. libri II. Rencensuit et emendavit O. Jahn. 8°. Lipsiae. 1852.
—— J. Flori Epitomae de Tito Livio bellorum omnium annorum D.C.C. libri duo. Recognovit C. Halm. 8°. Lipsiae. 1854.

Foerster, Paul Richard. Studien zu den Griechischen Taktikern. (*Hermes, XII.*) 8°. Berlin. 1877.
—— Die bildende Kunst unter Hadrian. (*Die Grenzboten.*) 8°. Leipzig. 1875.

Forbiger, Albert. Hellas und Rom. Populäre Darstellung des öffentlichen und häuslichen Lebens der Griechen und Römer. 8°. Leipzig. 1871.

Foy-Vaillant, Jean. Numismata Imperatorum, Augustarum et Caesarum a populis Romanae ditionis Graece loquentibus ex omni modulo percussa. 4°. Lutetiae Parisiorum. 1698.

Francke, Heinrich. Zur Geschichte Trajans und seiner Zeitgenossen. 8°. Güstrow. 1837.

Franz, Johann. Elementa Epigraphicos Graecae. 4°. Berolini. 1840.

Friedlaender, Ludwig. Darstellungen aus der Sittengeschichte Roms in der Zeit von August bis zum Ausgang der Antonine. 3 voll. 8°. Leipzig. 1888-1890.
—— Das Römische Africa. (*Deutsche Rundschau*, Heft 4 und 5.) 1883.

Froehner, Wilhelm. Departement des Antiques de la Sculpture Moderne. La colonne Trajane décrite par W. F. 8°. Paris. 1865.
—— Numismatique Antique. Les Médaillons de l'Empire Romain depuis la règne d'Auguste jusqu'à Priscus Attale. 4°. Paris. 1878.

Fronto, Marcus Cornelius. M. C. Frontonis opera inedita, cum epistulis item ineditis Antonini Pii, M. Aurelii, L. Veri, et Appiani; nec non aliorum veterum fragmentis, invenit et commentario praevio notisque illustravit A. Maius. Pars prior (Pars altera cui adduntur seu inedita seu cognita ejusdem Frontonis opera). 2 pt. 8°. Mediolani. 1815.
—— M. C. Frontonis Reliquiae, ab A. Maio primum editae ... iterum edidit B. G. Niebuhrius. 8°. Berolini. 1816.
—— M. C. Frontonis et M. Aurelii Imperatoris Epistulae L. Veri et Antonini Pii et Appiani epistularum reliquiae. Fragmenta Frontonis et Scripta Grammatica. Editio prima Romana ... curanti A. Maio. 8°. Romae. 1823.
—— M. C. Frontonis et M. Aurelii Imperatoris Epistulae et alia Scripta ... ed A. Mai. 8° Romae. 1846.

Gaius, the Jurist. Institutionem libri duo, cura E. Boecking: Institutionem commentarii quatuor cum commentariis J. F. L. Goeschenii. (*Corpus Juris Romani Antejustiniani.*) 4°. Bonnae. 1841.

Geib, Carl Gustav. Geschichte des Römischen Criminalprocesses bis zum Tode Justinians. 8°. Leipzig. 1842.

Gellius, Aulus. A. Gellii Noctium Atticarum Libri XX. Ex recensione et cum apparatu critico M. Hertz. 2 voll. 8°. Berolini. 1883-1885.

George Syncellus. Chronographiae ab Adamo usque ad Diocletianum ... collectio ex recensione G. Dundorfii, G. G. Bredorii dissertatio de Giorgio Syncellus ... ad Georgii Syncelli chronolog ... J. Goar digestus Jacobi Goar emendatione et annotationes. (*Corpus Scriptorum Historiae Byzantinae.*) *Gr.* and *Lat.* 8°. Bonn. 1828.

Gerhard, Eduard. Antike Bildwerke zum ersten mal bekannt gemacht von E. G. Text 3 Lieferungen. 4°. Stuttgart u. Tübingen. 1828-44.

Gibbon, Edward. The History of the Decline and Fall of the Roman Empire. With notes by Dean Milman and M. Guizot. Edited with additional notes by W. Smith. 8 voll. 8°. London. 1854-1855.

Graefenhan, Ernst August Wilhelm. Geschichte der klassischen Philologie im Alterthum. 4 voll. 8°. Bonn. 1843-1850.

Graetz, Hirsch. Geschichte der Juden von den ältesten Zeiten bis auf die Gegenwart. (*Institut zur Förderung der israelitischen Literatur.*) 11 voll. 8°. Leipzig. 1855, etc.

Grasberger, Lorenz. Erziehung und Unterricht im klassischen Alterthum mit besonderer Rücksicht auf die Bedürfnisse der Gegenwart. 8°. Würzburg. 1864.

Greek Anthology. Epigrammatum Anthologia Palatina ... apparatu critico instruxit F. Duebner. (A. F. Didot, *Scriptorum Graecorum Bibliotheca.*) 8°. Parisiis. 1864-1872.

Gregory, called Bar Hebraeus. Gregorii Abulpharagii ... Chronicon Syriacum : codicibus Bodleianis descripsit, maximam partem vestit notisque illustravit. P. J. Bruns edidit et parti vertit, notasque adjicit G. G. Kirsch. 2 voll. *Syr.* et *Lat.* 4°. Lipsiae. 1789.

Gregory of Nazianzus, Saint, Patriarch of Constantinople. Omnia opera. (J. P. Migne, *Patrologia Graeca*, tom. 35-38.) 4°. Parisiis. 1885, 1857, 1858.

Greppo, J. G. Honoré. Mémoire sur les voyages de l'Empereur Hadrian. Paris. 1842.

Gruterus, Janus. Inscriptiones Antiquae totius orbis Romani. 2 tom. Fol. Amstelaedami. 1707.

Guérin, Victor. Description géographique, historique, et archéologique de la Palestine, accompagnée de cartes detaillées. (Première partie—Judée, etc.) 8°. Paris. 1868-1880.

—— Voyage archéologique dans la Régence de Tunis, etc. 2 tom. 8°. Paris. 1862.

Guhl, Ernst. Ephesiaca. 8°. Berolini. 1843.

Haakh, Ad. Article ' Hadrian.' (Pauly, A. F. von, *Real Encyclopädie der classischen Alterthumswissenschaft.*) 8°. Stuttgart. 1839, etc.

Haenel, Gustav. Corpus legum ab Imperatoribus Romanis ante Justinianum latarum.... Accedunt res ab Imperatoribus gestae quibus Romani juris historia et imperii status illustratur. Ex monumentis et scriptoribus Graecis Latinisque collegit ... indicibus ... instruxit G. H. 2 pts. 4°. Lipsiae. 1857-1860.

Hardouin, Jean. Conciliorum collectio regia maxima ab anno Christi XXXIV. ad annum ; ad P. Labbaei et Cossartii labores ... emendationibus plurimus additis, ... ex codd. manuscriptis : cum novis ... indicibus. Studio J. Hardouini. 12 tom. Fol. Parisiis. 1715.

Hase, Carl August. Kirchengeschichte. 8°. Leipzig. 1837.

Hausrath, Adolf. Neutestamentliche Zeitgeschichte. 4 Theile. 8°. Heidelberg. 1868-1877.

Heineccius, Johann Gottlieb. J. G. H. ... Antiquitatum Romanarum jurisprudenciam illustrantium Syntagma.... Editio octava ... auctior. 4°. Genevae. 1746.

Helbig, Wolfgang. Untersuchungen über die campanische Wandmalerei. 8°. Leipzig. 1873.

Henzen, Wilhelm. *See* Orelli, Johann Caspar.

Herder, Johann Gottfried von. Ideen zur Philosophie der Geschichte der Menschheit. Dritte Auflage, mit einer Einleitung von H. Luden. 8°. Leipzig. 1828.

Hermann, Carl Friedrich. Lehrbuch der griechischen Antiquitäten. 8°. Heidelberg. 1875.
—— Zur Begleitung meines Lehrbuchs der gottesdienstlichen Alterthümer der Griechen.... 8°. Göttingen. 1846.

Herodian, the Historian. Herodiani ab excessu divi Marci libri octo, ab I. Bekkero recogniti. 8°. Lipsiae. 1855.

Hertz, Martin. Renaissance und Rococo in der Römischen Literatur. Ein Vortrag, etc. 8°. Berlin. 1865.

Hertzberg, Gustav Friedrich. Tituli Statuariorum Sculptorumque Graecorum cum prolegomenis, etc. 8°. Berolini. 1871.

Hieronymus, Saint. S. Eusebii Hieronymi opera omnia. (J. P. Migne, *Patrologia Graeca*, tom. 22-30.) 4°. Parisiis. 1857-1888.

Hirschfeld, Gustav. Tituli Statuariorum Sculptorumque Graecorum cum prolegomenis, etc. 8°. Berolini. 1871.

Hirschfeld, Heinrich Otto. Die Verwaltung der Rheingrenze in den ersten drei Jahrhunderten der römischen Kaiserzeit. (*Commentationes philologicae in honorem T. Mommseni. Scripserunt amici*, etc.). 4°. Berolini. 1877.
—— Untersuchungen auf dem Gebiete der römischen Verwaltungs Geschichte. 8°. Berlin, 1877.
—— Die Getreide Verwaltung in der römischen Kaiserzeit. (*Philologus, XXIX.*) 8°. Göttingen.

Hirt, Aloys Ludwig. Die Geschichte der Baukunst bei den Alten. 3 voll. 4°. Berlin. 1821-1827.

Hoeckh, Carl. Römische Geschichte vom Verfall der Republik bis zur Vollendung der Monarchie unter Constantin. Mit vorzüglicher Rücksicht auf Verfassung und Verwaltung des Reichs. 8°. Braunschwig. 1841-50.

Hudermann, E. E. Geschichte des römischen Postwesens während der Kaiserzeit. 8°. Berlin. 1878.

Huebner, Emil. Die antiken Bildwerke in Madrid, etc. 8°. Berlin. 1862.
—— Der römische Grenzwall in Germanien. (*Jahrbuch des Vereins für Alterthumsfreunde im Rheinland, LXII.*) 1878.

Humboldt, Friedrich Heinrich Alexander von, Baron. Kosmos. Entwurf einer physischen Weltbeschreibung. 5 voll. 8°. Stuttgart and Tübingen, 1845-62.

Irenaeus. Opera omnia. (J. P. Migne, *Patrologia Graeca*, tom. 7.) 4°. Parisiis. 1882.

Jahn, Otto. Aus der Alterthumswissenschaft. Populäre Aufsätze. 8°. Bonn. 1868.

Jost, Isaac Marcus. Allgemeine Geschichte des israelitischen Volkes, etc. **2 voll.** 8°. Berlin. 1832.

—— Geschichte des Judenthums und seiner Secten. 3 Abth. 8°. Leipzig. 1857-1859.

Jung, Julius. Die romanischen Landschaften des römischen Reiches. Studien über die inneren Entwickelungen in der Kaiserzeit. 8°. Innsbruck. 1881.

Justin, Martyr, Saint. Justini ... opera quae feruntur omnia. (Otto, *Corpus Apologetarum Christianorum saeculi secundi*, vol. 45.) 8°. Jena. 1876.

Justinian I., Emperor of the East (527-565). Corpus Juris Civilis. Editio stereotypa quinta. (Institutiones. Recognovit Paul Krüger.—Digesta. Recognovit Theodorus Mommsen.—Codex Justinianus. Recognovit Paul Krüger.) 4°. Berolini. 1888.

Kaibel, Georg. Epigrammata Graeca ex lapidibus conlecta. Edidit G. K. 8°. Berolini. 1878.

Keil, Heinrich. Griechische Inschriften. (*Philologus*, Suppl. II.) 8°. Göttingen. 1863.

—— Herodes Atticus. (A. F. von Pauly, *Real-Encyclopädie der classischen Alterthumswissenschaft.*) 8°. Stuttgart. 1839.

Kellermann, Olaus Christian. Vigilum Romanorum latercula duo Coelimontana magnam partem militiae Romanae explicantia edidit atque illustravit, appendicem inscriptiorum quae ad vigiles pertinent, laterculorum militarium hucusque cognitorium omnium et inscriptionum variarum militarium adj. O. K. 4°. Romae. 1835.

Kellner, Heinrich, of Treves. Hellenismus und Christenthum, oder die geistige Reaction des antiken Heidenthums gegen das Christenthum. Mit besonderer Rücksicht auf die Christenfeindliche Literatur des classischen Alterthums, sowie auch der Gegenwart. 8°. Köln. 1866.

Kiepert, Heinrich. A Manual of Ancient Geography, trans. by G. A. Macmillan. 8°. London. 1881.

King, Charles William. Antique Gems and Rings. 2 voll. 8°. London. 1872.

Klein, Josef. Fasti Consulares inde a Caesaris nece usque ad imperium Diocletiani. 8°. Lipsiae. 1881.

—— Bedenken gegen die Aechtheit des hadrianischen Christen Rescripts. (*Theologisches Jahrbuch.*) 1856.

Knaut, Dr. C., of Nordhausen. Hadrian als Regent und als Character. Ein Versuch. 4°. Nordhausen. 1871.

Koechly, Hermann August Theodor, and **Rüstow, F. Wilhelm.** Aelians Theorie der Taktik. Griechisch u. Deutsch. 12°. Leipzig. 1855.

Krause, Johann Heinrich. Νεωκορος. Civitates Neocorae sive Aedituae e veterum libris nummis, lapidibus inscriptis adumbratae, atque corollariis quattuor additio illustratae. 8°. Lipsiae. 1844.

—— Olympia, oder Darstellung der grossen Olympischen Spiele und der damit verbundenen Festlichkeiten ... nebst einem ... Verzeichniss der Olympischen Sieger ... und einigen Fragmenten des Phlegon aus Tralles, etc. 8°. Wien. 1838.

Kriegel, Carl Johann Albert. Antiqua versio Latina fragmentorum e Modestini libro de excusationibus ... in integrum restituta. Scripsit C. J. A. K. 4°. Lipsiae. 1830.

Kubitschek, Joseph Wilhelm. De Romanorum Tribuum origine ac propagatione. (*Abhandlungen des archäologisch-epigraphischen Seminars der Universität Wien*, Heft 3.) 8°. Wien. 1880.

Kuhn, Emil. Die städtische und bürgerliche Verfassung des Römischen Reichs bis auf die Zeiten Justinians. (Nachträge, etc.) 2 Theile. 8°. Leipzig. 1864, 1865.

La Berge, C. de. Essai sur la règne de Trajan. (*Ecole Pratique des Hautes Etudes*. Bibliothèque, etc. Fasc. 32.) 8°. Paris. 1877.

Laborde, Léon Emmanuel Simon Joseph de, Marquis. Voyage de l'Arabie Petrée par L. de Laborde et Linant, publié par L. de Laborde. (Flore de l'Arabie Petrée. Plantes recueillies par L. de Laborde ... décrites par M. Delile.) Fol. Paris. 1830.

Lacour-Gayet, G. Mélanges d'Architecture et d'Histoire. (*Ecole Française de Rome.*) Rome. 1881.

Lactantius, Lucius Caelius Firmianus. Opera omnia. (J. P. Migne, *Patrologia Latina*, tom. 6, 7.) 4°. Paris. 1844.

Lampridius, Aelius. *See* Augustan History.

Leake, William Martin. The Topography of Athens, with some remarks on its antiquities. With plates. 8°. London. 1821.

Le Bas, Philippe, and **Waddington, W. H.** Voyage archéologique en Grèce et en Asie mineure ... pendant les années 1843 et 1844 et publié ... par P. le Bas et W. H. Waddington. ... Itineraire, Inscriptions, Explications des Inscriptions. Fol. Paris. 1847, etc.

Lebrecht, Fürchtegott Shemaiah. Bether, die fragliche Stadt im Hadrianisch-jüdischen Kriege. Ein 1700 jähriges Missverständniss. Beitrag zur Geschichte und Geographie des alten Palästina mit historischen Beilagen in Hebräischer Sprache. 8°. Schmiedeberg. 1877.

Lenel, Otto. Das Edictum perpetuum ein Versuch zu dessen Wiederherstellung. 8°. Leipzig. 1883.

Lenormant, François. Recherches archéologiques à Eleusis exécutées dans le cours de l'année 1860. ... Recueil des inscriptions. 8°. Paris. 1862.
—— L'Antinous d'Eleusis. (*Revue Archéologique*.) 8°. Paris. 1874.

Letronne, Jean Antoine. La statue vocale de Memnon considérée dans ses rapports avec l'Egypte et la Grèce. Etude historique, faisant suite aux Recherches pour servir à l'histoire de l'Egypte pendant la domination des Grecs et des Romains. 4°. Paris. 1833.
—— Recueil des Inscriptions Grecques et Latines de l'Egypte étudiées dans leur rapport avec l'histoire politique, l'administration intérieur, les institutions civiles et religieuses de ce pays, depuis la conquête d'Alexandre jusqu'à celle des Arabes. 2 tom. 4°. Paris. 1842-1848.

Levezow, Conrad von. Ueber den Antinous dargestellt in den Kunstdenkmälern des Alterthums. Eine archäologische Abhandlung. ... Nebst 12 Kupfertafeln. 4°. Berlin. 1808.

Levy, M. A. Geschichte der jüdischen Münzen, etc. (*Institut zur Förderung der israelitischen Literatur.*) 8°. Leipzig. 1862.

Ligorio, Pirro. Ichnographia villae Tiburtinae Hadriani Caesaris, olim a P. Ligorio delineata et descripta, postea a F. Contucio ... recognita ... nunc denuo affabre aere incisa in elegantirrens ... formam redacta, addita expositione Latina. Pianta della villa Tiburtina de Adriano Caesaro, etc. *Lat.* and *Ital.* Fol. Romae. 1751.

Longpérier, Henri Adrien. *See* Prevost de Longpérier.

Luebcke, Wilhelm. Geschichte der Architektur von den ältesten Zeiten bis auf die Gegenwart, etc. Sechste vermehrte Auflage .. mit ... Holzschnitt Illustrationen. 2 voll. 8°. Leipzig. 1884-1886.

Lützow, Carl Friedrich Arnold von. Münchener Antiken. Fol. München. 1869.

Lumbroso, Giacomo. L'Egitto al tempo dei Greci e dei Romani. 8°. Roma. 1882.

Macrobius. Macrobius. F. Eyssenhardt recognovit. 8°. Lipsiae. 1868.

Madden, Frederic William. Coins of the Jews.... With 279 woodcuts and a plate of alphabets. 1881. (W. Marsden, F.R.S., *Numismata Orientalia*). 2 voll. 4°. London. 1874.
—— History of Jewish Coinage and of Money in the Old and New Testament, by F. W. M. ... With woodcuts and a plate of alphabets, by F. W. Fairholt. 4°. London. 1864.

Maffei, Paolo Allessandro. Gemme antiche figurate date in luce da D. de Rossi colle spositioni di P. A. M. 4 pt. 4°. Roma. 1707-1709.

Malala, Joannes. Joanniis Malalae Chronographia. (J. P. Migne, *Patrologia Graeca*, tom. 97.) 4°. Parisiis. 1865.
—— (*Corpus Scriptorum Historiae Byzantinae.*) *Gr.* and *Lat.* 8°. Bonnae. 1828.

Mannert, Conrad. Geographie der Griechen und Römer aus ihren Schriften dargestellt. 3 Theile. 8°. Nürnberg. 1788-1792.

Marcellinus, Ammianus. A. M. rerum gestarum qui de XXXI. supersunt libri XVIII. ... Omnia nunc recognita ab J. Gronovio qui suas quoque notes passim inseruit et necessariis ad Ammiani illustrationem antiquis nummis ac figuris ex ornari curavit. Fol. Lugduni Batavorum. 1693.

Mariette, Pierre. Traité des pierres gravées. 2 tom. Fol. Paris. 1750.

Marquardt, J. Cyzicus und sein Gebiet. Mit einer Karte. 8°. Berlin. 1836.

Marquardt, Joachim, and **Mommsen, Theodor.** Handbuch der Römischen Alterthümer. (Römisches Staatsrecht von Theodor Mommsen, voll. 1-3; Römische Staats Verwaltung von Joachim Marquardt, voll. 4-6; Das Privatleben der Römer von J. Marquardt, vol. 7.) 7 voll. 8°. Leipzig. 1887.

Marucchi, Orazio. Descrizione del Foro Romano e guida per la visita dei suoi monumenti. 8°. Roma. 1883.

Maspero, Gaston. Histoire ancienne des peuples de l'Orient. Quatrième edition. 8°. Paris. 1886.

Matter, A. Jacques. Histoire de l'Ecole d'Alexandrie, comparée aux principale écoles contemporaines. Ouvrage couronné par l'Institut. Deuxième edition. 8°. Paris. 1840-1844.

Meyer, Ludwig, Ph.D., of Berlin. Tibur, Eine römische Studie. (R. Virchow, and F. von Holtzendorff-Vietmansdorf, *Sammlung gemeinverständlicher wissenschaftlicher Vorträge*, Ser. XVIII.) 8°. Berlin. 1883.

Midrash. Bibliotheca Rabbinica. Eine Zammlung alter Midraschim, zum ersten male ins Deutsche übertragen von Dr. A. Wünsche. 12 parts. 8°. Leipzig. 1880-1885.

Milchhoefer, Arthur. Die Museen Athens. 8°. Athen. 1881.

Milman, Henry Hart, Dean of St. Paul's. The History of the Jews from the earliest period down to Modern Times. Third edition ... extended. 3 voll. 8°. London. 1863.

Minucius Felix, Marcus. M. Minucii Felicis Octavius. (J. P. Migne, *Patrologia Latina*, tom. 3.) 4°. Parisiis. 1886.

Mionnet, Théodore Edine. Description de medailles antiques grecques et romaines. 6 tom. (Recueil des planches. Supplément, 9 tom.) 8°. Paris. 1806-1837.

Mommsen, August. Athenae christianae ecclesiae prope Ilissum sitae. 8°. Lipsiae. 1848.
—— Heortologie. Antiquarische Untersuchungen über die städtischen Feste der Athener. 8°. Leipzig. 1864.

Mommsen, Theodor. Zur Lebensgeschichte des jüngeren Plinius. (*Hermes*, III.) 8°. Berlin. 1869.
—— Die Römischen Lagerstädte. (*Hermes*, VII.). 8°. Berlin. 1873.
—— De Collegiis et Sodaliciis Romanorum. Accedit inscriptio Lanuvina. 8°. Kiliae. 1843.
—— Inscriptiones Regni Neapolitani Latinae. Fol. Lipsiae. 1852.
—— Grabrede des Kaisers Hadrian auf die ältere Matidia. (*Königliche Akademie der Wissenschaften.*) 8°. Berlin. 1863.

Movers, Franz Carl. Die Phönizier. 2 voll. 8°. Bonn. 1841, 1856.

Mueller, Carl Otfried, Archaeologist. Handbuch der Archäologie der Kunst. Dritte ... vermehrte Auflage mit Zusätzen von F. G. Welcher. 8°. Breslau. 1848.

Mueller, Ernestus Henricus Otto. De P. A. Floro poeta ... Dissertatio ... quam publice defendet ... O. M. 8°. Berolini. 1855.

Mueller, Johann Jacob. Der Geschichtschreiber L. Marius Maximus. Eine kritische Untersuchung. 8°. Leipzig. 1870.

Mueller, R. O. Osymandias und sein Grabpalast. (Ersch und Gruber, *Allgemeine Encyclopaedie der Wissenschaften*). 4°. Leipzig. 1818.

Münter, Frederik Christian Carl Henrik, Bishop of Zealand. Der Jüdische Krieg unter den Kaisern Trajan und Hadrian. 8°. Altona und Leipzig. 1821.

Nardini, Famiano. Roma Antica. Editio quarta Romana ... con note ed osservazioni critico-antiquarie di A. Nibby ... e con disegni rappresentanti la faccia attuale dell' antica topografia di A. de Romanis. 8°. Roma. 1818-1820.

Neander, Johann August Wilhelm. Allgemeine Geschichte der christlichen Religion und Kirche. 6 voll. 8°. Hamburg. 1825-1852.

Neubauer, Adolf. La Geographie du Talmud. 8°. Paris. 1868.

Nibby, Antonio. Fabbriche antiche nei contorni di Roma misurate e pubblicate dall' architetto C. Pontani descritte dal professore Ant. Nibby. Distribuzioni. 4°. Roma. 1841.

Nicolai, Rudolph. Griechische Literaturgeschichte in neuer Bearbeitung. 3 voll. 8°. Magdeburg. 1873-1878.

Niebuhr, Barthold Georg. Lectures on the History of Rome from the first Punic War to the death of Constantine ... including an introductory course on the sources and study of Roman History. Ed. by L. Schmidt. 2 voll. 8°. London. 1844.

Nissen Heinrich. Das Templum. Antiquarische Untersuchungen.... Mit astronomischen Hülfstafeln von B. Tiele, etc. 8°. Berlin-Bonn. 1869.

Nompère de Champagny, François Joseph Marie Thérèse, Count. Les Antonins, ans de J. C. 69-180. Suite des Césars et de Rome et la Judée. 3 tom. 8°. Paris. 1863.

Noris, Enrico, Cardinal. Annus et Epochae Syromacedonum in vetustis Urbium Syriae nummis ... expositae. Additis Fastis consularibus anonymi. Accesserunt ... Dissertationes de Paschali Latinorum Cyclo annorum LXXXIV., ac Ravennate annorum XCV. 3 pt. Fol. Florentiae. 1691.

Occo, Adolphus, of Augsburg. Imperatorem Romanorum numismata ... ab Adolpho Occone olim congesta nunc ... aucta studio et cura F. Mediobarbi Biragi. Fol. Mediolani. 1683.

Orelli, Johann Caspar. Inscriptionum Latinarum selectarum amplissima collectio ad illustrandam Romanae Antiquitatis disciplinam ... edidit Johann Caspar Orelli. (Volumen tertium collectionis Orellianae .. edidit Gulielmus Henzen.) 8°. Turici. 1828-1856.

Origen. Origenis opera omnia. (J. P. Migne, *Patrologia Graeca*, tom. 11-17.) 4°. Parisiis. 1857, '62, '59, '63.

Orosius, Paulus. Pauli Orosii historiarum libri septem. (J. P. Migne, *Patrologia Latina*, tom. 31.) 4°. Parisiis. 1846.

Overbeck, Johannes Adolph. Geschichte der Griechischen Plastik für Künstler und Kunstfreunde. Mit Illustrationen gezeichnet von H. Streller, geschnitten von F. G. Flegel. Fol. and 8°. Leipzig. 1881-1883.

Pagi, Antoine. Critica historico-chronologica in universos Annales Ecclesiasticos Caesaris Cardinalis Baronii ... ab adventu Domini nostri J. C. ad annum 1198 studio et cura Francisci Pagi. Editio novissima, plurimis in locis emendata, cui accessit dissertatio hypatica, seu de consulibus Caesareis. 4 tom. Fol. Antverpiae. 1727.

Panvinio, Onofrio. Antiquae Urbis imago. (Graevius, J. G., *Thesaurus Antiquitatum Romanarum*, tom. 3.) Fol. Lugdunum Batavorum. 1694.

Parthey, Gustav Friedrich Constantin. Das Alexandrinische Museum. Eine von der Königl. Akademie der Wissenschaften ... gekrönte Preisschrift. 8°. Berlin. 1838.

Paulinus, Saint, Bishop of Nola. Opera omnia. (J. P. Migne, *Patrologia Latina*, tom. 61). 4°. Paris. 1861.

Pausanias. Pausaniae Descriptio Graeciae. Recognovit...J. H. C. Schubart. 2 voll. *Gr.* 8°. Leipzig. 1853-54.

Perrot, Georges, and **Guillaume, Edmond.** Exploration archéologique de la Galatie et de la Bithynie, d'une partie de la Mysie, de la Phrygie, de la Capadoce et du Pont, executée en 1861 et publiée ... par G. Perrot, E. Guillaume, etc. 2 tom. Fol. Paris. 1862.

Perrot, Georges. Inscriptiones inedites de la mer noire. (*Revue Archéologique.*) 8° Paris. 1874.

Peter, Carl. Geschichte Roms, etc. Dritte ... Ausgabe. 36 voll. 8°. Halle. 1870-71.

Petersen, Frederik Christian. Allgemeine Einleitung in das Studium der Archäologie. Aus dem Dänischen übersetzt von S. Friedrichsen. 8°. Leipzig. 1829.

Pfitzner, Wilhelm. Geschichte der römischen Kaiserlegionen von Augustus bis Hadrianus. 8°. Leipzig. 1881.

Philippi, Adolph. Ueber die römischen Triumphal Reliefe. (*Konigl. Sächsische Gesellschaft der Wissenschaften Abhandlungen*, vol. 6.). 1872.

Philostratus. Flavii Philostrati Opera auctiora edidit C. L. Kayser. Accedunt Apollonii epistolae, Eusebius adversus Hieroclem, Philostrati Juniaris imagines, Callistrati descriptiones. *Gr.* 2 voll. 8°. Lipsiae. 1870-71.

—— τὰ τῶν Φιλοστρατων λειπομενα ἁπαντα Philostratorum quae supersunt omnia. ... Accessere Apollonii Tyanensis Epistolae, Eusebii liber adversus Hieroclem, Callistrati descript. statuarum. Omnia ... recensuit, notis ... illustravit, versionem totam fere novam fecit G. Olearius. *Gr.* and *Lat.* Fol. Lipsiae. 1709.

Phlegon of Tralles. Phlegontis Tralliani opuscula Graece et Latine e recensione J. Meursii.... Iterum edidit, animadversiones ... adjecit T. G. F. Franzius. 8°. Halae-Magdeburgicae. 1775.

Photius, Patriarch of Constantinople. Φωτιου τὰ εὑρισκομενα παντα. Opera omnia. *Gr.* and *Lat.* 4 tom. (J. P. Migne, *Patrologia Graeca*, tom. 101-104.) 4°. Parisiis. 1860.

Pius II., Pope, Enea Silvio Piccolomini. Pii Secundi Pontificis Max. Commentarii rerum memorabilium, quae temporibus suis contigerunt, a J. Gobellino ... compositi (or rather begun by Pius II. and continued and edited by J. Gobelliniis), etc. Omnia ... nunc primum in lucem edita. 8°. Romae. 1584.

Plew, J. Marius Maximus als directe oder indirecte Quelle der Script. Hist. Aug. 4°. Strassburg. 1878.

Plinius Secundus, Caius. C. Plinii Naturalis Historia. D. Detlefsen recensuit. 6 voll. 8°. Berolini. 1866-82.

Plinius Caecilius Secundus. C. Plinii Caecili Secundi Epistularum libri novem, Epistularum ad Traianum, liber Panegyricus. Ex recensione H. Keilii. Accedit index nominum ... T. Mommsen. 8°. Lipsiae. 1870.

Plutarch. Πλουταρχου ... τὰ 'Ηθικα. Plutarchi ... Moralia, id est, opera, exceptis vitis, reliqua. Graeca emendavit ... item indices ... adjecit D. Wyttenbach. 8 tom. 4°. Oxonii. 1795-1830.

Polemon, Antonius. Polemonis Declamationes quae extant duae. Accedunt ... Isaaci Porphyrogenneti ... quae vulgo dicuntur Scripta. Recensuit H. Hinck. 8°. Lipsiae. 1873.

—— Πολεμωνος Σοφιστου Λογω. Polemonis Laodicensis sophistae laudationes II. funebres in Cynaegirum et Callimachum occisos in pugna Marathonia, Graece. Textum recognovit paraphrasin Latinam P. Possini ejusdemque et H. Stephani notas integras suasque et J. C. Orelli animadversionis adjecit J. C. Orellius, etc. *Gr.* and *Lat.* 8°. Lipsiae. 1819.

Preller, Ludwig. Römische Mythologie. 8°. Berlin. 1881.

Prevost de Longpérier, Henri Adrien. Mémoires sur la chronologie et l'iconographie des Rois Parthes Arsacides.... Ouvrage accompagné de 18 planches gravées. 4°. Paris. 1853-1882.

Prina, Benedetto. Nel primo centario di Angelo Mai. Memorie ... e documenti pubblicati per cura dell' Ateneo di Bergamo il 7 Marzo 1882. 8°. Bergamo. 1882.

Procopius of Caesarea. Procopius ex recensione Gr. Dindorfii. *Gr.* and *Lat.* 2 voll. (*Corpus scriptorum Historiae Byzantinae*, pars 10.) 8°. Bonnae. 1833-1838.

Prudentius Clemens, Aurelius. Carmina. (J. P. Migne, *Patrologia Latina*, tom. 59, 60.) 4°. Paris. 1844.

Prutz, Hans Georg. Aus Phönizien. Geographische Skizzen und historische Studien.... Mit 4 lithographirten Karten-Skizzen und einem Plan. 8°. Leipzig. 1876.

Ptolemaeus, Claudius. Claudii Ptolemaei ... opus Geographie noviter castigatu et emaculatu additiöibus ... necnon cū tabularum in dorso jucunda explanatione.... Hoc bona mente L. Phrisius ... in lucem jusut prodire, etc. Fol. Argentorati. 1522.

—— Claudii Ptolemaei Geographiae libris octo.... Edidit F. C. Wilberg (Socio adjuncto C. H. F. Grashofio). Fasc. 1-6. 4°. Essendiae. 1838-45.

Ptolemaeus, Claudius. Géographie de Ptolémée, reproduction photolithographique du manuscrit grec du Monastère de Vatopédi au Mont Athos … précédée d'une introduction historique sur le mont Athos … par V. Langlois. Fol. Paris. 1867.

Puchstein, Otto. Epigrammata Graeca in Aegypto reperta. Retractavit O. Puchstein. (*Kaiser Wilhelm-Universität. Dissertationes philologicae.*) 8°. Strassburg. 1880.

Puchta, Georg Friedrich. Cursus der Institutionen (of Justinian). Achte Auflage … besorgt von P. Krüger. 2 voll. 8°. Leipzig. 1875.

Ranke, Leopold von. Weltgeschichte. 7 Theile. 8°. Leipzig. 1881-1886.

Re, Antonio del. Dell' Antichita Tiburtine capitolo V., etc. 4°. Roma. 1611.

Regent, Joseph. De C. Suetonii Tranquilli vita et scriptis. Diss. inaug. 8°. Vratislaviae. 1856.

Renan, Joseph Ernest. Histoire des Origines du Christianisme. 8 voll. 8°. Paris. 1863-1883.
   Saint Paul. Vol. 3. 1869.
   Les Evangiles et la seconde generation Chrétienne. Vol. 5. 1877.
   L'Eglise Chrétienne. Vol. 6. 1879.
   Marc Aurèle et la fin du monde antique. Vol. 7. 1883.
—— Mission de Phénice dirigée par M. E. Renan. 4°. Paris. 1864.

Renier, Charles Alphonse Léon. Inscriptions Romaines de l'Algérie. Fol. Paris. 1858.
—— Recueil de Diplômes militaires, publié par L. Renier. 4°. Paris. 1876.

Ritschl, Friedrich Wilhelm. Die Alexandrinischen Bibliotheken unter den ersten Ptolemäern, und die Sammlung der Homerischen Gedichte durch Pisistratus. … Nebst literarhistorischen Zugaben über die Chronologie der Alexandrinischen Bibliothekare, etc. 8°. Breslau. 1838.

Ritter, Carl, Geographer. Die Erdkunde im Verhältniss zur Natur und zur Geschichte des Menschen; oder allgemeine vergleichende Geographie. … Zweite … Ausgabe. 8°. Berlin. 1822-1859.

Robinson, Edward, D.D. Biblical Researches in Palestine, Mount Sinai, and Arabia Petræa. A journal of travels in 1838, by E. R. and J. Smith. … Drawn up from the original diaries, with historical illustrations, by E. R. Third edition, with new maps and plans. 3 voll. 8°. London. 1867.

Rohde, Erwin. Der Griechische Roman und seine Vorläufer. 8°. Leipzig. 1876.

Rossi, Giovanni Battista de, Cavaliere. La Roma Sotterranea Cristiana descritta ed illustrata. 4°. Roma. 1864, etc.
—— Piaule icnografiche e prospettiche di Roma anteriori al secolo XVI. raccolte e dichiarate da G. B. di Rossi. (*Institute di correspondenza Archeologici.*) Fol. and 4°. Roma. 1879.

Rudorff, Adolph August Friedrich. De juris dictione edictum. Edicti perpetui quae reliqua sunt. Constituit, adnotavit, edidit A. P. Rudorff. 8°. Lipsiae. 1869.

Savigny, Friedrich Carl von. Geschichte des Römischen Rechts im Mittelalter. 7 voll. 8°. Heidelberg. 1834-1851.

Scaliger, Joseph Juste. Thesaurus temporum, Eusebii ... chronicorum canonum omnimodae historiae libri duo. ... Ejusdem Eusebii utriusque partis chronicorum canonum reliquiae Graecae ... opera ac studio J. J. Scaliger, etc. Fol. Lugduni Batavorum. 1606.

Schliemann, Heinrich. Ilios, the city and country of the Trojans: the result of researches ... on the site of Troy ... in the years 1871, '72, '73, '78, '79. Including an autobiography of the author. With a preface, appendices, and notes, etc. With maps, plans, and illustrations. 8°. London. 1880.

Schneiderwirth, Johann Hermann. Die Parther. Oder das neupersische Reich unter den Arsaciden. Nach griechisch-römischen Quellen. 8°. Heiligenstadt. 1874.

Schoell, Maximilian Samson Friedrich. Histoire de la Litterature Grecque profane, depuis son origine jusqu'à la prise de Constantinople ... suivie d'un précis de l'histoire de la transplantation de la litterature grecque en occident. Seconde édition. 8 tom. 8°. Paris. 1823-1825.

Schuerer, Emil. Lehrbuch der neutestamentlichen Zeitgeschichte. 8°. Leipzig. 1874.

Seneca, Marcus Annaeus. Annaei Senecae Oratorum et Rhetorum Sententiae, Divisiones, Colores. Recognovit A. Kiessling. 8°. Lipsiae. 1872.

Sepp, Johann Nepomuk. Jerusalem und das heilige Land. Pilgerbuch nach Palästina, Syrien, und Egypten. Zweite ... Auflage mit Illustrationen, etc. 2 voll. 8°. Schaffhausen, Regensburg. 1873-1876.

Severus, Sulpicius. Opera omnia. (J. P. Migne, *Patrologia Latina*, tom. 20.) 4°. Paris. 1845.
—— Sulpitii Severi libri qui supersunt recensuit ... instruxit C. Halm. (*Kaiserliche Akademie der Wissenschaften. Corpus Scriptorum Ecclesiasticorum Latinorum*, etc. Vol. 1.) 8°. Vindobonae. 1866.

Sibyls. Χρησμοι Σιβυλλιακοι Oracula Sibyllina, textu ad codices manuscriptos recognito, Maianio supplementis aucto ... commentario perpetuo excursibus et indicibus: curante C. Alexandre. 2 voll. 8°. Parisiis. 1841-1856.

Sickler, Friedrich Carl Ludwig. Geschichte der Wegnahme und Abführung vorzüglicher Kunstwerke aus den eroberten Ländern in die Länder der Sieger. Ein Beitrag zur Kunst- und Kultur-Geschichte. Erster Theil. Geschichte der von den Griechen, Persern und Römern erbeuteten und weggeführten Kunstwerke. Nebst tabellarischen Uebersichten. 8°. Gotha. 1803.

Socrates, Scholasticus. Σωκρατους Σχολαστικου, Ἑρμειου Σωζομενου Ἐκκλησιαστικη Ἱστορια. Socrates Scholastici, Hermiae Sozomeni, Historia Ecclesiastica. H. Volesius. ... Latine vertit, notis illustravit, cujus editionem criticis observationibus locupletavit G. Reading. (J. P. Migne, *Patrologia Graeca*, tom. 67.) 4°. Parisiis. 1857, etc.

Sozomenus, Hermas. *See* Socrates, Scholasticus.

Spanheim, Ezechiel, Baron. Illustrissimi E. Spanheimii ... Dissertationes de praestantia et usu Numismatum antiquorum. Editio nova, etc. 2 voll. Amstelaedami. 1717.

Spanheim, Friedrich, the Elder. F. Spanhemii. F. Summa Historiae Ecclesiasticae a Christo nato ad saeculum XVI. inchoatum. Praemittitur Doctrina Temporum, cum oratione de Christianismo degenere. 2 tom. 12°. Lugd. Batavorum. 1689.

Spartianus, Aelius. *See* Augustan History.

Spon, Jacob. Voyage d'Italie, de Dalmatie, de Grèce, et du Levant, fait es années 1675 et 1676 par J. Spon ... et G. Wheler, tom. 1-3. (Suite de Voyage de Grèce de J. Spon, etc., tom. 4.) 4 tom. 12°. Lyon. 1678-1680.

Stark, Carl Bernhard. Gaza und die philistäische Küste. Eine Monographie, etc. 8°. Jena. 1852.

Stephan, H. Das Verkehrsleben im Alterthum. (*Raumers Historische Taschenbuch.*) 8°. Leipzig. 1868.

Stephen of Byzantium. Stephani Byzanti, Ἐθικῶν quae supersunt. *Gr.* Edidit A. Westermann. 8°. Leipzig. 1839.

Strabo. S. Geographica Recensuit, commentario critico instruxit G. Kramer. *Gr.* 3 voll. Berolini. 1844-1852.

Suetonius, Tranquillus, Caius. C. Suetonii Tranquilli praeter Caesarum libros reliquiae. Edidit A. Reifferscheid, etc. 8°. 1860.

Suidas. Indices tres Lexicon Suidae compendiose repraesentantes. (J. P. Migne, *Patrologia Graeca*, tom. 117.) 4°. Parisiis. 1894.

Tatian. Oratio adversus Graecos. *Gr.* and *Lat.* (J. P. Migne, *Patrologia Graeca*, tom. 6.) 4°. Parisiis. 1884.

Tertullianus, Quintus Septimus Florens. Quinti Septimii Florentis Tertulliani opera omnia. (J. P. Migne, *Patrologia Latina*, tom. 2.) 4°. Parisiis. 1879.

Teuffel, Wilhelm Sigmund. Geschichte der Römischen Literatur. 2 voll. 8°. Leipzig. 1890.

Themistius, Euphrada. Themistii Orationes ex codice Mediolanensi emendatae a Gulielmo Dindorfio. *Gr.* 8°. Leipzig. 1832.

Theodosius II., Emperor of the East, 408-450. Codex Theodosianus. Ad LIV. librorum manuscriptorum et priorum editionum fidem recognovit et annotationi critica instruxit G. Haenel. Novellae constitutiones Theodosii II., Valentiniani III., etc. (*Corpus Juris Romani Antejustiniani.*) 4°. Bonnae. 1841.

Tobler, T. Topographie von Jerusalem und seine Umgebungen. 2 voll. 8°. Berlin. 1854-5.

—— Dritte Wanderung nach Palaestina im Jahre 1857. 8°. Gotha. 1859.

—— Golgotha. 8°. St. Gallen. 1851.

Ukert, Friedrich Augustus. Geographie der Griechen und Römer von den frühesten Zeiten bis auf Ptolemäus. ... Mit Karten. 3 Theile. 8°. Weimar. 1816-1846.

Ulpianus, Domitius. D. Ulpiani quae vulgo vocantur fragmenta sive ex Ulpiani libro singulari regularum excerpta. Ex Jurisprudentiae Antejustinianae reliquiis separatim edidit E. Huschke. 8°. Lipsiae. 1874.

Ungarelli, Luigi Maria. Interpretatio Obeliscorum Urbis. With notes by N. F. Rosellini. Plates. 2 tom. Fol. Romae. 1842.

Vidal-Lablache. Hérode Atticus. Étude critique sur sa vie. 8°. Paris. 1872.

Vitruvius Pollic, Marcus. M. V. P. de Architectura libri decem. Ex fide librorum scriptorum recensuit, emendavit suisque et vivorum doctorum annotationibus illustravit. J. G. Schneider. 3 tom. 8°. Lipsiae. 1807-1808.

Vogüé, Charles Jean Melchior de, Count. Syrie Centrale. Architecture civile et religeuse du 1er au 7e siècle, par le Compte M. de V. (et W. H. Waddington). 4°. Paris. 1865, etc.
—— Syrie Centrale. Inscriptions sémitiques. Publiées par le Compte de V. Planches. 4°. Paris. 1868-1877.
—— Le Temple de Jérusalem, Monographie du Haram-ech-Chérif, suivie d'un essai sur la topographie de la Ville-Sainte, par le Comte M. de V. Fol. Paris. 1864.

Volkmar, Gustav. Handbuch der Einleitung in die Apokryphen. 8°. Tübingen. 1860.

Volkmann, Richard. Leben, Schriften, und Philosophie des Plutarch von Chaeronea. 2 Theile. 8°. Berlin. 1869.

Vopiscus, Flavius. *See* Augustan History.

Wachsmuth, Curt. Die Stadt Athen im Alterthum. 8°. Leipzig. 1874.

Waddington, William Henry. Fastes des Provinces Asiatiques de l'Empire Romain depuis leur origine jusqu'au règne de Dioclétien. 8°. Paris. 1872.

Wallon, Henri Alexander. Histoire de l'esclavage dans l'antiquité, etc. Deuxième édition. 8°. Paris. 1879.

Warsberg, Alexander von, Baron. Eine Reise durch das Land des Sarpedon. (*Oesterreichische Rundschau.*) 8°. Wien. 1883.

Welker, Friedrich Gottlieb. Alte Denkmäler erklart. 5 Theile. With plates. 8°. Göttingen. 1849-64.

Werner, Carl. Geschichte der apologetischen und polemischen Literatur der christlichen Theologie. 5 voll. 8°. Schaffhausen. 1861-67.

Westermann, Anton. Geschichte der Beredsamkeit in Griechenland und Rom. 2 Theile. 8°. Leipzig. 1833-1835.

Wetzstein, Johann Gottfried. Reisebericht über Hauran und die Trachonen. Nebst einem Anhange über die Sabäischen Denkmäler in Ost-Syrien. 8°. Berlin. 1860.

2 C

Wieseler, Carl. Die Christen Verfolgungen der Cäsaren bis zum dritten Jahr-hundert, historisch und chronologisch untersucht. 8°. Gütersloh. 1878.

Wilmanns. Die Römischen Lagerstädte Africas. (Philologus.) 8°. Berlin. 1877.

Winckelmann, Johann Joachim. Geschichte der Kunst des Alterthums. 4°. Wien. 1776.

Wood, John Turtle. Discoveries at Ephesus, including the site and remains of the Great Temple of Diana. With … illustrations. Appendix in 8 parts. Greek and Latin inscriptions from Ephesus, etc. 8°. London. 1877.

Zeller, Edward. Die Philosophie der Griechen in ihrer geschichtlichen Entwick-elung dargestellt von Dr. E. Zeller. 8°. Leipzig. 1892.

Zoega, Georg. Numi Aegyptii imperatorii prostantes in Museo Borgiano Velitris, adjectis praeterea quotquot reliqua hujus classis numismata … colligere obtigit. 4°. Romae. 1787.

Zumpt, August Wilhelm. A. W. Z. Commentationum epigraphicarum ad antiqui-tates Romanas pertinentium volumen. (Volumen alterum.) 2 voll. 4°. Berolini. 1850-1854.

Zumpt, Carl Gottlob. Ueber den Bestand der philosophischen Schulen in Athen und die Succession der Scholarchen. 4°. Berlin. 1843.

INDEX

Abae in Phocis, 365.

Abonotichus, 295 *sq.*

Abydos, 71, 140.

Achaia, 34, 77, 78, 79.

Adane, 103.

Adiabene, 17.

Adramyttium, coins of, with Antinous, 309.

Adria, 1.

Adriana, *see* Hadriana.

Adrianopolis in Thrace, 85.

Advocati fisci, 198.

Aeclanum, 356.

Aegae, 103, 313.

Aegina, 140.

Aelia, name granted to cities, 46, 91, 356, 366.

Aelia Capitolina, 28, 159 *sq.*, called by Emperor Commodus "Commodiana," 163, 164; long survival of the name, 356; *see* also Jerusalem.

Aelia Mursa, 59.

Aelian, Sophist of Praeneste, 236.

Aeliopolis, name granted to cities, 356.

Aelium Aquincum, 59.

Aelium Carnutum, 59.

Aerarium, 39, 198.

Aezani, 102.

Africa, province, 89; cities enumerated, 90, 91.

Agri decumates, 55, 57.

Agricola, Cn. Iulius, 11, 60.

Agrippa, M. Maenius, 60.

Akiba, Rabbi, 111, 145, 158.

Alabaster, coloured, used for busts, 342.

Alani, war with the, 165 *sq.*, 247.

Albanians, 70.

Alcibiades, 47.

Alcinous, 282.

Alexander the Great, 72.

Alexander of Abonotichus, 294 *sq.*

Alexander of Troas, the sophist, 266.

Alexandria, 47, 126 *sq.*, centre of learning and philosophy, 238; its library, 240; destroyed by fire, 240; coins of, with Antinous, 309.

Alexandria Troas, 68, 73.

Alimenta Italiae of Trajan, representation in relievo, 345.

Amasia, 69.

Amastris, 299.

Amisus, 69, coins with Antinous, 309.

Amphictyonic League, 84; its members, 85.

Amphipolis, 140.

Ancyra, 69; coins with Antinous, 309.

Anemurium, 140.

Antigonia, *see* Alexandria Troas.

Antigonus, 73.

Antinoe, 307, 308, oracle at A. in honour of Antinous, 307; built in honour of Antinous, 357.

Antinoopolis, *see* Antinoe.

Antinous, 49, 87, 187, death of, at Besa, 131 *sq.*; honoured as Iacchus, 142; remarks on the deification of, 305 *sq.*; statues of, 350.

Antioch, 16, 17, 28, 67, 105.

Antiochus, 72, 105.

Antium, Villa of Hadrian at, 370.

Antoninus Pius, Emperor, 62, 63, 76, 181 *sq.*, 276, inscription at Jerusalem bearing his name, 163.

Antoninus, Titus Arrius, 11, 182, 237.

Apelles, 97.

Aphrodisias, 142.

Apollinaris, C. Sulpicius, 252.

Apollo, oracles of, 102, 301, 302.

— Didymeus Temple of, 101.

Apollodorus of Damascus, 12, 33, 247, 376.

Apollonius, philosopher, 235.

Apollonius, rhetorician, 235

Apollonius of Tyana, 262, 281, 313.

Apollonius, Dyscolus, 252.

Appian of Alexandria, 72, 248.

Apronianus, Cassius, 21.

Apuleius, 90, 237, 280.

Aqueducts at Troas, 355; at Dyrrhachium, 356; built by Hadrian, 356; at Alexandria Troas, 359; at Athens, 364; at Corinth, 364; at Olympia, 365; at Canisium, 365.

Aquitania, 54.

Ara Ubiorum, 56.

Arabia Petraea, 14, 114, province retained, 25.

Architecture under Hadrian, 354 *sq.*

Arelate, 263.

Argentoratum (Strassburg), 55.

Argos, oracle of Apollo at, 77, 83, 85, 302.

Aristides, apologist, 328.

Aristides, P. Aelius, rhetorician, 72, 262, 374.

Ariston of Pella, 151.

Arles, 54.

Armenia, province of, 17; abandoned, 25.

Armenia, Minor, 69, 70.

Army, Hadrian's reforms, 47, 48.

Arrian, Flavius, 69, 72, 163 *sq.* 243 *sq.* his *Enchiridion*, 246.

Art among the Romans, 332 *sq.*; Hadrian's relation to, 12, 332 *sq.*; Activity in art in the Empire, 333 *sq.*; Greek artists in Rome, 334, 336; character of, in Hadrian's age, 338; under Trajan, 12.

Artemidorus Daldianus of Ephesus, 280.

Artemion, 18.

Artemis, 97.

Artemisium, 97.

Asia, province of, 68.

Asclepios of Byblus, 266.

Aspendus, 102.

Asper, M. Antonius, 91.

Assyria, 25.

Athenaeum, 88, 241.

Athenagoras, 293.

Athens, 15, 47, 49, 85; Hadrian's first visit to, 81; second visit to, 95; third visit to, 139; description of, 81; seat of philosophy and rhetoric, 237 *sq.*; Pantheon at, 360; Odeum at, 365.

Atra, temple of the Sun at, 20.

Attianus, Caelius, 6, 14, 21, 22, 29, 35, 42, 222.

Attica, 77.

Augurinus, Sentius, 11.

Augusta Rauracorum (Basel), 55.

Augustus Caesar, 69, 70, 78, 81; his journeys, 45; attitude toward the Senate, 216; hieroglyphic inscription, 306; represented on a relievo at Ravenna, 307.

Auranitis, 104.

Aurum Coronarium, 38.

Auximum (Osimo), 366.

Avitus, 299.

Baalbek (Heliopolis), 28, 108.

Babylon, 17.

Baden-Baden, built by Trajan, 55.

Baetica (Hispania ulterior), 6, 64.

Baiae, 35, 370.

Barcocheba, 146, 147, 149, 154, 155.

Basel (Augusta Rauracorum), 55.

Basilica of Neptune, 375, 376.

Basilides, 331.

Baths at Corinth, 364; at Thermopylae, 365.

Belgica, 54.

Berytus, 106, 107, 108.

Besa (Antinoe), 308.

Bether, 144, 145, 154.

Bithynia, 68, 70, 71, 299, 356.

Bithynium (Claudiopolis), 71; coins of, with Antinous, 309.

Boeotia, 77, 84.

Borbetomagus (Worms), 55.

Bordeaux, 54.

Bosporus, 169; the Thracian, 169; the Cimmerian, never a Roman province, 170.

Bostra, 28, 117.

Branchidae, oracle of, 302.

Brigantes, 60.

Brigetio, 59.

Britain conquered by Claudius, 60; visit of Hadrian to, 61; Hadrian's wall, 62, 63.

Bronzes, scarcity of, in H.'s time, 342.

Buildings of Hadrian in Jerusalem, no remains of any, 163.

Byzantium, 170.

Caecilia Metella, tomb of, 380.

Caesar, C. Julius, 60, 72; consecrated, 306.

Caligula, 78, 84.

Camalodunum, 60.

Cameos, 341.

Campania, 43; temple of Isis in, 126.

Canisium, aqueduct at, 365.

Cappadocia, 69, 70, 104; Arrian governor of, 246; Severian governor of, 297.

Caracalla, 276, 310.

Caria, 68, 76, 101, 356.

Carthage, assumes the name of Hadrianopolis, 90.

Casper, Flavius, 252.

Cassius, Avidius, 105.

Castle of S. Angelo, see Mausoleum.

Castra Vetera, 61.

Castricius, 256.

Catana, 86.

Catti, 57.

Catullinus, Q. Fabius, 91.

Celer, Velleius, 235, 252, 256, 310.

Celsus, P. Juventus, 223.

Celsus, L. Publius, 14, 21, 34, 35.

Celsus, 313.

Cerasus (Pharnacia), 69, 169.

Cerealis, Petilius, 60.

Cephalion, 247.

Chaennus, 278.

Chaeronea, 84; birthplace of Plutarch, 243.

Chersiphron, 97.

Chosroes, 25, 70.

Christianity, 322 sq.; declared by Trajan a religio illicita, 326; Hadrian's rescript regarding, 326; doubts as to its authenticity, 326, 327; arguments in favour of authenticity, 328.

Cibyra, 102.

Cilicia, 68, 104.

Cipollino, 375.

Circus Maximus, 373.

— of Hadrian, 379.

Cius, 71.

Clarus, oracle of Apollo at, 297, 302.

Clarus, C. Septicius, 43, 63, 222, 251.

Claudiopolis, 71.

Claudius, Emperor, 65, 78, 84; conquest of Britain by, 60; arrangement of Danubian provinces, by, 59.

Clemens, Pactumeius, 228.

Cohors I., Flavia urbana, 195.

Cohortes urbanae, 222.

Coins of Hadrian's time, 50 sq., 339, 340.

Coliseum, 373, 379.

Cologne (Colonia Agrippina), 9, 55, 56.

Colophon, 101.

Columella, L. Junius Moderatus, 64.

Commagene, 69.

Commodiana, name given to Aelia Capitolina.

Commodus, Ceionius, see Verus, Lucius Commodus.

Consilium, judicial, under Hadrian.

Conspiracy of the Consulars, 34, 35.

Constantine, 48, 73; indictions of, 40; arch of, 377.

Constitutiones principum, 228.

Consul suffectus, Quietus appointed, 19, 228.

Controversiae, 255.

Coptus, 134, 135.

Corduba, 64.

Corinth, 79, 80, 83, 84, 85; coins of, with Antinous, 309; baths and aqueduct built by Hadrian at, 364; theatre by Herodes Atticus, 365.

Coronea, 94.

Cotys, coins of, 170.

Crito of Pieria, 247.

Ctesiphon, 17, 70.

Curator actorum Senatus, 13.

Cursus vehicularius or *publicus*, 199.

Cynic philosophy, 288.

Cyprus, 140; copper mines in, 17; rising of Jews in, 18.

Cyrenaica, 89, 356,

Cyrene, province of, 17.

Cyzicus, 95; called *Philosebastos* and *Adriane*, 74; Olympian games at, 140; coins of, with Antinous, 309; temple at, 358, 359.

Dacia, Hadrian in D. with Trajan, 12, 13, 30; conquest of, 13; threatened by the Roxolani, 32; divided into two provinces, 33.

Dacians, first war against, 12; second war against, 13.

Daemons, belief in, 314.

Dalmatia, 30; separated from Moesia, 32.

Damascus, 28, 108, 109.

Damis, biographer of Apollonius, 313.

Decebalus, 13, 14.

Decoration of houses, 339 *sq.*

Decrianus, 378.

Delos, oracle of Apollo at, 301.

Delphi, 84, 85, 301; coins of, with Antinous, 309; Stadium at, built by Herodes Atticus, 365.

Demonax, 81, 288, 289.

Didymae near Miletus, 302.

Dies imperii of Hadrian, 22.

Dinocrates, 97.

Diogenes of Heraclea, 247.

Dion Cassius, 2, 47, 143, 249, and *passim*.

Dion Chrysostom, 12, 75, 263, 264.

Dionysia, 82.

Dionysius, Aelius, of Halicarnassus, 252, 277.

Dionysius of Miletus, 239, 265.

Dioscurias, *see* Sebastopolis.

Disciplina Augusti, 48.

Dium, 140.

Dodona, 85.

Domitia Calvilla, 183.

Domitia Lucilla, wife of L. Commodus Verus, 175.

Domitia Paulina, mother of Hadrian, 6.

Domitian, 8, 9, 12, 78, 260; *limes* of, 57.

Domitius, 252.

Doris, 84.

Dyrrhachium, aqueduct at, 356.

Eburacum, 60, 63.

Edessa, 19.

Edictum perpetuum, 226 *sq.*

Egypt, 18, 120 *sq.*, 356.

Elagabalus, 321.

Eleusinian mysteries, 81, 95.

Eleusis, first visit of H., 84; second, 94, 95, 142.

Emerita, 64.

Epaminondas, 47, 83.

Epaphroditus, 283.

Ephesus, 140; first visit of H. to, 67; second visit of H. to, 95; history and description of, 98 *sq.*; temple built by H. at, 359.

Epictetus, 234, 284.

Epicuraeans, 315.

Epirus, 85.

Equites, 216 *sq.*; as constituted by Augustus, 216; as constituted by Hadrian, 217.

Ergastula, 230.

Erycius of Thessaly, 276.

Euboea, 85.

Euphranor, 97.

Euphrates, philosopher, 183, 283.

Euphrates, 17 *sq.*; boundary of Roman Empire in Asia, 24.

Evodus of Rhodus, 276.

Fadilla, Arria, 182.

Faliscus, Arrianus, 276.

Faustina, Annia Galeria, 183.

Faventia, 35.

Favorinus, 237, 264 *sq.*, 268, 303.

Fiscus, 39, 197, 221.

Flaccus, Calpurnius, 256.

Fleet, 195.

Florus, Julius, 250.

Florus, L. Annius, poet, 11, 274.

Forlanum, 366.

Forum, Adriani, 59.

— the Roman, 373.

— Augusti, 375.

— Trajani, 37, 375.

Fronto, M. Cornelius, 90, 214, 235, 256, 257.

Frugi Crassus, 21, 29.

Frumentarii, 63.

Fulvus, Aurelius, 182.

Fundanus, C. Minucius, 327, 328.

Furniture of Hadrian's time, 337.

Gades (Cadiz), 6.

Gaius (Caligula), policy of, towards Senate, 218.

Gaius, jurist, 228.

Galatia, 69, 70.

Galen, Claudius, 252.

Gaul, 54, 63.

Gellius, Aulus, 237, 242, 258; pupil of Favorinus, 263, 293.

Gens Aelia, 32.

Gentianus, Terentius, 174.

Gerasa, 28.

Germania, 9, 55 *sq.*

— *superior* and *inferior*, 9, 55; coins, 57.

Giallo antico found in Africa, 89, 374.

Gladiators, 13.

Glevum, 63.

Gnosticism, 125, 331.

Gordyene, 17.

Granianus, Licinius, 327.

Greece, 77 *sq.*

Gruttae, 366.

Gymnasia, built by Hadrian, 356; at Athens, 361; at Smyrna, 356.

Hadria, 6.

Hadrianus Afer, P. Aelius, father of Emperor, 6.

Hadrian, Emperor, his portrait, 1-8; his character, 2, 4, 186-188; birth, death of father, school in Rome, 6; return to Spain, recalled to Rome, fond of chase, 8; tribune, 8; military tribune, 9; quaestor, 12; in first Dacian war, 12; *Curator actorum Senatus*, 13; tribune, legionary legate in second Dacian war, 13; praetor, exhibits games, praetorian legate of Lower Pannonia, 13; consul, 13; adjutant general to Trajan, 14; Athens elects him archon, 15, 78; in Parthian war, 16; at Antioch, 16; in supreme command of eastern army, 20; adopted by Trajan, 21; legions hail him Imperator, 22; remains at Antioch, 22; character and policy as emperor, 23; surrenders the lately acquired provinces of Trajan, 24; travels westward and settles affairs in Pannonia and Dacia, 30-33; arrival in Rome, 36; the great remission of debt, 38-40; second consulate, 40; third consulate, 41; celebrates gladiatorial games, 41; his journeys, 45 *sq.*; his military organization, 47, 48, 56, 57; administration of justice, 48; visits Gaul, 53, 54; visits Germany, 55 *sq.*; visits Raetia and Noricum, 58, 59; in Britain, 60 *sq.*; through Gaul to Spain and Mauretania, 64 *sq.*; first journey to the East, 67 *sq.*; in Greece and at Athens, 77 *sq.*; goes to Africa, 87 *sq.*; second journey to the East, 93 *sq.*; in Syria, 102 *sq.*; in Judaea and Arabia, 111 *sq.*; in Egypt, 120 *sq.*; on the Nile, 128 *sq.*; revisits Athens, 138 *sq.*; last years in Rome, 173 *sq.*; death of Sabina, 174; adoption and death of Aelius Verus, 178 *sq.*; adoption of Antoninus and death of Hadrian, 183 *sq.*

Hadrianeum at Alexandria, 358.

Hadrian of Tyre, sophist, 271.

Hadriana or Hadrianopolis in Cyrenaica, 92.

Hadriana, a name granted to cities, 46, 69, 71, 74, 356.

Hadriane, 71.

Hadrianis, name of a new Athenian tribe, 94; name of a new Megarian tribe, 94.

Hadrianotherae, 71; coins of, with Antinous, 309, 356; founded by Hadrian, 356.

Hadrianopolis, name granted to cities, 356.
Halicarnassus, 74, 277, 379.
Harpocrates the Gnostic, 331.
Harpocrates, 235, 309, 310, 348.
Heliodorus, Avidius, 224, 234, 252, 265.
Heliopolis in Egypt, 128, 130; oracle at, 302; obelisk erected there by Hadrian, 347.
Heliopolis (Baalbek), 28.
Helvetia, 55.
Hephaestion, 235, 252.
Hermippus of Berytus, 278.
Herodes Atticus, 73, 235, 264, 268, 272; *corrector* of the cities of Asia, 355.
Herodianus, Aelius, 252.
Hierapolis in Syria, 302; coins of, with Antinous, 309.

Iamblichus of Syria, 280.
Iberia, 70.
Ilium, 47, 71.
Illyricum, 30, 356.
Imperator, title assumed for second time by Hadrian, 156.
Imperium proconsulare, 179, 220.
Inscriptions from Greek cities, 140.
Ionopolis (Abonotichus), 294, 299.
Iseum et Serapeum, 126.
Isis, 126.
Istria, 132.
Isthmus, cutting of, 269, 270.
Italica, 6, 9, 11, 65.
Italy, Pliny's praise of, 191; no troops in, 195.
Izates, 17.

Janus, temple of, closed, 45.
Jason of Argos, 247.
Jazyges, 31.
Jerusalem, 28, 112, 113, 144, 163, 164, 356.
Jews, 27, 28; rising in Mesopotamia and Cyrene of, 17; rising in Cyprus, 18; rising under Barcocheba, 143 *sq.*
Joshua ben Chananja, 144.
Journeys of Hadrian, remarks on, 45 *sq.*, *see* also Hadrian.

Judaea, governed by a procurator, 197.
Julia Balbilla, 129.
Julianus, Salvius, 90, 223, 226, 227.
Julianus, Antonius, 151, 256.
Julian, Emperor, 311; his sketch of Hadrian, 186.
Jurisprudence, 226 *sq.*
Jurists, Roman, 227, 228.
Jus gladii, 196.
— *latii*, 210.
— *quiritium*, 231.
— *respondendi*, 227.
— *trium liberorum*, 232.
Justin Martyr, 330.
Justinian, 79.
Juvenal, 11, 62.

Kehlheim, 57.

Laberius Maximus, 21, 29.
Lambaesis, 90, 91.
Lanuvium, temple of Diana and Antinous at, 310.
Laodicea, 140.
Lateran Museum, 351.
Latinus Junianus, 231.
Leander Nicanor of Alexandria, 247.
Lebadea, oracle of Trophonius at, 84, 302.
Legati Aug. iuridici, 197.
— *Aug. pro praetore*, 196.
— *Aug. praetorii*, 196.
— legionary, 197.
Leges Juliae of Augustus, 196 *sq.*
Legions, *Minervia*, I., 13.
    Trajana II., 121, 151.
    Adjutrix II., 8.
    Augusta III., 89, 90, 91.
    Cyrenaica III., 117, 151.
    Gallica III., 151.
    Scythica IV., 151, 152.
    Macedonica V. 9, 31.
    Ferrata VI., 163.
    Victrix VI., 61, 62.
    Claudia VII., 152.
    Gemina VII., 64.
    Gemina X., 59, 152.
    Fretensis X., 19, 20, 113, 145, 151, 163.

Legions, *Fulminata* XII., 69, 166.
  Apollinaris XV., 69, 166.
  Flavia Firma XVI., 69.
  Valeria Victrix XX., 62.
  Deiotariana XXII., 9, 121.
Lex, *Aelia Sentia* 204, 230, 231.
— *de Imperio*, 219.
— *Furia Caninia*, 204.
— *Julia*, 211.
— — *de adulteriis*, 230.
— — *Municipalis*, 211.
— *Junia Norbana*, 205, 231.
— *Petronia*, 229.
— *Plautia Papiria*, 211.
— *Regia*, 219, 221.
Libertini, 205.
Library at Athens built by Hadrian, 361;
  of Alexandria, 240; in Rome, 240;
  in Hadrian's villa, 367.
Libri Catachannae, 277.
Limes, Germanicus, 57.
— *Raeticus*, 57.
Literature under Hadrian, 234 *sq.*,
  273 *sq.*
Livianus, 14.
Locris, 84.
Lollianus of Ephesus, 237, 266.
Londinium, 63.
Lucan, 64.
Lucian, 75, 80, 242, 278, 280, 282, 290,
  299, 317-320.
Lucius Patrensis, 280.
Lucuas, 17.
Lugdunum (Lyons), 54.
Lupiae, harbour built at, by Hadrian,
  366.
Lupus, Julius, 182.
Lupus, procurator, 18.
Lusitania, 64.
Lusius Quietus, 14, 65; quells the
  Jewish rebellion in Mesopotamia, 19,
  20, 25; removed from Palestine, 26;
  conspiracy and death, 34, 35.
Lutetia (Paris), 54.
Lycaonia, 68.
Lycia, 102, 356.
Lydia, 68, 100, 101.
Lysimachus, 72, 73, 74.
Lysippus, 97.

Macedonia, province of, 30, 78, 84, 85,
  356.
Macer, Baebius, 29.
Maecianus, Volusius, 228.
Magnesia on the Meander, 101.
Major, C. Julius, 91.
Mantinea, 83, 94; seat of the Antinous
  cult in Greece, 308; coins of, with
  Antinous, 309; temple of Poseidon
  Hippius at, renewed by Hadrian, 365.
Marble, coloured, much used in Rome,
  341; imported from Numidia, 341;
  Numidian, 374; Carystian, 375.
Marcellus, Publius, 152.
Marciana, 8, 10.
Marcomanni, 57.
Marcus Aurelius, 81, 181; extends the
  remission of debt, 40; makes no men-
  tion of Antinous, 309.
Marcus of Byzantium, 262, 266, 267.
Marius Maximus, 249.
Martial, 11, 64.
Massilia, 54; walls built by a private
  citizen, 355.
Matidia, 8, 10, 22; death of, 43.
Mauretania, 65; governed by a pro-
  curator, 197; *Caesariensis* (Algiers),
  18, 65; *Tingitana* (Tangier), 65.
Mauri or Moors, 65.
Mausoleum of Hadrian, 379 *sq.*
Maximus of Aegae, 313.
Mayence (Moguntiacum), 55.
Mazaca, 69.
Medallions of Hadrian's time, 340.
Mediolanum, 366.
Megara, 85, 94; temple of Apollo at,
  rebuilt by Hadrian, 364.
Melissa, 47.
Melissus, Aelius, 252.
Melitene, 69, 70.
Melito, bishop of Sardis, 101, 324, 328.
Memnon, statue of, 47, 133, 134.
Memnonium, 133.
Memphis, 129, 130.
Mesomedes of Crete, 276.
Mesopotamia, 17; abandoned, 25.
Messana, 86.
Miletus, 101, 140.
Miltiades, 47.

Mines (opus metalli), 230.

Mithridates of Bosporus, 69, 97.

Moeragenes, 313.

Moesia, Hadrian tribune in, 9, 30; extent of province of, 31; threatened by the Roxolani, 32; Lower Moesia, 32; united with Hellas and Macedonia, 78.

Moguntiacum (Mayence), 55, 56.

Moles Hadriani, *see* Mausoleum.

Mopsvestia, 103.

Mosaics from the Tiburtinum, 342, 369.

Municipium, 209.

Mursa, *see* Aelia Mursa.

Museums, Torlonia, 335, 346; the Vatican, 335, 347, 348; the Lateran, 311, 335, 351; National, at Athens, 352; at Naples, 351; Kirchner, 369.

Musonius Rufus, 283, 288.

Myra, 102.

Myron, 97, 348.

Mysia, 68.

Myus Hormus, 134.

Naarda, 17.

Naples, cult of Antinous, 311; splendid buildings in, 355.

Narbonne, 54.

Narbonensis, 54.

Nemea, 83.

Neocaesarea, 69.

Neocoria, 98, 101, 306.

Neoplatonism, 283.

Nepos, Aulus Platorius, 14, 62, 174.

Nepos, Titus Haterius, 224.

Nero, Emperor, 78, 84, 85.

Nerva, Cocceius, Senator, subsequently Emperor, 9; his death, 9; exempted Italy from the support of the Imperial post, 199.

Nicaea, 71; restored by Hadrian, 359.

Nicanor of Cyrene, 252.

Nicomedia, 71; birthplace of Arrian, 245; coins with Antinous, 309; restored by Hadrian, 359.

Nicopolis, 74, 84, 85; coins with Antonius, 309.

Nigrinus, Avidius, 14; conspiracy and death, 34, 35.

Nile, Hadrian's voyage on, 59, 128.

Nisibis, 17, 19.

Nismes, 54, 63, 142.

Noricum, 30, 59.

Noviodunum, 59.

Novum Ilium, 71, 72.

Numenius, 276.

Numidia, 89; coloured marble obtained from, 341.

Octavianus (*see* Augustus), 3.

Odessus, 171; Roman fleet stationed at, 31.

Odeum at Athens, 365.

Oenomaus of Gadara, 282, 288, 302.

Olbia, 102.

Olympia, 78, 83; aqueduct at, 365; celebration of the, by Hadrian, 140 *sq.*

Olympieum, 82; dedication of, 140; built by Hadrian, 362; description, 362, 363.

Olympus in Lydia, 102.

Oracles, 84, 301, 302.

Oratory, Roman, 233 *sq.*

Orion, 252.

Orsova, 33.

Osroëne, 17.

Ostia, statue of Antinous as Vertumnus found at, 311; favoured by Hadrian, 366.

Paintings in the Artemisium at Ephesus, 98; at Tiburtinum, 342.

Pales, 140.

Palestine, province, 19, 111 *sq.*

Palilia, 43, 44.

Palma, Cornelius, 14, 20, 21; conspiracy and death of, 34, 35.

Palmyra, 28, 109, 110; colonnades at, 355.

Pamphylia, cities in, visited by Hadrian, 68, 71, 102.

Pancrates, 137, 239, 276.

Panhellenia, 141, 360.

Pannonia, 30, 59; Lower, 13, 30; Hadrian legate in, 13, 30.

Pantheon, 375; containing list of Hadrian's buildings, 360, 361.

Panticapaeum, 170.

Paphlagonia, 294, 296, 356.

Parium, 68, 71.

Parrhasius, 97.

Parthamaspates, 25.

Parthia, legions withdrawn from, 25.

Parthian war, 16.

Patara, 102.

Pater patriae, 38, 88.

Patras, 79.

Paulina, sister of Hadrian and wife of Servianus, 6, 173.

Paulus, Julius, 275, 276.

Pausanias, 72, 77, 83, 84, 142, 278.

Pavonazetto, 374.

Peloponnesus, 77, 83.

Pelusium, 47, 118, 119.

Peraea, 117.

Peregrinus Proteus, 290 *sq.*

Perga, 102.

Pergamum, 74, 95.

Perpetual Edict, 226, 227.

Petra, 116, 117.

Petronius Arbiter, 255.

Pharasmanes, 70, 165, 166, 169; visit of, to Rome, 166.

Phaselis, 102.

Phidias, 97, 376.

Philadelphia, 100.

Philo of Byblus, 249.

Philo, Herennius, 247, 278.

Philosebastos, 74.

Philosophy, 282 *sq.*

Philostratus, Flavius, 73, 238, 261, 267, 313.

Phlegon of Tralles, 248, 278.

Phocis, 77, 84, 94.

Photius, 248, 263, 280.

Phrygia, 68.

Pinara, 102.

Pisidia, 68, 102.

Piso, 11.

Pisistratus, 261.

Pliny the elder, 46, 72, 191.

Pliny the younger, 11, 43, 237, 303; his *Panegyricus*, 10.

Plotina, 8, 10, 14, 21, 63, 64.

Plotinus, 283.

Plutarch, 12, 72, 84, 243 *sq.*, 265, 287, 313-315; friend of Favorinus, 245.

Pola, 32.

Polemon of Smyrna, 100, 140, 238, 239, 264, 267, 268; unfriendly to Favorinus, 264.

Poliorcetica, 376.

Pollio, Valerius, 252.

Polycletus, 1, 97, 348.

Pompeiopolis, 140.

Pompey, 47.

Pomponius Sextus, 227.

Pons Aelius, 62.

Pontifex Maximus, 221.

Pontus, 69.

Porphyry, used in architecture, 342.

Portraiture in marble, 343.

Potestas patria, 232.

— *tribunicia*, 41, 179.

Praefectus, 198.

— *praetorio*, 223.

— *urbi*, 222.

— *vehicolorum*, 200.

— *vigilum*, 222.

Praeneste, villa of Hadrian at, 370.

Praetorian guard, 219.

Praxiteles, 84, 97, 349.

Priscus, Javolenus, 228.

Priscus, 20.

Priscus, Neratius, 223, 228.

Proconsular power, 196, 220.

Procurator ad curam gentium, 18.

— *a rationibus*, 198, 223, 224.

— *a libellis*, 223, 224.

— *ab epistolis*, 223, 224.

Provinces, number of, at Hadrian's accession, 195; Senatorial and Imperial, 195; government of, 195 *sq.*

Provincial diets, 201.

Ptolemy, Claudius, geographer, 251, 252.

Publius Celsus, 14, 21, 34; death of, 35.

Puteoli, 366.

Quadratus, a pupil of the apostles, 328.

Quaestorship, 197.

Quintilian, 12, 64, 255, 259.

Quintilius Condianus, 271.

Quintilius Maximus, 271.

Raetia, 30, 58, 59.

Ramaseum, 133.

Rasparasanus, King of the Roxolani, 32.

Regilla, Appia Annia, 271.

Relievo, historical art of, 344.

Religion, *see* Christianity.

Remission of debt by Hadrian, 38-40; represented in relievo, 345.

Responsa prudentum, 227.

Rhammius Martialis, 136.

Rhetoricians, Schools of, 253 *sq.*

Rhodes, 75.

Roads built by Hadrian, 355, 356; from Beneventum to Aeclanum, 356; to Myus Hormus, 357; over the Isthmus, 365; *via Cassia*, 366; *via Augusta*, 366.

Roemetalces, son of Cotys, 170.

Roman empire, 191 *sq.*; Aristides' panegyric on, Tertullian's opinion of, population and extent, its civilization, its languages, its division into E. and W., art, religion, philosophy derived from E., 191-194; military forces of, trade and commerce in, 195, 196.

Rome, 211 *sq.*

Rosso antico, 348.

Roxolani, expedition against, 31, 32.

Rufus, Caninius, 11.

Rusticus, Q. Junius, 40.

Rutilianus, 298, 299.

Sabina, 10, 38, 49, 54, 69, 88, 129, 174, 175, 381.

Sabinus, L. Vibius, 10.

Sabinus, T. Pontius, 60.

Sabinus, 266.

Salamis in Cyprus destroyed, 18.

Salinator, Cn. Pedanius Fuscus, 40, 173, 177.

Samosata, 69.

Samothrace, 71.

Santiponte, *see* Italica.

Sardis, 61, 95, 100, 101, 142.

Sarmatians, 13, 31.

Sarmizegetusa, 33.

Satala, 69, 70.

Saturninus, 331.

Scaurus, 235, 252.

Scopas, 349.

Scopelianus, 266, 268.

Sculpture, Ideal in the age of Hadrian, its cosmopolitan character, repetition of ancient masterpieces, description of, in the Tiburtinum, 346, 347, 348; in the temple of Ephesus, 99.

Sebastopolis, 140.

Secundus, P. Metilius, 90.

Seleucia on the Tigris, 17.

Seleucus Nicator, 105.

Selinus (Selinti), 20, 21, 22, 29.

Senate, 196 *sq.*, 219 *sq.*

Senatus consultum Claudianum, 230.

Senatorial provinces, 78.

Seneca, 64, 254, 283.

Senecio, C. Sossius, 11, 243.

Senecio, S. Attius, 152.

Septa, 375, 376.

Serapeum, 238.

Servianus, L. Julius Ursus, 6, 173; legate of Upper Germany, 9; consul third time, 42; Hadrian's letter to, 124.

Sestus, 71, 140.

Severianus, 297.

Severus, Alexander, 81, 180, 222, 321; refused to admit freedmen to the equestrian order, 217; favourably disposed towards Christianity, 329; aqueduct at Tyrrhachium restored by him, 356.

Severus, L. Catilius, 30, 182.

Severus, Julius, 152, 157.

Severus, Tiberius Julius, 152, 157.

Severus, Septimius, 62, 89, 106, 321; exempts the provinces from the burden of the imperial post, 199.

Sextius, Q., 283.

Sextus, philosopher, 235.

Sicily, 86.

Sicyon, 85.

Side, 102.

Sidon, 107.

Sigia, *see* Alexandria Troas.

Silius Italicus, 11.

Similis, Sulpicius, 29, 42, 222.

Simon, son of Giora, 149.

Sinope, colony of Miletus, 169.

Slavery, 204.

Smyrna, 47, 95, 99, 100, 140; seat of sophistry, 100; gymnasium at, built by Hadrian, 355-360; coins of, with Antinous, 309.

Sophists, Greek, great builders, 355.

Soranus, 274.

Sorrento, 366.

Sosius Papus, 14.

Sosus of Pergamum, Roman copy of mosaic, 343.

Spain, 6, 8, 64.

Sparta, 77, 78, 79, 83, 94.

Spartianus, 2, 30, 35, 57, 88, 234, 249, and *passim*.

Spira (Speier), 55.

Spurinna, 11.

Stadia at Delphi, 365.

Statius, 11.

Statues in honour of Hadrian, 15, 33, 65, 82, 84.

— Trajan, 78.

Stoicism, 282 *sq.*

Stones, precious, 341.

Strabo, 46, 73, 86.

Stratonicea restored by Hadrian, 359.

Suetonius Paulinus, 60.

Suetonius Tranquillus, 11, 42, 49, 63, 224, 249.

Suidas, 247.

Suovetaurilia, 345.

Sura, L. Licinius, 10; death of, 14.

Syracuse, 86.

Syria, 103 *sq.*, 356.

Tacitus, Cornelius, 55; his *Germania*, 11.

Talmud, 26, 28.

Tarracina, 35.

Tarraco, 64, 65, 201.

Tarsus, coins of, with Antinous, 309.

Tauromenium, 86.

Taurus of Tyre, 268, 282.

Teano, 366.

Telephus of Pergamum, 235, 252.

Telmessus, 102.

Temples:—

Olympian Zeus, 361 *sq.*

Divi Trajani, 375.

Diana and Antinous at Lanuvium, 310.

Zeus Panhellenius and Hera at Athens, 360.

Rome and Venus, 376 *sq.*

Genius of Rome at Ephesus, 359.

Apollo at Megara, 364, at Xanthus, 102, at Abae, 365.

Poseidon Hippius renovated by Hadrian, 365.

Antinous at Mantinea built by Hadrian, 365.

Bona Dea, 376.

deified Augustus at Tarraco, 64, 65.

Peace, 379.

Dea Cupra, 366.

Genius of Rome and Augustus, 79.

Caesar and Augustus, 79.

Octavia, 84.

Tertullian, 46, 192.

Thasos, 140.

Theagenes of Patrae, 292.

Thebes, 84.

Thebes in Egypt, 174.

Theodotus, sophist, 272.

Theon, 282.

Thermae, 86.

Thespiae, 84.

Thessaly, 84, 85.

Theveste, military road to, 90.

Thrace governed by procurator, 85, 197, 356.

Thyatira, 101.

Tiberius, emperor, 38, 69, 78, 219.

Tiburtinum, 366 *sq.*; description of, by Pope Pius II., 370.

Timocrates, 282.

Tineius Rufus, 113, 147, 153.

Tomi, 31.

Torlonia Museum, 346, 348.

Toulouse, 54.

Trachonitis, 28, 104.

Trajan emperor, 6, 47, 60, 69, 78; adoption, consular legate of Upper Germany, emperor, 9; return to Rome, 10; first and second Dacian campaign, 12, 13; conquests, 14;

Parthian war, leaves Italy for the East, 16; reaches Persian Gulf, 17; homeward journey and illness, 20; his adoption of Hadrian and death, 21; ashes burned, 37; column of, 15, 19, 375.
Tralles, 68, 101.
Trapezus (Trebizond), 47, 167, 168, 359.
Treves, 54.
Tribunicia potestas, 41.
Tributum capitis, 197.
Troas, aqueduct built by Herod. Att. at, 355.
Troesmis, 31.
Turbo, Q. Marcius, 68, 222; crushes rebellion of Jews, 18; sent to Mauretania, 27; summoned to Dacia, 32; prefect, 42.
Turnu Severin, 33.
Tyana, 69; coins of, with Antinous, 309.
Tyras, colony of Miletus, 31.
Tyrants, the thirty, 321.
Tyre, 107.

Ulpia Trajana (Sarmizegetusa), 33.
Urbicius Q. Lollius, 152.

Valens, legate of leg. xv., 166.
Valens, Aburnus, 228.
Valentinus, 331.
Valerius Asiaticus, 182.

Vatican Museum, 346, 348.
Vectigal, 197.
Verus, Lucius Commodus (Caesar), called Aelius Verus, 34, 175, 176, 178 *sq.*
Verus, Lucius, son of L. Commodus or Aelius Verus, 34, 175, 181.
Verus, Annius, father of Marcus Aurelius, 181.
Verus, M. Annius, *see* Marcus Aurelius.
Verus, Vindius, 228.
Vespasian emperor, 6, 64, 76, 78, 102, 219, 256, 282.
Vestinus, L. Julius, 224 note, 239, 252.
Victor, sex. Aurelius, 174, 249.
Villa of Hadrian, *see* Tiburtinum.
Vindobona (Vienna), 59.
Vitiges, 379.
Vaconius, 275.
Vologeses, 165.

Wall of Hadrian, 61, 62.

Xenophon, Commander of Roman troops against the Alani, 166.
Xenophon, 47.
Xanthus, oracle of Apollo at, 102, 302.
Xiphilinus, 2, 50, 249.

Zeno, the stoic, 283, 286.
Zenobia, 110.
Zenodorus, 378.
Zeuxis, 97.

ERRATA.

P. 9, l. 4, *For* 'Imperial law suits' *read* 'Prosecutions for treason.'

P. 12, l. 6 from bottom, *For* 'from whóm he had refused to take the tribute accepted' *read* 'to whom he had refused the subsidy granted.'

P. 19, third footnote, *For* '(propraetorian legate)' *read* '(inter praetorios allectus).

P. 34, l. 8, *For* 'consuls' *read* 'consulars.'

P. 65, l. 2 from bottom, *For* 'festivals' *read* 'thanksgivings.'

P. 101, l. 6, *For* Neocoria' *read* 'Neocorate.'

P. 105, l. 12, *For* 'of Orontes' *read* 'in the Orontes.'

P. 161, l. 1, *For* 'The Aelia established' *read* 'The new Aelia determined.'

P. 193, ll. 5-12 should read, "The history of the peoples round the basin of the Mediterranean Sea was written in the creation of many forms of States. All were embraced in the empire of Rome, and as the Romans, in their insatiable desire for aggrandisement, extended the borders of their State in ever widening circles to include Germans, Britons, Slavs and Arabs, they thus erected bulwarks which protected these old Mediterranean lands against barbaric invasion."

P. 195, l. 2, *For* 'established' *read* 'regulated.'

P. 197, l. 20, *For* 'increased power' *read* 'high authority.'

l. 28, *For* 'rulers' *read* 'officials.'

P. 201, l. 13, *For* 'spirit' *read* 'genius.'

P. 203, l. 10, *For* 'Latinum' *read* 'Latii.'

P. 211, l. 4, *For* 'league' *read* 'community.'

P. 223, l. 29, *For* 'board of secretaries' *read* 'head of the secretariat.'

Last line, *For* 'of the courts' *read* 'from officials.'

P. 224, l. 4 from bottom, *For* 'furnish' *read* 'institute.'

P. 226, ll. 2-3, *For* 'the philosophic maxims which it established on its basis' *read* 'the philosophic principles which it applied to legal relations generally.'

P. 227, l. 13, *For* 'jurisdictions' *read* 'courts.'

l. 20, *For* 'make theses of law' *read* 'lay down legal maxims.'

P. 252, ll. 1-4. The sentence should run 'Under the Antonines, when the great catalogue of roads was made, geography was elevated by the genius of Claudius Ptolemaeus to the rank of a mathematical science together with astronomy and chronology.

P. 259, l. 9, *For* 'was a free art of polite letters and of literature' *read* 'retained its title to be called a fine art of polite letters and was in consequence productive.'

P. 261, l. 18, *For* 'fifty-six years of its life after the death of Polemon' *read* 'death of Polemon at the age of fifty-six.'

P. 270, l. 18, *For* 'less' *read* 'more.'

P. 271, l. 7 from bottom, *For* 'Quintilians' *read* 'Quintilii.'

P. 285, last two lines, *For* 'The Aesthesis' *read* 'Sensation': *For* 'the Hormesis *read* 'passion.'

P. 287, l. 28, *For* 'paradox' *read* 'contradiction.'

P. 306, l. 26 and in second footnote, *For* 'Emperor-worship' *read* 'Caesar-worship.'

l. 4 from bottom, *For* 'Neocoria' *read* 'Neocorate.'

P. 311, l. 3, *For* 'priesthood belonging to' *read* 'guild of worshippers of.'

l. 5, *For* 'priesthood' *read* 'similar guild.'

P. 323, l. 28, *For* 'a particularly' *read* 'everywhere.'

P. 334, l. 3, *For* 'displayed' *read* 'illustrated.'

P. 350, l. 31, *For* 'by Mondragone' *read* 'of Mondragone.'

P. 352, l. 25, *For* 'by Mondragone' *read* 'of Mondragone.'

1898

UNIVERSITY·PRESS
ROBERT·MACLEHOSE
JAMES·J·MACLEHOSE
GLASGOW